The House of Kanoo

A Century of an Arabian Family Business

The House of Kanoo

A Century of an Arabian Family Business

Khalid M. Kanoo

THE LONDON CENTRE OF ARAB STUDIES

First published by
The London Centre of Arab Studies
Vicarage House
58-60 Kensington Church Street
London W8 4DB

ISBN 1 900404 03 6

Typeset by South Bucks Photosetters.
Printed by Oriental Press, Dubai.

To my Father

In writing the story of the first 100 years of the Y.B.A.Kanoo family
business, my aim has been to capture a sense of the exciting
pioneering spirit exemplified so energetically by my late father,
Mohamed Jassim Kanoo, and to whose fond memory I dedicate this
book. He was a serious, yet sensitive man. He and his 'brothers'
Ahmed, Abdulla, Mubarak, Abdulrahman, Abdulaziz and Hamed
took over a company which was almost financially bankrupt yet rich
in reputation and built it up to be one of the leading companies in
the Gulf. Ahmed Kanoo was the visionary but my father was the one
who implemented his ideas and made them a reality. He was the
company engine that drove the organisation. He was the 'cannon', as
the late Shaikh Sulman Al Khalifa, the Emir of Bahrain used to call
him. If you needed something done you gave it to Mohamed.
Sombre he was not. He was fun-loving, kind, generous and caring.
Above all he was a leader of men who would do anything for him.
So in my father's spirit I have tried to blend formality with a little fun
to create a relaxed, illustrated story of our company and of our
homeland and so take readers on a journey through a century of
change, challenge and, sometimes, even crisis. If this mix tempts my
own children and their cousins to cherish their heritage as I do, then
this book will have been one project well worth finishing.

Khalid M. Kanoo

Contents

Foreword

Personal considerations alone make it a great pleasure for me to introduce this exciting book on *Bait Kanoo* (the House of Kanoo). My own family and the Kanoos have been friends for a very long time, the friendship moving from one generation to the next. I have vivid memories from my early childhood of visits exchanged between the elders of the two families. I often accompanied my father on these occasions. I met the author of this book, Khalid, before either of us was ten years old (I am a year or two older) and although our paths didn't cross often, I remember him as a very energetic, and naughty boy.

My professional career brought me closer to some aspects of the Kanoo enterprises. When I was the Director of the Saudi Rail Road in the mid-seventies, I was in charge of running the Dammam Port. I came to watch and admire the efficiency with which the company handled its operation in the port. Abdulla Kanoo was a frequent visitor to my office and I greatly benefited from his wise advice. Later on, as the Minister of Industry and Electricity, I was very happy to inaugurate personally the manufacturing projects that came into being through joint ventures the Kanoos formed with leading international companies.

All those who come to know the Kanoos quickly admire the traits all members of the family share: unfailing courtesy, unbounded hospitality, and an always-helpful attitude. I know of no other family where it is customary to travel hundreds, at times thousands, of miles, just to attend a wedding, or a funeral, of a friend. As far as observing the social niceties, the Kanoos are becoming a legend in their own lifetime.

Yet personal and professional considerations aside, I strongly feel that this is a very important book. With accurate sensitivity, it traces the fortunes of one of the most prominent merchant families in Arabia over a century of ups and downs. While Arabians have been traders since the dawn of their history, the twentieth century presented them with unparalleled challenges and opportunities. Yusuf bin Ahmed Kanoo is one of the few family enterprises that met the challenges head on and made the best possible use of the opportunities. It is a case study of how family business should be conducted.

While the author did not intend to write a history of the Arabian Gulf, interesting pages of that history unfold as the story of the company is related. We see in absorbing detail how the thriving capitals of the Gulf grew, from very modest origins. Those who did not see the transformation themselves would find it impossible to believe that such stupendous changes took place in the short span of three decades. Khalid and I, although in different places and from different perspectives, are lucky to have been 'present at the birth'.

This book will be of great value to many categories of readers. For historians there is a mass of information. For non-Arabs wishing to do business with Arabs, it is almost a manual. For the general reader, it is a fascinating look at a society in transformation. For management consultants, there is a heady brew of the latest business theory mixed with very ancient traditions. I suspect, however, that Khalid wrote his book mainly for the benefit of the new generation, that of my children and his. It is a lovely gift – and the recipients should treat it with affection and gratitude.

I wish the book the success it deserves, and I heartily commend Khalid and his writing partner on a job very well done.

Dr Ghazi A. Algosaibi
Ambassador
Royal Embassy of Saudi Arabia, London

Preface

During 1990, when the Yusuf bin Ahmed Kanoo family business reached one hundred years of uninterrupted trading, many people suggested that it was time to publish a book which documented the origins of the House of Kanoo. Such a book should trace the evolution of the business, explain how this business operation was interwoven with the affairs of the local community and, especially, how its rapid development after the Second World War coincided with the accelerated economic growth of the Arabian Gulf region.

We were lucky to locate very old company papers, most of which had lain forgotten in one of our warehouses. The oldest existing documents date back to the end of the nineteenth century. These tell a story of how the Kanoo business began as a humble one, selling basic materials such as rice, sugar, dates, wood and rope, until the time when Haji Yusuf bin Ahmed Kanoo took over the company in 1890. Thereafter, he progressively modernised and developed the business until it became an enterprise of international repute.

Haji Yusuf bin Ahmed Kanoo had the foresight to see that for a business to grow, one has to open one's eyes and see what is happening around one, grasp the opportunities that arise and then explore these to the full. Hence, the Kanoo family became traders with very strong international links. Haji Yusuf's reputation for honesty made him well-known and sought after, both domestically and abroad. He set a path which we still follow: that of being concerned about business; helping and assisting those in need, and being in the forefront with those who support the community for whatever it needs, with both our time and money.

After Haji Yusuf died in 1945, his nephews Jassim and Ali took over the leadership of the company. It was an exciting time as the whole Gulf region, with the help of oil revenues, slowly modernised to become a dominant influence in world economic markets and international power-politics.

When I took over the company in 1952, together with my cousin, Mohamed, the path was already paved and the goals were set. All we had to do was to work harder with my brothers and cousins to progress the company so that it could evolve into what it is today, a very diversified multi-million-dollar operation, strong in both reputation and finance.

It is now the turn of our sons and daughters to carry the torch and continue what was started by our founder Haji Yusuf bin Ahmed Kanoo, to maintain our tradition of being assertive in our business dealings, but kind and generous with the community.

I hope you will enjoy our family story as related by my nephew Khalid. Little did he know, or myself for that matter, that it would take some five years of research and compilation to create this book, accurate in detail and providing a flavour of the region in which the business of Yusuf bin Ahmed Kanoo has developed over a century.

Ahmed Ali Kanoo
Group Chairman
Yusuf bin Ahmed Kanoo

Ahmed Ali Kanoo

Acknowledgements

When I decided to write a book on the Kanoo family business some five years ago, I did not realise the amount of work and research which was needed in addition to the actual writing. Actively managing a company and writing a historical book was just too time-consuming. I needed help. After an international search I found Angela Clarke in Bahrain. Angela is an author and a historian of the Arabian Gulf. I learnt a lot from her and without her help I would not have had the time to complete the research, let alone write 120,000 words of text. Angela was a hard taskmaster but a pleasure to work with.

The easy part was to rescue boxes of old abandoned company documents, invoices, letters, shipping manifests and bills of lading. Add to that all the old pictures of the family, company premises and dignitaries which I was accumulating. Sorting the assembled pile was not so easy, or much fun!

While Angela and I have no idea how many sheets of paper we catalogued, I do know that we used thousands of plastic files and dozens of archive boxes to store them all. Space for storage, sitting and studying simply ran out because of the needs of these documents, reports, books, and the transcriptions of many hours of oral history recorded on tape. Now, after building an extension to my library at home, many metres of shelving are devoted to preserving our family archive, a unique reservoir of Arabian family history.

Three years were spent making sense of it all, shaping and structuring the material into readable form. Again, I thank Angela for the hundreds of hours she spent working at her computer creating, as it were, the warp on the loom so that I could spend many a long weekend designing and weaving the weft of my story. Eventually, my 'carpet' was complete.

Of course there were many others who were kind enough to help me with my research. Let me give special thanks to members of my family – Ahmed Kanoo, Mubarak Kanoo, Abdulaziz Kanoo and Fawzi Kanoo. Thanks to eminent family friends such as Dr Ghazi A. Algosaibi, Mr Yousuf Al Shirawi, Mr Mohamed Juma, Mr Hussain Yateem and Mr Mohamed Saleh. My thanks to many specialists including Dr Frauke Heard-Bey – Center for Documentation, Abu

Dhabi, Mr Abdulla Ismael and Mr Abdulaziz Al Khadar and to companies which made their archives available: British Airways (through Mr Robert Ayling), ARAMCO, BANOCO and ADNOC. Many thanks to our company research 'volunteer' staff such as Chris Ramsden, John Skinner, Nick Lane, Jassim Khalaf, Alf Johnson and N. A. Khan. To them and to all those people who helped, my sincere thanks.

I gradually learnt to write the history of our family, its business and environment over a hundred years, most of the early part undocumented by us. Finding those who remember the old days, or have documents was frustrating and needed perseverance.

Finally, I thank my wife Salwa for her patience and support through all the late nights and weekends I spent at home tied to my library throughout this long and time-devouring process.

Haji Yusuf bin Ahmed Kanoo

Chapter 1

The Rising Son

Nearly two centuries ago, most of the Arabian peninsula and the archipelago of Bahrain were occupied by fishing and agrarian communities settled in small villages, together with nomadic bedouin tribes which roamed the length and breadth of the region. Then, as now, the Bedu did not keep many records. Instead, they depended mostly on what the elders said and remembered, just like the American Indian tribes in the USA. Many historical documents relating to this period were recorded only by the British, and only about matters of interest to them. Since the Kanoo family name is unique and cannot be easily attributed to a natural ethnographic source, not surprisingly, opinion varies as to the precise origins of our family.

From what I have heard, my ancestors seem to have migrated from north of Riyadh (now in the Central Province of Saudi Arabia), north to Kuwait, briefly into Mesopotamia (modern Iraq) before heading east and then south along the eastern coast of the Arabian Gulf which formed the southern boundary of Persia (now Iran). Since many Arabs lived there, they were able to maintain the Arabic language and their traditions.

A few generations later during the mid-nineteenth century, the Kanoo family began to make its way back to Arabia, via Bahrain which was intended as a 'stop-over'. Instead, the family settled on the island, led by Hilal who began to sell consumer products in his small shop. Before long, the Persian soldiers and settlers teased him for trading according to the accepted rules and the law, Qhanoon. Since they could not pronounce the Arabic letter Qh, they substituted a K sound, hence people referred to Hilal as Kanoon. In time, the last N was dropped and the name was shortened to Kanoo. While this is an interesting and logical conclusion, unfortunately I have no means of substantiating the claim. Then, in 1950, some family members returned to Saudi Arabia where the migration had first begun, thus completing a 'full circle'.

When my story begins, in the late nineteenth century, there were few cities in Arabia as we understand the term today, except for

Mecca and Medina which were focal towns even before the advent of Islam and the growth of their significance for Moslem pilgrims from all over the world. Elsewhere, remains of cities built and abandoned in antiquity could be seen: Ur and Nineveh (now in Iraq); Failaka island (part of Kuwait) and the Dilmun cities in Bahrain, to mention just a few sites excavated in modern times.

In the mid-nineteenth century, when my ancestors settled in Bahrain, the Arabian peninsula's only prosperous towns were coastal ports. Jeddah, Hodeida, Aden, Kalba, Muharraq, Kuwait and Basrah were active then, as they are today. The urban communities of Bahrain comprised two small towns: Muharraq, then the capital and the focal point of the most northern island of the same name; and Manama, the commercial centre, now the twentieth century capital located in the north-east sector of Bahrain island from which the country takes its name. Among the remaining fertile areas of the archipelago's thirty-three islands, including the Hawar group which itself embraces some sixteen isles, small isolated villages dotted the landscape. There, the fishing and agrarian communities lived, worked and worshipped, and to some extent traded.

During the late nineteenth century, Bahrain's economy was based mainly on maritime industries: fishing, pearl-diving and boat-building. According to the Government of India's Administration Report for 1889-90, of the 4,500 pearling dhows (locally-built wooden boats) operating throughout the Arabian Gulf's pearl banks, one third were based in Bahrain. By any standards, 1,500 vessels is no small fleet.

Household commodities such as charcoal, cutlery, china and candles, together with bolts of white cloth, twist and gold thread, dyes, indigo, raw silk and woollen goods were imported. The islands' indigenous date crops were plentiful, as were fish and mutton. Nonetheless, the local diet was supplemented with other imports such as coffee, fruit and vegetables, grain and pulses, rice, dried lemons, spices and sugar. Hides, skins, tobacco, medicines and perfumes were needed too. Of necessity, villagers made long journeys by donkey to the Customs House in Manama, then the distribution centre for imported and exported goods. At that time, the port had neither a jetty nor a warehouse. It was not until 1902 that the construction of a stone pier was considered seriously, let alone built. As for a shed to store and protect goods from the elements, this was not completed until 1912. It was in this economic climate that my great-great-uncle, Haji Yusuf bin Ahmed Kanoo, took over the small family business in 1890 at the age of twenty-two.

Born in 1868, Haji Yusuf grew up learning about the business which his father, Ahmed bin Mohamed, had inherited from his own father Mohamed before him. Although a modest trader in foodstuffs, Ahmed Kanoo was not a wealthy man. Nevertheless, he was religious and a highly-respected member of Bahrain's community. Apparently, when Haji Yusuf joined the family business (which later assumed his name), it was 'just a little thing' to import basic goods to support the islands' maritime industries, all of which required canvas, ropes, timber and tools. It would seem that many other traders and merchants in Bahrain were content with what they had and did not feel inclined to expand their businesses. Ahmed bin Mohamed's son, Haji Yusuf, had other aspirations. Young and shrewd, he recognised commercial opportunities waiting to be developed.

As soon as he took over from his father, Haji Yusuf began to modernise the enterprise, starting slowly until business gained momentum. He chartered a boat to import commodities from Kerala, south-west India. Often the vessel sailed south along the East African coast, calling into Mombasa (now Kenya's main port). Sometimes, it continued south to Zanzibar, an island some 200 kilometres south of Mombasa, then ruled by an Omani Sultan. Like the Malabar Coast of Kerala, Zanzibar is famous for rich spices, coconut groves, and exotic timber, particularly mangrove which is still used in traditional Bahraini roof construction and boat-building. Closer to home, Haji Yusuf's chartered vessels called into ports along the north-west coast of India where he bought bales of cotton piece-goods, rice, tea and other consumables. Since other merchants in Bombay had long-established trading links with Arabian Gulf ports, he avoided competing with them.

As the British Raj still controlled the Arabian Gulf region from India, Haji Yusuf soon recognised the strategic and economic importance of developing diplomatic and trade links between the two areas, even though the Arabian Gulf region was a relatively unexplored part of the world. In 1862, Sir William Mackinnon founded the British India Steam Navigation Company (BISN) so that he could extend his service (already operating between Calcutta, Bombay and Karachi), to include Bahrain, Basrah and Bushire. The formation of the BISN had been made possible because the India Office, in 1861, agreed to subsidise a steamer service to serve the Arabian Gulf. Without this subsidy in the form of a mail contract, steamers were uneconomic to operate, even with full cargoes, simply because the steamers' low-pressure engines consumed huge amounts of coal and were mechanically unreliable.

3

The British were also apprehensive of Russian expansion. It was clear, then, that the BISN mail contract aimed to uphold British commercial interests in the Arabian Gulf region and reinforce existing British political representation. By 1885, British India Steam Navigation Company steamers were competing with the British-registered, but locally-operated, Bombay and Persia Steam Navigation Company, the Persian Gulf Steam Navigation Company, French steamers, and a miscellany of other smaller shipping companies. Thus, the value of imports into Bushire, the terminating port at the head of the Gulf, increased by 300 per cent from 1873 to 1903. A knock-on effect was that the economy of Bahrain improved, an entrepôt located more or less mid-way along the southern coast of the Arabian Gulf. Meanwhile, the Persian port of Lingah developed and prospered as a trans-shipment centre for traffic to and from Bahrain, as well as serving the Trucial Coast (now the United Arab Emirates).

At first, BISN's representatives at the main Gulf ports were Gray Paul & Co. and Gray Mackenzie & Co., two merchant partnerships. (Gray Paul's office in Bahrain opened in 1883.) By the 1890s, the BISN mail steamers had created a new trade up and down the Arabian Gulf, an opportunity which Haji Yusuf recognised and soon developed to his advantage. By 1898, he realised that if he were to progress in the British Raj-controlled territory, then he must learn English. To this end, he associated himself with the first British representative in Bahrain, Haji Ahmed bin Abdel-Rasool, by working as an unpaid messenger and clerk. Haji Yusuf learned quickly. As a well-informed and respected member of the community, he advised Haji Ahmed on local affairs; acted as a 'sounding-board' among other Bahraini traders; conveyed the Bahraini point of view to the British; and even assumed the role of arbitrator in local trading disputes or disagreements between the British authorities and the Bahrainis.

In 1900, Mr J. Calcott Gaskin (lately British Vice-Consul in Bushire) was assigned to Bahrain as the islands' first resident Assistant Political Agent. The British Political Department considered this posting purely temporary until an officer on its 'graded list' could be selected. Before long, Gaskin was reported to be on friendly terms with the Ruler of Bahrain. This confirmed Lord Curzon's view expressed in 1899, that Gaskin was the right choice, remarking: 'it no more matters whether he is a gazetted officer than whether he wears whiskers'.

At first, Haji Yusuf acted as interpreter between the Assistant

Political Agent and the Ruler of Bahrain, Shaikh Isa bin Ali Al Khalifa. After 13 December 1901, when Gaskin's permanent appointment was approved by the British Secretary of State, Haji Yusuf developed his relationship with the Political Agency, thus gaining experience and status. In October 1904 Gaskin's tour of duty ended and Captain F. B. Prideaux, an Indian Army officer, succeeded him. In 1905 his post was upgraded to that of Political Agent (PA). Prideaux, it seems, was also well liked. However, Haji Yusuf's relationship with successive PAs was not always cordial.

Haji Yusuf – shipping and travel agent

For most of the 1890s, long-established shipping companies faced little competition, particularly the British India Steam Navigation Company whose mail boats called into Bahrain on their way up and down the Arabian Gulf. By 1901, however, three other companies were each scheduling one or two vessels per month to transport cargo to Bahrain. These were the Bombay and Persia Steam Navigation Company, the Anglo-Arabian and Persian Steam Navigation Company, and the British and Colonial Steam Navigation Company Limited.

The official Administration Report for 1901 says that that year was 'the most prosperous year in the annals of the islands' of Bahrain, principally because of the large volume of Indian rice imports and a successful pearling season. The year was also remarkable for the largest importations of cotton piece-goods on record. At that time, Bahrain supplied the adjacent Arabian mainland coast from where trade routes ran to Nejd and beyond. Slowly, tea was becoming more popular. Meanwhile, the demand for coffee had increased considerably, with Brazilian brands competing well against their Indian and Ceylonese competitors.

The introduction of a new feature in the classification of shells was of particular interest to traders, the hope being that it would be more comprehensible to the merchants who traded in the commodity, such as Haji Yusuf. Mother-of-pearl, mussels and a certain quantity of oyster shells, known to the trade as Lingah shells, were imported from Qatar, and the island of Dalma near Abu Dhabi. Oyster shells exported from Bahrain were considered to be the best obtainable in the Arabian Gulf, being of a better-than-average quality and heavier than those shipped from other ports. Mother-of-pearl and mussels were sold by weight and oyster shells by measure. Both, in various forms, were used by craftsmen around the world to beautify jewellery, paper knives, cutlery, inlaid woodwork and other forms of decorative art.

In time, Haji Yusuf widened his network of international trade links by talking to German, British, Belgian and even American businessmen who passed through Bahrain. He became a regular traveller himself, mostly to India where he purchased goods for shipment to his own clients, as well as to other merchants in Bahrain. Once the goods were sold, a portion of the income was sent to Haji Yusuf. He bought more items, and so a cycle of trade began. Often, Haji Yusuf's trading trips lasted for four, even six months.

Before long, friendships he had developed with traders in India were transformed into more structured business arrangements. For example, through some friends, Haji Yusuf secured an agency to buy coffee and tea in large bags, send them to Bahrain and then sell the commodities loose by weight through distributors. Thus he operated as both a retailer and a wholesaler in the procurement of goods. From Bahrain, many of these were distributed to other regions such as Nejd, Al-Hasa, Qatif, Kuwait, Qatar and Sharjah. Apart from being known as a devout Moslem, Haji Yusuf earned a reputation for being trustworthy and careful. Frequently he was asked to act on behalf of other traders to buy goods for them, as well.

While all this was taking place, another sequence of events was unfolding during the first two years of the twentieth century which was of more than passing interest to Haji Yusuf: the first steps towards the re-establishment of safe trade-routes across Arabia.

During the autumn of 1901 in Kuwait, where the Al Saud family was living in exile, the Amir Abdul-Aziz Ibn Saud assembled a force of some forty relatives and retainers. He aimed to recapture Riyadh by force. Late that year, the raiding party ventured south to the remote oasis of Jabrin. There, Ibn Saud and his followers quietly observed Ramadhan and prepared themselves for their mission. After the Holy Month had ended, Ibn Saud led his party to the outskirts of Riyadh. Then, shortly after dawn on 16 January 1902, in a brief, violent assault, the walled town measuring some 700 yards square (582 metres square) was successfully recaptured. Thus, the first step had been achieved towards the return of his family from exile. (It was this same Amir Abdul-Aziz, Sultan of Nejd, who was proclaimed King of the Hijaz, Nejd and its dependencies, on 18 January 1926. Six years later, on 23 September 1932, the Kingdom of Saudi Arabia was proclaimed.)

As our family business grew, agency agreements with foreign shipping companies became Y.B.A.Kanoo's 'senior service'.

Although Haji Yusuf began to deal with shipping lines soon after he took over the family business, it was not until the early twentieth century that he formalised these arrangements. The earliest surviving shipping documents in our family archive confirm that during 1911, Haji Yusuf corresponded regularly with a newly-formed company: Arab Steamers Limited. Although this Bombay-based company owned just one vessel, it was eager to provide Yusuf bin Ahmed Kanoo, its agent in Bahrain, with a regular service. By July 1911 two more steamers had been ordered, 'in every way comfortable and much larger' than the SS *Budrie*. Now having a 'capable fleet', it intended to offer a weekly or fortnightly service, provide competition for the British India Steam Navigation Company and, above all, recover some of its investment. To achieve this latter end, it would seem that Arab Steamers' Managing Director, Mr M. A. W. Mishari, assumed that Haji Yusuf would play the game according to their rules.

First, the company decided to maintain its cargo and passenger rates at exactly those of the British India steamers. The price marked on relevant tickets, bills of lading, and so on, had to correspond exactly with the British India Steam Navigation Company's charges. But this was not the end of the matter. Only if Haji Yusuf managed to 'secure' more than a dozen passengers to travel at the same time, was he allowed to instruct the shipping company's agent in Basrah to send SS *Budrie* via Bahrain, *en route* back to Bombay. As such diversions required more coal, Arab Steamers' policy was that the cost of the ship's fuel should be covered. But when the 'BI people' threatened to lower their rates and still offer a regular service, life became more complex for Haji Yusuf. On the occasions when he managed to book some passengers, but fewer than the minimum quota, Arab Steamers would not provide the transport. Much to Haji Yusuf's embarrassment, passengers then had to switch to the competition. Predictably, he told Arab Steamers just how disgusted he felt about this 'irritating irregularity'.

Sometimes, Haji Yusuf was asked to act as a local courier. A letter dated 1911 describes four share certificates issued in Bombay for 'Abdoola bin Hasan Al-Doosaree of Bahrain'. Once Haji Yusuf received them, he was requested to deliver them safely. Abdoola (now usually spelt Abdulla), was a leading member of the powerful and proud Al-Doosaree (Al-Dosari) Arab tribe which inhabited Bahrain, eastern Saudi Arabia and Qatar. (Today, the family remains influential, with several of its members appointed to senior private and government positions. Among them was Mr. Yousuf Rahma Al-

Dosari who, until his death in October 1995, had been the President of the Amiri Court of Bahrain for many years.)

By all accounts, 1911 was regarded as a successful first year of co-operation between Arab Steamers and Haji Yusuf. By the year end, the shipping company had acquired new premises (Arab Lane, Grant Road, Bombay); a new telephone number (Bombay 1533); re-designed stationery; and had five vessels in service ready to start a regular fortnightly service to Bahrain in January 1912. Meanwhile, Haji Yusuf had something else to look forward to. As requested, Mishari had bought 'a good typewriting machine' for him, due to be sent by the next steamer leaving Bombay. This, I later learnt, was the first typewriter to be imported by an Arab into Bahrain, or elsewhere in Arabia.

If Haji Yusuf was optimistic about the opportunities which Arab Steamers' increased service would offer him, he was also aware of the difficulties being experienced among Bahrain's shipping fraternity. Discharging cargo and disembarking passengers offshore into lighters (engineless inshore boats) and dhows without damage and injury, was becoming a major concern. In the interests of a quick turn-round and the safety of vessels, steamer captains preferred to anchor in deep water several kilometres offshore, too far out to sea for the practical convenience of inshore craft. As a result, particularly during rough weather, both people and packages tended to fall into the sea during the transfer process. On such occasions, Haji Yusuf often mediated in disputes between steamer and dhow captains. Later, he negotiated a compromise whereby steamer captains were instructed to moor as near to Mina Manama (Manama Port) as possible, without risking damage to their ships from submerged reefs, or being grounded in shallow sea.

Nevertheless, disasters still happened. During the afternoon of 7 May 1912, the Bahrain-based lighter, *Shaikh Isa,* went alongside the SS *Queda* to load 500 bags of rice. As *Nawkhadha* (Captain) Jabar bin Ahmed Jalahmi began his task, a strong northerly wind, the *shamal,* blew up. The captain managed to transfer the cargo from steamer to lighter and set sail for Mina Manama. But, just before sunset as the boat neared the wharf at high tide, a fierce gust blew the lighter onto some sharp rocks. With its hull ripped open, the boat lay impaled in less than half a metre of water. Next day, porters waded out to the wreck to discharge the sea-sodden cargo onto the wharf. It fell to Haji Yusuf, the shipping company's agent, to request Gray Paul & Co., Lloyds agents in Bahrain since 1904, to survey the loss. They concluded that 49 bags of damaged goods should be sold by public auction, duty payable only on the sale's proceeds. In consideration of this service, Haji Yusuf was charged two guineas: £2 2s.

One week later, Haji Yusuf dealt with a far greater calamity. On 14 May four lighters loaded with cargo, again discharged from SS *Queda*, sailed for Mina Manama. As it was low-water, the boats anchored outside the harbour to wait for the next high-tide. Unfortunately a storm blew up during the night making it impossible for the boatmen to reach the shore in safety. Two of the dhows, both from Qatif on the Arabian mainland, sank with all their cargo. Another dhow was driven onto the reef close to the harbour, leaving the *nawkhadha* and his crew stranded. The fourth dhow, also blown onto the reef, was partly submerged. In the confusion many bags of rice were jettisoned, although some were later recovered from the sea. Again, it was Haji Yusuf's task as the shipping company's agent to organise a salvage operation, arrange a loss assessment and make an insurance claim through Lloyds agents, Gray Paul & Co. The report does not mention the captains and crews, so I assume that they were rescued.

In late 1912 the Government of India directed the Political Agent in Bahrain to revise the port landing procedures immediately. Although these would do nothing to help dhow captains struggle with rough weather, at least the landing of goods might become more efficient. The main new procedure required shipping company agents, like Haji Yusuf, to be given the option, upon payment of 5 per cent on the gross landing fees, to discharge cargo onto the pier in an officially organised manner.

To achieve this, the Ruler of Bahrain appointed a Customs Director to supervise operations and to assess and collect duty. The Ruler also appointed a Warehouse Superintendent to receive consignments onto the jetty from the shipping companies' agents and to have the goods sorted and stored, then issued to the consignees who, in turn, were responsible for removing their shipments from the port. As a temporary measure, the Ruler nominated Ali bin Abdullah (one of his employees), to organise the lighter arrangements. On 6 April 1913 the new system came into effect.

Some Boat Notes, dated 17 April 1914, provide another insight into contemporary maritime affairs. For those unfamiliar with the term, a Boat Note is a form which numbers and itemises the cargo discharged from a steamer into a local lighter, including a description of the packages, their contents and in what condition they were received. Having signed the Boat Note, the Discharging Officer then handed it to the Head Boatman (the procedure printed on the form) who, in turn, delivered the Note to the shipping company's agents, in this case, Haji Yusuf.

Tins of tallow and ghee, bags of rice and black pepper, bundles of candles and cardboard were nothing unusual. It was an unfamiliar commodity, capots of charcoal, which made me curious. Three separate Boat Notes referred to the considerable quantities involved: 89, 110 and 130 capots. As to the column which invited comments concerning the condition of the cargo, each Note contained the same message: 'several covers torn and contents running out.'

Since it seemed that a capot was neither robust, nor well-suited to transporting charcoal, I wondered what they were and why they were used. Apparently, charcoal used to be shipped in straw mats, sewn together in the shape of a barrel and stitched at both ends, this type of straw packaging being called a capot. Interestingly enough, the steamer from which the cargo had been discharged was another 'old faithful': the SS *Budrie,* owned by Arab Steamers.

Another example of an agency agreement negotiated between the House of Kanoo and a foreign company was that signed in 1913 by Haji Yusuf and the Anglo-Persian Oil Company (APOC). The Mahadi Namazi Line had already begun a service between Basrah and Bahrain on behalf of the oil company. When Haji Yusuf's new agreement became effective, *de facto* he represented the Mahadi Namazi Line in Bahrain, too. Later, this shipping company integrated with the Mogul Line for which Haji Yusuf was the agent in Bahrain and whose main activity was the transport of pilgrims to and from Jeddah.

By the outbreak of the First World War, Haji Yusuf had established a substantial portfolio of shipping agencies. At the same time, the shipping company owners had created a complex web of corporate identities through successive acquisitions, mergers and name-changes. In 1903, Frank C. Strick & Co., the Bucknall Steamship Lines and J. E. Guthe & Co. (owners of the West Hartlepool Steam Navigation Company) came to a joint agreement which lasted until 1909. When this contract expired, Guthe & Co. withdrew from the arrangement. Meanwhile, in 1908, the Ellerman Line acquired Bucknall Steamship Lines. Thus, from 1909 until the outbreak of the Second World War in 1939, Frank C. Strick & Company and the Ellerman Line together operated a competitive service between the United Kingdom and the Arabian Gulf: the Strick-Ellerman Line.

The number of shipping company changes which occurred during the early years of this century often caused confusion and lost business, as the next episode illustrates. Soon after the First World

War began Haji Yusuf signed a contract to represent the Bombay & Persia Steam Navigation Company. (By 1916, this had merged with Arab Steamers to operate a joint service. Later, it became part of the Mogul Line.) Before long, Haji Yusuf had also negotiated an agency agreement with the Persian Gulf Steam Navigation Company Limited creating a conflict of interest.

Adding to the confusion of the similar names was the fact that both rivals had been registered in 1870. The only helpful hint as to their separate identities was that the home port of the Persian Gulf Steam Navigation Company was London, and that of the Bombay and Persia Steam Navigation Company was, not surprisingly, Bombay.

Perhaps because of the risk of mistaken identity, rather than the threat of lost business, Haji Yusuf's latest agency acquisition caused the owner of the Bombay and Persia Steam Navigation Company to complain that it was not corporate policy to allow its agents to represent rival shipping lines. Eventually Haji Yusuf resolved the matter by giving up the smaller agency, that of the Persian Gulf Steam Navigation Company.

Although, at this time, not all Haji Yusuf's work involved commercial affairs at sea, more often than not his business was connected with it. Two pages of text, dated 28 November 1913, sent to Major Trevor, the British Political Agent in Bahrain, represent an example of how Haji Yusuf became indirectly involved with a visiting Admiral's recreational pursuits.

The invoice and receipts refer to no less an event than a two-day camping expedition to A'ain Al-Ghar, led by the British Admiral Sir Edmund Slade, then visiting Bahrain. Apparently, this *a'ain* (a fresh-water spring) owes its name to a smell of *ghar* (bitumen). The water may have been polluted with oil, indicating that this may have been the first sign of oil reserves in Bahrain, as suggested by Guy E. Pilgrim in his geological account published in 1908. A'ain Al-Ghar, now covered by a road, was situated a few miles south of Jebel Ad-Dukhan (Mountain of Smoke), and the site of Bahrain's first oil-well which came on stream in 1932. The *a'ain* would have been a very remote place for the Admiral's camp-site, but not so far from another lone phenomenon: the Tree of Life. (Botanically classified as a *Prosopis juliflora*, even today, the irrigation source of this isolated member of the bean family, a relative of the Central American mesquite tree, remains a mystery.)

For the use of the donkeys and donkeymen in the Admiral's party, Haji Yusuf was required to send the following articles to the camp-site: half a bag of rice, four bundles of dates, fresh grass for two days, fat and prawns, tobacco, onions, coffee and halwa. The Admiral's party itself was supplied with rice, bread, two bundles of dates, six baskets and one capot of charcoal.

Haji Yusuf's comments in his covering letter to Major Trevor add an interesting postscript to the episode: 'I have paid each man separately, as I thought if I paid the money in one's hand for distribution to the others, they might afterwards grumble that they have not received their amounts properly, hence the different receipts.' According to Major Trevor's wish that Haji Yusuf should recommend deserving people, he chose Khal (Uncle) Mohamed, Mubarak bin Saad bin Ramul and Abdulrahman bin Abdul Latif. Haji Yusuf's charge for the entire service was just 634 rupees.

On a regular basis, Haji Yusuf also operated as a travel agent for pilgrims sailing to Jeddah. The procedure depended on close liaison with his shipping agency counterparts in Basrah and Bushire, Muscat and Karachi. The Ottoman authorities added a complication by levying a tax of ten piastres on each pilgrim who arrived in the Hijaz region. As this tax was based on passenger manifests, shipping companies' agents had to collect both taxes and ticket payments from pilgrims, before they were allowed to leave their originating port. Thereafter, it was the responsibility of steamer captains to pay the taxes to the Turkish authorities immediately upon their arrival in Jeddah. Inevitably, there was resentment and resistance to the scheme, but in the prevailing political circumstances, little could be done to alter the situation.

An added frustration developed in mid-September 1911. The roads from Yanbu were closed because of hostilities between the Sherif of Mecca and the Bedouin. As a result, pilgrims were obliged to disembark at Rabigh, some 100 kilometres south of Yanbu and so nearer to Mecca. Nevertheless, steamer tickets had to be issued so that they were available for both ports. One wonders how Haji Yusuf reacted to Mishari's distant directive despatched from his Bombay office: 'Do your best to lessen the inconvenience of customers and patrons, but of course with proper precaution.'

The British Political Agency

In addition to Haji Yusuf's shipping and travel agency activities, there was another side to his public life: the relationship between the House of Kanoo and the British Government. There is little doubt that the Political Agents had not met anyone like Haji Yusuf and did not know how to deal with him. Already, his unpaid services as interpreter and communicator between Political Agents and the Ruler of Bahrain were useful. But before long, the Political Agents considered that his opinions should be treated with special caution. If Haji Yusuf did not follow their instructions, he was viewed as an 'intriguer'. He was in a bind or, one might say, a lose-lose situation.

The point of saying this is not to open old wounds or to settle scores, but simply to illustrate how power play evolved between Haji Yusuf and successive Political Agents. Naturally they protected British principles and interests which still embraced a wide sphere of political and economic influence. Haji Yusuf, just as naturally, saw his role as a protector of Bahraini interests. The alignment of the two conflicting parties demonstrates that each had its 'battle lines' drawn. It is reasonable to suppose, therefore, that neither side was likely to deviate from its position willingly. Even as early as 1911, it was clear that things were not well, although not beyond repair.

That year, Captain D. L. R. Lorimer, Political Agent in Bahrain, reported that Haji Yusuf had 'declined to give assistance' and 'he is believed' to be in 'the Arab camp'. However, during 1912, Lorimer's final year as Political Agent in Bahrain, he recommended that Haji Yusuf's services to the British Government should be recognised. When Lorimer's successor wrote the Agency's Administration Report for 1912, Major A. P. Trevor noted: the Kaiser-i-Hind Medal of the Second Class had been awarded to Yusuf Kanoo, an Honorary *Munshi* (a go-between between the Agency and the Ruler). The medal, an Indian decoration awarded by the British to non-British dignitaries, was a Coronation honour presented to Haji Yusuf with due ceremony on King George V's birthday. Clearly alluding to previous strains between the Political Agent and Haji Yusuf, Major Trevor also remarked that relations between the Agency and Haji Yusuf had gradually become easier during that year, 1912.

Five years later, writing on 7 August 1917, Captain P. G. Loch informed Haji Yusuf: 'It is with great pleasure that I send you the Badge, Ribbon and Sanad of the title of Khan Sahib which has been conferred on you by the Government of India in recognition of your services.' (This title is equivalent to 'Sir' and is used in the same way.) Then, on 3 June 1919, Haji Yusuf became a Member of the Order of the British Empire (MBE). Three days later Captain N. N. E. Bray, the incumbent Political Agent, departed on a special mission to England. For the next five months Indian Assistant Syed Siddiq Hassan held office at the Agency. Then, on 6 November 1919, the 'Dicksonian' era began.

Major H. R. P. Dickson was well known as a man who either loved someone or hated him. Unfortunately, Haji Yusuf fell into the latter category. Each time he wrote to, or about, Haji Yusuf, Dickson did so in derogatory terms. Major Dickson was an arrogant man who felt that the local population should do what he ordered without question, or he would punish them. For example, one day he had a big circle marked with rocks on the road between Manama and Gudaibiyah and ordered that no-one should cross the road by going inside the circle. There was no apparent reason for this except, perhaps, to demonstrate his authority. When Major C. K. Daly became the Political Agent in 1921, he began a campaign to break Haji Yusuf, principally because he was in the 'Arab camp' and actively supported it.

Neither Dickson nor Daly liked Haji Yusuf and so created trouble for him. Both were military intelligence officers who had previously served in Iraq. Both were later transferred from Bahrain after the people and the Shaikh of Bahrain petitioned the British Government for their removal. In Dickson's case, the dismissal was abrupt. During what he thought would be a temporary absence from Bahrain for the purpose of escorting his wife from Iraq, an order for his removal from office was prepared. When Dickson returned to Bahrain, he was shown the order and instructed to return to Iraq on the same steamer from which he had just disembarked. Dickson's tenure in Bahrain had lasted just over a year: from 6 November 1919 to 28 November 1920. In Daly's case, after a policeman made an attempt on his life in 1926, he was replaced by Major C. C. J. Barrett.

While British Political Agents often disliked Haji Yusuf's rebellious spirit, they also feared him for two significant reasons: most obvious was Haji Yusuf's close relationship with the Ruler of Bahrain; less evident, but equally influential, was the high regard which Bahraini citizens held for Haji Yusuf as a benevolent merchant and a religious leader. It is therefore not surprising that Haji Yusuf faced problems with Dickson and Daly, in particular, as did many other Bahrainis. As a merchant and a leading member of the community, Haji Yusuf was targeted on several occasions. In an attempt to break him, many derogatory reports were sent to London in the Political Agents' official correspondence. Haji Yusuf survived the intrigue, but not the backlash. He had been 'stained', notably by a character assassination written in 1920.

By now, Haji Yusuf's relationship with the Political Agency in Bahrain had deteriorated. Being a proud man and not someone to be pushed around, Haji Yusuf would not always comply with what successive Political Agents wanted. They resented him because he was influential enough to make trouble. Yet they would not admit openly to a bad relationship with him. Arabs value their self-esteem and the British did not understand why Haji Yusuf was 'somewhat of a touchy nature in which his dignity is a concern.' As both the British and Bahrainis energetically defended both their pride and privileges, political power play was often the root of the struggle.

A decade later, the ugly spectre of British ill-will became evident again. By now, the 1930s economic depression had affected the Arabian Gulf, including Bahrain. Haji Yusuf saw much suffering and starvation and vowed to do what he could to help. After repaying all his debts, he gave to the needy to the extent that he became cash-poor himself. When he requested Rs 20,000 as a bridging-loan to tide him over until he was paid by debtors and could generate more cash, the Ruler of Bahrain agreed. But the Ruler's adviser, Charles Belgrave (who, incidentally, arrived in Bahrain six months before Major Daly's departure in 1926), recommended against it. Hence Haji Yusuf had to do what he feared most, approach the Eastern Bank for a loan with interest, a non-Islamic practice. This was granted, but being a commercial enterprise, the bank levied hefty interest. To pay this, Haji Yusuf had to sell much property but even so, he could not repay the bank fully. When the Bahrain Government eventually gave him an interest-free loan, both his business and health had been affected.

This situation is largely explained by the fact that, until the independence of India in 1947, British dominance of the Arabian Gulf area was overpowering. What the British dictated, through the Government of India's offices in Calcutta and Delhi, was what happened. Few people opposed them. One person who resented this authoritative hand was Shaikh Qasim Al-Mihza, the Chief Justice of Bahrain. He opposed the British because of what he saw as their interference in local matters and citizens' lives.

All this being said, there were moments of pleasing politeness. One such example took place in 1923 when Haji Yusuf was decorated with the CIE (Companion of the Order of the Indian Empire), an honour conferred by King George V.

Arch-rival Gray Mackenzie

In January 1920 Haji Yusuf had been honoured to attend the Court of Abdul-Aziz Ibn Saud in Riyadh, an episode I describe later. For now, suffice it to say that it is unlikely that Haji Yusuf knew of the

Mesopotamia Persia Corporation's formation during that same month. On the face of it, the two events are unconnected. However, it should be noted that the incumbent British Political Agent, Major Dickson, had attended the audience too. Whether thoughts of potential rival business interests occurred to Haji Yusuf and Major Dickson as they left Riyadh, we shall never know. What history has shown is that the Mesopotamia Persia Corporation became the forerunner to the arch-rival of Y.B.A.Kanoo's shipping agency: Gray Mackenzie & Company.

This rivalry was manifest in Bahrain, but it also surfaced in Arabia, Abu Dhabi, Dubai, Muscat and Sharjah where both companies operated as part of an extensive agency network. As mutual irritation between Y.B.A.Kanoo and Gray Mackenzie did not become apparent until several years later, I shall not digress here. However, it is helpful to understand the background to this rivalry. It also helps the flow of my story if I sketch a simple evolution and framework of company names which, during the 1920s and early 1930s, became part of this growing predicament.

In the immediate years preceding the First World War, the British had become increasingly concerned about the growth of German influence in the Arabian Gulf. For instance, in the late nineteenth century Robert Wonckhaus, agents for the Hamburg-Amerika shipping line, established a branch in Bahrain. Early in the twentieth century, the Wonckhaus agency was competing fiercely with the British India Steam Navigation Company, whose Chairman was then Lord Inchcape.

As tensions rose in Europe, the British Government decided to encourage British enterprise in the Arabian Gulf region more vigorously. So it was that Lord Inchcape played a key role in the negotiations between two Boards of Directors, those of the Baghdad Railway Company and the Ottoman River Navigation Company. The details of the agreement reached in 1913 concerning railway construction and the creation of a commercial traffic monopoly on the Tigris and Euphrates rivers, are irrelevant to my story. The significant point is that these plans were made in conjunction with Lynch Brothers who, with Lord Inchcape, were to hold a 40 per cent interest in part of the project.

Once the First World War began, the project was put on ice. After hostilities ended in 1918, the British Government urged Lord Inchcape once more to do what he could to strengthen British interests in the development of what had become Iraq. He, together with W. B. Buchanan (a senior partner of Gray Mackenzie and Gray

Paul) and F. W. Parry (an executive director of Lynch Brothers) created a new entity: the Mesopotamia Persia Corporation Limited (MPC), formed in January 1920.

But as it turned out, expectations did not match experience. Although it was hoped that this new enterprise would contribute much to the region's post-war economic recovery and expansion, the realities were different. The amalgamation of these business interests did not reap the expected economies in office staff and the elimination of duplication. Even worse, management conflict and a lack of co-operation between Gray Mackenzie and Lynch Brothers caused MPC to suffer heavy financial losses from the outset. The two firms never managed to work together in a harmonious or profitable fashion. By 1924, the liquidation of MPC was discussed but never implemented. The ultimate demise of the Mesopotamia Persia Corporation took place in 1936 when the firms involved reverted to their original identities.

Out of this transformation, the two merchant partnerships of Gray Mackenzie & Company and Gray Paul & Company were converted in 1936 into one limited liability company registered in the United Kingdom: Gray Mackenzie and Company Limited. It so happened that their registered office was shared with those of the British India Steam Navigation Company (BISN) and Peninsular & Oriental Steamship Company (P & O) shipping lines at 122 Leadenhall Street, London. But during the 1920s, as the Mesopotamia Persia Corporation wrestled with its internal problems, it was clear that our comparatively modest family business in Bahrain could expect to encounter hostility and cynicism from this British competitor.

Haji Yusuf – benefactor and diplomat

Despite Haji Yusuf's business success, there was sadness in his life since he and his wife were unable to have children of their own. Equally unfortunate was the early death of Haji Yusuf's younger brother, Mohamed, a victim of the devastating plague, cholera and influenza epidemic which struck Bahrain during 1903 and 1904. Of the estimated 600 occurrences of the disease, 301 deaths were recorded. Just twenty-five years old, Mohamed died leaving two sons, Ali and Jassim, and a daughter Mariam. So it was that Haji Yusuf assumed responsibility for raising his nephews and niece.

As an even closer family bond formed between them all, the children no longer called Haji Yusuf 'uncle' but 'father'. As my story evolves, Jassim and Ali's sons will be introduced as they begin to participate in the business but, for now, suffice it to say that my father was Jassim's eldest son. It so happens, therefore, that I am the oldest of the fifth generation of family members to become involved in the business. (Figure 1 on page 310, a simplified abstract from our family tree, explains these relationships more clearly.)

During the second decade of the twentieth century, Haji Yusuf became a prominent member of Bahrain's community in affairs unrelated to trade. For example, in November 1912 a subscription was raised for the Red Crescent Society. Some 104,000 rupees were collected, of which the Ruler of Bahrain, Shaikh Isa bin Ali Al Khalifa, had subscribed 10,000 rupees. Merchants and members of the Bahrain community subscribed handsomely also. At the end of 1912, Haji Yusuf and Shaikh Abdul Wahab Zayyani were appointed to transmit the money to Constantinople in person. Fearing that the Wali of Basrah might interfere in the matter *en route,* the travellers took the precaution of landing in Bushire. From there, they sent a telegram to the Sultan in Constantinople giving him details of the donation, the total sum of money which had been collected and the circumstances of its collection. The money, it was made clear, had been donated by both the Ruler and the citizens of Bahrain for the sole benefit of the Red Crescent Society. Apart from ensuring that the Wali of Basrah could not claim the money for his own use, perhaps the travellers also wished to document that, as a nation, Bahrainis concerned themselves about the suffering of others living far beyond their shores.

Haji Yusuf was among the first few people to support the idea that a municipality should be formed in Manama. In 1917, he helped his close friend, Mohamed Ali Zainal Alireza, to establish Al Falah, the first private school for boys in Bahrain. (Al-Hidaya Al-Khalifeya School, the first Government school in the Arabian Gulf region, opened in Bahrain during 1919.)

Later, Mohamed Ali Zainal Alireza set up similar schools in Jeddah and Dubai, also called Al Falah. (Interestingly, in the mid-1920s, Amir Abdul-Aziz ibn Saud arrived outside Jeddah with the intention of persuading the city to join his unification of Arabia, by force if necessary. On 17 December 1925, Mohamed Ali Zainal's uncle, Haji Abdulla Alireza, the Governor of Jeddah, persuaded the city's elders to join Ibn Saud, and so led a delegation to his camp at Ragamah, some ten kilometres out of Jeddah. A series of meetings and negotiations followed. On 23 December 1925, the citizens of Jeddah first paid homage to Abdul-Aziz Ibn Saud. Haji Abdulla Alireza formally handed the key of the city to Ibn Saud without a fight, along with his own resignation as Governor. Abdul-Aziz, however, recognised the old man's mission to organise resistance for over a year, and so reinstated his governorship in a gesture of reconciliation. Jeddah had capitulated after a long siege. Thereby the Hashemite rule of Hijaz ended and the modern history of Saudi Arabia began.)

Haji Yusuf was also renowned for calming local disturbances although, understandably, he did not enjoy sitting on committees of enquiry which were established for the purpose. Sometimes, he was asked to arbitrate outside Bahrain, an example of which I heard about in 1971 from the late Shaikh Khalid Al-Qasimi, then Ruler of Sharjah. After I had been introduced to Shaikh Khalid by my late uncle, Hamed Kanoo, the Ruler reminisced about his first meeting with Haji Yusuf many years earlier. Apparently, Haji Yusuf was asked if he would arbitrate between two tribes who were fighting over the ownership of a water-well in Ras Al-Khaimah. He willingly obliged and set sail to Sharjah.

On his arrival, after hearing the case from both sides, he insisted that he should see the disputed well for himself before making judgment. Unaccustomed as he was to riding a camel, the only mode of transport available, Haji Yusuf found the journey a cumbersome procedure. Nevertheless, the party duly set off from Sharjah, riding through Um Al-Qawain until they entered Ras Al-Khaimah. As the group neared a small fortress, Haji Yusuf accidentally fell off his camel. Steadfastly he refused to travel further and conducted the arbitration on the very spot where he had fallen, the top of a sandy hill. Even today, this place is called Nidd Kanoo (Kanoo's Rise).

Chapter 2

Business Blooms

Early in the twentieth century Bahrain was the centre of the Arabian Gulf pearl industry. Merchants arrived from all over the region to buy and sell pearls, not only for the local markets but also to trade with international markets such as Bombay and Paris. Often, foreign traders opened an account with a Bahraini pearl merchant through whom they bought pearls. If a foreign trader knew a friend or family member stationed locally, then he might ask that friend or relative to act as a local agent to buy pearls on his behalf. But there were risks to such arrangements. There were no banks and no secure place for people to deposit their valuables for safe-keeping.

Years ago, Haji Yusuf told Ahmed Kanoo (now the Group Chairman) how dangerous the situation had become before the First World War. People were afraid to keep money in their homes because often thieves broke into houses where they knew the occupants stored money and valuables, stole what they wanted, killed the owners and escaped, the culprits believing that they could make off with the goods without being caught.

In about 1910 when people became more fearful for their lives and their property, Haji Yusuf decided to build a strong-room in Bahrain for the use and benefit of the islands' inhabitants and travellers. Coincidentally, oil had been discovered in Persia during 1908. During 1909, the Anglo-Persian Oil Company (APOC) was formed and the Eastern Bank established in London to serve trading links with India. In 1910 the bank's first branch was opened in Bombay. (In 1912 and 1915 the Eastern Bank opened two more branches: the first in Baghdad and the second in Basrah.)

Haji Yusuf – banker of Bahrain and Bombay

Perhaps it was a coincidence that Haji Yusuf began his 'banking' service in Bahrain at much the same time. Nevertheless, he was well aware of the new Eastern Bank's presence in Bombay and monitored its activities closely. He would also have recognised the potential of becoming an agent for APOC, which he did in 1913.

However, for now, my focus is on part of the ground floor of our large old family house in Manama where Haji Yusuf had established his office. (The old house occupied the site on the Tijjar Road where Al-Zainah Plaza stands today.) Having purchased a Goodridge safe from England, complete with a huge, walk-through steel door, Haji Yusuf installed this next to his office. Merchants were allowed to deposit their money, gold and pearls in what became his famous strong-room, secured with thick steel panels, the heavy door and big locks, guarded by a watchman who sat outside. In this small way, Haji Yusuf's safe-deposit service began. (Now, the safe is displayed in Bahrain's Heritage Centre, just a couple of blocks away from our main Manama office.)

So it was that many people came to Haji Yusuf with their sealed boxes of silver coins which had been shipped from India. As demand increased, Haji Yusuf had rows of shelves installed in his strong-room to accommodate more of these wooden boxes. Each box, featuring two rope handles and secured with a padlock, contained 4,000 rupees divided equally between two bags.

Although it would be interesting to convert this sum to Bahrain's present currency, it is very difficult to do so. However, an alternative, although imprecise modern comparison can be made. Many elderly market traders still speak of rupees, not Bahrain's present unit of currency, the dinar. If I were to buy a bunch of parsley from such a trader, he might ask me for one rupee although he would know that, broadly speaking, the equivalent legal tender is 100 fils (one tenth of a dinar). For him, the 100 fils coin is conveniently similar to the rupee coin which the trader is used to counting. My grandmother's recollection is that fifteen rupees fed the entire Kanoo household for one month. For instance, a sack of rice (50 kilograms) cost three rupees.

Large amounts of coins were not counted individually, but were weighed on a conventional set of scales such as those still used by souq traders to weigh fruit, nuts, spices and tobacco leaves. The clattering ring of coins being poured into one of the scale's brass pans (the other being occupied by weights), is a sound I still remember. It is interesting to note that all such transactions which involved our family, were made in front of Haji Yusuf in his large open office where all could witness the proceedings.

Several reasons help to explain why Haji Yusuf's 'banking' service was much sought-after. Many Arab merchants preferred to stick with their traditional trading customs which they believed worked well enough for them. Since they all spoke Arabic and operated on a one-to-one basis with Haji Yusuf, communication was not a problem either. As a result, traders and travellers used Haji Yusuf's safe-deposit facility and often placed their valuables with him for safe-keeping. Haji Yusuf did not charge a fee for this service but provided it for the prestige he would gain.

Haji Yusuf became known as a banker in both Bahrain and Bombay where he had established offices. The system seems to have worked this way. Shaikhs, merchants and individuals might send their 'cheques' (personal promissory notes) to Haji Yusuf, instructing him to pay 'so and so' an amount of money, on the promise that the account would be settled later. Conversely, Haji Yusuf might do the same in reverse.

In this way, Bahraini importers could deposit funds with Haji Yusuf in Bahrain, travel to India, purchase what they required and then pay their creditors by drawing on their own accounts maintained in Haji Yusuf's Bombay office. In this way, the physical shipment of hard currency was kept to a minimum. When it did move, the process was straightforward since the money was already bagged and boxed. This system operated throughout the Asian sub-continent and the Arabian Gulf ports.

It was customary for Bahraini pearl merchants to travel to India during the winter months to sell their pearls. Having done so, they could establish an account with Haji Yusuf by depositing the sale-proceeds in his Bombay office. In the spring the pearl merchants could then go to Haji Yusuf's office in Bahrain and draw on their accounts held in Bombay. In this way, they could advance money to the dhow captains who, in turn, advanced expenses to the divers, pullers and other members of the pearl-fishing crews. Sometimes, Haji Yusuf might commit himself to ventures, such as financing an entire pearling voyage. In this type of speculative deal, Haji Yusuf would agree to underwrite the dhow captain's venture, and to partake in his profit or loss (whichever applied). Conversely, Haji Yusuf might finance a dhow captain's trading voyage in the same way. This Islamic banking principle is known as *mudharaba,* not to be confused with *murabaha,* which is a short-term loan for a specific, defined purpose with minimum risk. An example would be a deal in which Haji Yusuf lent some money to a local merchant who, as a commission agent, wished to buy goods from a manufacturer and sell them to a retailer, on the understanding that the loan would be repaid to Haji Yusuf with part of the merchant's profit.

Although Haji Yusuf kept meticulous accounting books, few people in Bahrain could read or write at that time. To overcome this, he sometimes adopted an accounting system which did not depend on paperwork. So, when dhow captains, divers, traders and travellers entrusted Haji Yusuf with a sum of money, or pearls, often they identified their property by tying several knots in the red handkerchief in which they had wrapped their belongings. Haji Yusuf's accountant identified each owner by the number of knots attributed to each person, as noted in our record books. During long absences from Bahrain, Bahrainis might also arrange for Haji Yusuf to pay their families a regular allowance, or leave a 'will' so that if a traveller died while away, Haji Yusuf would pass the deceased's money onto his heirs.

In time, Haji Yusuf became a financial 'authority' in Bahrain. By receiving currency and commodity prices from agents in London, he could advise his clients throughout the Arabian Gulf region, including Muscat and Oman. He also kept a watchful eye on other banking activities, not least of which was the Eastern Bank's interest in opening a branch in Bahrain.

Competition – the Eastern Bank

In 1916 the Eastern Bank applied to open a branch in Manama. As the bank expected no resistance in Bahrain, it came as a surprise when permission was refused. When, in 1917, Mr MacPhail, the Eastern Bank's representative, met Shaikh Isa bin Ali Al Khalifa, the Ruler, he was told that some Bahraini merchants opposed the establishment of a formal bank in Bahrain. No doubt Haji Yusuf was among this number since he, and many others, believed that banks should follow Islamic principles: no interest should be charged. Instead, a banker should take an agreed amount of his client's profit, nowadays called the Islamic banking method. Apart from this objection, Haji Yusuf did not welcome the idea of a foreign bank operating in Bahrain since he recognised the proposal as a serious threat to his own 'banking' business.

Wartime rationing was also making it very difficult for anyone to obtain shipments of specie (coins as opposed to paper money) from India. Nevertheless, in July 1918, the Political Agent in Bahrain, Captain N. N. E. Bray, invited all the islands' leading merchants to a meeting to hear him explain the additional trade facilities and advantages they would gain, as would the pearling fraternity, if a conventional commercial bank were to be established in Bahrain. At the end of the meeting, the merchants, including Haji Yusuf, were asked to sign a list according to their wishes: stating their approval or opposition to the project. The official British view, according to the Annual Administration Report, was that all the merchants consented willingly since they understood the value of having a conventional, international commercial bank operating in Bahrain. The Ruler, Shaikh Isa bin Ali Al Khalifa, was approached regarding the proposal and readily agreed that a branch of the Eastern Bank should open in Bahrain.

The Eastern Bank saga is a long one. For the purposes of my story, it is sufficient to say that many Bahrainis maintained their position: they did not want a non-Islamic type of bank established on the island. The Political Agent, however, felt that it would be strategically important to the United Kingdom if a British bank replaced Haji Yusuf's operation, thus making international trading and financial control easier for them. Haji Yusuf led the resistance in a quiet way. Even so, the Political Agent formally asked him to give up his opposition.

Thereafter, Haji Yusuf continued privately to resist the Eastern Bank's establishment in Bahrain, although officially he no longer objected strenuously to its presence. Perhaps this explains his co-operation in 1918 as a co-signatory to the merchants' document of approval. Haji Yusuf was not happy with the decision since he concluded that a foreign bank's presence would reduce his sphere of influence and his prominence in the local community. However, he was wise enough to concede that, sooner or later, proper banking would be established in Bahrain, with or without him.

On 1 July 1920, the Eastern Bank commenced business in a house in the Manama souq, located on the site of the present Oriental Palace Hotel. The property was leased from Abdul Rahman Algosaibi for an annual rent of Rs 250. Mr N. R. Newsum, the bank's first manager, had arrived during June to conclude this arrangement and to purchase some essential items: a safe from India, a safe-door from Basrah, and six Yale padlocks from an unrecorded source.

An entry in the Office Furniture Account stating 'cost of lantern for guard' indicates that the building was guarded. Then in January 1921, a revolver and cartridges were purchased. As to whether this was a response to, or an anticipation of, unwelcome trouble, the records are silent.

Supplies of both goods and cash came mostly from the Bombay, Basrah and Baghdad branches. As late as 1924, some account-opening forms still had 'Basrah' scored out and 'Bahrain' written over the top. In addition to sundry furniture, the Bahrain office boasted a *pankah* (ceiling-fan), a table call-bell, scales with copper pans, and a typewriter which had cost Rs 200.

Newsum was replaced in April 1921 by Mr M. W. Himsworth whose apartment was on the upper floor of the leased property. He, too, enjoyed the luxury of a *pankah*, as well as a soda-water machine and an ice-cream freezer. BISN 'slow mail' boats brought supplies of drinking water from Bombay. As the boats anchored a mile or so offshore, individuals' water drums were sent out by launch so that they could be filled from the fresh-water tanks on board the ship.

Almost from the start, a major problem faced the Eastern Bank: the volume of silver coins required to serve business needs in Bahrain. Eastern Bank's Inspector of Branches reported during 1920, that 'all evidence at our disposal goes to show that the merchants in Bahrain are not accustomed to notes, and that silver has been, and is still practically the only circulating medium'. Nevertheless, within a few years, the residents of Bahrain apparently began to appreciate the advantages which the Eastern Bank offered, particularly the direct import of goods from Europe, facilitated by payment against shipping documents, received through the bank.

With the benefit of hindsight, it can be argued that Haji Yusuf missed both the opportunity and the advantage of requesting a licence to establish his own proper bank and so pre-empt the Eastern Bank's first application several years earlier. Personally, I doubt that this possibility had escaped Haji Yusuf's attention. Since he was a deeply religious man, a more likely explanation is that the concept of charging interest would have been his greatest concern. Nevertheless, within his own interpretation, Haji Yusuf's 'bank' continued to work in parallel with the Eastern Bank until his death in 1945. In any case, old habits died hard. Many merchants preferred to stick with Haji Yusuf's system which they knew, and felt more comfortable communicating in Arabic. New-fangled forms and the English language were often considered by the traditionalists as confusing complications which they could easily live without.

Pearls, protectionism and progress

While the Eastern Bank had been negotiating to open its branch in Bahrain, on 9 November 1918, an Armistice was signed to the effect that at the eleventh hour on the eleventh day of the eleventh month, the last shot of the First World War would be fired. Almost immediately after hostilities ended, so great was the rush to buy pearls that the prices shot up 50 per cent above those for 1917. Although

Bahrain's 1918 pearl-harvest was smaller than average because of bad weather, the war-time prohibition of pearl exports from India to Europe had a marked effect on the Bahraini economy. At the end of Bahrain's 1918 diving season, which more or less coincided with the expected end of the war, wealthy Arab merchants who owned substantial gold reserves and who could easily afford to wait for a return on their investments, purchased almost half of the available pearls in Bahrain as a form of speculative stockpiling. From mid-November 1918 to the end of the year, it was estimated that practically all the Arab and Indian pearl merchants in Bahrain sailed for Bombay taking with them pearls worth £450,000, leaving behind just £61,000 worth to be shipped in unaccompanied consignments. But behind this post-war euphoria that business was booming again, this apparent 'silver cloud' had a sinister lining for the Arabian Gulf's natural pearl industry. The name of Mikimoto was beginning to make an impact.

Born in 1858, Mikimoto seemed predestined to succeed. His first name was Kichimatsu. *Kichi* means luck and *Matsu* means pine-tree, a symbol of prosperity in Japan. As he became interested in the fishermen who dealt in natural pearls, he became a pearl buyer. His taste for perfection led him to select the finest pearls, some of which were noted by the Empress at an exhibition in Tokyo in 1887. The resultant publicity suddenly generated a new fashion and enormous demand, so much so that Mikimoto feared that the natural oyster-beds would soon be exhausted. So, for the next twenty-three years, he struggled to perfect an old Chinese method of introducing a small piece of mother-of-pearl into each oyster in order to create an irritation. To protect itself, the oyster secretes a liquid around the irritant. The longer the secretion is produced, the bigger the resultant pearl.

By January 1916 Mikimoto had perfected his technique and began to produce round pearls. During the next few years, cultured pearls became much cheaper and quicker to produce than natural pearls, and so the livelihoods of pearl-divers throughout the world were devastated. The Arabian Gulf's natural pearl industry could never compete against this onslaught which, even by the mid-1920s, was being felt. To put this in perspective, out of an entire three-month diving season in the Arabian Gulf, the combined efforts of one dhow's crew might harvest enough pearls for one excellent, and two or three good pearl necklaces. The rest of the catch would be of lower quality.

Throughout the 1920s, the pearl industry in Bahrain continued to oscillate between boom and gloom. During 1922, there was an unexpected revival in trade, so much so that the large stock of pearls which had accumulated because of the depression of previous years, was entirely disposed of. Selling prices advanced between 30 to 40 per cent on those of 1921. One single pearl found that season, sold for one lakh, that is, Rs 100,000. Then in 1924, the pearl market reverted to stagnation for two reasons. There was first the uncertainty of the exchange-rate between India and France, the major clients for Bahrain's best pearls; and, secondly, important European buyers showed distinct caution because of the appearance on the market of Japanese cultured pearls. These, they feared, were mixed with the natural Arabian Gulf variety.

The Bahrain Government responded quickly. It banned the import of cultured pearls into the country and issued a stern warning. If such 'mixing' continued, the Deputy Ruler would be advised to purchase X-ray equipment and hire an expert to detect such fraud. (Cultured pearls when X-rayed, or cut in half, do not display layers within them, as do natural pearls.)

Although these moves helped to protect Bahrain's volatile pearl industry, smuggling was extremely difficult to control. Even experts found that when cultured pearls were mixed with genuine Arabian Gulf pearls, the non-indigenous varieties were not easy to detect simply by studying their size, colour and shape.

In 1925, although general trade in Bahrain had been brisk, there was a considerable decline due to yet another poor pearling season. Ironically, the number of boats which had headed for the pearling banks had been unusually large, but throughout the season, the weather had been unfavourable. On one occasion, a severe cyclone blew up during which it was estimated that between thirty and forty boats were sunk with great loss of life. The season was a disaster resulting in many bankruptcies. So it was that 1925 became known in Bahrain as *Sinat Al-Taba'a,* the 'Year of the Sinking'.

This episode only served to emphasise that the absence of any stable industry, other than pearl-fishing, was the cause of great hardship among several Bahraini communities. Since the pearl-fishing season lasted for four months and ten days only, even during a good year, this meant that many of the islands' inhabitants were without occupation for the rest of the year. Unless they could use their time profitably in other ways, they had no income.

The answer for many dhow crews was to rest for a month or so after the pearl-diving season ended, then to embark on trading trips to Muscat, India and beyond, or south to Aden, and even all the way to Zanzibar. At each port, they sold whatever goods they were carrying on board. Then with the proceeds, they bought items which they thought would sell at the next port, and so on. In time, a chain of coffee-shops was established in the various ports where the *nowaakhdha* (captains) gathered to exchange news about what was going on and what products were in demand at other ports nearby. For example, they often took dates and mother-of-pearl to Bombay and returned with wood, rice and spices. (At sea the dhow captain was the *nawkhadha,* while on land he was a trader.)

Some years previously, canvas-weaving for boat-sails had been a fairly prosperous industry in Bahrain but this had declined because of heavy taxation which had driven up the cost of raw materials. By the mid-1920s there were signs of a revival. Meanwhile, some sixty Bahraini weavers had established themselves in Budaiya village. This confidence soon stimulated new canvas-making centres to open in other local villages, particularly Diraz, Al-Markh and Bani Jamra, where fabric-weaving later became a handicraft tradition. But for all this, Bahrain's economy remained fragile. New business initiatives were needed. Nevertheless, there had been some positive prospects for prosperity, at least for Haji Yusuf.

As international business began to pick up after the end of the war, Haji Yusuf was appointed the Frank C. Strick Line's agent in Bahrain. Several years earlier, the Strick Line had established a trading arm in Basrah (then Mesopotamia's most southern city), to represent many British companies, especially in consumer products.

While Strick exported foodstuffs such as dates, barley and other grains grown along the fertile banks of the Tigris and Euphrates rivers, it also imported mechanical goods such as generators from India for Iraq. For Haji Yusuf, this business was 'right up his street', enabling him to become Strick's agent in Bahrain, sourcing his orders through their Basrah office. These included a variety of goods needed for Bahrain's market, as well as for the markets which Haji Yusuf had developed in Saudi Arabia, Qatar and Dubai.

Some of the cargo manifests which I rescued from the ravages of ants, mice and mildew make fascinating reading. In particular, those of the Persian Gulf Steam Navigation Company, headed with a striking Gothic typeface, reveal that bags and bales packed with peppermint and Java sugar regularly made their way to Bahrain, as did Jamboo oil stored in drums. Add twine, turmeric and tallow (for making candles and soap), and we have an intriguing insight into aspects of life in Bahrain more than seventy years ago. The manifest for SS *Zayani,* Voyage 59A, sailing from Karachi to Bahrain on 11

January 1920, is a good example. Originated by the Persian Gulf Steam Navigation Company and sent to Y.B.A.Kanoo, the shipping line's agent in Bahrain, the document reads simply: 'Dubai to Bahrain, one tin of golden coins, value 20,000 rupees.'

Also in January 1920, Yusuf bin Ahmed Kanoo was honoured by the special event mentioned earlier: an invitation to attend the Court of Abdul-Aziz Ibn Saud in Al-Hasa, together with Major Dickson, British Political Agent. Accompanied by Abdulaziz Al-Qusaibi, Ibn Saud's agent in Bahrain, the party sailed for the mainland on 29 January 1920. Haji Yusuf Kanoo was already well known to Abdul Aziz Ibn Saud's Court since, for some years, he had supplied it with goods and services. Orders were received either directly via cables from Riyadh, or through Abdulaziz Al-Qusaibi. But, as yet, although Haji Yusuf was a close friend of Shaikh Abdulla Al-Sulaiman, the treasurer and *wazir* of Ibn Saud, he had not met Abdul-Aziz Ibn Saud.

Almost certainly, this visit to Arabia would have provided Haji Yusuf with new business contacts and prospects. Among these was an indication that, should Ibn Saud's expressed wishes come to pass, Haji Yusuf would have the chance to expand his shipping agency network to Saudi Arabia. Apparently, Ibn Saud had stated a desire to improve the port of Ojair by building a wharf and a beacon, and to arrange for fortnightly calls by the British India Steam Navigation Company's steamers. At that time, Ojair was the only port serving the Provinces of Al-Hasa and Nejd, which, in turn, depended upon Bahrain and Kuwait for their imports. Dammam, 120 miles north-west of Ojair, was just a small coastal village.

The essence of Ibn Saud's purpose was this: if Ojair port was enlarged so that goods could be imported directly into Arabia from India, the two provinces could be served directly without involving agencies in Bahrain and Kuwait. On the one hand, Haji Yusuf could see the potential loss of some of his trans-shipment business originating from Bahrain. On the other hand, if Ibn Saud's idea took shape, then foreign shipping companies would require agents to handle their affairs. If Ojair proved to be unsuitable for expansion, then Jubail and Qatif were to be considered since both offered adequate landing facilities for cargo-steamers. The main drawback to all three candidates was that each of their approaches was very shallow so that even the smallest of steamers had to anchor some seven or eight miles offshore. Obviously, it was of little or no concern to Haji Yusuf as to which of the three contenders might be chosen. The important point was that, with this shipping intelligence, he could monitor progress. It is reasonable to suggest that when Haji

Yusuf visited Riyadh in January 1920, the idea of expanding his shipping agency network to mainland Arabia had already crossed his mind.

From what we know today, it is hard to imagine a time when the modern port of Jubail was anything less than a modern industrial terminal. Equally, when I consider the Y.B.A.Kanoo organisation today, heavily weighted in the Kingdom of Saudi Arabia in terms of size and diversity, it is just as remarkable to imagine a time when our family business had no business interests established anywhere along the coast of Arabia opposite Bahrain. But in 1920, none of this could have been foreseen.

Another highlight to the new decade for Haji Yusuf was a visit to Bahrain by the British Civil Commissioner from Baghdad. His arrival at the beginning of 1920 attracted our interest not because of his personality, but because of the implications of his visit for the role of the British Royal Air Force (RAF), now just two years old. The British Government was now beginning to explore the possibility of creating an aerodrome in Bahrain.

Equally significant was an event which took place during 1919. Two intrepid pioneers, one pilot and one passenger (a reporter from the *London Evening Standard*), had boarded a de Havilland DH44 aircraft at Hounslow Heath, near London and flown to Le Bourget, just outside Paris. This memorable two-and-a-half hour flight launched both Aircraft Transport and Travel Limited (forerunner of British Airways) and the world's first daily scheduled international air service between the two European capital cities. No one needed a crystal ball to predict that, sooner or later, commercial air travel would embrace the world, including Arabia. But, for the time being, the immediate implications of an RAF presence in Muharraq were of more interest to Haji Yusuf. As APOC's agent in Bahrain, he was ideally placed to bid for business as the RAF's refuelling agent.

The Civil Commissioner, during his short stay, sanctioned the laying out of an 'aeroplane ground and plot' measuring 650 yards long (594 metres) and 400 yards (365 metres) broad. Pillars, the central white circle and the T-cloth to indicate wind direction, were ordered and by April 1920 the ground was ready. In June that year Air Vice-Marshal Sir W. G. Salmond visited Bahrain to survey the new 'aeroplane ground'. He saw immediately that it was too narrow and asked for it to be widened. The Civil Commissioner approved further expenditure and the ground was prepared.

On this subject, there is nothing in the Bahrain Government records, nor our archive, which illuminates further progress during the next four years. However, we do learn that on 1 April 1924, Britain's four main fledgling airlines merged to form Imperial Airways. Almost immediately, the new airline contemplated inaugurating a service between London and India.

On 8 June 1924 three aeroplanes from RAF Shaibeh (in Iraq) arrived in Bahrain. During this four-day public-relations visit the Deputy Ruler, Shaikh Hamad bin Isa Al Khalifa, and the Political Agent were taken on a flight which lasted one-and-a-half hours. For the first time, the Deputy Ruler viewed the 'whole of his dominions' from the air, and over-flew the Bahrain pearling fleet which was then at work some forty miles from the main island.

The experience was greatly appreciated by Shaikh Hamad who invited the RAF officers to repeat their visit whenever possible. They, in turn, had found the landing-ground to be satisfactory. The consensus was that Bahrain's favourable position made it worthy of consideration as a future air-station. And so, in 1926, as APOC's agent in Bahrain, Haji Yusuf began to supply the RAF with Imperial Aviation Spirit (aircraft fuel).

Haji Yusuf's APOC agency

During 1927 business was brisk: 60 cases of aviation fuel costing Rs12 6a. each, were consigned to Haji Yusuf on the SS *Khuzistan,* for sale 'on account and risk of the Anglo-Persian Oil Company Limited'. A notice of loading dated 4 September 1928, lists some 500 cases of B.P. Motor Spirit (petrol), 7,000 tins of Palm Tree Kerosene and 40 cases of Standard Aviation Blend, the last a somewhat unusual request.

Too late to telegraph Haji Yusuf, APOC had received notice that an Imperial Airways aeroplane was due to land in Bahrain. Upon its arrival, all the reserve stock of Imperial Aviation Spirit kept in Bahrain, some 300 gallons, would be required for refuelling. Thus, APOC was sending Haji Yusuf replenishments, reassuring him that the Standard Aviation Blend was exactly the same as Imperial fuel, consisting of 60 per cent Aviation Spirit and 40 per cent Benzol. The difference was simply a name-change for marketing purposes!

Between 1913 (when Haji Yusuf became APOC's agent in Bahrain) and until oil was discovered on the island in 1932, most of Bahrain's imported petroleum-based products were purchased by Haji Yusuf from APOC's Abadan refinery. I say most, because in one respect, the oil company faced competition from none other than Haji Yusuf's cousin, Khalil Kanoo. In June 1928 Khalil Kanoo told Ashraf Brothers in Bahrain that he had received quotations for a minimum quantity of 25 cases of Flit insecticide sprayers for direct shipment from New York. The product was offered in variously sized containers: half-pint, pint, quart, gallon, 5-gallon, 30-gallon and 55-gallon drums.

By 1929, APOC was making strenuous efforts to encourage Haji Yusuf, their Bahrain agent, to promote the oil company's own-brand insecticide: Imshi. During August that year, he was asked to submit a monthly sales statement; a report on the prospect for further sales, and a sales statement regarding competing brands, if any. Insecticides apart, APOC was also earnestly trying to increase its product distribution. Kerosene for cooking, motor spirit (petrol) and benzine (aviation fuel), were all imported in tins and drums from APOC's refinery in Abadan. Each product was easily identified on the containers: a lion usually indicated motor spirit; a picture of a palm tree explained the initials P.T. on kerosene tins; and those marked with a red cross were filled with aviation fuel.

APOC owned a few large vessels, each with a capacity of some 500 tons. One of these was the SS *Khuzistan* which, for many years, regularly dropped anchor in Suwaifiyah Bay, near to Manama's modern Central Market. Throughout the 1920s, this bay was the discharging focal point for Bahrain's imported petroleum products, away from urban Mina Manama. (Only after the Standard Oil Company of California (SOCAL) built the Sitra marine terminal and the Bahrain refinery in the 1930s, did this arrangement lapse.) APOC's SS *Taraqqi* was another regular visitor to the bay. Often, Ahmed Kanoo saw this small coaster riding at anchor, just about where the Pearl roundabout now stands in Manama on land reclaimed from the sea.

To the delight of APOC, imports into Bahrain increased by 50 per cent during 1927 as Haji Yusuf (their agent) offered extensive credit to purchasers. (Why, I do not know.) In the same year, APOC built an oil-storage tank to cope with the rise in demand. The usual routine was that the oil company's ships anchored offshore and then small dhows came alongside. As there was no crane, the tins were discharged by hand, several thousand at a time, and not all of the same product. For example, in January 1928 the SS *Khuzistan* arrived again, this time loaded with 1,100 tins of B. P. Motor Spirit (costing Rs 4 7a. each); and two grades of Palm Tree kerosene identified by different types of containers: 1,000 cases (Rs 7 each) and 3,000 tins (Rs 3 3a. each).

During the 1920s, Kanoo also received orders from merchants in Arabia and Qatar to supply them with fuel, particularly kerosene. By now Ojair had become Arabia's main east-coast port. Even then, port regulations governing the movement of benzine (aviation fuel) were very strict. Under no circumstances was it allowed to be carried by sailing vessels of 'the Gulf type' (meaning wooden dhows), motor launches, or similar craft. Only the SS *Khuzistan* was permitted to transport benzine up and down the Arabian Gulf. So, in 1929, when Messrs Algosaibi in Arabia placed an order for the product, and offered to send a motor launch from the mainland to Bahrain to collect it, APOC still followed the rules. Haji Yusuf was asked to tell his client that, under these circumstances, APOC very much regretted that it was unable to meet the client's requests.

Meanwhile, Bahrain's first petrol pump had been installed in Manama on a site which today is occupied by the Kanoo Phase 2 building. (A gift shop called Novelty now occupies the ground floor.) The pump was later moved to a site on Government Road (now Avenue) where the City Centre has been developed. (Until recently, this was called the Shaikh Mubarak Building, opposite Manama Municipality.) Ahmed Kanoo, our Group Chairman, remembers the days he spent on that street corner working as a hand-pump attendant, delivering kerosene from the designated 4-gallon tins and petrol from 22-gallon drums. His salary was Rs 70 a month. Contrary to what many people believe, it was not until after the Bahrain refinery began production in 1936 and so supplied the local market that, in 1938, Hussain Yateem opened his first filling station, also on Government Avenue.

New Kanoo family enterprises

On the subject of cars, the first to arrive in Bahrain was delivered to the Ruler, His Highness Shaikh Isa bin Ali Al Khalifa. In 1920, a second car appeared on the island, a Ford (Model A) and our first family motor vehicle. Since the Political Agent in Bahrain had no motor transport of his own, Haji Yusuf agreed to lend our Ford to Major Dickson for three months.

In due course we acquired a Plymouth car and a small Wolseley saloon. During 1925, the number of motor cars on the roads of Bahrain had increased to the extent that the Government introduced a licensing system: drivers were now required to pass a driving-test. Licence Number 9123 issued from Bombay on 17 March 1925 is a unique survivor among our family records. Inside, the text simply reads: 'Licence to drive a motor car throughout British India.' The fortunate owner of this rare document was none other than Khalil bin Ebrahim Kanoo, Haji Yusuf's first cousin and my wife's grandfather. It is said that he was one of the few licensed Bahraini drivers at that time.

Regulations were issued governing taxi fares. Rules were also introduced to control motor traffic in the towns, a necessity because of the narrow and tortuous streets which, with increasing traffic, had caused very many accidents. By the end of 1926, the authorities estimated that there were some 140 cars and 4 motor lorries plying the islands. The majority of these were Fords but some merchants were contemplating the import of more expensive, higher powered types, mainly American. No doubt Khalil bin Ebrahim Kanoo was among that number, since records in our archive document his contacts with European car manufacturers and suppliers of accessories. As early as 1925, for example, Khalil Kanoo was corresponding with Citröen in France.

Yet, even towards the end of the decade, the Political Agency in Bahrain still did not own a motor vehicle. In his book, *Taste of the Past,* Mahdi Abdulla refers to Haji Yusuf kindly placing his car at the disposal of the British Political Agent, when it was required. In *Personal Column,* Charles Belgrave mentions our Ford being lent to the Political Agent in the late 1920s, specifically so that he could drive to Sakhir to visit the Ruler of Bahrain at his desert retreat.

During 1928 motor car imports into Bahrain declined, the island being considered well stocked. Nevertheless, during that year our family became the regional Studebaker agent, despite some tough correspondence on the part of Ali bin Mohamed Kanoo (Haji Yusuf's nephew). Early in 1928, Ali Kanoo had begun to negotiate with the Studebaker Corporation in the USA. In March, he then wrote: 'It is not quite clear to me as to why I should communicate with one of your representatives in India, if I wish to take up your dealership for this territory [Bahrain]'. Ali Kanoo could not understand why he was prevented from communicating directly with Studebaker, and so gain the benefit of dealer's prices for their cars, rather than pay extra, namely the profit of Studebaker's representatives in India. Another frustration was that Studebaker required a cash deposit from my grandfather. Why? he asked. Other big companies, such as Ford, had not required a deposit from their Bahrain agents (meaning Khalil Kanoo, the Ford agent.)

Despite all this, negotiations continued and Ali Kanoo placed his first order with Studebaker. By early June 1928, a Director Tourer Royal (a seven-seater passenger car), had arrived in Bahrain. But, as he reported to Studebaker, 'it has not created a great impression. So

I am not able to say what the future possibilities will be'. Clearly, Studebaker acquiesced in Ali Kanoo's reservations for, on 22 June 1928 he was pleased to note that the company no longer required a cash deposit with the Agency Agreement, three copies of which he had duly signed and returned to America, as requested.

On the other side of the Atlantic Ocean, the Daimler Company, based in Coventry, England, was discussing the possibility of selling exclusive limousines to Khalil Kanoo. In September 1928 Powell & Hanmer, another British company, acknowledged Khalil Kanoo's payment for 24 double-twist car horns and 12 motor spot-lamps, complete with universal fittings and canvas-lined tropical bulbs. The company's export manager confidently explained that Powell & Hanmer's *de luxe* model spot-lamp was the finest on the market, being fitted with the added benefit of a round mirror, 4 inches (10 cm.) in diameter.

Another order placed by Khalil Kanoo, this time with the Dunlop Rubber Company from whom he usually bought car tyres, particularly caught my eye. Who, I wondered, needed 'one dozen stitched tennis balls in a tin case, absolutely necessary to preserve them', and one dozen Maxfli golf balls? Both orders were to be sent by parcel post to the customer and the cost 'drawn on him' through the Eastern Bank in Bahrain. The client, it transpired, was Bahrain's Director of Customs, Mr C. C. de Grenier.

A contrasting but less surprising anecdote told by Sulman Kanoo, relates to his father's Ford agency. During the 1920s or early 1930s, Khalil bin Ebrahim Kanoo often delivered Ford cars to Riyadh from Bahrain. Helped by Sulman Garata, Ebrahim Taqi and Abdulla Al-Zain, they would sail from Bahrain, land at Ojair on the east coast of Arabia and then drive to Riyadh. But in those days, before paved roads were commonplace in Arabia, the desert surface was often so soft that motor vehicles just sank. The solution was to hire camels so that they could pull the cars over straw mats laid out across the sand.

Meanwhile, by early 1927, efforts to tap Bahrain's underground fresh-water supply had proved to be very successful. Fourteen wells had been sunk, seven each in the towns of Manama and Muharraq. These supplied plentiful drinkable water, an immense boon to the community. During the same year, representatives of the Eastern and General Syndicate appeared in Bahrain again, some years after their first arrival on 6 August 1920. This time, their purpose was to bore more water wells on the Arabian Mission's compound (now the American Mission Hospital) and on the property of Ali Yateem, a Bahraini merchant. Our family saw the chance to compete at a cheaper price. Haji Khalil bin Ebrahim Kanoo (Haji Yusuf's cousin) imported suitable plant and drilled a few water wells at a very much lower cost than the Eastern and General Syndicate. Much encouraged, Khalil Kanoo and Mohammed Yateem combined their efforts during 1928 and conducted several more water borings. The strength of the gush in Mohammed Yateem's garden at Barbar was so remarkable that he energetically and enthusiastically launched himself into a challenging new enterprise: experimental vegetable gardening.

As an aside, it is worth commenting on what seemed to be inconsistent behaviour on the part of the Eastern and General Syndicate, a consortium of British businessmen registered as a British company to acquire and operate oil concessions in the Middle East. In May 1923 the consortium was granted a concession in the Al-Hasa province of mainland Arabia by Ibn Saud (Sultan of Nejd). In May 1924, a similar concession was allowed in the Kuwait-Nejd Neutral Zone. Then, on 2 December 1925, Shaikh Hamad bin Isa Al Khalifa, Deputy Ruler of Bahrain, granted the consortium an exclusive oil exploration licence for two years. The Eastern and General Syndicate's short-sightedness is legendary. Remarkably, in hindsight, it concluded that there was no future in oil exploration in Bahrain and so transferred its activities to Kuwait. On 30 November 1927, it assigned the Bahrain concession to Eastern Gulf Oil (a subsidiary of the Pennsylvania-based Gulf Oil Corporation). Eager to start work, Eastern Gulf Oil despatched a senior geologist, Ralph Rhoades, to Bahrain. In 1928, he concluded that if a test-well were to be favourably located on the Bahrain anticline then it 'may reasonably be expected to encounter oil.' His optimism was to prove well-founded.

Why the Eastern and General Syndicate now favoured water drilling projects in Bahrain is unclear, particularly in view of growing local competition. For Jassim Kanoo (Haji Yusuf's nephew and my paternal grandfather) had also been studying a well-boring venture. In a letter of 18 August 1928, to Mr Karunakaran, he noted that it was good of him to have found a 'very clever man in boring [good at his job], but too clever a man [over-qualified] will not be suitable for us'. Despite this reservation, my grandfather asked for the gentleman's full address, and as much information about him as possible. Was he a Muslim, Hindu or Anglo-Indian, for instance?

Whether this overture developed further, I do not know. However, by the end of 1928, some fifty-five wells had been sunk throughout the islands of Bahrain, with the towns of Manama and Muharraq being well equipped with suitable water for drinking and irrigation.

Nonetheless, the haphazard practice had caused much water to be wasted. It was the opinion of some that, if the number of wells greatly increased, the head of water would fail and the wells would not operate. Some had even run dry already. So, during 1929, the Government introduced measures to stop random drilling.

Despite this set-back, on 29 September 1929, several shaikhs arrived in Bahrain from Oman. Having heard much of Khalil Kanoo's drilling equipment, they had made their long journey for the sole purpose of buying some apparatus from him. The Administration Report for the year states that the Omani shaikhs could have seen similar plant in India where they could have bought it more cheaply. But, instead, they 'had to see their brother Arabs using it, to be convinced.'

Chapter 3

Fragile Fortunes

When news was received in Bahrain that Imperial Airways had opened a new route from England to Karachi, there was the exciting prospect that Bahrain might, before long, become a scheduled stop for Imperial Airways. From 1929, passengers with a penchant for oriental adventure could purchase a single ticket for £130, board an Armstrong-Whitworth Argosy aircraft at Croydon airport (opened in 1928) and take off to Basle in Switzerland. There, a Genoa-bound train transported passengers to Italy. They then embarked on a Calcutta-class flying boat destined for Alexandria. In Egypt, passengers boarded a DH66 Hercules which flew over Gaza and the oil pipelines of Iraq and Persia, landing for overnight stops at selected fortified desert camps. Finally, the Hercules hugged the eastern shore of the Arabian Gulf, before flying inland to its final destination: Karachi.

'The Suez Canal of the air'

In 1932 the establishment of a civil air-route along the eastern shores of Arabia greatly enhanced Haji Yusuf's APOC fuelling agency. Following a feasibility study, Imperial Airways transferred its entire operations, including its wireless stations, to what they called the southern coast of the Arabian Gulf. By early October, all was ready for the new service to be inaugurated between Kuwait, Bahrain, Sharjah and Gwadur (in present-day Baluchistan). After 25 September 1932, no Imperial Airways 'machine' flew along the Persian coast, not least because 'trigger-happy tribesmen were likely to take pot shots at aircraft'.

Then, on 6 October, the first commercial flight passed through Bahrain. *Hanno,* an aeroplane of the Hannibal-class arrived on schedule, but more dramatically than expected. It transpired that just a fortnight earlier, a Hannibal pilot had reconnoitred the Manama landing-strip and concluded that it was too soft for that class of aircraft. For some reason the pilot's warning report to Imperial Airways was ignored. *Hanno* sank into the treacherous surface of the

Manama landing-ground and only after a tremendous effort during the next day were the wheels freed.

Rather embarrassed, Imperial Airways then sought permission from the Bahrain Government to share Muharraq's landing facilities, already used by the RAF and other occasional charter flights. Again Imperial Airways showed no inclination to hurry. By the end of 1932, it had neither chosen a permanent aerodrome, nor finished equipping its new rest house. Nevertheless, the new strategic civil air-route along the Arabian Gulf to India was soon heralded as the 'Suez Canal of the Air'.

During 1933, Imperial Airways continued their weekly service both east and west. With the exception of a few forced landings, no incidents of a serious nature occurred. Royal Air Force Flying Boats of No. 203 (Flying Boat) Squadron, paid frequent visits to Bahrain, while Wapitit aeroplanes of the RAF's No. 84 Squadron landed on several occasions. On 25 July 1933, an RAF Wapitit aeroplane suffered the same fate as *Hanno*. It, too, sank into the now notorious soft surface of the Manama landing-ground. This time, the damage was a broken propeller. Thereafter, RAF and Imperial Airways' heavy aircraft always used the Muharraq landing-ground.

In 1934 the rulers of Bahrain, Kuwait and Muscat met to negotiate a regional Air Agreement since Imperial Airways' and the RAF's existing use of Sharjah airstrip made it clear that air travel via the Arabian Gulf was bound to expand. The outcome was that air facilities were granted in Dubai although, the Ruler of Dubai was not present at the meeting.

Given Haji Yusuf's APOC agency business in Bahrain, much of it now being a refuelling service for civil and military aircraft, these developments in aviation were of great interest to him. A natural progression from this would be the establishment of a travel agency in Bahrain. But for the time being, this could only be a daydream for Haji Yusuf. The financial fallout from the Wall Street collapse had by now affected most of the world, and our family.

The Wall Street crash

On 24 October 1929, in a wave of fear, confusion and panic, nearly 13 million shares changed hands on the New York Stock Exchange. The city's bankers blamed the panic and subsequent 'crash' on the technical inadequacy of the ticker-tape system to process such massive-volume trading. The spree of easy money and over-confidence was over. Many small investors on Wall Street had lost all.

Throughout 1930 the Anglo-Persian Oil Company became increasingly unpopular after significantly raising petrol and kerosene prices in Bahrain, as compared with those charged in Persia. As APOC's agent in Bahrain, Haji Yusuf was caught up in the dispute as he faced a flood of angry customers. According to the 1931 Annual Administration Report, most Arabs felt that they were being 'fleeced' by APOC, since many knew that the company had come to a regional agreement with its competitors, particularly the Iraq Petroleum Company. Whatever business deal had been made, only APOC's petroleum products were imported into the Arabian Gulf region. This monopoly applied as much in Bahrain as it did in the Trucial States. This irked local merchants and consumers even more since they knew well enough that until oil was discovered somewhere in Arabia, perhaps even in Bahrain, APOC's firm grip on the market could not be relieved.

Merchant shipping trade in Bahrain still held its own, although not as briskly as before. During 1931, 116 British, 1 Norwegian and 10 German ships called into Bahrain, compared with 123 British and 121 German vessels in the previous year. By now, British India Steam Navigation Company 'down' steamers began to call into Bahrain on a weekly basis, instead of once a fortnight. This welcome change was much appreciated by the local trading community.

But, as prophesied, 1930 proved to be disastrous for the Arabian Gulf's pearl industry. Consequently for Bahrain, pearls reached only 30 per cent of their 1929 value. Although the catch had been above the average, there was next to no buying. Almost the entire season's harvest remained unsold except for some cheaper grades which were bought fairly freely. It was believed that merchants who took their pearls to India were unable to sell even half of them, igniting fears that conditions would worsen in the following year. Merchants who had a capital of ten or fifteen lakhs had nothing left but pearls for which there were no purchasers. It was little consolation to Bahraini traders to reflect that their neighbours were worse off. To all intents and purposes, both Qatif (the Arabian port), and the Qatar peninsula were economically ruined.

A clutch of letters exchanged between Haji Yusuf and Ebrahim Moledina (merchant and commission agent in Bombay) chronicled similar tales of woe. For example, up to 5 June 1930, Moledina had been unable to dispose of eight bundles of sharks' fins, even for culinary use (such as speciality soup) and medicinal preparations. The Bombay market was very low and the Chinese market was also dull. Haji Yusuf's consignment (most likely caught in the Arabian Gulf) was expected to realise less than Rs 50 per hundredweight (50 Kg). If he wished to sell the fins at this price, Moledina would oblige. Otherwise, Haji Yusuf might wish to consider storing the goods until the October auctions. A week later he opted for the latter course of action. Within a month the shark-fin business was at a standstill because of the monsoon.

Meanwhile, the sugar market which Haji Yusuf had traded in for several years was in no better shape. According to Moledina, the rate offered in July 1933 for transhipping Java sugar to India was not favourable. He could advance no opinion as regards the future as the situation in Bombay was 'getting very complicated'.

In June 1933 Pittar, Leverson & Co., diamond, pearl and precious stone brokers, distributed their new market report from London, a copy of which arrived on Haji Yusuf's desk in Bahrain. No doubt it would have heartened him to learn that analysts had noted a considerable improvement in business.

This upward movement had been led by the USA since the effect of America leaving the gold standard was exactly the opposite of what many had anticipated. Instead of restricting business, inflation had caused a greater demand for all kinds of commodities, and a consequent increase in their prices. The rally in the American commodity markets had caused the European markets to follow this upward trend, albeit more slowly and cautiously. The gradual return in confidence had also stimulated American buyers to reappear in the market after an absence of nearly three years. This upturn had created more demand in the USA, with many commodity dealers taking the view that it was preferable to hold goods rather than dollars, the latter having continued to depreciate.

The pearl market had shown increased activity, but only for certain types of goods, particularly pearls of cheaper quality. These were much more in demand, provided that the colour was rosy or cream. Shapes and marks were of less importance. This applied to pearls of good colour in prices ranging from between Rs 50 and Rs 150 per *chaw*. It transpired that Pittar, Leverson & Co. had received offers on many such items, both in necklaces and bunches. Very white or very tinted bunches or necklaces remained very difficult to move. Pittar, Leverson & Co. believed that shippers should be encouraged by this brighter business outlook. But it would seem that for all its optimism, this firm was unaware that Bahrain's economic future was far less bright. Other commodity markets with which Haji Yusuf had dealings did not share the London brokers' analysis either.

For instance, in early December 1933, a sale of mother-of-pearl shells took place in Manchester (England) with the usual majority of continental buyers attending. While the demand had been fair, the realised prices were 50 per cent less than expected. Few varieties of Bombay shells were presented: only 78 packages were offered for auction of which just 12 were sold.

A letter from J. M. Shasha to Haji Yusuf on 6 December 1933 illustrates the shell-trade position. As Manchester-based merchants, manufacturers, importers and exporters (with whom Haji Yusuf had traded for some time) they were preparing him for the likely outcome of the upcoming auction in January 1934. When Haji Yusuf's shipment arrived in Manchester, subject to the quality, Shasha would recommend that either he should sell 'on the spot' or hold it back. Unfortunate trends at recent auctions showed that 'fair quantities' of shells were being carried forward. Shasha believed that *all* prices for *all* commodities would stiffen, even though they had 'no basic factors to justify the view'.

These cameos demonstrate that while Haji Yusuf participated in a variety of international commodity markets when it seemed appropriate, his ability to do so depended on maintaining a delicate balance between cash-flow and credit. As 1933 drew to a close, this feat had become almost impossible for him to sustain.

Pearls, debts and depression

Our family was not directly involved in the pearl trade according to Ahmed Kanoo. However, we did work on a brokerage basis. We had our agencies, just as we did in the shipping industry. Haji Yusuf went further by becoming closer to the local pearl merchants who were buying and selling among themselves. If, for example, a Bahraini merchant needed money available to him in India, he might deposit funds with Haji Yusuf's office in Manama which, in turn, sent a draft to the Kanoo office in Bombay. This office then ensured that the Bahraini merchant's receiving party in India collected the money. The system also worked in the opposite direction.

However, when the 1930s recession really began to bite, these procedures were no longer straightforward. Say, for example, a merchant had borrowed Rs 10,000 from Haji Yusuf until he could sell his stock of pearls. When the value of Arabian Gulf pearls declined, many people found themselves in debt. Instead of being able to repay his loan at the appointed time, a merchant might ask Haji Yusuf to lend him another Rs 5,000. Meanwhile, that merchant would still try to sell his pearls, even at a reduced rate.

Although Haji Yusuf's *mudharaba* fund was not a large one, sufficient money was tied up in this kind of trading arrangement so that when the 1930s recession hit hard, it became a major liquidity problem for him. In Ahmed Kanoo's words: 'We were stuck'. At one time, Haji Yusuf's business was worth twelve lakhs of rupees. By the time the recession had degenerated into world-wide depression, much of that money had been committed to merchants. As they had no money to repay their debts, nor any source of income because of the collapse of world commodity markets, many merchants gave Haji Yusuf their unsold pearls. But as there was no market for them, nobody wanted to buy them. They were worthless to him at that time. As a result, Haji Yusuf lost most of his money.

He used what was left to support the large Kanoo family and to keep his business ticking over. Any residue he gave to those families who were finding it difficult to survive, as any good Moslem would do. In 1933 Haji Yusuf's financial situation worsened and he was obliged to mortgage some property to the Eastern Bank for Rs 75,000. When that loan fell due at the end of the year, he was unable to repay either the loan or the accrued 9 per cent interest. It seems that all this reached a crisis in 1934.

By then the Arabian Gulf pearl trade was noted as being 'bad'. Since buyers no longer visited Bahrain, the catch was taken to Bombay for sale. Only 316 pearling craft were licensed during 1935, compared to 340 in 1934, clear evidence of a continuing decline. Four decades earlier in 1889, 1,500 pearling dhows were registered in Bahrain; the fleet had thus declined by over 80 per cent.

Haji Yusuf's growing financial problems were closely monitored by the British Political Agent in Bahrain who conveyed the news to the Political Resident in Bushire, Lieutenant-Colonel T. C. W. Fowle. Whereas relationships between Haji Yusuf and various PAs during the 1920s were strained, on this occasion the mood was, by now, more mellow. Not only did Captain G. A. Cole seem concerned about Haji Yusuf's plight, but he also appeared to show willingness to try and ease the financial pressures facing him, if Haji Yusuf would mortgage his property.

By early 1934 Haji Yusuf's request to the Bahrain Government proved to be successful. It was prepared, if the worst came to the worst, to lend him Rs 20,000 on the security of certain real estate. It so happened that this corresponded to the sum which Haji Yusuf's Bahrain agency owed to the Anglo-Persian Oil Company at that time. Captain Cole intended to ask APOC to bide its time in pressing for payment, since he realised that if the company did not hold back, it was likely to bring about Haji Yusuf's bankruptcy which, in turn, would result in heavy loss to all concerned. As Haji Yusuf's debts had reached a total sum of half a lakh, in early February 1934 he travelled to Kuwait to try and secure a loan and 'save the situation'. Meanwhile, Cole expressed the hope that Haji Yusuf would weather the storm.

By mid-April 1934, Haji Yusuf had obtained for APOC, a lien on property belonging to him as well as his nephews, Jassim and Ali. Meanwhile, APOC was now owed a further Rs 20,000. This time, the oil company insisted on having the debt secured on more Kanoo property. Haji Yusuf even owed Hilal Al-Mutairi, his Kuwaiti merchant friend, Rs 180,000. Financially, Haji Yusuf was cornered. So it was that our family sold many of its assets to pay off debts. For instance, at that time we owned a prime city block which stood on the site of the present Citibank. Ahmed Kanoo tells me that this was sold to Haji Hilal, in either 1935 or 1936, for Rs 270,000. Likewise, the building opposite the main entrance to our Head Office in Manama, was sold for Rs 80,000, much less than the actual cost of its construction.

The money generated from these sales did not suffice. An added factor was Haji Yusuf's strong religious commitment. He did not want it on his conscience that he had not paid his creditors, especially the small ones who were also facing financial crisis. So Haji Yusuf was forced to borrow further from the bank. But in so doing, he had to pay interest which, apart from being against his religious beliefs, proved to be a major struggle because of the recession, and later because of restrictions and rationing imposed during the Second World War.

As Haji Yusuf's ability to repay his debts became more limited, he even looked to rentals from his remaining properties to relieve the situation. But even they did not yield what Haji Yusuf had reasonably expected. In the end other family properties were sold to repay our bank overdrafts, interest on business loans, and outstanding debts related to his various agency commitments.

On 7 December 1940, Haji Yusuf wrote to the Anglo-Iranian Oil Company (AIOC), formerly the Anglo-Persian Oil Company until 21 May 1935. Haji Yusuf explained: 'It is not possible for me to pay more than Rs 1,000 monthly towards the liquidation of my debt to the company. This is because of the present war conditions and the consequent slackness in trade.' Furthermore, Haji Yusuf still had other debts to settle. As soon as this was achieved, he would pay more into the oil company's account against his indebtedness. On a positive note, Haji Yusuf felt that AIOC would be pleased to hear that 'because of our strenuous efforts, we are today holding more than two-thirds of the market for your products.'

Despite this positive achievement, it would appear that AIOC was unimpressed. By now, Haji Yusuf had reached the twilight of his life. In a poignant letter written to AIOC, he referred more graphically to the 'fag-end of my life'. This comment, together with the whole tone of the letter, clearly reveals the extent to which Haji Yusuf had become worn down and depressed by the whole process of debt. The following extract is a potent reflection of just how he felt.

Having expressed his hope that the company would not place him in an embarrassing situation by demanding more than the agreed monthly repayments, Haji Yusuf explained: 'My debt to you was originally Rs 135,000. This has now been brought to the very low figure of Rs 26,500. This being the case, it pains me very much when you press me to pay more than Rs 1,000 monthly. I am myself very anxious to clear my debt to you but in my present straightened circumstances, I am paying you to my utmost limit. My last request to you at this old age is to permit me to carry on with your agency and to pay you monthly, Rs 1,000.'

Ahmed Kanoo remembers well how his grandfather, Haji Yusuf, set 1940 as the target year by which he should have repaid all his debts. However, this proved to be a forlorn hope for reasons outside his control. I have no doubt that, had it not been for the onset of the Second World War which so affected trade and Haji Yusuf's ability to maintain repayments, he would have achieved his objective. But that is to gaze into a crystal ball, not at a bank statement. The only properties which he refused to sell in order to raise money, were our big old family house on Tijjar Road, and other premises behind our present Head Office in Manama, then occupied by family members.

All this being said, despite the financial difficulties which faced our family, Haji Yusuf was well aware that many other families were worse off than his own. Although he was not a pearl merchant himself, over the years he had acquired many pearls of various grades. So it was that during the depression years, he frequently gave less valuable pearls to impoverished Bahraini families who were in greater need than ourselves. Haji Yusuf also gave money and food whenever he could, and so helped to avert the threatened starvation of families who had no income due to the complete absence of work in the pearl-fishing industry.

Before his death on 21 December 1945, Haji Yusuf had managed to repay most of his loans. The few outstanding debts were paid off by his successors, nephews Jassim and Ali Kanoo. With the family wealth having all but disappeared, they had no choice but to rebuild the company, starting with the money that was left: just Rs 10,000.

Oil discovery in Bahrain – cause for optimism

While business prospects in Bahrain during the 1930s were far from rosy, it would be wrong to suggest that trade and progress on the island came to a halt. Despite the global recession, Y.B.A.Kanoo (with other Bahraini companies) benefited from several commercial opportunities before wartime restrictions gripped the nation in 1940. Not least of these were developments in Bahrain's oil industry.

As mentioned earlier, on 2 December 1925, the Bahrain Concession had been granted by the Deputy Ruler of Bahrain to the British Eastern and General Syndicate Limited. When, in 1927, the syndicate assigned the Concession to the Eastern Gulf Oil Company, the agreement's terms stated that the Americans had the option to exercise oil exploration rights in Bahrain, until 1 January 1929. For various complicated reasons to do with finance and Anglo-American politics, Eastern Gulf Oil was unable to follow this through. Just ten days before the exploration rights expired, it transferred the option to the Standard Oil Company of California (SOCAL) on 21 December 1928.

In the nick of time, the way had been prepared for the formation of the Bahrain Petroleum Company (BAPCO). However, there was another complication: the British insisted that BAPCO should have British nationality. After much discussion, the Americans overcame this difficulty by registering the company in a British Dominion, (the name given to a self-governing territory of the British Commonwealth). Thus, on 11 January 1929, the Charter of the Bahrain Petroleum Company Limited was sealed in Ottawa, Province of Ontario, Canada. While the nationality requirement had been fulfilled, in practice BAPCO was a wholly-owned subsidiary of SOCAL which maintained its head office in San Francisco, USA.

The way was now prepared for the Americans to begin earnest exploration in Bahrain. In June 1930 geologists William Taylor and Fred Davies arrived to conduct a survey on behalf of the Standard Oil Company of California. During one particular dinner conversation with two pearl merchants, they learned of the grievances within the islands' pearl-diving community. The geologists' two dining companions explained that in the course of their business operations, they consumed at least 100,000 cases of petrol a year, as well as large quantities of kerosene. This represented about half of the Bahrain pearling industry's requirements. The merchants confided that they 'heartily disliked' the Anglo-Persian Oil Company from which they had to buy all their supply. Consequently, they would welcome any competition which would reduce the price.

Fred Davies and William Taylor left Bahrain on 21 July 1930, without making a definitive statement. However, it was understood that they were optimistic about the possibilities of finding oil in Bahrain. In his subsequent report, Fred Davies wrote that he had detected a large, definitely closed 'domal' structure, in other words, an anticline. This compared favourably with other oil-bearing structures which were known elsewhere in the Middle East. With caution, Davies concluded that Bahrain could be considered a likely wildcat venture, if the structure was of the steep-dip variety (a geological expression to describe a particularly steep anticline where the sides slope sharply from the crest of the structure).

The outcome was that in 1931, an advance drilling party arrived in Bahrain and set up camp below Jebel Ad-Dukhan (Mountain of Smoke), more or less in the centre of Bahrain island. About a thousand tons of equipment were shipped from the USA. On 16 October 1931 Well Number One was 'spudded in'. His Excellency, the Deputy Ruler, Shaikh Hamed bin Isa Al Khalifa, then operated the drill for the first few blows. By early 1932, the well had become something of a tourist attraction. Then, at six o'clock in the morning of 1 June 1932, oil flowed from a depth of 2,008 feet (612 metres). Before the well was shut off, it obtained a flow of 70 tons a day. Edward Skinner, SOCAL's representative in Bahrain, remarked that it was a 'driller's dream'.

While an even greater flow could have been achieved, as the oil concession stood at that time it did not pay SOCAL to do so. Nevertheless, when on 9 December 1932, the Ruler of Bahrain, His Excellency Shaikh Sir Isa bin Ali Al Khalifa died, he did so knowing that oil had been found in his country, the first discovery of its kind anywhere in Arabia.

One might say that when oil was discovered in Bahrain on 1 June 1932 it was also a banker's dream come true. At that time, the Eastern Bank's first purpose-built building in Bahrain was in the final stages of construction with just three weeks to go before the official opening on 23 June. The bank's new premises represented a new era in Bahraini construction, being built of steel and reinforced concrete at a cost of Rs 75,000. The Political Resident commented in his annual report that 'it will be interesting to see how the cement responds to the climate, since the air and water have hitherto undermined the best that can be produced'.

Bankers and traders in Bahrain could have wished for nothing better than the discovery of oil. Now they had good reason to hope that perhaps this was the silver lining to the dark cloud of recession. As it turned out, after Bahrain's oil revenues began to increase later in the decade, the nation began to show signs of economic recovery.

On 22 February 1934, the *El Segundo* tanker dropped anchor off Sitra island, laden with supplies and staff of the Standard Oil Company of California. From this mooring some 4,880 metres offshore, the men used the tanker as their dormitory and supply base while they constructed an onshore marine loading-terminal, a pump-house and three crude-oil tanks with floating roofs, and laid a submarine pipeline.

When all was done, BAPCO's first shipment of crude oil was loaded onto the *El Segundo*. To the applause of those who had worked so hard for the previous four months, the tanker left Sitra anchorage on 7 June 1934, destined for Yokohama, Japan. Thus, Sitra anchorage and jetty became (and remains sixty years later) Bahrain's only loading facilities for oil tankers.

Meanwhile, the people of Bahrain continued to suffer financial hardship until the oil industry really began to take off some two years later. For instance, despite the Eastern Bank's improved facilities, it still faced operating difficulties, particularly its ability to import the large supplies of silver required by businessmen in Bahrain. A retired bank officer recalls that, throughout the 1930s, a continual ringing was heard throughout each day as customers and cashiers bounced silver rupees on the bank's cement floor to check the coins' purity.

Haji Yusuf, among other traders, would also have been keenly aware of the marginal difference between the value of a rupee showing the head of Queen Victoria (who died in 1901) compared with those minted with a King's head: either that of her son Edward VII (who died in 1910), or her grandson George V (who reigned until 1936). Apparently, the late Empress of India was at a disadvantage on account of her sex, despite the rarity value attributed to such coins.

From the mid-1930s, several of BAPCO's construction projects combined to provide many Bahrainis with retraining opportunities and settled employment on land. This was apart from BAPCO's increased drilling operations and greater activity at Sitra terminal from where crude oil was exported. By the end of 1935, fifteen tankers of four nationalities (six Norwegian, five American, three

British and one Danish) had exported 1,766,388 tons of crude oil from Bahrain; the construction of Bahrain's refinery was scheduled for completion in mid-1936; and the development of Awali, BAPCO's township, was well under way. Meanwhile, Haji Yusuf had assumed a new, somewhat unusual role: geological expedition quarter-master.

A loading notice dated 24 February 1935, sent by the Geological Section of the Anglo-Persian Oil Company to Y.B.A.Kanoo, turned out to be more than a simple inventory. After studying the listed contents of one despatch box and four hampers, I re-created a vivid picture of how a geological team camped and worked in the desert.

The first hamper contained the essentials of comfort: one bedcamp (I presume, a camp-bed); one Kopak mattress; two roll-up tables; a rooki chair (whatever that may have been); a new mosquito pole; a Wolsely valise (portmanteau, or leather trunk, which opens into two parts to store clothes); a ground-sheet, together with a wash-stand, basin and canvas bucket.

The contents of the second hamper suggested that these geologists were not inclined to lead a spartan life. Brown blankets, a sand-fly net, a sleeping-bag, pillow-cases and bed-sheets were ordinary enough. But the inventory also stipulated that both bath-towels and face-towels should be supplied, and the pillows had to be soft. Clues that a scientific expedition was involved appeared later in the list: 200 sample bags; a haversack and leather map-case; two new aluminium water bottles, and a pair of field-glasses.

Hamper number three seems to have been the office, if not the hub of the expedition. I tried to envisage how several metres of drawing paper-canvas, field-note books, sheets of square paper, even a Summary Receipt Expenditure Book, would have survived the dust and humidity, or even the bottles of ink in six colours: blue, black, green, yellow, carmine (crimson pigment made from ground cochineal) and vermilion (a brilliant red pigment made from ground cinnabar). Apart from black-leaded pencils, there were eight coloured crayons: purple, ultramarine, red, pink, yellow, azure, sepia and light green. Draughting equipment included instruments, mapping and quill pens, drawing pins, adhesive tape, art-gum, an eraser and a Louis and Gaunt table.

Serious work in the desert required alidades for surveying and mapping; a circular protractor; a level; an oil prismatic compass and a telescopic clinometer (for measuring slopes). A barometer and a cylindrical map-case, a ball of thin cord, a straight edge, spares for the range-finder, a geological hammer, prickers, measuring tape and scales were included, too. I assume that the primus stoves (and spare burners), a torch and batteries (with two spare bulbs), and three hurricane lamps were for use in the camp.

The fourth hamper indicated culinary conventions at the camp. A pudding bowl, fancy cake-tins, sugar bowl, bread tins, kettles, tea-cups and saucers, not forgetting the four-pint and two-pint teapots, all suggested to me that afternoon-tea was quite a ritual. For lunch and dinner, soup plates, meat plate, a set of carvers, dessert plates and cheese plates, knives and forks, gave the impression that a four-course European-style meal was quite usual. Breakfast cups and saucers came as no surprise, nor did the basting spoons, jam-jars, tin-openers, cork-screws, cook's knife, frying pan and tumbler glasses. Clearly, few concessions were made, even to the desert. Wisely, a medicine chest was included, too.

The despatch box contained a dinner-suit, two dress-shirts (complete with four collars and a black tie) and one pair of black socks. For everyday wear, two summer suits, a khaki coat, two pairs of shorts (white and khaki), and two pairs of stockings, seem to have comprised the basic kit. A topee and a pair of jodhpurs added to the character sketch of the 'best-dressed geologist' wandering about Bahrain in 1935. Curiously, there appeared to be no requirement for shirts, shoes and sandals, or even saucepans. Perhaps they were the subject of another loading notice.

I wonder what Haji Yusuf made of it all? Perhaps dealing with this shipment was a welcome diversion from his usual routine as APOC's agent in Bahrain, such as handling mundane tins of fuel. However, a much more exciting event occurred in 1935. Oil was discovered in Saudi Arabia. After years of financial depression, perhaps Haji Yusuf now had good reason for cautious optimism.

Oil strike in Saudi Arabia – a blessing and a boon

While some spectators viewed this discovery as an immediate blessing, serious speculators knew that the Saudi Arabian wells were not producing oil in commercial quantities. Bahrain's oil industry, just three years old, was still in its infancy and awaiting the completion of BAPCO's new refinery, due in 1936. For now, the Anglo-Persian Oil Company still had no competition in Arabia.

So much so that, in February 1935, F. A. Davies, on behalf of BAPCO, asked Haji Yusuf to resume APOC's monthly shipments of gas oil to Bahrain. To this end, Haji Yusuf placed a standing-order for 250 tins of gas-oil on the next, and each subsequent, trip of the

SS *Khuzistan* from the Abadan refinery. (Incidentally, it was geologist Fred Davies who, with remarkable perception, determined to within six feet (two metres) the precise place where oil-well number one in Bahrain should be placed, and would successfully strike oil. Years later, he was appointed Chairman of the Arabian Oil Company (ARAMCO).

By March 1935, Haji Yusuf had become very concerned about the arrival of American kerosene in Bahrain, apparently imported from Muscat. While APOC regretted that it had no control over the independent (unidentified) merchant concerned, they understood that this 'rogue' shipment was an accumulation of consignments which their competitors in Muscat had imported from Karachi, and then found impossible to sell. APOC did not think that Haji Yusuf should be too apprehensive since they had no news to suggest that further supplies had been shipped from Karachi. In any case, APOC had found out that the kerosene's quality was 'definitely inferior' to its own brand Palm Tree, both in colour and burning properties.

In bizarre contrast, by June 1935 the Rafidain Oil Company in Basrah, Iraq, (formerly Khanaqin Oil Company based in Baghdad, by now part of BP) decided that Muharraq aerodrome needed a face-lift. As the Rafidain Oil Company's agent in Bahrain, Haji Yusuf was told that one five-gallon drum of khaki paint had been despatched to the island for the purpose of smartening up the Nissen hut stores at Muharraq aerodrome. 'We believe that wire brushes are in your possession and these should be used to remove old paint or rust on the surface, before applying a fresh coat.'

Meanwhile, Arabia's oil industry had taken on another new aspect. On 8 November 1933 in Delaware, USA the California Arabian Standard Oil Company (CASOC) had been incorporated. In 1934 CASOC acquired an exclusive concession from the Standard Oil Company of California: that which King Abdul-Aziz Ibn Saud had granted to SOCAL some years earlier. (Until 1940 CASOC was a legal entity only; SOCAL conducted the practical development of the Saudi Arabian oil-field. During the Second World War the US Government created the Petroleum Reserves Corporation which attempted to buy a controlling interest in CASOC. After protracted negotiations failed, the company ceased to exist on 31 January 1944 when its name was changed officially to the Arabian American Oil Company. Thus, ARAMCO was born.)

Throughout 1935, CASOC prospected for oil in various parts of the Al-Hasa region of Saudi Arabia, urged on by the fact that Bahrain was now exporting crude oil, albeit in small quantities. By 1937, Fred

Davies had transferred from BAPCO to CASOC. On 18 January 1937, writing from Al-Khobar, he responded to Haji Yusuf's request for information concerning the approximate number of steamer passages which CASOC might expect to book each year. At that time, there were no travel agencies or airlines serving Saudi Arabia. So when CASOC sent their employees off on home-leave after three years' service in the Kingdom, they set off for Beirut where they connected with the American Export Lines which sailed directly to the USA. The snag was that all this travelling took a long time. So, by way of finding an alternative, Fred Davies told his 'old friend' Haji Yusuf that he would appreciate information on the following: the sailing dates of steamers from Bahrain; their size, particularly relative to available accommodation; the names of interconnecting shipping lines; the number of days' delay in each port *en route*; the length of the entire voyage to the USA in days; the cost; which ports on the Pacific coast of America the steamers represented by Haji Yusuf called into; and which places these vessels stopped at *en route*.

In February 1937 another request landed on Haji Yusuf's desk, this time from the Anglo-Iranian Oil Company (AIOC). (Prior to the official country name-change of Persia to Iran on 21 May 1935, AIOC had been Haji Yusuf's old 'friend', APOC.) Having decided to provide all main aerodromes within its areas with BP wind-indicators, they asked Haji Yusuf to find out: who owned the existing windsleeves; whose permission had to be sought to erect AIOC's own indicators at the aerodrome; assuming these could replace the existing ones and, supposing permission were to be granted, how much would it cost to erect the new windsleeves?

More or less at the same time, Mr C. H. Service of the Rafidain Oil Company wrote to Haji Yusuf, yet again expressing his concerns about corporate image: he ordered all Kanoo's regular (non-casual) refuelling staff to be kitted-out with new uniforms. According to Haji Yusuf's expense statement, the eight uniforms required 40 yards (37 metres) of khaki-drill, and lining; eight *agals* (black circular head-bands to secure the head-dress); eight cotton 'shawls' (the head-dress); eight pairs of canvas shoes and eight pairs of socks. The total bill, including stitching charges, came to Rs 65 4a.

By early 1938, the early optimism which Dammam's first test-well had stimulated, had all but dissipated. Although oil had been struck in Saudi Arabia on 27 August 1935 the result had been disappointing. Many people were seriously thinking of abandoning the whole enterprise. Despite some oil and gas shows, there had been no big strike. However, King Abdul-Aziz was not prepared to give up, nor was Max Steineke, a CASOC field geologist. Encouraged by the King, and driven by his own determination, Steineke persevered. Finally, on 3 March 1938, at a depth of 4,727 feet (1,441 metres), oil started gushing out of Dammam's Well Number 7. At last Saudi Arabia's oil industry had taken off.

Petroleum products – Haji Yusuf's 'bread-winners'

Despite the renewed enthusiasm which this discovery inspired, two cables sent to Haji Yusuf during 1938 offer contrasting 'readings' of the commercial climate prevailing in Arabia at that time. Both were sent by the Anglo-Iranian Oil Company. The first, sent in June, informed Haji Yusuf that it had heard reports to the effect that dealers in Bahrain were 'contemplating' filling AIOC's empty tins with BAPCO-produced kerosene, and then selling them as if they were intact AIOC-originated tins. Their message to Haji Yusuf ended with the instruction: 'What action would you wish to take against these dealers? ... Decision at once.'

The second cable confirms that, even in October 1938, the Government of Saudi Arabia still depended on imported oil products: in this case, BP Motor Spirit (petrol) and Palm Tree kerosene bought from the Anglo-Iranian Oil Company, via Y.B.A.Kanoo in Bahrain. Nevertheless, during 1938, Saudi Arabia began exporting crude oil to Bahrain from a small storage and shipping terminal located at Al-Khobar. There, the oil was received from a pipeline, transferred into containers, and transported by barge to the Bahrain refinery. Oil had been discovered in Kuwait, too, with the prospect of a large oil-field which 'may, in time, rival Bahrain!'

In the same year, on 26 September, a flying era came to an end. Haji Yusuf heard from the Rafidain Oil Company that, shortly, he should expect the last RAF-registered 'Sunderland' flying boat for delivery to Singapore, to arrive in Bahrain. Haji Yusuf was asked to supply the aircraft with 1,125 gallons (5,114 litres) of aviation fuel and 30 gallons (136 litres) of lubrication oil for the final stage of this nostalgic flight. However, Haji Yusuf remained AIOC's agent in Bahrain, re-fuelling other RAF and Imperial Airways' aircraft. Until 1936, Mesopotamia Persia Corporation (MPC) was Imperial Airways' appointed passenger-handling agent in Bahrain. It also managed The Landing Company, a firm owned by the British India Steam Navigation which operated Manama port. When MPC ceased trading in 1936, its successor Gray Mackenzie & Company took over these two roles.

Continuing the oil and aviation themes, it is worth describing exactly what refuelling entailed, even though one's first reaction might be, so what? Let us pause to think of conditions in the 1930s. No mechanised bowsers and high-speed fuel-injection systems were available. At Muharraq aerodrome, six men had to hand-pump the inflammable contents of several hundred fuel tins into an aircraft's tanks in a matter of a few minutes, often when the weather was intensely hot and humid. Now imagine carrying out the same operation from a small wooden launch tethered alongside a flying-boat. In such circumstances, the effort involved assumes a different dimension.

But before these procedures could begin, the necessary aviation fuel and lubricating oil (imported from APOC's Abadan refinery, discharged at Suwafiyah Bay near Manama, and stored in a godown (warehouse) had to be loaded onto a local launch. With no cranes or forklifts available, this job required several coolies (unskilled labourers). Throughout the trip from Suwafiyah Bay to Muharraq aerodrome, or the RAF Pier, a watchman stood guard. To put this procedure into a wider perspective, an average daily throughput (from store to aircraft) was 400 tins of aviation fuel and 40 drums of lubricating oil. Occasionally, as many as 1,000 tins of aviation fuel were needed.

At Muharraq jetty, the tins and drums were off-loaded from the launch into hired cars and taken to the aerodrome. Petrol for the cars had to be carried too. At the landing-ground, six different coolies carried out the re-fuelling operation, over-seen by a *tindel* (supervisor). All these men were hired by Haji Yusuf. Often, two aircraft landed during a day: one eastbound in the morning and one westbound in the afternoon. It was also Haji Yusuf's responsibility to provide food for the seven men throughout their day-time duty, either at the aerodrome or the pier; to buy rope for bundling the tins and pay the labour charges incurred; and to pay for the bundled empty containers and the labourers to be returned to Suwafiyah Bay. (At the end of each month all expenses were reclaimed.)

The refuelling process was equally labour-intensive, and more hazardous. Take *Hadrian, Hannibal, Hanno, Helena, Hengist* and *Horsa*, for instance. All six aircraft, fitted with Jupiter engines, plied Imperial Airways eastbound and westbound routes through Bahrain until the beginning of the Second World War. The stop-over time varied considerably, as did the quantity of fuel taken on board. As an example, I picked one day at random. Eastbound *Hadrian* arrived in Bahrain from Basrah *en route* for Sharjah. The stop-over was 72 minutes, during which time, 256 gallons (1164 litres) of BP Aviation Spirit (fuel) and 8.5 gallons (39 litres) of lubricating oil were loaded in 13 minutes. Later that day, westbound *Hannibal* arrived from Sharjah, *en route* back to Basrah. This stop-over was 18 minutes less than *Hadrian's* (54 minutes), yet the aircraft took on more fuel: 406 gallons (1846 litres) of BP Aviation Spirit and 210 gallons (955 litres) of lubricating oil. Obviously, refuelling took longer, 20 minutes in all.

As for the flying-boats (or sea-planes), the refuelling process was similar to that carried out at Muharraq aerodrome, but seven, not six, labourers were needed because the fuel-tins and the men were afloat. The extra man minded the small wooden boat, while the six labourers hand-pumped fuel into the moored, but moving flying-boat – quite a tricky procedure.

An interesting experiment was carried out in November 1934. APOC shipped a consignment of six barrels, not tins, of aviation fuel to Haji Yusuf for Imperial Airways' use. Haji Yusuf was then asked to inform APOC, by return airmail, of the barrels' condition when they arrived in Bahrain and their general suitability for handling aviation fuel. Subsequent expense statements until 1939 refer to tins (not barrels) of aviation fuel, suggesting that the experiment had not worked as planned. Since barrels are larger and heavier than tins, perhaps they were too cumbersome to handle.

Although Haji Yusuf's expense statements submitted to Imperial Airways and the RAF no longer mean much in financial terms, they tell us a great deal about the passenger facilities available during the 1930s. For instance, we learn that in 1936 Imperial Airways gave up the building they maintained in Manama as a rest-house. Instead, tents were erected on the aerodrome, then known rather formally as the Civil Landing Ground. There, passengers could eat their meals, and sleep 'in case of an emergency'.

Some of the names of people who flew in and out of Bahrain are equally noteworthy. One unique Kanoo family possession reveals that Haji Yusuf was, to use modern jargon, a 'frequent flyer'. Writing to Haji Yusuf Bin Ahmed Kanoo from the airport of London, Croydon on 7 June 1935, Captain Walters of Imperial Airways said: 'I think you will be interested to know that on the occasion of Their Majesties' Silver Jubilee on May 6th, when you travelled on my aircraft from Sharjah to Bahrain, I caused the following Airadio Telegram to be wirelessed: "To Their Majesties The King and Queen of England. Passengers, Officers, Crew, R.M.A. "Hannibal" flying Persian Gulf, send loyal congratulations – Walters, Commander [of the aircraft]".'

In reply, Buckingham Palace thanked the Commander for his good wishes, addressing their letter to 'Captain Walters, Royal Mail Aircraft "Hannibal", c/o Imperial Airways'. Now transferred to London, Walters added that he would miss the pleasure of seeing Haji Yusuf so regularly at various points on the Arabian coast. (Incidentally, an air ticket Bahrain–Basrah–Bahrain, invoiced to Haji Yusuf in 1939 by Imperial Airways' office in Rue des Fatimites, Alexandria, cost £20 sterling.)

On 26 March 1937, the famous aviator Colonel C. A. Lindbergh, accompanied by his wife, arrived in Bahrain from Delhi, flying his own aeroplane. The next day, after Haji Yusuf had refuelled the aircraft (powered by an American-made Minasco 200 HP engine), he left for Basrah *en route* to the United Kingdom.

Throughout the 1930s, RAF and Imperial Airways flying-boats landed in Khor Qalai'yah and moored at the RAF Pier (now, more or less between the Grand Mosque and the Marina Club). RAF Blenheims, Vincents and Valencias were regular visitors. As for Imperial Airways' flying-boats, fascinating names crop up such as *Calypso*, *Corsair*, *Coolanghata*, *Carpentaria*, *Ceres*, *Corio*, *Cleo*, *Coogee* and *Cordelia*. By 1939, Imperial Airways' regular destinations beyond Bahrain included Delhi, Hong Kong, Singapore, even Brisbane in Australia. For the pioneers who participated in Arabia's fledgling civil aviation and oil industries, including Haji Yusuf, the 1930s had been a memorable decade.

Chapter 4

Surviving our
Cash Crisis

As I sorted through many boxes of neglected family papers relating to the 1930s, a remarkable range of trading activity presented itself. Although these papers have no monetary value as collectors' pieces, their inherent value is as a group of contemporary documents. I was pleasantly surprised to find that they comprise a fascinating commentary on our trading activities around the world, not what one normally expects to find in an incomplete set of business letters, invoices and expense statements!

It seems that, despite the onset of the 1930s depression and its impact on both Bahrain and our family business, Haji Yusuf continued to develop his international business contacts. Not least of these was with the Crescent Tool Company of Jamestown, State of New York which eagerly promoted its products: pliers 'of the types most generally used by mechanics in all industries'. In Bahrain, electricians, car and aircraft mechanics, plumbers, carpenters, and even youngsters tinkering with their bicycles would find pliers to suit their needs. Crescent Tool Company assured us that not only did the range fit 'the modern trend', but also it represented a very moderate investment.

Certainly, the oak display-case was a work of art in itself, including the oak-veneer panel-back. The tools were mounted by clips and wing nuts, so that each item was easy to remove. The door of the case, complete with a lock, comprised a solid frame which held a sheet of clear glass in place and so revealed the displayed tools kept clean and bright.

We now travel to Birmingham, England where J. A. Phillips & Co. manufactured bicycles. An illustrated leaflet showed its most popular line of pedal-powered transport, the 'Phillips Supreme', a class of machine expected to appeal to Haji Yusuf's market. Phillips 'trusted' that its price was competitive and that Haji Yusuf would favour them with a trial order. (In 1935, a gentleman's bicycle cost 47s 6d. Ladies had to pay more, 48s 9d. I never discovered why.)

As for petrol-powered transport, on 15 October 1935, the President of the Studebaker Export Corporation notified Haji Yusuf that the company hoped to start manufacturing 1936 passenger car models within the next thirty days. Similarly, their new 1936 trucks would start production within fifteen to thirty days thereafter. The President added: 'I am sure you will agree that it would be to your advantage to start operations as a Studebaker distributor with our newest offerings. We hope to be able to write you within the next two weeks with quotations and literature on both passenger cars and trucks'. We had, of course, been the Studebaker agent in Bahrain since June 1928 when Ali bin Mohamed Kanoo signed its Agency Agreement.

If variety is the spice of life, then our family certainly could not have complained. Even Vicente Domarco based in the southern Spanish town of Novelda had identified Yusuf bin Ahmed Kanoo as a potential client. Now, he had much pleasure in quoting prices for the new saffron crop. In complete contrast, London-based Williams, Ellis and Company enthusiastically promoted its 1936 catalogue: 'Welcome Jig-saw Puzzles' (costing sixpence, and one shilling), together with the 'Gee-Wiz' Jigsaw Race Game (three shillings each), looked intriguing enough.

New portfolio – tobacco agencies

Although our finances were greatly diminished in the aftermath of the recession, Haji Yusuf's eagerness to find new business remained buoyant. In particular, our portfolio of tobacco agencies, later became one of Y.B.A.Kanoo's most profitable lines of business. Although my father, Mohamed Kanoo, was just thirteen years old in 1935, many years later his name was synonymous in Bahrain with British American Tobacco (BAT). This agency, to quote a Kanoo company director, was my father's 'baby'.

Reverting to 1935, a letter to Haji Yusuf from Mr W. Baldwin of Cherrydown Avenue, Chingford, London opens up the whole subject of tobacco agencies. Writing on 31 May, Baldwin says: 'Your name has come to me through dealing with the despatch of cases of cigarettes to you from the tobacco factory [not specified] in which I am employed. As I am greatly interested in stamps, I should be very much obliged if you could introduce me to somebody who could help me to obtain some Bahrain stamps in exchange for others.' Clearly Haji Yusuf had, by now, established himself as a cigarette importer.

From England, my story moves to Greece. On 12 August 1935, Papastratos Cigarette Manufacturing Company of Piraeus thanked Haji Yusuf for a copy of his letter addressed to Mr Mohamed Omer Bazara, their agent in Aden. They hoped that Haji Yusuf would create 'an interesting collaboration' with Bazara. Papastratos also wished to know if their Greek products were suitable for Bahrain's market, samples of which (Virginia brands, Hellas Blue and Red Cock) were on their way.

This convoluted round of communication seems to have arisen because Papastratos was 'not in a position' to quote Bazara 'C.I.F.' (cost, insurance, freight) to Arabian Gulf ports through a direct Bill of Lading. Hence, Greek cigarettes were shipped first to Aden and then to Bahrain. Not surprisingly, Bazara took this opportunity to introduce his own 'very good cigarettes of Egyptian taste'. Naturally, and gladly, he would supply Haji Yusuf with samples and quotations.

Coincidentally, my grandfathers were eager to generate complementary business with a German company in Köln-Sülz (Cologne). On 9 September 1935, Kölner Werkzeugmaschinen-Fabrik Von Wilh. Quester wrote to Jassim and Ali Mohamed Kanoo: 'I am glad to see you are interested in tobacco and cigarette manufacturing machinery'. Quester claimed the company had been building this specialised class of machinery for the last 80 years. His own considerable experience had enabled him to bring the machines to a high standard of perfection. As he was not represented in Bahrain, my grandfathers were free to quote the machines for resale. Quester added that he had several second-hand cigarette machines of the well known UK and Triumph make in stock, all in excellent condition and thoroughly repaired like new machines. If these were of interest, he would be glad to quote and awaited news with much interest.

Towards the end of 1935, Haji Yusuf tried to persuade the United Kingdom Tobacco Co. (1929) Ltd. to offer him more competitive prices. Haji Yusuf believed that he could increase his turnover of My Princess cigarettes considerably if he were allowed to sell them on competitive terms with 3 Roses. While both parties were equally keen to do business with each other, the UK Tobacco company pompously reminded Haji Yusuf that since, already, they had lowered their prices to him for the My Princess brand, they found it 'quite impossible' to make further reductions.

After taking this stand, the company conceded that there was a big demand for a lesser-priced line. To help Haji Yusuf (and presumably themselves) 'to capture a share of this business', they offered to reduce the price of My Princess cigarettes, if Haji Yusuf accepted a slightly different blend and changed the packaging. If he also arranged cash payments to be made against documents in London, then they could offer a further concession. I assume that an acceptable compromise was negotiated since the two companies continued to correspond with each other.

More or less simultaneously, Haji Yusuf had also been trying to secure an agency agreement with yet another UK cigarette manufacturer: R. & J. Hills. In August 1936 he heard from Shasha & Co. (the Manchester-based exporters and commodity brokers) that Hills were prepared to grant a limited agency to Shasha for one year. The 'stick' to this arrangement was that it would apply to Bahrain and Sharjah only, since Hills was already doing business with another agent in Dubai and Muscat. The 'carrot' was that if Haji Yusuf's turnover was satisfactory during the next twelve months, then Shasha would obtain the R. & J. Hills cigarette agency for the 'whole territory'. (Whether this was intended to embrace more than the four Arabian locations just mentioned is not stated.)

A letter sent to Haji Yusuf on 22 December 1936 by the Premier Export Tobacco Co. based in London takes the tobacco story further. In a recent issue of the British *Board of Trade Journal,* Haji Yusuf had advertised his interest in selling cigarettes in Bahrain and the Arabian Gulf. The Premier Export Tobacco responded by telling Haji Yusuf that they were large manufacturers of cigarettes for export markets, particularly Virginia, Turkish, Egyptian and American blends varying in price from 27s 6d to 6s per thousand. With some knowledge of the Bahrain market, Premier Tobacco did not think Haji Yusuf would be interested in their higher-priced brands. Instead, they quoted for Smoke Cloud and 12 O'Clock, two of their cheapest lines. These, they believed, would compete successfully against rival brands: Oceanic and Air Mail. The competitor was none other than R. & J. Hills.

Haji Yusuf kept his options open. That is, he sold both Premier Tobacco's brands, and those of R. & J. Hills. Whether he was forced to select one agency or the other, I do not know. However, by mid-1937, Gallaher Limited of London (manufacturers of high class tobaccos, cigarettes and snuff) was on the agency trail, too. When they wrote to Yusuf bin Ahmed Kanoo on 7 June, already one parcel of sample Three Birds, Homeward Bound and Torchlight cigarettes, supplied gratis and not for resale, was on its way to Bahrain. The elaborate, flamboyant invoice-heading suggests that their cigarettes and tobacco were equally impressive!

Japan – A tempting trader

We now switch gear to a very different culture and style of business, the Japanese. The chosen examples demonstrate both the ambitions of Japan to expand its trading links west to Asia and Arabia, and its confident attitude towards potential agents.

I begin with two letters from T. Hayakawa Metal Laboratories in Osaka, Japan, both dated 30 March 1935 and sent to Jassim and Ali Kanoo. After thanking my grandfathers for their enquiry, Hayakawa's promotion began: 'Being the pioneers and the largest manufacturers in radio engineering in this country, we have been engaged in foreign trade for many a year. Now our Sharp Dyne radio receiver has won a good reputation for their superior selectivity and sensitivity as well as their competitive prices in overseas markets.' Predictably, its catalogue and export price-list were already on their way to Bahrain.

After years of research, Hayakawa Metal Laboratories was also pleased to say it was now producing 'Ever' electric clocks in its newly-equipped factory. Economy was an outstanding feature of the product: only 2 watts were needed to operate these refined mechanisms. Quoting from its second promotion: 'Your territory is open for these products and we are desirous of talking over with you the sole agency for our mutual profit.'

From the refinements of radio receivers and electric clocks, I was impressed by the Toyo Trading Company's more practical products: ten selections of rayon elastic garters. Mailed from Kobe in Japan during December 1936, samples of cotton machine threads and glass tumblers were included in the parcel. While drawing our attention to cement and black-tea, Toyo Trading also drew our attention to the strong fluctuations in these commodity markets. A partial explanation for this appeared in Mitsubishi Shoji Kaisha's letter from its Bombay branch, dated 21 December 1936. This company, a subsidiary of the Mitsubishi Trading Company Limited, explained: 'We thank you for your offer of 150 cases of Japanese black tea, but regret to note that the price is very much out of line. The market in Japan is strong due to the failure of the crop this season owing to the cold weather.'

Meanwhile, as requested by Haji Yusuf, the Bombay branch of Mitsui Bussan Kaisha Limited had sent him samples of Shizuoka black tea, packed in veneer chests of 100 lb. (45 kg.) net, each wrapped with hessian covering. Haji Yusuf was urged to try them and then 'wire' his requirements. In return, Mitsui Bussan Kaisha would do their best to put through the business. Until then, they anxiously looked forward to Haji Yusuf's 'esteemed commands.'

If tea was an uncertain commercial proposition, then Meiji's milk caramels were no less a risk. It seems that, in February 1937, Haji Yusuf was somehow convinced of the wisdom of buying 50 cases of the confectionery: 5 pieces in a packet, 200 packets in a tin and 16 tins in a case, a grand total of 800,000 milk caramels!

Haji Yusuf's letter of 23 April 1937 to Mitsubishi Shoji Kaisha in Bombay, contained no surprises: 'I do not know what manner to express to your goodselves the difficulty I have taken in canvassing the above order for 50 cases of caramels. The mere reason is due to the fact that dealers, or rather my clients at this end, have been accustomed to import most of their requirements through their agents or friends from Bombay. I observe that they are always obtaining lower rates in Bombay than that quoted by your goodselves, although I understand that you are sharing a part of the business. Permit me to venture and ask you of the necessity for trying my utmost to canvass and popularise various of your products?'

Referring to the balance of 50 cases of Meiji's milk caramels, Haji Yusuf explained: 'I have left no stone unturned to dispose of the balance of your kind offer, but I find the dealers do not show much interest owing to the market being adequately stocked.' After strenuous efforts, he managed to persuade one dealer to buy the remains of the lot for a much reduced price. But, as Haji Yusuf concluded: 'This is the utmost I could do in this respect'.

Not the least put off by this difficulty, the same Bombay branch of Mitsubishi Shoji Kaisha encouraged Haji Yusuf to start selling ready-made mosquito nets. In May 1937, he placed a trial order for two cases, ten dozen in each case (a total of 240 nets). Back came the reply that the order could not be confirmed because Mitsubishi Shoji Kaisha had no ready stock in Bombay and the requested quantity fell short of the required minimum order. It was at this point that I recognised a recurring pattern: the Japanese perception of a sensible minimum order for the Bahrain market was not realistic, nor did it coincide with what Haji Yusuf had in mind.

The following story illustrates just how big a headache Japanese export marketing quotas became for our family business. On 9 March 1937, the Bombay branch of Mitsubishi Shoji Kaisha began pushing Haji Yusuf hard on cigarette sales. Their bottom line was a minimum order: 10 cases of each kind of cigarette. The seven 'kinds' comprised 3 brands packaged in various ways. So far, the mathematics were easy: a minimum order was 70 cases.

Rather cleverly, Mitsubishi Shoji Kaisha first quoted the prices per thousand pieces, for each of the seven kinds (variations according to brands and packaging). Then the company altered course, and listed the quantities packed in each wooden case. This meant that Haji Yusuf first needed to establish how many thousands of cigarettes would be packed in those 70 wooden cases, before he could calculate how much it would cost him to buy the stipulated quantities of the seven different kinds.

To simplify the story yet tell the tale, I begin with the Akatsuki cigarette brand: 20 pieces packed in a box, 10 boxes in a carton, 100 cartons in one wooden case, thus 20,000 cigarettes in each case. The quantities in each wooden case containing varieties 2, 3, 5 and 6 worked out to be the same: 20,000 cigarettes per case.

The difference in these four varieties was the brand-name, price and packaging. Brands Cherry and Hope (kinds 2 and 5) were packed in cellophane-wrapped boxes, while the same brands were also packed in un-wrapped boxes (kinds 3 and 6). All four variations were packed 10 pieces to a box, 50 boxes in a can, and 40 cans in a wooden case. Since the minimum order was 10 cases per kind, obviously variations 2, 3, 5 and 6 generated 40 cases. With 20,000 cigarettes in each, take my word for it, the sub-total is 800,000 pieces!

Add the Akatsuki minimum order of 200,000 cigarettes (10 cases containing 20,000 items in each), and the total has now reached one million cigarettes. But that is not all. The Hope and Cherry brands were also packed in slender-roll cans (kinds 4 and 7): 50 pieces in a can, 10 cans in a carton, 20 cartons in a wooden case, (10,000 items per case). These two varieties multiplied by 10 cases each, total 200,000 cigarettes. So, according to my calculations, Haji Yusuf had to buy no fewer than 1,200,000 cigarettes, just to get started!

Since the price-list quoted the cost of each variable that calculation would have been another nightmare, quite apart from the capital investment. However, the big surprise was not the complex presentation of the entire promotion (enough to deter most newcomers to the export business), but the emphatic tone of its penultimate paragraph. Haji Yusuf was asked to 'please note' that the prices offered were 'the best ones and no reduction will be possible' because the cigarette industry in Japan was monopolised by the Japanese Government.

In much the same dictatorial style, the Bombay branch of Mitsubishi Shoji Kaisha told Haji Yusuf: 'Sacrifice a portion of your commission and see that business is done.' I cannot imagine Haji Yusuf taking too kindly to such arbitrary language, particularly since the commission on offer was just 3.5 per cent, before any 'sacrifice' was made. Even allowing for quirks in translation, the examples just mentioned are an interesting insight into Japanese export marketing during the 1930s. Such an approach is worlds away from the current Japanese practice of customer-oriented marketing.

In contrast, Haji Yusuf had developed a new interest: candle importing. In February 1937 he wrote to Frank C. Strick & Co. (Busra) Limited (which also had branches in Baghdad, Khorramshahr and Abadan). Providing that the prices of 8 oz. (227 g.) and 10 oz. (284 g.) white candles were acceptable to him, Haji Yusuf appears not to have been concerned about the candles' country of origin. Strick took a different view.

They replied that they could offer a reduced price on the candles they had in stock (origin unstated) to stop competitors entering the Bahrain market with Japanese candles. Thus prompted, Haji Yusuf identified one competitor (un-named) whom he suspected. Although the dealer appeared 'quiet', Haji Yusuf believed that he was simply waiting for a direct shipment to arrive from Japan. Haji Yusuf informed Strick that he was watching movements carefully and would not hesitate to report fully when anything transpired.

At the same time, Haji Yusuf had secured an order for coloured candles (from whom, I do not know). These were required by the first available steamer from Basrah: 100 cases, each candle weighing 8 oz; 200 cases of white candles of similar weight were ordered too.

Meanwhile, anxious to find out just how serious a threat the Japanese candles were to their own principals' products, Strick's office in Basrah was busy having samples of the Japanese candles analysed. On 30 April 1937, they confidently told Haji Yusuf that their principals (the manufacturers) had examined the candles and concluded: the Japanese variety had two disadvantages compared with their own candles. Firstly, the burning-time of the competitive candles was very much less than that of their own products. For example, the burning-time of a 10 oz. Japanese White Star candle was 5.13 hours, compared with 6.38 hours for Strick's variety. Secondly, the Japanese candles contained large proportions of Stearine (a by-product of fish oil) which, as Haji Yusuf had no doubt noticed, gave the candles 'a rather disagreeable smell'. Of less concern, the Japanese candles were very opaque. However, as the manufacturers remarked, it did not necessarily follow that buyers would be prejudiced against Japanese candles for these reason alone.

Strick believed that Haji Yusuf could obtain 'appreciable' prices for the candles they supplied, despite the competition, because of another discovery. White Star brand-labels stated that the candles had been made for Becharada Govindji & Co. (Bombay). After all, they were not of Japanese origin. Haji Yusuf was asked: 'Please continue to watch the situation and keep us closely advised.'

Later in 1937, Haji Yusuf's candle importing assumed a different character. On 19 November, he wrote to Strick: 'I have received an enquiry for black candles required for use during the coming *Muharram* days. I shall be thankful if you would kindly let me know whether manufacturers are in a position to supply these as required by the dealers here. ... I do not know whether or not you will be able to arrange for a shipment of black candles to arrive here a week before the *Moharram* [Muharram] Festival which falls on about 11th March 1938.' Haji Yusuf needed fifty cases of black candles to fulfil orders already placed with him. It would seem that Frank C. Strick did not know of their significance.

In a simplified explanation, Haji Yusuf replied that the word *Ashoora* refers to the first ten days of Muharram during which period Shia Moslems burn candles in large quantities. As the file in our archive is incomplete, I do not know whether or not Haji Yusuf was supplied with black candles. Maybe he was, and perhaps they were of Japanese origin, too.

Cables and wireless – confidential communication

In the 1930s, one has to remember that speedy communication, in written form, could only be achieved by telegraphy: transmission by cables (many of which lay on sea-beds), and international wireless signals. Of course, ticker-tape networks existed, such as those used to record quotations on the New York Stock Exchange. Today, we take telex, teleprinters and facsimile machines for granted, equipment which also depends on public telecommunications networks.

By their very nature, telegrams (or cables, as they are often called) could be read by virtually anyone who handled them *en route* between the originators and the recipients: typists, message-boys, wireless-operators and office-clerks. It was a very public type of communication. However, the period under discussion was a time when civil aviation was in its infancy, and so speedy delivery of documents by air was, as yet, a limited facility.

Those countries and companies which did have access to telephone systems, knew well enough that telephone-operators had 'free and easy' listening as well. Only when networks became busier and direct-dial facilities became more widely available, did eavesdropping become less likely. (By 1982, for example, there were 181 million telephones in the USA, and 60 million in Japan.)

So, if speed was of the essence, cablegrams were the only alternative form of communication. When confidentiality was an equal factor, many companies coded their messages prior to despatch. Recipients then translated them, using relevant manuals which listed the cyphers. Of course, there was, and remains, another aspect: expense. The shorter the message, the less it costs to send, whatever system is used. In the case of coded cables, one cypher of three or five letters often translated into a phrase, even a sentence.

Random searches among correspondence exchanged between Y.B.A.Kanoo and organisations with whom we communicated, demonstrate that coding was general operating practice. The range of codes was extensive, too. Take the Yusuf bin Ahmed Kanoo letter-head used in the 1930s, for example. This lists no fewer than nine codes: ABC 5th Edition, Acme Commodity & Phrase, Bentley's Complete Phrase, Bentley's Second Phrase, Lombard, Mosse Condenser, Oriental 3-Letters, Private and Rudolf Mosse.

In a series of cables sent to Haji Yusuf during 1935, the Ottoman Bank in Basrah, Iraq, 'advertised' five telegraphic codes, including Broomhall's Imperial Combination, Lieber's 5 Letter, and Peterson's 3rd Edition. S. Samuel & Rosenfeld (commodity merchants in Hamburg with whom Haji Yusuf had dealings) used several codes just mentioned, plus Commercial Telegraph, and Tanner's Council Edition. And so the list goes on, with some most unusual names such as Stella and Zebra.

With the aid of manuals, often hundreds of pages long, correspondents were able to translate the cables, cypher by cypher. One telegram from APOC to Haji Yusuf illustrates this well. Referring to page 785 of the Supplement to the Lombard Code (not even the main manual), Haji Yusuf was asked to insert *TARAQQI* (an APOC steamer's name) at the top of certain columns.

For many people in Bahrain, including members of my family and our employees, the tedious process of translation is well within living memory. This ranged from the comparatively simple message to the complex. The following example is taken from a message hand-written by the Master of the SS *Khuzistan*, then anchored off Bahrain, and delivered to Haji Yusuf: 'Will you please send the following telegram to the Kuwait Agency from me'.

Since the date was 24 December 1935, by now the Anglo-Persian Oil Company had changed its name to the Anglo-Iranian Oil Company. Thus, AIOC's agent in Kuwait would have received the following cyphered telegram (left column) from his counterpart in Bahrain, Haji Yusuf. After translation (right column), the Kuwaiti agent would have known when to expect the SS *Khuzistan* to arrive and what was required:

YJIWE	Khuzistan
UBWJA	15
EKESZ	coolies
AOJNY	and
JBZAY	lighters
HUULJ	for
AABOT	arr.
OOFCC	26th Sept.
UXEJN	7,500
ALETU	packages

Having come across a ten-page list of three-letter cyphers, many of which de-code as names and phrases, I will end this theme with a little light relief. As the first page was missing (and also the name of the code), I began at letter B. Immediately I saw similarities between some cyphers, but not their translations. Consider BXA and BZA: de-coded, they became Bahrain Petroleum Company, and Bahrain Government. An incoming cable simply saying VYK, would tell me that the market in Paris was very dull. Conversely, VYM would indicate that it 'showed an improvement'. While I could not find cyphers for members of our family (perhaps listed on the missing page one), I did see Mohammed Yateem discreetly disguised as FCA.

Commodity markets – risks and rewards

In May 1937 Erdmann & Sielcken (Javanese commodity brokers and analysts based in Soerabaja, but with other offices in Batavia and Semarang) had reported to Haji Yusuf a general feeling of financial uneasiness. This overshadowed world-wide commodity markets for the rest of the year. Even slight improvements were not strong enough to generate a positive upward trend.

As for sugar, things began to look more favourable after a quota system was agreed and fears were allayed that the annual Sugar Conference in London might fail. Sugar values in London advanced after a more optimistic view was taken, but in New York, the market was erratic. While Shanghai came out of its reserve in May 1937, followed by considerable volume trading in molasses for forward months, Hong Kong 'did not participate in the buying mood of its northern neighbour'. The Japanese sugar market remained lifeless. In

India, of the few enquiries received, all led to nothing because of the disparity of prices which was too great to bridge.

By November 1937, Erdmann & Sielcken had concluded: 'The aspect of things generally still lacks signs of a more hopeful nature and it is at present extremely difficult to venture an opinion as to the trend of further development which might influence commercial sentiment in the near future.'

Lately, exchange-rates had not been quite so steadfast. Values in London had declined slightly. Nevertheless, fluctuations seemed to indicate that there was increased resistance to recession. New York was quiet, but steady. The Java sugar market recorded satisfactory sales. Buying continued in Hong Kong on a small scale, but purchasers appeared to be greatly influenced by the uncertain political situation in the Far East, causing them to refrain from making larger commitments. So for the time being, bulk sugar which had been one of Haji Yusuf's 'safe' purchases, no longer offered him the same guarantee.

In February 1938, hopeful news came from J. M. Shasha in Manchester, UK. They could possibly dispose of Haji Yusuf's 80-ton shipment of *kasha* fish which remained in storage. Shasha reckoned that in early March 1938 they could sell the consignment at £11 10s per ton. Their export manager wrote to Haji Yusuf: 'Really, I am not too satisfied with this price, but I am finding it extremely difficult to make buyers believe that our quality is the same as the standard grade which has, in the past, been shipped to their markets. ... It will be advisable to accept the offer as, by so doing, we will establish confidence with our buyers and no doubt secure their further orders when they are next in the market'.

Since the invoice cost was only £9 per ton, the profit of £2 10s would be shared between Shasha and Haji Yusuf. Shasha considered this to be fairly reasonable, and even believed that it ought to encourage Haji Yusuf to go into this business on a larger scale since they had several interested clients.

In late March 1938 Haji Yusuf received word that the sale for the first 80 tons of *kasha* fish had gone through. But, because of substantial accrued storage charges, and the fish having dried out (causing a weight-loss of two tons), the profit was not as great as expected. Nevertheless, considering the large amount of capital involved, Shasha were sure that they had established Haji Yusuf's mark on the market, and that they would be able to conclude forward sales at a satisfactory price later in the year. To this end, Haji Yusuf was encouraged to make extensive purchases of both *kasha* and *dhoma* fish, since there seemed to be no reason why both he and Shasha should not capture the bulk of this business. Confidently, Shasha stated that they were the largest buyers of this commodity and believed they could obtain forward orders for at least 1,000 tons of both types of fish, just as soon as Haji Yusuf was able to make some satisfactory offers during the coming season.

While *kasha* and *dhoma* fish were regarded as a good proposition, the mother-of-pearl shell market had shown signs of instability. Late in 1936, Haji Yusuf had arranged for twenty cases of pearl shells and seventy bags of Lingah shells to be shipped from Kobe, Japan, to London by SS *Suwa Maru* 'by order and for account and risk' of Y.B.A.Kanoo, Bahrain. On 17 December 1936, Mitsubishi Shoji Kaisha notified Haji Yusuf that it very much regretted it could not comply with his request to sell his consignment of pearl and Lingah shells, simply because of the substantial difference between his required price and the market price obtainable in London. Nevertheless, the consignment was shipped to Trieste and Venice for storage, as he had requested.

By late February 1937 Shasha was still finding great difficulty in disposing of the shells. One client had offered nine shillings per hundredweight, but then the Italian Government cancelled all import licences because of the nervousness 'hanging over Europe'. In the event of war, Italy, like every other country, would need all her sterling for necessities, and not what customs authorities considered to be luxuries. No one knew whether this restriction was temporary or not. Meanwhile, Haji Yusuf was asked to assure his clients that everything possible was being done in their interests. By way of added reassurance, J. M. Shasha's judgment was that none of their competitors could have acted differently under the circumstances.

By mid-September 1938, buying trends at London auctions had steadily improved. Large quantities of Persian Gulf shells had been offered for sale, and fairly satisfactory clearances made. As for better quality mother-of-pearl shells, the achieved price was higher than before. Unfortunately, the same could not be said for Lingah shells since fewer continental buyers had attended the sales than usual. In Shasha's view, the market would possibly decline still further in the near future, simply because of the large accumulated stocks which would have to be carried over to future sales.

However, the situation was not all gloom. In October 1938 Haji Yusuf learned that the UK importers had received an enquiry for Indian and Persian Gulf un-ground dried prawn shells. If he was interested in this commodity, then would he send a large-size sample, and make Shasha an offer for 50 tons of the commodity for November and December shipments from London (a total of 100 tons). Since dried prawn shells were sold on an analysis basis, it was necessary for Haji Yusuf to state the guaranteed composition: the minimum content of protein, and maximum percentage of sand, water and salt. If no laboratories existed in Bahrain from which this data could be obtained, then the tests could be carried out in London. Despite this complication, Shasha believed that dried prawn shells could generate good sales and so anxiously hoped that Haji Yusuf would give the matter his immediate attention.

Reflecting on the events of 1938, clearly the relationship between Shasha and Haji Yusuf had had its difficult moments. Nevertheless, in a conciliatory frame of mind, the Manchester-based company suggested that since, at all costs, both parties wished to keep their business friendship, they had decided to meet Haji Yusuf's wishes by crediting his account with the various items he had requested. Of course, they realised that it would be better for everyone if all their respective shell stocks could be sold. In that event, their account could be closed entirely and a new slate started afresh on new business. In closing, J. M. Shasha told Haji Yusuf: 'I can assure you, however, that I expect you to have as much confidence in me as I have in you, and as I have adjusted matters in the matter desired, I hope we will now be able to continue our business relationship together. ... I think it foolish for business to come to a standstill when there are only minor adjustments to be made'.

Judging by the flurry of subsequent letters, business did not come to a standstill. Shortly afterwards, Haji Yusuf asked Shasha to issue an inspection order in favour of Johann Schlintz for 125 bags of shells lying in Hamburg port. Haji Yusuf was interested in buying them and was willing to pay in Reichmarks. As for the shells still in Venice, Shasha assured Haji Yusuf that no stone would be left unturned in an effort to sell them. However, restrictions in force at that time made any headway impossible. Better success was hoped for the shells in Trieste, despite one sale having fallen through because the interested client could not pay in sterling. Outlets in London and on the continent of Europe remained extremely quiet. Prices in the Arabian Gulf area were reported as 'easier', although shells offered 'on the spot' in Bahrain, Lingah and Muscat now attracted no interest. For all their differences of opinion, J. M. Shasha and Haji Yusuf agreed on one matter: both hoped for better news soon.

Appetising imports – Australian fruit and vegetables

In February 1939 W. A. Robertson (manufacturers' representative in Batavia, Java, North East Indonesia) introduced themselves to Haji Yusuf. According to what Robertsons had been told, Hadden & Co. and the Stoomvaart Mij Nederland now shipped fresh vegetables to the Arabian Gulf region. Would Haji Yusuf like to become a fruit and vegetable importer? If so, then Robertsons would gladly co-operate to any reasonable extent.

In presenting their credentials, Robertsons remarked that although they had no experience as exporters, for many years they had been the largest importers of fresh fruits into Java, their sales amounting to between 30,000 and 35,000 cases per year. With connections in Soerabaya, Semarang and Batavia, they considered themselves well-positioned to supply Haji Yusuf with really good quality produce for every steamer sailing to the Arabian Gulf. As for the vegetables which they considered suitable for Bahrain, the list was most varied: cabbages, cauliflowers, maize, carrots, cucumbers, sweet potatoes, leeks, tomatoes, red beans, lobak (type of turnip), ojong (a popular Javanese vegetable known as 'crew vegetable' because of its use on ships as green food for the crews), terrong ('egg plant' or aubergine), marrow, beetroot, spinach and red peppers.

Tempted by this overture, Haji Yusuf placed his first order on 21 March. However, business with W. A. Robertson did not get off to a good start, partly because the best price they could obtain for potatoes in the Javanese market was not suitable for Haji Yusuf. As for fresh fruits, Haji Yusuf's offer was considered 'entirely out of line' with prevailing conditions in the same market. The only apples recommended for shipment to Bahrain were green Granny Smiths and red Democrats. As for Australian oranges, shipment from Adelaide could not begin until the middle of May 1939.

Despite this inauspicious beginning, Robertsons wrote: 'It is unfortunate that we did not get together earlier in the season, but now that we are in communication, it is quite possible that next season we can do a very fair Australian business with you. Right at the moment all Australian early fruits are now finished due to the heat-wave which struck that country just as the fruit was forming on the trees. There is a shortage and prices are, in our opinion, enormously high in consequence.'

By late May, Robertsons ran into further difficulties. Regular fruit shipments from Australia had been disrupted. The political situation had generated a great demand for cold storage foods, particularly frozen meat, to supply the British garrison in Singapore. Thus, many of Robertson's clients had had their orders reduced from 50 per cent to 40 per cent because Australian fruit exporters were no longer able to book refrigerated space for civilian requirements. There was another complication. From time to time the Silver Java Pacific Line temporarily withdrew its steamer service to the Arabian Gulf, leaving no other vessels available with cold storage facilities for the long voyage. Thus, as Haji Yusuf could not be guaranteed regular supplies, this uncertainty might make the business of fruit and vegetable importing uninteresting to him.

W. A. Robertson's only alternative was to purchase locally in Java, but by doing so, their prices would have to include duty since the Indonesian Government gave no rebate, even on produce destined for export. Yet, despite these hurdles, the company remained anxious to try out this business with Haji Yusuf. As a start, they proposed to buy fruit from Western Australia. Although pears and grapes from there were considered unsatisfactory, Granny Smith and Democrat apples were good. They suggested supplying four cases of each type, and oranges too, even though Western Australian oranges were not as good as those from the south.

At last, in mid-June, Haji Yusuf heard that his requested shipment of fruit had been ordered: ten cases of Granny Smith green apples; five cases each of Democrat red apples and mandarin oranges. By early August, he reported back that the apples had arrived in Bahrain in good condition. So pleased was he that, immediately, he ordered further supplies, including Josephine pears. But, as Robertsons warned, 'the season is all but over until next March. In any event, it must be clearly understood between us that no shipment will be made if, in the writer's opinion, the fruit is not strong enough to withstand the journey from here to Bahrain and arrive in a saleable condition'.

In the end, the company exceeded Haji Yusuf's expectations. The Samarang and Second Samarang Marine and Fire Insurance Companies insurance certificate for this shipment tells us that no fewer than 60 cases of mandarin oranges, 30 cases of apples, 5 cases of pears, as well as 1 crate each of mangoes, avocado pears and papaya (a total of 98 cases) were shipped to Bahrain by the steamer *Bengkalis* on 25 August 1939. A week later, Haji Yusuf was asked by the exporters to report on the condition of the fruit upon its arrival in Bahrain. The mandarins, as shipped, were green, but 'we assure you if you keep them for a time, they will come out yellow, very appetising and good eating'.

Robertsons were sorry to learn that the previous two shipments of vegetables had arrived in a very bad condition, probably because they had been kept too long in the packing cases before being placed in cold storage in Java. Meanwhile, they had written to 'friends in America' to find out how they handled cabbages for long-distance shipments. If Americans could land this vegetable in good condition in Java after a five-week trip, Robertsons reckoned they could land their cabbages in Bahrain at the end of a four-week trip, also in good condition. The company realised that business could not be built up in a day: Haji Yusuf was asked if he would spare a little of his very valuable time and send full reports on the shipments received, the complaints which he had received and the 'troubles' he had discovered when the produce had been unpacked.

Haji Yusuf – commercial connoisseur

Throughout 1938 and 1939 Y.B.A.Kanoo still attracted a diversity of interest from European companies, several of which were German. For instance, while centrifugal irrigation pumping-sets were nothing strange to Haji Yusuf, perfume and pumice stones were unusual departures from his normal agency interests. A letter from Vanillin-Fabrik in Hamburg, dated 24 November 1938, is an example: 'We beg to refer to your advertisement in the official newspaper of the local Chamber of Commerce. ... We do not supply perfumery goods ready for sale in the shops but we can only offer the raw materials for making perfumes. Perhaps you are interested?'

It would seem that Haji Yusuf was interested, but not in making the perfumes himself. Haarmann & Reimer in Holzminden, Germany, seemed to offer more what Haji Yusuf had in mind. Writing on 26 April 1939, the company were glad to note that Haji Yusuf intended to begin trade in their synthetic perfumes and perfume compositions: 'We feel confident that, going into the possibilities of business in your market, you will find that something can be done'. By way of an introduction, Haarmann & Reimer wished to show Haji Yusuf 'some fine perfume compositions at moderate prices, and will send you samples of the following: Chypre of Orient, Nights of the Bosphorus, Gardinia of Carior, Rêve de Pompeia and Rose of Chiraz'. There were even some exotics: Exota Extra, Cubanita Extra, Eau de Cologne Jasminée and Fougère Royale.

If Haji Yusuf wished to become a connoisseur, it was explained that the fine scents were best tested in solutions. The German company recommended using a 10 per cent dilution of industrial alcohol to create finished handkerchief-perfumes. Solutions of 2-3 per cent achieved toilet-waters, lotions and so on. In certain perfumes, such as Chypre of Orient, slight impurities had to be eliminated. In other words, these solutions had to be filtered.

Haarmann & Reimer also specialised in various perfumes for soap but pointed out that 'the compounding of perfumes for soaps is sometimes a difficult task'. Nevertheless, their perfumery laboratory would readily assist Haji Yusuf at any time, if he required perfumes of a special character. (Later, he did commission original perfumes. One special fragrance was called Fananah, meaning 'performing artiste'.)

Supposing that Haji Yusuf wished to secure their agency in Bahrain, the Germans added that they also manufactured fruit-flavours and aromatic products used in chocolate-bonbon and sweet manufacturing, aerated waters and lemonade. Did Haji Yusuf have any good connections for this line of business, they wondered.

After perfume fragrances, I discovered Gamburg synthetic pumice stones: 'the best', used all over the world and not excelled by any other brand (so the company claimed), they were absolutely free from all the impurities so frequently found in the natural or volcanic pumice stone. The grain and grades of these stones are very irregular and often spoil an expensive piece of work. In contrast, Gamburg pumice stones were smooth and made in ten different grades, suitable for rubbing, smoothing, facing and polishing. While Haji Yusuf would have envisaged painters, decorators, furniture manufacturers, carpenters, cabinet-makers, tin-workers, metal-polishers, marble-cutters and polishers among his clients, the other trades which Gamburg catered for were, as yet, not operating in Arabia. Nevertheless, it was interesting to know that the needs of railway-car and carriage builders, manufacturers of leather and patent leather, oilcloths, felt and hats, stucco-workers and even sculptors were all catered for.

A variation on the same theme was a letter dated 31 March 1939 from African and Eastern (Near East). The catalogue of coloured cements (now on its way), illustrated the unpolished floor grade, finished with a steel or celluloid trowel as described in the manufacturer's pamphlet, *Colour in Everyday Construction*. The polished floor grade was also shown, laid in accordance with the recommendations outlined in their complementary brochure *Colour Floors Walls and Coving*. A shade-card was enclosed but, as African and Eastern warned, the materials usually assumed a darker tone when polished. They waited with interest to see if Haji Yusuf would be able to place any business for these articles.

In mid-summer 1939, Haji Yusuf was back in his familiar role as shipping agent. Hadden and Company, agent of the Silver Java Pacific Line in Batavia, had replied to a most bizarre request: how Y.B.A.Kanoo might ship a Persian cat to San Francisco. Hadden and Company suggested a freight rate of US$35, plus US$5 attendance fee. This rate included food and water for the animal in question, but we were required to provide the necessary basket. We also had to obtain documents to the effect that the animal had a clean bill of health. If the cat was being shipped to the USA for breeding purposes, then we had to obtain permission beforehand from the Department of Agriculture in Washington. No suggestions were offered as to how these requirements could be fulfilled without much frustration.

If perfume and pumice stones, coloured cement and a Persian cat suggest that Haji Yusuf had, indeed, become a commercial connoisseur, his orders for everyday needs were no less unusual, for example, 50 cases of Japanese-made glass tea-cups, no fewer than 60,000 items. All these products (and the pet cat) demonstrate how, in the 1930s, Haji Yusuf was dealing with many organisations around the world. Each country, company and commodity market had its varied and complex business procedures. To trade with them successfully, Haji Yusuf had to grasp the essential fundamentals of these procedures. In contrast, very, very few of his contemporaries were engaged in any form of international trade at that time.

By the late 1930s anyone who had been contemplating entering foreign markets for the first time could be excused caution. For quite some time international observers had been following disturbing political developments in Europe. The pessimists, or the realists, depending on one's point of view, predicted war on a global scale. The optimists, and the naïve, believed that such a catastrophe could be averted. Neville Chamberlain, Prime Minister of the United Kingdom, supported the latter opinion.

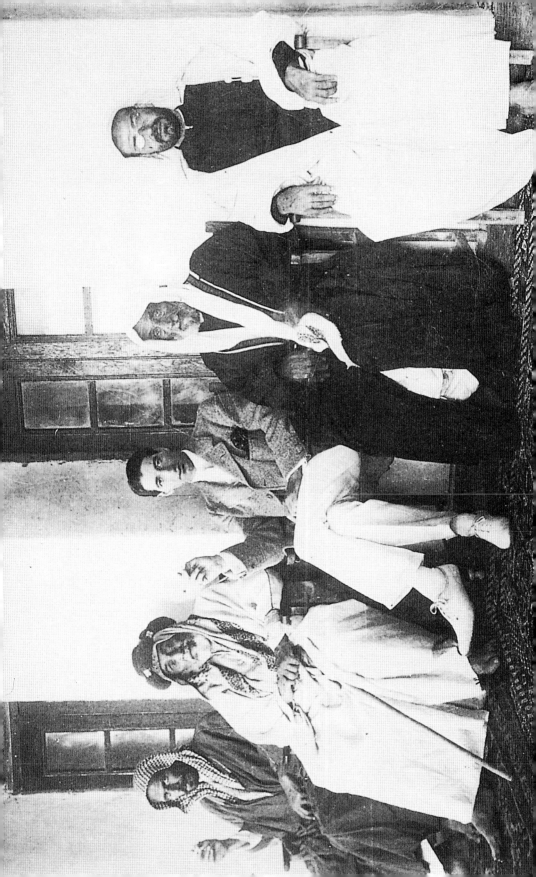

GRAY MACKENZIE AND COMPANY LIMITED.

THE MESOPOTAMIA PERSIA CORPORATION, LIMITED.

INCORPORATING:
STEPHEN LYNCH & Cº
LYNCH BROTHERS, CF
GRAY, MACKENZIE & CF
AND GRAY, PAUL & CF

Telegraphic Address:
"MESPERS"

Codes used:
Bentley's Complete Phrase Code.
Bentley's Second Phrase Code.

IN REPLY PLEASE QUOTE
Nº W/457

Bahrain, 7th June, 19 39.

Haji Yusuf Bin Ahmed Kanoo,
Bahrain.

Dear Sirs:

With reference to your letter 0/162 of 1st
instant, we enclose herewith our receipt in duplicate for the
oils received by us on account of Messrs Petroleum Developmen
(Qatar) Ltd.,which we trust you will find in order.

Yours faithfully,
for GRAY MACKENZIE AND COMPANY LIMITED.

AGENTS

المراكب العربية المحدودة
THE ARAB STEAMERS, LIMITED.

Telegraphic Address
"ASTLID."

Telephone No. 1896.

MANAGING DIRECTOR
Mr. M. A. W. Mishari.

A. B. C. Code
5th Edition.

نمبر الفنستن سركل ٭ القلعه ٭ بمبی
15, ELPHINSTONE CIRCLE, FORT;
Bombay, 28th December 1912.

To,
The Agent, Mr. Yosoof bin Ahmed Kanoo
BAHREIN.

Dear Sir,

S.S.Inchanga

The S.S.Inchanga arrived here on the 26th instant.
She is leaving Bombay on Saturday next for Karachi.
After discharging there some home cargo she will take
cargo for all Persian Gulf Ports and Busserah. So,kindly
when the ship arrives at your port try and give her some
cargo and passengers. We have no doubt that you will
give her quick despatch.
She will return from Busserah to Bombay and will
call at all Persian Gulf Ports.

Yours faithfully,
The Arab Steamers Ltd.
Managing Director

left Kanoo's first Shipping Agency:
The Arab Steamers Ltd (1911).

above The Mesopotamia Persia
Corporation Ltd. became Gray
Mackenzie in 1936 but paper
shortages prevented reprinting of
stationery.

previous page M. Cartier in Bahrain
buying natural pearls. On his right,
Mujbil Al Dhukair, Ebrahim Matter,
on his left Sulaiman Matter and Haji
Yusuf Kanoo (1918).

Top *El Segundo* arrived in Bahrain with
building material, oil pipes and tanks, and
left for Japan with the first shipment of
Bahraini crude oil (1934).

Above Hannibal-class aircraft were regular
visitors to Bahrain in the 1930s.

opposite Waiting to receive the first aircraft in Manama, Bahrain. Shaikh Hamed bin Isa Al Khalifa, Deputy Ruler of Bahrain, with Mohamed Zainal and Haji Yusuf Kanoo (1924).

above First Bahrain Muharraq Airport (1930's). The bell rang once for the arrival of the aircraft and twice for its departure.

top Haji Jassim Kanoo (r), with Khalil Al Moayyed, two leading merchants in the Gulf (1925).

right Haji Ali Kanoo with his children Ahmed, Abdulla and Sharifa (1925).

top right Letter from Bombay Telephone Company restricting use of telephone to Haji Yusuf Kanoo and his servants.

back row Ahmed, Fatima, Haji Jassim, H.P.S. Van Ketwick, Abdulla, Haji Yusuf, Mr Alinas, Mohamed Kanoo.
front row Abdulaziz, Hamed, Abdullatif, Abdulrahman and Mubarak Kanoo.

above Oil concession agreement between Bahrain and Eastern & General Syndicate (1925).

left Damman Well No. 7, first oil-producing well in Saudi Arabia (1938).

below Oil surveyors' Fairchild airplane in Jubail (1934).

top Mohamed Kanoo at the entrance of our Travel and Trading office (1946).

right Condolences from the American Consul, on the death of Haji Yusuf. (21st December 1945.)

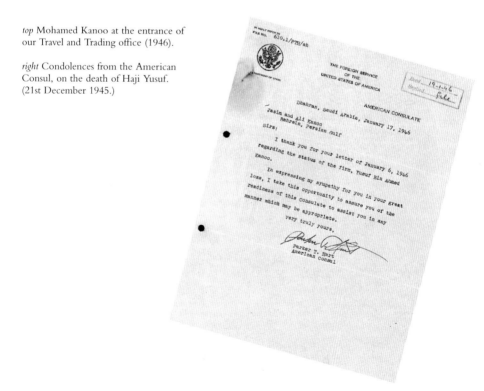

Chapter 5

The Handshake
then the Hurricane

Neville Chamberlain's historic meeting on 30 September 1938 in Munich with Hitler, Mussolini and Daladier had ended in a handshake and a signed promise. Chamberlain's famous declaration to the British Parliament upon his return to London that night, 'I believe it is peace for our time', turned out to be a grave miscalculation. Many British Members of Parliament scorned the agreement as a 'sell-out' to Hitler; the latter had been appeased, while the Czechs themselves had received nothing except a guarantee that the remains of their country would be protected against aggression. The deal was that on October 1st, German troops would march into the Sudetenland, which they did. Teschen-Silesia was annexed by Poland, while Hungary laid claim to much of Czechoslovakia's territory lying north of its common border.

This international crisis made a profound impression on the rulers of Arabia. In late 1938, they earnestly considered emergency plans for the defence of their homelands and oil-fields. By now, these rumblings were seriously affecting European commodity markets, upon which Haji Yusuf's business relied. Nevertheless, in 1939 it seems that some companies among the international business fraternity barely expected the impending new catastrophe: Germany's invasion of Poland, and all that followed.

Take for instance, a letter from Johann Schlinz of Bremen to Messrs. Yusuf bin Ahmed Kanoo. It was not our claim (via Schlinz) against a certain German manufacturer (for quoting us the wrong internal diameters for ten tons of bright steel wire) or Haji Yusuf's assumed potential for selling galvanised buckets which caught my eye, but the question posed by Schlinz to Haji Yusuf: 'Are you interested in the hurricane lantern business?' Since this was from a German company, I cannot recall having come across a more prophetic analogy, given the date of the letter: 5 May 1939. Less than four months later, the 'hurricane' had indeed begun.

Four days prior to this letter being written, on 1 May, in the presence of King Abdul-Aziz, the first crude oil to be exported by tanker from Saudi Arabia was loaded onto the American vessel *D. G. Scofield*. But the euphoria surrounding this event soon disappeared. On 3 September 1939 the Second World War began when the British ultimatum to Hitler expired.

The impact of the Second World War

The destructive implications for the Arabian mainland and Bahrain were obvious: possible bombing and invasion by the Axis forces. However, Haji Yusuf took a more constructive view, soon recognising a commercial opportunity for his company: supplying BAPCO and CASOC (two regional oil companies) with fruit and vegetables. Almost certainly, their own regular shipments from Europe and America would be disrupted, if not discontinued. To this end, W. A. Robertson (manufacturers' representative based in Java) followed up Haji Yusuf's suggestion and sent sample-sets of produce so that he could deliver one each to BAPCO in Bahrain and CASOC in Saudi Arabia. As local produce prices in Java had risen sharply, Robertsons doubted if they could supply Haji Yusuf at the previous rates. Nevertheless, they were assessing the situation and promised to advise Haji Yusuf of their findings: the bottom line was they would endeavour to keep costs down to the lowest possible minimum, despite the imposition of War Risk insurance.

Haji Yusuf was realistic enough to understand that under the circumstances, any supply was better than no supply, despite the price increases. By the end of September 1939, he heard that his most recent fruit and vegetable order had been shipped: five crates each of leeks, beans and carrots; three crates each of sawi and mangoes; and two crates each of oranges, beet and radishes. All, except the carrots and beets, were basket-packed which Robertsons believed would ensure that the shipment would arrive in 'first class condition'.

The exporters explained that this was a new form of packaging and suggested how the cargo handlers in Bahrain should open the crates which contained baskets: take one basket out from one side, then turn the crate over and remove the second basket from the other side. Experiments had shown that delicate vegetables shipped in this way arrived in a much better condition. However, Haji Yusuf was urged not to be afraid 'to tell us if anything does not arrive right'. In so doing, he was asked to consider two main features: the type of packaging, and the temperature at which the goods were carried for long periods of time. Robertsons could control the packaging, but only advise on the temperature on board ship although, gradually, the engineering crew of the carrying steamers were willing to co-operate as much as possible.

Meanwhile, by mid-September, Haji Yusuf had received a circular from the Silver Java Pacific Line's Basrah office. This notified him that fares would increase by 50 per cent throughout October 1939, and by 100 per cent thereafter. Reservations for steamer passages could be made for terminal ports only. Bookings for destinations which required trans-shipment could not be accepted. Already, the effects of war were being felt on the Arabian mainland and the archipelago of Bahrain.

Then, as had been feared might happen at some stage in the war, the Bahrain oil refinery was bombed at 3.45 a.m. on 19 October 1940. Three Savoia Machetti SM 82 bombers of Italy's Regia Aeronautica had approached the islands of Bahrain from a north-westerly direction. After circling over the refinery at some 2,000 to 3,000 feet, the pilots sighted their target and executed their bombing 'run'. The next day, the Italian Broadcasting Service claimed that Bahrain had been 'destroyed'. The reality was rather different.

Within a few days, BAPCO had surveyed the area and produced a drawing which showed that the aircraft had flown more or less south over Bahrain island and then veered west into the direction of their attack, more or less one aircraft behind the other. After dropping their payload of eighty-seven bombs, only three of which failed to explode, the aircraft headed for the Arabian mainland. There they joined up with a fourth compatriot who had also flown from their originating base in Rhodes. In this case the pilot had headed for the flares of Dhahran refinery on Saudi Arabia's east coast and released forty bombs, remarkably fracturing just one water-main and an oil pipeline. The four aircraft then flew west across the Kingdom to their destination: Zula airfield in Italian Somaliland, virtually on the western shore of the Red Sea at its southern extremity.

Apparently, several days before, BAPCO had received a warning that the Italians had been told to bomb the flares, and had moved one near to the coke-pile, outside the refinery fence. By the time the aircraft arrived, this and only two other flares were burning. The small-calibre devices created a spectacular firework display, but only four of them landed well within the refinery perimeter. A few other explosions occurred around the skimming-pond. The rest were spread out more or less in line over some 1,500 yards (1372 metres). No casualties were caused, nor any destruction.

Years later, Phil McConnell (BAPCO's Assistant General Manager of Oil Production at the time) remembers how the three unexploded bombs were dealt with. Judiciously, if crudely, a rope was attached to the bombs, and then hitched to a truck. The driver then accelerated across the empty desert, driving over as many bumps as possible until the devices exploded. Such was Bahrain's bomb disposal technique in those days! Now, as he admits, the whole episode sounds like a comic opera affair, but at the time, this was no joke, simply inspired improvisation.

Various stories were circulated as to who was responsible for the mission, ranging from Count Ciano (Mussolini's nephew) wishing to enhance his war record, to Italian tanker captains who, during peacetime visits to Sitra wharf, would have seen the position of the refinery's flares from their berths, and so could have reported such observations to their principals in Italy. In reality, the raid was masterminded by Captain Paolo Moci and led (with Mussolini's approval), by Major Ettore Muti, a high-ranking Fascist leader. But the theory which seems to have captured the imagination most, was the notion that Father Irzio Luigi Magliacani (an Italian priest living in Bahrain), had relayed key intelligence to Rome. Whether or not the priest had engaged in espionage became irrelevant. After the raid, feelings ran so high within the community in Bahrain that less than a month later, the Political Agent could no longer guarantee Magliacani's safety, and so the Italian was deported to India for his own protection.

After this incident, while BAPCO continued to run the Bahrain refinery, oil operations in Saudi Arabia gradually came to a halt until 1943 when activity resumed in a limited way. In the autumn of that year, plans for a 50,000 barrels-per-day refinery at Ras Tannurah were announced. But considering military intelligence gathered during 1942 which suggested that Rommel's North African Army might advance south (the German General's aim being to control Arabia's oil-fields), the proposed new refinery seemed out-of-step with the times. The Allies devised a contingency plan: a 'scorched-earth policy'. This brain-child of the War Office in London and the Tenth Army in Baghdad planned three phases of 'oil denial'. The first involved plugging key oil-wells in Arabia. A 'grave emergency', phase two, required all wells to be immobilised permanently. Phase three, if invasion was imminent, was to blow up various oil installations, including the Bahrain refinery.

Rommel did not advance through Arabia, so the plan was never implemented. But for a while, Bahrain and her neighbours, were hardly waiting comfortably. For those who believe that history tends to repeat itself, what better example do we have than the extraordinary events in 1990. Once again, the Arabian peninsula braced itself against invasion following Iraq's overnight occupation of Kuwait. As in 1942, the aggressor's targets were Arabian oil facilities. A 'scorched-earth' policy was even mooted again, this time by Saddam Hussein.

Rationing and restrictions

The main problem for Bahrain's residents during the Second World War was lack of food and a steep rise in the cost of living. Food quotas based on previous years' consumption were allotted to the Arabian Gulf area, supplied from India. Rationing was introduced and export controls tightened. Rice, wheat, flour and sugar were most affected.

According to the Political Resident of the day, '1943 was probably the most dismal year in the history of the Gulf administration'. Early in January, the Government of India had caused the utmost consternation by its decision to stop the export of cereals. Thus, the Arabian Gulf region was obliged to sever its age-old food-trading connections with India and look for other sources of supply.

These were eventually organised by the British Government through the Middle East Supply Centre, whereby the necessary cereals were back-loaded from Basrah, Iraq's southern port. Due to shortages, these shipments included a high proportion of Iraqi barley, formerly sold as animal fodder. An added frustration was that the British Government had to pay more for this low-grade barley than for better-quality Australian wheat. But because of wartime restrictions, the latter was not available to Arabia. Eventually, the British Government was forced to grant a food subsidy to help offset the high cost of the barley, to the extent that it spent eight million rupees buying essential food-stuffs: wheat, barley, flour, rice, sugar and dates. The Bahrain Government also stepped into the breach by purchasing large quantities of standard types of Indian cotton piece-goods which were then sold at just 5 per cent above cost to help clothe the poorer members of the community.

During 1944, the cereal ration was maintained at 20 pounds (9 kg.) per head each month. Rice disappeared almost entirely from the menu whereas before 1942, Bahrain's inhabitants were almost exclusively rice eaters. Almost overnight, residents of the Arabian Gulf region were forced to change their diet to one of cereals which they had never eaten before, and so found the greatest difficulty in both preparing and digesting them. Unsuccessful representations were made to procure rice from Egypt or even from India since a British Government decision said that both Egyptian and Indian rice had to be supplied to rubber-plantation workers in Ceylon. For an obscure reason which apparently, 'could not be made available', this concession was granted neither to those who worked in Arabia's oil industry, nor to the starving residents of the region.

But this was not the end of the story. Owing to the failure of the winter rains in southern Iran during the 1943–44 season, the quality of meat obtained from that country was of the lowest, and even then the quantity was much less than the local demand in Bahrain. As a result, during the late summer and early winter of 1944, meat shortages occurred, the situation having worsened because earlier that year, butchers in Bahrain had consistently refused to sell meat at controlled prices. In the end, the Bahrain Government purchased all the imported meat, and then sold it directly to the public through Government-salaried butchers at the meat market.

Meanwhile, until 1941, the Kerr Steamship Company of New York still maintained a service to the Far East. This meant that Y.B.A.Kanoo, the Bahrain agent for the Kerr-Silver Line which operated out of Batavia, was still able to import fresh vegetables, particularly cabbages, french beans and carrots. There were occasions when shipments were incomplete or inaccurately discharged, as happened in peacetime. For instance, on 12 January, 1941 the Silver Java Pacific Line received a 'tracer' from Haji Yusuf, regarding a shortfall of four bags of coffee and four nongs of fabricated pipe-bend. As for excesses, forty-six bags of sugar and one of black pepper had been over-delivered, while six cases of vegetable oil had been landed at Aujan and Kuwait by mistake.

Expense statements occasionally produced oddities, such as a miscellany submitted to Y.B.A.Kanoo in June 1941 from the Kerr-Silver Line. Items included a sum of money to purchase white papers, envelopes and pins; the *Baladiya* (Municipality) tax on the filling station (for services such as street cleaning and garbage collection); and the rent on the *Baladiya* (Municipality-owned) godown at Suwafiyah, not forgetting the cost of two tins of Brasso polish to smarten up the premises. The strangest claim of all, was the 'repetition charge' levied on Y.B.A.Kanoo for one word which had been unnecessarily repeated in a telegram sent from an unnamed source in Abadan.

From the Silver Java Pacific Line's office in Bushire, Y.B.A.Kanoo received a startling request in wartime from M. K. Dashty: 'I shall be glad', he wrote on 5 April 1942, 'if you will kindly buy from Mr. Khalil Kanoo at your place, four tyres size 650 x 16 for a Chevrolet touring car and send same by the first steamer.' Three weeks later, Haji Yusuf told Dashty that under instructions from the Government of Bahrain's Food Controller (who also controlled other exports considered essential to the country's needs), Kanoo was not allowed to export tyres from Bahrain to Bushire.

If wartime circumstances created some strange anomalies, one of the most wasteful was that relating to the disposal of 1,600 empty fuel tins. On 15 January 1942 the Gulf Inspector for the Anglo-Iranian Oil Company told us: 'In view of the fact that purchasers do not accept our conditions that the above tins should not be used for storing food-stuffs, you are therefore requested to arrange to dump this quantity into the sea, after they have been punctured to render them useless in my presence'. Why the tins could not have been returned to Abadan, or put to good use other than food storage, is not mentioned.

Another incident involving fuel containers occurred on 3 July 1945. On this occasion, the Anglo-Iranian Oil Company had applied to the Commanding Officer of H.M.S. *Juffair* (the British Royal Naval Base in Bahrain) through Yusuf bin Ahmed Kanoo for all empty oil drums supplied to the base to be returned to the Abadan refinery. (Because of Bahrain's strategic location, the British had maintained a naval base on the island for more than a century, and did so until the British Government withdrew its forces from 'East of Suez' some twenty-five years later.)

Since, in 1945, the British Navy no longer bought gasoline and oil from AIOC which, itself, was suffering from a chronic shortage of supplies, this seemed a reasonable request. Commander Irwin's reply was not what AIOC or Haji Yusuf had expected. An increase in Navy personnel, combined with a lack of other containers, had caused the empty oil drums to be used for storing drinking water. (The taste was good. It was the cockroaches that 'spoilt' it!) It was regretted, therefore, that the drums could not be returned to Abadan but, by way of compensation, the Navy would refund the cost-price upon receipt of an appropriate invoice.

From one kind of fuel to another: matches. Wartime shortages had obliged us to seek new sources. The Lion Match Company in Durban seemed a possibility. But with regret, as there was a serious shortage of matches in South Africa also, the company was not allowed to export them for the time being. The same applied to British-made Mackintosh chewing gum. On behalf of Haji K. M.

Dawani, Y.B.A.Kanoo had been asked to order fifty cases of the confectionery. Mackintosh regretted that the export of chewing gum from the UK was not permitted until further notice.

But the answer was not always 'no'. In June 1943, the New Customs House in Bombay issued Khan Saheb Yusuf Kanoo with an export licence. This allowed him to take to Bahrain one necklace of seven pearls, valued at Rs 550; two diamond rings (value Rs 250); one emerald ring (value Rs 200); one gold pocket-watch and chain ('old', so not valued) and one small bioscope. The Export Trade Controller's authority was valid for fifteen days only.

Two years later, on 29 March 1945, our application to export some 'controlled articles' from Bahrain was granted, remarkably just two days after Haji Yusuf had submitted his request. The   articles concerned were no less than thirty cases of Japanese-made enamelled rice-plates, ordered by Mr. Sasoon Khedouri in Khorramshahr. The export licence was granted with the proviso that the plates should leave Bahrain, by motor launch, within one month of the licence being granted. Other than this stipulation, the Bahrain Government had 'no objection' to our request.

Keeping the lines of communication open

In complete contrast, I should recount the incident which occurred during 1942, when Y.B.A.Kanoo (an Arab company) tried to compete with Gray Mackenzie (a British company). The problem began on 14 March when Haji Yusuf wrote to the Director of Customs and Port Officer, Bahrain, asking for his sanction to carry out agency work for two steamship companies: the Netherlands Shipping and Trading Committee (then chartered to the British Ministry of War Transport), and the Holland-British India Line.

The Director of Customs appended a memorandum of his own to our letter, and sent it to Charles Belgrave, then adviser to the Ruler of Bahrain. The gist of the missive was that the Director of Customs recommended that the agencies should be granted to Messrs Gray, Mackenzie & Company, and not to Y.B.A.Kanoo. The Director of Customs believed that Haji Yusuf did not have enough or sufficiently experienced staff to handle a steamship company's agency 'at such time as the present' (meaning wartime), when the speedy clearance of ships was of great importance. The Director argued that Gray Mackenzie had a complete organisation of lighters, tally-clerks and supervisors available for this service and that, also, they were the agents for the Silver Java Line at Ras Tannurah. This gentleman appeared not to know that Haji Yusuf was the Silver Java Line's agent in Bahrain.

Gray Mackenzie contributed to the friction by complaining to the Political Agent that it was against the interest and strategy of the British 'Raj' for a local company to be given the right to hold a shipping agency. Charles Belgrave did not wish to have a 'run-in' with Haji Yusuf, so side-stepped the issue by forwarding the complaint to the Political Agent for his opinion. Belgrave explained: 'I am reluctant to deal with the matter myself as foreign interests are concerned and also I feel quite sure that Yusuf Kanoo would regard any suggestion of this kind from me as a personal matter.' Surprisingly, the PA favourably supported Y.B.A.Kanoo's case (upon advice from India): if the shipping agencies concerned wished to employ Haji Yusuf Kanoo as their agent, the PA could see no objection to their being allowed to do so. He commented that if the shipping companies found Kanoo's handling of their affairs to be inefficient then, no doubt, they would take it upon themselves to appoint another agent.

We regarded the episode as an extension of the British 'displeasure' with Haji Yusuf dating from the days of Major Dickson in the 1920s, and now carried forward. As it turned out the company performed well, to the extent that some voices among Gray Mackenzie's lobby conceded that, perhaps, Haji Yusuf had exceeded the service which they were able to offer at that time.

If lines of communication between the House of Kanoo and Gray Mackenzie were somewhat frayed, those between Haji Yusuf and the Anglo-Iranian Oil Company seemed to be in good shape. For example, early in November 1943 the oil company notified us that they were to send us 97,000 tins of 100-octane civil aviation fuel (possibly all marked RAF), during the next few months. The point of this advance warning was to advise us of the phased delivery of these supplies, aboard their vessel Harris, so that we could make plans to receive these 'rather large quantities of fuel'.

A separate shipment of 100-octane fuel, probably 27,000 tins, would arrive by barge in Bahrain by the end of November 1943. To make handling easier for us, AIOC would endeavour to arrange matters so that the *Harris* and the barge did not arrive in Bahrain simultaneously. Later, the balance of the shipment would be despatched by *Nelson,* or by barge. For our part, we were asked to make adequate arrangements for discharging, reconditioning and storage undercover, well in advance of the fuel's arrival.

Meanwhile, in December 1943, BOAC's Station Manager, E. N.

Chase, requested us to arrange, through Basrah or Abadan, to keep a small stock of bitumen for the airline's sole use, say a maximum of ten drums. Apparently, this was constantly needed for marine and general maintenance. BOAC anticipated that these ten drums would amount to approximately one year's supply.

Although commercial airlines suffered from disruption during the Second World War, the world's shipping industry was affected more harshly. Passenger steamship services were cut to a minimum and merchant shipping was frequently torpedoed and sunk. At the height of the U-boat assault during 1943, the German High Command made a calculated assumption: if 800,000 tons of Allied shipping could be sunk each month, then the war against the Axis would be doomed. This was no wild fancy. During a crippling series of torpedo attacks in March 1943 alone, the Germans claimed that they sank no less than 650,000 tons of merchant vessels.

While Bahrain was several thousand miles away from this aspect of the conflict, some of the shipping lines which plied the North Atlantic route in peacetime, were also those which called into the Arabian Gulf ports of Muscat, Dubai, Doha and Dammam. The same applied to Bahrain where Y.B.A.Kanoo remained the local agent for the New York-based Kerr Steamship Company. In the Pacific rim, Y.B.A.Kanoo continued to serve the Silver Java Pacific Line which, even in 1941, still called into Indonesian ports (Batavia, Semarang and Sourabaya) and North American ports (Los Angeles, San Francisco and Vancouver), before sailing west to Colombo, Bombay, Karachi, Ras Tannurah, Basrah, Bushire and Bahrain. But these were exceptions to the rule. By now, many American and European shipping companies were unable to maintain their services to the Middle East.

One limiting factor was that a high percentage of most Allied shipping lines' vessels had been requisitioned for military purposes. Rationing had precipitated a huge reduction in the availability of commodities for consumption in their countries of manufacture and overseas. This spawned a new genre of traders, the black market operators from which Bahrain suffered as much as anywhere else in the world, including an influx of gold smugglers. Although the most prolific offenders were caught and imprisoned, genuine traders, importers and shipping agents in Bahrain all had a hard time throughout the war, as did all the islands' consumers.

Similarly, great confusion and dislocation was caused by the disintegration of the Arabian Gulf air and sea-mail services. The region's scattered ports depended on trade with India and Europe, and with each other. However, the co-ordination of this vital network nearly came to a halt when the work of the Gulf Residency was almost brought a standstill. The cause was the British Ministry of War Transport's unwillingness to listen to requests: 'They, at no time, showed any grasp of, or interest in, local problems and constant resort had to be made to both the British Government and that of India to bring pressure to bear'.

This being said, before the main post office was opened near to Bab Al-Bahrain (Gate of Bahrain) in central Manama, the British Political Agency provided a small room where an Indian clerk sorted all the mail which arrived in, or left Bahrain by sea and air. While sea-mail was well organised, airmail was less so. One reason was that, until the final span of the swing-bridge was completed in 1942, there was no road-link between the islands of Bahrain and Muharraq. All supplies and personnel needed at the aerodrome, had to travel by boat between Manama and Muharraq.

The British Political Agent paid Y.B.A.Kanoo Rs 300 every month to take the mail from the post office to the airport and bring incoming mail back. It was only a small bag as there were very few letters. This arrangement became the basis of Kanoo's early relationship with British Airways Limited, a new airline formed in 1936 after several small independent airlines merged to rival Imperial Airways. In 1939, following a British Government enquiry, the two rival airlines were obliged to merge. The result was the formation of the British Overseas Airways Corporation (BOAC), effective on 1 April 1940.

Throughout the war, regular air traffic continued to pass through Bahrain, as various shipping manifests and refuelling expense statements confirm. The Anglo-Iranian Oil Company's oil refinery in Abadan continued production for civil as well as military use. BOAC continued to order its fuel requirements in Bahrain through Y.B.A.Kanoo.

During 1943 BOAC planes still managed to transport some 800 passengers, together with 8,500 kilograms of diplomatic, military and civilian mail, to and from Bahrain. In 1944 BOAC traffic increased considerably, including the re-appearance of 'Ensign' class aircraft, (although, in 1946, BOAC finally withdrew them from its schedules to Bahrain.) The airline even managed to increase its east and west-bound weekly services from two Sunderland flying-boats and one land-plane service at the beginning of 1944, to seven flying boats and one land-plane service, by the end of the year. So much so, that it was not unusual to see three to four flying-boats moored near to each other during any given night-stop. Unfortunately, there was no proper accommodation for the passengers so that much discomfort had to be accepted by the many civilian and service personnel who used the services.

Even so, the RAF pier (also available to BOAC's flying-boats) was extended so that it could carry a road out to the sea end where new terminal buildings and a restaurant had been constructed. It was noted that BOAC's accommodation at the landing ground of Muharraq island still left much to be desired. A hint of improvement was a rumour, 'They are moving from their present weather-board hut to more substantial and imposing quarters in the coming year', meaning 1945.

BOAC's passenger and crew rest house had been well advanced before the Second World War began, as Haji Yusuf knew. For, in June 1939, the General Manager of African and Eastern (Near East) asked him: 'With reference to the Rest House which Imperial Airways are building in Bahrain, we are agents for the U.S. Airco air-conditioners, thousands of which already have been sold in America, Egypt and elsewhere. Is there any prospect of our getting an order to supply the Rest House? We can arrange to send down a qualified engineer'.

Once the rest house was ready for occupation in 1945, various members of the Kanoo family regularly visited BOAC's office there to collect and deliver airmail bags. Two or three people, whom my father knew well, remained good friends of the company for many years. Like other similar rest houses which the airline built around the world, it became known as Speedbird House, adopting the name of BOAC's logo.

Help from Hercules

Despite the difficulties experienced by merchant shipping companies, especially on trans-Atlantic routes, Haji Yusuf was determined to find a way round some of the difficulties he now encountered. Not only was limited transport a problem, but also wartime rules which governed the concept of 'essentiality'.

By early May 1944 Hercules Export and Import Company based at 42 Broadway, New York, were interested to receive Haji Yusuf's enquiry about the possibility of their exporting commodities such as confectionery, silks, toilet articles, Camay soap, perfumes, menswear, stationery, woollen goods and canned fruits. In late June, Haji Yusuf informed the American company that he had been granted the necessary permit to import six Dodge motor cars into Bahrain. But this was only half of the story. Hercules needed a licence to export the cars from America, a stumbling block which Haji Yusuf was to discover could not be overcome. Yet, Haji Yusuf had already found out that some of his competitors were frequently importing various other items from the USA, all unaffected by American export restrictions or Bahraini import requirements. In particular, Lucky Strike and Chesterfield cigarettes arrived in Bahrain at regular intervals. (It was not until 1976 that we were appointed as Brown & Williamson Tobacco Corporation's distributor in Bahrain and, in 1981, in Abu Dhabi. Lucky Strike was one of their brands, as were Pall Mall, Viceroy, Kool and Sir Walter Raleigh Smoking Tobacco.)

Anxious not to miss any such opportunity himself, Haji Yusuf asked Hercules if they could arrange to ship good quality cigarettes to him on a regular basis, even by post. He concluded that 'we shall be initiating ourselves into some business' and if the 'essentiality' problem did not apply, there was other much more lucrative business to be done. Perhaps, for instance, Hercules could ship textiles from their South American friends. The main hurdle was that we could not comply with the minimum-order requirement: equal in value to US$0.5 million. Nevertheless, Haji Yusuf reassured Hercules: 'Still, consistent with the capacity of an island of our size, with a population of 100,000, we shall endeavour to give you a bumper order'.

This being said, our company remained much more interested in the possibility of importing cars. Apparently, we were in a position to accept no fewer than fifty vehicles, provided that Hercules could manage to ship them to us. We did not mind from where they were shipped, perhaps even via South America. Our preference, according to one letter, stated that we favoured the following makes of cars: Ford, Chevrolet, Chrysler, Dodge (five and seven-seaters and station-wagons). This was apart from Nash vehicles for which we were the agent already. If Hercules did not insist on an 'Essentiality Certificate', we were also interested in refrigerators, chewing gum and canned fruits.

By November 1944, Hercules were anxious that they had not heard from Haji Yusuf since August. However, they had not pressed the issue since they had been awaiting the outcome of their application to export six Dodge Sedan automobiles. Now, with regret, Hercules told Haji Yusuf that the India Supply Mission had rejected their application because 'passenger cars' had not been manufactured in the USA since 1942. The country's remaining stock of new cars could not even meet America's domestic and foreign requirements. Thus export applications were being refused, except for those related to the war effort's most urgent needs.

The fact that Hercules' application had stipulated that these vehicles were to be used to transport personnel involved in the production and supply of petroleum for the war effort, seemed to have cut no ice with the India Supply Mission. Not put off, Hercules considered this an adequate justification and lodged an appeal. Meanwhile, we were urged to secure some other worthwhile business for which export restrictions might not apply.

But this was not the last hurdle. Hercules knew how difficult it might be for Y.B.A.Kanoo to remit funds to America. But, if we were able to do so, a considerable volume of goods could be despatched to Bahrain by parcel-post, one parcel weekly to each customer of a net value of one dollar each. Items might include men's and women's rayon hosiery; women's rayon slips and other garments; razor blades, cigarettes and saccharine. Hercules remarked that this business could not be operated practically or profitably on a letter-of-credit basis, simply because of the serious shortage of manpower and facilities needed to prepare drafts and documents required by the banks, and because each parcel would be of a relatively small value.

On 29 December 1944, we received an airmail letter from Hercules, posted one month earlier. The contents were expected, but not welcome: 'We exceedingly regret to advise you that our appeal concerning the rejection of our application for an export licence of the six Dodge sedans has likewise been rejected for the same reasons indicated before.' All this was academic, since the American exporter had also been told by the Dodge factory, whose aid they had enlisted in their efforts to obtain the licence, that their supply of passenger cars was now exhausted. Since it was impossible to foretell when production could resume, all Hercules could say on the subject of cars was that they hoped this may be 'real soon'. However, all was not lost. Dodge had resumed its truck production. While these could be exported only for the use of foreign governments, or to oil companies engaged in producing petroleum products for the war effort, we were asked if we might find any interested buyers. If so, Hercules would gladly quote.

Replying on 5 January 1945, Haji Yusuf commented that he was sorry about the car situation but not too discouraged. Instead, he was placing an order for cigarettes and refrigerators. No doubt with some feeling, he added: 'We shall be glad if you will let us know which goods you will be able to supply us without these formalities of licences. We would like to know all the regulations about the despatch of postal parcels and in what way you would like to receive payment in such shipments. The undersigned is thinking of going over to the United States on a business trip as soon as the necessary passport formalities have been gone through. We have requested Nash Motors, whom we represent here, to apply for a visa and we enclose a copy of the application form'. (Since this was the final year of Haji Yusuf's long life and his nephew, Ali Kanoo, was responsible for our car business, presumably it was he who was planning to travel.)

Peace and recovery

On 7 May 1945, at 2.41 a.m., peace descended on a battered Europe. Anticipation of the announcement, combined with an anxiety to celebrate, had caused many people in Bahrain to 'jump the gun'. According to the Political Agent, when the official announcement was made, there was a tinge of anti-climax since people had already been celebrating for some time. Nevertheless, flags during the day and light at night made a brave show. The squibs were old and damp, but their dullness served only as a reminder that material for making them was for use in sterner fireworks.

The days of 9, 10 and 14 May were declared public holidays in Bahrain, the last day being selected by British Government representatives to host an Arab dinner for His Highness Shaikh Salman bin Hamad Al Khalifa, the new Ruler of Bahrain (since his father's death in 1942.

When hostilities ended, regulations controlling trade and currency were considerably relaxed. At last, merchants and the banking authorities could trade again 'normally'. Bank-rates had to be competitive. Demands for foreign exchange more than doubled immediately, and increased further towards the end of 1945. In particular, exchange on India was in great demand during the last three months of the year. Nevertheless, many wartime restrictions still applied. Shipping space was scarce. Steamer communication throughout the Arabian Gulf was inadequate and irregular. Commodities were in short supply, particularly food, clothes and construction materials. Rationing was still in force. Even the oil companies were affected by shortages.

After the war ended in the Far East during August 1945, there was no further need to fly service personnel to that area. Thus, BOAC's frequency of flights to that region declined, as did the services which passed through Bahrain. Yet, in October 1945, BOAC extended its

Sunderland services from Calcutta to Rangoon which meant that the number of transit passengers through Bahrain increased, most of whom were civilians. With this change in emphasis, it was expected that before long a commercial trunk-route service from the United Kingdom to the Far East, calling at Bahrain thrice-weekly, would be introduced. It was also thought likely that a weekly Lockheed Lodestar service between Cairo and Bahrain, calling at Basrah, Baghdad and Damascus, might be instituted.

As 1945 ended our family drew comfort from the fact that some 108 times that year, RAF Sunderland flying-boats had used Bahrain's landing facilities, as had Catalina aircraft on 27 occasions. A combination of Sunderland, Dakota, Lancastrian and Lockheed civilian aircraft had served Bahrain just short of 1,500 times. All had used our agency services, particularly refuelling. Over 3,000 passengers had embarked at Bahrain. Some 2,500 had disembarked. As for air-cargo, 283,394 kilograms of freight, stores, civil and troop mail, diplomatic bags and precious consignments were handled.

Also in 1945, despite wartime restrictions, the RAF had managed to acquire materials to improve the Muharraq runway by laying perforated steel sheeting along its edge. (These steel plates had been salvaged from wartime emergency landing strips which had been built hurriedly by the Allies in Normandy.) Later, a firm of Palestinian contractors repaired the main runway. This involved laying a bitumen and sand foundation, on top of which similar pierced steel sheeting was laid. While this seemed a good idea at the time, it later proved to be hazardous rather than helpful. Quite simply, the intensity of the sun's rays tended to curl the steel. When this happened, take-off and landing were interesting experiences!

Until 1942 crossing from Muharraq island (where the civil aerodrome was located) to the main island (Bahrain) and Manama (the capital) had been no simple procedure either. Before the swing bridge linking the two islands was completed that year, passengers had to be rowed across the channel in small boats. But even after the swing bridge became operational, travel between Muharraq and Bahrain islands was always delayed when the bridge was opened for an hour at noon, and again at midnight, to allow dhow and barge traffic to pass along the sea channel. BOAC's flight was scheduled to land at 11.00 p.m. at night. If it did, everyone (passengers, crew, airport staff and Kanoo representatives) making their way from the airport to Manama would find the road across the bridge still open to vehicle traffic. If the flight was late, or there were other delays, then everyone had to wait on Muharraq island until one o'clock the following morning, a discipline which required much patience, particularly after a long flight.

Way back in the mid-1930s, Imperial Airways' company regulations stated that overnight accommodation was available for its personnel in the company's rest house at Bahrain. At that time, aircraft called at both Bahrain and Sharjah, the latter destination being the only place of the two where passengers could stay overnight. It was not until early 1939 that reference is made to building progress on passenger accommodation in Bahrain, presumably Speedbird House. In August that year, it was reported that the new facilities were becoming habitable and that a steward had arrived in Bahrain. By 1945 Speedbird House in Bahrain was complete since the Bahrain Government Report for that year refers to the premises being almost permanently full of BOAC crew. The only commercial hotel in the country at that time was the Bahrain Hotel, located in the heart of Manama souq. Its ornamental wooden façade was a delightful landmark for many years.

A letter in our archive, sent almost two months to the day after the German surrender was one of the first indications we received in Bahrain that merchant shipping was reverting to a peacetime status. Writing on 6 July, the General Agent of Java Bengal Line (Area Representatives Netherland Shipping and Trading Committee Ltd based in Calcutta) informed Y.B.A.Kanoo that the end of hostilities in Europe had caused the termination of the Charter with the British Ministry of War Transport and BMWT/US War Shipping Administration. All requisitioned ships were to be released from military charter, with the exception of those presently commissioned as troop and hospital ships. A month later, the Java Bengal Line circulated its seventeen shipping agents, including Y.B.A.Kanoo in Bahrain, informing them that eleven more steamers and ten tankers had been redelivered from British Ministry of War Transport charter.

At last, the market in Bahrain began to emerge from the dull, static period enforced by the war. The international trading world was becoming active again as companies clamoured to kick-start their businesses into post-war recovery. Documents in our family archive illustrate how quickly this process took shape.

In September 1945, we received a comprehensive price-list from J. A. Afriat, a UK trading company operating from 109 Jermyn Street, London. This provided an intriguing commentary on contemporary product prices and commodities which might be used in Bahrain: blotting paper at 1s 6d per pound; 12-inch electric table fans (67s 6d each); 56-inch ceiling fans (£7 19s 6d each) ; pure hide glue in cake form (£135 per ton); best quality smoothing-irons (30s 6d per hundredweight); and so on. Fish-hooks, hair-clippers, hurricane lamps, insecticides, cast iron safes, locks and keys, printing and stencil inks, rivets and eyelets for boots and shoes, smoking-mixture, stoves, table-telephones, toothbrushes, even tennis racquets and racquet-presses, were available. Regrettably, earthenware and china were temporarily out of stock.

Barely another month passed before Yusuf bin Ahmed Kanoo was approached by the Export Co-ordinator of York Corporation, 'specialists in mechanical cooling since 1885', based in Pennsylvania, USA. York Corporation informed him that various catalogues had been sent to him inviting orders for bespoke air-conditioning units. As each had to be individually engineered to specification, 'you will understand our inability to furnish you with prices'! This was a far cry from the 100/250 volt ceiling fans offered by Messrs. Afriat in London, for less than £8 each.

On 18 December 1945, the United Kingdom Tobacco Company, advised us that, at last, 900,000 cigarettes had been shipped to us on the SS *Empire Stuart,* in part execution of our 'valued order' dated 17 April that year. A subsequent letter revealed that this had only been made possible because former restrictions had been waived: 'We are very glad to see the end of the complicated regulations which so hampered exportations to your territory and we hope that labour conditions and shipping facilities at this end will shortly improve.' The balance of our requirements was shortly to be completed.

As for the promised samples of Greys cigarettes, we had found these to our taste and so immediately placed an order by cable: one million flat tins and one million round tins of Greys, to be sent to Kuwait, via Basrah, and another quarter of a million of flat and round tins to Bahrain. However, this interest in Greys cigarettes 'on a considerable scale' created a handicap for the United Kingdom Tobacco Company. Our order, confined to hand-packed lines, would take time to process because of a labour shortage. The company offered 'quicker execution' if packets of 10 and 20 Greys cigarettes would be acceptable to us. These could be made up in hermetically sealed tin 'outers' of 1,000 cigarettes capacity, the object being to give protection against atmospheric conditions.

In December 1945, Lever Brothers (India) in Bombay told us they had made half a ton of their allocation of soaps available to us for supply during 1946, the proviso being that we were required to obtain an import licence to cover the quota. Certificate of Origin 5267, issued by the Bombay Chamber of Commerce on 4 July 1946, told us that seven cases of Lifebuoy soap and six cases of Lux toilet soap would leave on the SS *Barala* during the month, marks and description of goods for Yusuf bin Ahmed Kanoo, Bahrain.

Meanwhile, the Netherlands Ministry of Shipping & Fisheries (moved to London during the German occupation of Holland) advised us that twenty of its steamers had been redelivered to them. A further thirteen vessels had been 'found' and would be sent as soon as they were ready for service. In early November, the management and administration offices of Nederland Line were transferred back to Amsterdam, having spent the war years in New York. But for the time being, Java Pacific Line and the Java New York Line maintained their management offices in the USA. Then, in March 1946, the Dutch shipping company N. V. Stoomvaart Maatschappij 'Nederland' notified Kanoo that its Government had relinquished four of the company's vessels, with ten more due to be de-requisitioned shortly.

Meanwhile, a significant era in the history of our family had quietly ended. On 21 December 1945, Haji Yusuf passed away. Such was the community's respect for him, all the merchants closed their shops and offices for the day of his funeral. It seemed as if everyone in Bahrain attended. Shortly before his death, Haji Yusuf had summoned his nephews Ali and Jassim to his side, together with his great-nephews. Already, he visualised a very different future for our company compared with that which he and the family had known. The impact of the 1930s depression and the restrictions of the Second World War had added to Haji Yusuf's recognition that the destiny of his family, and the company to which he had given his name and had modernised, depended on careful planning. For, while Haji Yusuf died poor in financial terms, he had repaid his debts and followed the teaching of Islam. Spiritually strengthened, Haji Yusuf felt that he could now 'face Allah'.

According to Mubarak Kanoo, one of his great-nephews who was present at the family gathering, Haji Yusuf told his family that he foresaw much change. Recent oil discoveries in Bahrain, Saudi Arabia and Kuwait would have far-reaching benefits for the economies of the region. But, for now, Haji Yusuf reported to his family that there were only a few thousand rupees left in the bank, his role was over and it was now up to them to carry on. He urged that the family members should be good Moslems; the elder members must be kind to the young members of the family; and the younger ones must respect their elders.

Thus, in the final months of Haji Yusuf's long life, he selected 'young' Ahmed Kanoo as the leader of the young generation. Haji Yusuf spent time telling Ahmed how he wished him to behave within the family. In his business dealings, he should fear God, be firm but fair, and be kind to those weaker than himself.

When the time came for Ahmed Kanoo to assume this role, one of his first decisions was to decree that the family would never be put into a position of financial hardship, such as that experienced during the 1930s recession. During that time, many families and businesses throughout the world were affected, not just ourselves. As explained earlier, depressed financial and commodity markets, together with the demise of the Arabian Gulf's natural pearl industry, were major contributory factors. While oil revenues helped to finance Bahrain's post-war economic development and create many new jobs, the lessons of dependence upon one industry were still being learnt, and heeded by the Kanoo family. We would not borrow from banks. The company would expand into different business disciplines and establish itself in other countries. Thus, our corporate policies of diversification and self-financing were born.

As post-war recovery evolved into pioneering progress, Ahmed Kanoo led his brothers and cousins into uncharted business territory. Initially, they strengthened our core shipping business, launched our travel agency and created a Gulf-wide network. Then Ahmed began to travel overseas to secure new business. Over the next few decades, our family diversified into insurance, construction and associated equipment, oil-field supplies and mercantile activities. During the 1950s and 1960s, offices were opened in Saudi Arabia, Kuwait, Dubai, Abu Dhabi, Sharjah and Ras Al-Khaimah. After the mid-1970s, we established a presence in Oman, London and Houston. Property investment and joint ventures also became part of our business. Today, retailing, petrochemicals, water-treatment and manufacturing are part of our portfolio. As Ahmed Kanoo had envisioned, diversification on a big scale was put into practice.

Chapter 6

Exploring
Far Horizons

The environment of my childhood and that in which the family business grew is so different from that of today. I am not old enough to remember my great-grandfather Haji Yusuf, for he died when I was about three years old. However, even at that age, I still recall our grand old house and original office below it. (This used to stand on the site of the present Zainah Plaza shopping centre and the Kanoo Tower, right in the centre of Manama). The house extended some 80 metres along the main road, and was about 130 metres wide. Being an adventurous child, I used to explore a warren of storage rooms, staircases, family living 'wings', kitchens and internal open spaces, all on different levels. The offices and the historic strong-room were on the ground floor. Haji Yusuf used to sit there on one side with his clerks and accountants. Other managers and staff of the newly established travel department, sat on the other side.

Our family house was in a traditional Arabic courtyard design. The ground floor comprised the office and the storage area where the family food supplies (rice, sugar, flour and ghee) were kept, as well as products associated with the family's trading business. The passageway which led from the office provided access to these ill-lit stores. Passing the strong-room which was linked to the office, a long dark passage from the office led to the central kitchen on the ground floor. This ended with a two-flight staircase which gave access to the middle of the house. At this end of the property, the family entrance for the house gave access to the side road through, what seemed to me as a child, a gigantic wooden door with a traditional small postern gate incorporated within it.

The ground-floor kitchen was supervised by Mr Abol, the cook, who orchestrated food for family and business dinner parties. When I was a child his phenomenal cooking pots, some one and a half metres in diameter, were a source of my constant curiosity and investigation! It was quite routine for Mr Abol and his assistants to cook for fifty people, menus which included 100 kilograms of rice, six whole sheep, chicken and vegetable curries, sambosas, as well as salads, fruits and cream caramel.

The next floor up comprised an open space, the upstairs kitchen and the sitting room, as well as two living quarters: one each for Haji Yusuf and Haji Jassim and their families. Above this, on several more floors, our huge house accommodated some six families in different 'wings'. In the allocation of apartments my father's wing was right at the top, Ahmed Kanoo's apartment was across the hallway and Mubarak Kanoo lived on the floor below. From any of the wooden balconies I could look onto the interior of the house and watch members of the family go about their daily lives.

My great-grandmother Lulwa bint Majid, Haji Yusuf's wife, ruled the family household. Being the eldest lady in the family, she decided what we should eat, distributed the food according to family size, shared out the family supplies and anybody with a problem would go to her.

Before going to bed we, the children, used to sit around my grandmother Fatima (wife of Haji Jassim) and listen as she told us stories. Often they were religious narratives about the Prophet Mohamed and how the individual leaders of Islam lived, how they suffered and how they set an example to others. Grandmother Fatima used to sprinkle among them the scary stories that old women tell children the world over, such as the tale of the 'green woman' who eats children who misbehave. Leaving her to go to our wing upstairs, I would run as fast as I could, looking behind me imagining some ghost was chasing me. Like other families in Bahrain we did not have air-conditioning at that time. During the summer we lay on our beds in the open air and gazed up at the wonderful star-filled sky before drifting off to our night-time dream-world.

Poised for post-war development

To some readers, my childhood memories may seem old-fashioned or quaint. My own children and their cousins sometimes find it hard to relate what they see around them today to the 'old days' which, after all, were not so very long ago. We only have to look around us to see the impact of rapid economic, technological and urban development and cultural change. However, to appreciate the radical transition which Bahrain and the other Gulf states have experienced on an unprecedented scale during the last half century, such comparisons are relevant.

For example, little more than fifty years ago, Y.B.A.Kanoo

imported the first generator into Bahrain. According to Ahmed Kanoo, every room in our house was supplied with enough electricity to illuminate just one bulb and drive one fan. In Ramadhan, the generator was moved to the mosque nearby. We also imported a pump to distribute water throughout the house. After boring a well in the courtyard, we then had it covered so that we could pump clean water through pipes to our house so that every bathroom, at last, had one stand-pipe with a tap. In those days, this was advanced technology.

This reminds me of a story told to me by Ahmed Masood, the late head of a prominent family from Abu Dhabi who died in the early 1980s. 'Abu Dhabians who visited Bahrain used to tell us about all these strange and wonderful things they had seen, like this pipe on the wall which you turn and water comes out. You touch the wall, and light comes on.' One has to appreciate that societies in the United Arab Emirates and Saudi Arabia, even more so than in Bahrain, were still very bedouin-oriented because of the vast tracts of desert inhabited by nomadic families. In the late 1940s, urban life with its 'new' sophistication was very curious and special.

It was not until the end of 1945 that Bahrain took delivery of a new 206 kW generating set which the Ruler 'set working' during April, 1946. Later that year, a new 100 kW substation for the use of BOAC was connected to the main electricity supply. The new wing of Manama Palace was also connected to the supply, as were the residential quarters of those employed by the Bahrain Government and Gray Mackenzie; four new flour mills, and 116 private consumers of which our family, luckily, happened to be one.

However, proposals to install an automatic telephone system in Bahrain had not progressed. According to the 1946 Bahrain Agency Report, some 131 telephone subscribers 'had to suffer for another year from the accumulated defects of the obsolete equipment still in use.' Meanwhile, Cable and Wireless had 'noted' Y.B.A.Kanoo's request for various telephone lines. But it was not until 1948 that the company commissioned an automatic telephone system capable of serving the towns of Manama and Muharraq. In 1949 this became operational and a line was installed in our office. The telephone number was 25.

It is against this background that the key phase in our family company's development took place. In Ahmed Kanoo's view, the fifteen years between 1945 and 1960 were an era of firm leadership, dedication and struggle. The latter part of this period coincided with my teenage years. Many of my school holidays were spent learning about the company, although obviously at that age I was not involved with the business on a daily basis. However, I do know that the modern Kanoo company began to evolve during Haji Yusuf's lifetime, helped by his nephews Jassim and Ali. It then took off after Haji Yusuf's death under the leadership of his great-nephews: Ahmed Kanoo and my father, Mohamed. Ahmed assumed the role of 'thinker' and financier, while my father became the operations man who put into action and managed whatever they both decided to do.

For both of them, and for other members of the family, life was hard. Often, my father left the house at seven o'clock in the morning and did not return until midnight. As a result, my cousins, my sister and I hardly ever saw our fathers during our childhood years. They were always working at establishing new connections with foreign companies; strengthening previously developed relationships and exploring new areas of business, such as opportunities created by the new regional oil companies (BAPCO in Bahrain and ARAMCO in Saudi Arabia). But then is it not true that the children of entrepreneurs and owner-managers of family companies the world over, suffer the same fate?

There is no doubt that Ahmed Kanoo's ability to speak, read and write English was a great help to him. From what he has told me, after the end of the Second World War foreign companies sought to widen their world-wide network of contacts, particularly in the Middle East. They tried to locate people in those countries with whom they could communicate in English directly, rather than rely on Indians to act as their interpreters and translators.

A good example of how Ahmed Kanoo developed new international connections, often with other family businesses, is a letter dated 3 April 1946, sent to him by the New York-based Lewis International Corporation. For some years, Y.B.A.Kanoo had advertised in Chamber of Commerce lists around the world, and in commercial directories, such as *Kelly's*. Foreign companies often used these references as their starting point to approach us with a view to establishing new business links. Writing from 11 Broadway, New York City, Mr B. G. Lewis had this to say: now that the war was over, he presumed that firms like ours would make plans to initiate, or resume, buying goods from the USA. Since, for some time to come, America would be the only country able to provide goods for export, Lewis believed it to be of the 'utmost importance' to an organisation like ours to have proper buying representation in the USA. 'While, prior to the war, you might have had suitable connections with manufacturers and suppliers, today and for a long period of time, goods will continue to be scarce.' Lewis suggested that it would prove to be in our best interests, and more economical in the long run, if we appointed a buying agent in the USA to represent us. To this end, Lewis International wished to assume this role on a 5 per cent commission basis, cable costs for our account. (This arrangement was quite normal.)

As I read about the items which Lewis exported, a chemistry lesson would have been helpful. Powdered sodium perborate, powdered Indian magnesite calinced, menthol-homo crystal, magnesium oxide heavy calinced, paradichlorobenzene, powdered potassium chlorate and triacetin. Cream of tartar, soap flakes, bleaching powder, potash and paraffin wax were more familiar. As for dichloro-diphenyl-trichloro-ethane, I have often wondered what the initials DDT stood for. Now, I know.

Y.B.A.Kanoo – *focus of worldwide interest*

In contrast, particularly as I am a vintage-car enthusiast, I enjoyed reading the *Tallyho* booklet which I found in our archive attached to a letter dated 18 June 1946. Written by Nash Motors and sent to their export distributors, including ourselves, both documents are nostalgic commentaries of the period.

The booklet, published by the Automobile Club of Michigan to celebrate the 50th anniversary of the motor car, claims to contain the most nearly complete listing of American-made automobiles ever recorded (up to 1946). The booklet's old-fashioned rhetoric declares: 'It is a parade of accomplishment perhaps best told by a perusal of the mortality list of twenty-five hundred names that once flew proudly from the mast-heads of motor cars only to run afoul of the reefs of time, and vanish.'

Such exaggerated prose was part of Nash Motors' 'business lesson' intended to stimulate the interest of overseas automobile distributors. Their Export Manager, Mr S. I. Carlson, stated with astonishing self-confidence: 'Nash has earned the right and is proud to be among the handful of manufacturers comprising the automotive industry today. To become an automotive leader requires the concentrated efforts of our entire organization. In other words, it behoves all of us, from the production line to the dealer, to get ready now for the competitive market which is certain to come and not let the current lush market throw us off the track.'

A glance through our Nash file suggests that, despite restrictions imposed by the US War Shipping Administration on practically all steamship lines operating from America, Y.B.A.Kanoo had not been unduly 'thrown off track'. Even if raw materials, US dollars and shipping capacity were in short supply, Nash had plenty of eager customers in Bahrain. By early August 1946, Carlson had penned a new missive of encouragement, complete with a photograph of the 'Automotive Pioneers'. This, we were told, was suitable for framing as it was felt that every distributor would 'want this picture to hang in either his showroom or his office'. More likely, the enclosed photographs of the new four-door sedan trunk model in the Nash Ambassador and the Nash '600' series appealed to my father and uncles more. Certainly, they tempted our customers, so much so that on 10 August we ordered five of the '600' series and one Nash Ambassador. Two weeks later, Nash Motors confirmed receipt of our payment (money orders, cash and cheques totalling $2273.40), hastening to tell us that this was 40 cents more than the amount we had stated in our letter! Meanwhile, the ordered cars were on their way from Kenosha, Wisconsin, to New York from where they would be shipped.

A related episode occurred soon afterwards. On 11 September 1946 we introduced Mr C. F. Jarrett of the Bahrain Petroleum Company to Nash Motors. During his forthcoming annual leave in the USA, Jarrett hoped to buy a Nash car in the '600' series from our allocation. Our one stipulation to Nash Motors was that the deal should include the recovery of our $465 'control profit' from Jarrett, in addition to the cost of the car. We found out later that he agreed to pay only $250 commission. It would seem, however, that this was the least of our worries for, during October 1946, the US Government imposed a quota system to relieve a shortage of raw materials. This more or less coincided with a maritime strike in the USA and a shortage of US dollars in Bahrain. The combined effect prompted us to send an agitated cable to Nash Motors: 'All our buyers are getting out of hand. Stop. Telegraph shipment remaining six cars. Urgent!'

Good luck prevailed. It transpired that the quotas for Bahrain and Kuwait were separate. So, to overcome the imbalance in supply and demand, Nash suggested that some of the cars we required should be shipped to Kuwait. Their two provisos were that Kanoo should arrange for the vehicles' onward trans-shipment to Bahrain and, of course, the necessary dollars had to be made available in sufficient time. It would appear that we were able to comply.

Meanwhile, other North American businessmen began their export drives to Arabia. New York-based Holland-Nahas Import &

Export Company wrote to us in July 1946 offering a range of items manufactured in the USA, some quite bizarre variations on a familiar theme. Given the nature of Arabian society, and the phase of our country's development at that time, handbags, bathing suits, cosmetic cases, sun-glasses and suspenders were a curious choice of products to launch upon Bahrain. Whether or not we did business with Holland-Nahas, I have not discovered.

An even more remarkable approach came from Stevis Manufacturing Co. of Montreal in Canada. Given the nature of Bahrain's indigenous jewellery industry and our Islamic culture, either Stevis Manufacturing were ill-informed, or they had not considered the relevance of their mail-shot. Apart from imitation gold jewellery manufactured from base metals such as brass, copper and bronze, the company also offered religious articles such as rosaries, crucifixes, and crosses.

In contrast, a letter from Bell Sales Co. of Montreal demonstrates that the urge to generate international business was not all one-way. Ben B. Bell advised us that, further to our letter of 27 June, Y.B.A.Kanoo had been appointed Bell's representative for Roumania. There were some unusual items in the product-list: plastic dice, collar-holders, tie-slides, powder puffs, even three-piece play suits, whatever they were.

Meanwhile, throughout 1946, our family company received a curious range of other promotions. From Bombay B. M. Chadha & Co., ship's-chandlers, manufacturers and government contractors, offered us seeds, spices and skins, together with oils, paints and hardware. With leisure time in mind, Karia Brothers, exporters, importers and general merchants, were pleased to supply six types of playing cards. Meanwhile, M. A. Mullick & Co. had pleasure in introducing themselves as one of the leading Muslim Export-Import firms with influential connections both in India and abroad. Of interest to us was the fact that the Indian authorities had recently lifted the ban on the export of essential oil-seeds, spices, talc and shellac (a thin flaky substance which, when melted, was used for making varnish). Interestingly, black pepper and cinnamon were still prohibited export items.

Four other letters, two from Bahrain and one each from Iraq and Iran, add new dimensions to our trading activities for 1946. Bahraini merchant and commission agent, Khalil bin Haji Murtez Dawani, asked us to instruct our London agents to ship to him, on his account: 25 cases of Flower Basket Swedish safety matches, size 8 white sticks, brown dips, each case containing 75 gross, together with

50 cases of Mackintosh's Chewing Gum, peppermint flavour. In contrast, Dr Paul W. Harrison, Chief Medical Officer of the American Mission Hospital in Bahrain, asked my maternal grandfather, Ali Kanoo, to procure two drums of Vaseline for the hospital, at his earliest convenience. (For many years Vaseline was a common ointment applied to medical dressings.)

From Baghdad, Vladimir Sigal & Sons billing themselves as high-class goldsmiths, silversmiths, engravers, enamellers, jewellers, art metal workers, diamond merchants and bullion dealers, wrote: 'We are in receipt of the sample for Mother of Pearls forwarded to us by our friend Mr J. C. W. O'Brien for which we thank you and wish to point out that he has asked us to correspond with you regarding prices etc.' The goods which Y.B.A.Kanoo had sent to Baghdad on O'Brien's behalf were required by a well-known, unspecified English firm which Sigal & Sons represented. We were reminded that our quotes should include Sigal's 3 per cent commission. In return, they were happy to offer us a prompt service at all times.

The eccentric prose contained in the promotion from trading firm, Mohammad Nader, captured my imagination. On 27 July 1946, the Import Manager wrote from Tehran: 'Being in touch with the address of your firm as general exporter-importer of Bahrain, we seize this opportunity of our extreme desire in establishing firm business with your esteemed house.' After further preamble and claims to have valuable experience, to be well-placed in the market and in a position to undertake transactions of great importance to us, Mohammad Nader's correspondent came to the crux of his letter: the firm needed 200 tons of mother-of-pearl (*sadaf*) of high quality 'without worm holes, without decay and not being in a dead state'. The company looked forward with 'deep interest' to hearing from us.

As shipping lines and manufacturers began to reinstate peacetime services and production, at the end of 1946 the Bahrain Government declared confidently that the country had 'experienced a large and steady demand for all classes of products' from the United Kingdom. Hardware, radios, cement, toilet articles, electrical fittings, toys, shoes and biscuits had been of particular interest. Rather than wait for foreign representatives to visit the island, already some Bahrainis had visited the UK to make contact with commercial firms personally.

Although rationing was still operative, the price control on luxury goods had been abolished. Not surprisingly, merchants took this opportunity to maximise their profits, causing the prices of consumer goods to rise quickly and remain very high. Meanwhile, the Government of Bahrain now permitted the re-export of more categories of goods than previously allowed in order to encourage traders to stimulate the country's economy.

The impact was impressive. Flying under the flags of nine nations, no less than 566 commercial vessels put into Bahrain during 1946. Total imports for the year amounted to 51,825 tons, while 192,375 tons of exports included 184,908 tons of petroleum coke, a solid residue produced during the oil-refining process, one of BAPCO's profitable by-products at that time.

Business had also resumed with some other European countries, besides the UK. In the latter months of 1946, credits were opened by local banks with companies in France, Holland and Italy. Australian imports, mostly foodstuffs, were arriving too. Y.B.A.Kanoo, the Bahrain agent for J. G. Thompson & Co. in Melbourne, were able to import limited supplies of beans, asparagus, beetroot, cauliflowers, carrots and even luncheon beef but, like other importers, we still experienced difficulties owing to limited shipping capacity. This forced banks to extend credit to local companies, although exchange rates remained steady throughout 1946, except in India.

The Eastern Bank still dominated the island's banking activities, although the Imperial Bank of Iran was making its presence firmly felt. During 1945 alone, we are told that more than 100 new accounts were opened at the branch. The Imperial Bank of Iran's first branch in Bahrain opened in Manama during 1944. Hussain Yateem told me that the bank first rented premises in the 'Hilal' building. Until Haji Yusuf sold the property to Haji Hilal Al-Mutairi in the mid-1930s to help pay off his debts, this was our 'old' building, (simply called 'The Building' so as not to be confused with our big family house described earlier). In 1949, the Imperial Bank of Iran changed its name to the British Bank of Iran and the Middle East. Then, in 1952, the name was shortened to the now familiar name: the British Bank of the Middle East (BBME). (Incidentally, nearly two decades later, on 17 January 1970, Citibank opened its Bahrain branch in our 'new' building, described in a later chapter.)

It was a curious coincidence when I found two separate but relevant documents in our archive. One, a bill of exchange dated 27 June, 1946, was drawn on the Eastern Bank Limited, Bahrain, for ten Egyptian pounds. This was to be honoured by Barclays Bank, Cairo, in favour of my uncle Abdulrahman Kanoo. The other document dated 8 July 1946, is a memorandum from the Imperial Bank of Iran, Bahrain, to my maternal grandfather Ali Mohamed Kanoo asking him to 'please note that we have received for collection the following bill on you. Kindly arrange to pay Rs 7,000 (seven thousand rupees) as soon as possible to Mr Selim Ebrahim Nonoo, Basrah', a member of the well-known family of Jewish money-brokers which owns and manages the Bahrain Financing Company in Bahrain.

Moving forward to the following year, Ahmed Kanoo remembers 5 October 1947 very well. For the first time, he travelled to England by flying-boat, to make his first visit to London and 'score' what he considers to be our first major international success after the Second World War.

At that time, no white refined sugar was available in Bahrain. People did not want to buy dark brown, unrefined sugar, particularly Iranians and Iraqis who were the major consumers of refined sugar in the region. As a result, several agents had approached Y.B.A.Kanoo in the hope of securing a sugar deal. One of these was Samac Agency Limited whose offices were at 172 Buckingham Palace Road, London, near to the BOAC terminal in Victoria. (This was not our family's only business contact with Samac. Certainly by 1949, my grandfather, Jassim Kanoo was 'sourcing' British Portland cement through the agency, confirmed in a letter dated 12 April that year.)

Samac was run by three Austrian-Jewish refugees, Messrs S. Munz, C. Munz and M. Weisselberg. After escaping from Hitler's tyranny, these gentlemen had established themselves in business in London. During the course of negotiations in Bahrain, the directors convinced my uncle that Y.B.A.Kanoo should buy several thousand tons of British granulated white sugar. Ahmed Kanoo agreed and took the risk by selling, in advance, 20,000 tons of sugar to various merchants in Bahrain, Saudi Arabia, the UAE and Iran. After collecting the regional merchants' advance payments for the consignment, Ahmed transferred the money to Citibank in New York, via his London bank, as requested by Samac. Meanwhile, the Austrians had returned to London and changed their minds. They wished to increase the price.

After taking advice from the Manager of the Eastern Bank in Bahrain, my uncle flew to London to discuss the problem face to face with the agency. In short, if Samac's directors wished to renege on the previously agreed fair price, then Y.B.A.Kanoo would take its business elsewhere. Not surprisingly, the Austrians modified their stance and offered to abide by the original agreement, but only if Ahmed Kanoo paid them cash. My uncle refused, unless he could pay by cheque drawn on his London bank account. A complicated, drawn-out disagreement then followed. Eventually, the dispute was resolved through independent arbitration in Luxembourg.

Then the next problem emerged. How could my uncle transport the sugar from Europe to Bahrain? So, his next port of call, quite literally, was Rotterdam where he visited the offices of the Holland-Persian Line. There he managed to charter two ships and arrange for the sugar to be shipped. Even today, Ahmed Kanoo insists that, despite the 'hassle', this contract was the basis of a very good start for our company as we explored new international markets.

Letters from Jassim Kanoo's mail-bag

During the late 1940s, Jassim Kanoo was also active making new business contacts around the world, mostly through correspondence rather than travelling himself. He received constant enquiries from foreign companies whose range of interest in our family business was remarkably diverse: pocket-watches and perfumes, slippers and samovars, cars and coffee-grinders were all promoted with enthusiastic endeavour.

For example, through the introduction of a business friend, Evergreen Sales in Hong Kong discovered that Y.B.A.Kanoo was 'one of the largest importers in Bahrain'. Thus, on 30 June 1948, they took the initiative by writing to make some preliminary business connections with us. As so often was the case then, the usual 'old faithful' items were offered for export, such as cotton piece-goods. However, there were some interesting 'newcomers' to the usual range on offer: drill pants, cotton singlets, torch bulbs, thermo socks, cotton quilts, banzo (storm) lamps, sarongs, Chinese medicine, gallnut, aniseed and honeycombs.

Two weeks earlier, we were approached by the Yau Sun Shoe Factory, also from Hong Kong. Established for more twenty years, the factory manufactured and exported many varieties of footwear, all of which were widely used in Hong Kong and abroad. For several decades our company had imported canvas shoes from India, but this was the first promotion to suggest that ladies' embroidered evening wear and slippers might find a niche in Bahrain.

Also in July 1948, this time from Vienna, Y.B.A.Kanoo heard from Johnsons (Anglo-Belgian) Agencies. Having found our entry in *Kelly's* trade directory, they introduced themselves as a British firm of importers and exporters with a branch in Austria. They claimed that their range of pocket-watches had found 'a considerable market overseas', particularly in Europe before the war.

Always on the look-out for the unusual, I enjoyed reading J. Boh. Cástek's letter to Haji Jassim, written in Prague on 12 August 1948.

Anxious to encourage my grandfather's interest in their special coffee-grinders for mocca, this Czechoslovakian company drew his attention to their 'interesting novelty', a traveller's samovar, 'especially suitable for people travelling on horse-back or on camel-back in the desert'.

Although my grandfather had also developed a lucrative business importing cement from various suppliers, by July 1949 it would appear that, like Haji Yusuf ten years earlier, he was developing an informed interest in perfumes, particularly miniature bottles of Evening in Paris. Responding to Jassim Kanoo's enquiry, Parfumerie Bourjois in Croydon, England, explained that this particular range was handled by their Paris factory. From England the Parfumerie offered a range of soaps which were also 'finding favour' in the Arabian Gulf market.

In complete contrast, Jassim Kanoo had extended his enquiries to Aden. There, it would appear, Ebrahim Abdulla Barahim was sourcing American and British-made cars. Eager to import a variety of these into Bahrain, my grandfather's letter expressed his specific interest in Chevrolet, Dodge and Ford automobiles, and British-made Austin, Morris, Hillman and Standard cars. (Nash and Studebaker were not mentioned.) Similarly, Armstrong Siddeley Motors in Coventry, England, corresponded with Jassim Kanoo during 1949, on the subject not of cars but of air-cooled diesel engines.

By coincidence I came across a clutch of other letters exchanged between our family and old friends abroad. Through their reminiscences of the past and contemporary comments of the day, a clear picture emerged as to how our family business was faring as 1949 drew to a close. On 14 September, Jassim Kanoo contacted his old business acquaintance, David Bienenfeld, with whom he had dealt for over twenty years, (this assumption being based on Bienenfeld's promotion of pocket-watches in 1928.) Writing to 62 Rue Lafayette, Paris, my grandfather wrote: 'Mr Lieberman arrived in Bahrain on the 11th and gave me your salaams. I have connected this gentleman to Mr. Hassan Mudaifa who has been good enough to accommodate him in his own office and who has assured me that every kind of help will be given in buying pearls. But this is not the season for pearl-buying, as all the divers are out at sea. Mr. Lieberman had the idea to go to Dubai to buy pearls so I wired to my friend Abdulla Owais there, but as he has also replied, there are no pearls available now.'

As the divers were due back in Bahrain by the end of September in time for *Eid Al-Adha* (the Moslem feast and second annual holiday), my grandfather hoped the divers would have pearls to sell which would enable Lieberman to make some bargain purchases for the Paris and American markets.

As a point of interest, the Mudaifa family was famous in Bahrain, particularly for its involvement in the pearl business and 'Mudaifa Jewellery'. (The shop still trades today.) Abdulla Owais was a famous pearl merchant in Sharjah, a very kind and generous man who also became famous for importing gold from Europe and exporting it to neighbouring countries.

However, it was not so much the prospect of a revived pearl industry which occupied my grandfather's thoughts, but the great pleasure with which he recalled the good old days when Mr Bienenfeld had been on the island: 'I am wondering if I will have the good fortune to see you again in Bahrain which I should say with great pride has improved much beyond your expectations. It has become a very important port in the Gulf and has built up a good business. I am sure, by the grace of God, all of you are keeping in good health and continued prosperity. Give my salaams to Mr Adam if he is in Paris, or convey to him when writing'. (Adam Frenel was an American family acquaintance living in New York.)

By September 1949, our business had grown to the extent that Y.B.A.Kanoo was now the agent for twenty-two shipping lines and six airlines, in addition to other business. In the letter just quoted, my grandfather explained that his sons, and those of his brother Ali, were looking after the business under Ali's direct supervision, referring to my grandfather only on important matters. Jassim Kanoo ended: 'I am writing all this as I am sure you will be very pleased to know about our present position'.

At the same time in New York, Adam Frenel heard from his friend Simon Lieberman who was visiting Bahrain. Within days, Frenel contacted my grandfather: 'It is a long time since I was in Bahrain, but I will always remember your kindnesses and friendship with the greatest pleasure. It is my hope that you may be able one day to visit America and see our great city. I was glad to hear from Mr. Lieberman that you are prospering well. I would like to tell you, in case you are interested to do business with him, that he is a reliable and substantial merchant, good for any requirements. I have known him and worked with him for many years.'

Adam Frenel added: 'I would also like to be remembered to your Uncle Yusuf Kanoo'. Given wartime restrictions on trade and travel, and relatively primitive telecommunications, perhaps it did not occur to Lieberman that Adam Frenel in New York might not have heard of Haji Yusuf's demise some four years earlier. In reply, my grandfather made no mention of this, but simply remarked: 'It was a very pleasant surprise to receive your letter. It took me back to the good old days of our friendship and contacts. The desire to meet and spend a few days with old friends is reciprocal.' He looked forward to that day.

Despite the gaps in communication, Mr Frenel was no stranger to our family. He had first seen Jassim Kanoo's eldest son Mohamed (my father) and his eldest nephew Ahmed (my uncle) as toddlers. Now that both 'toddlers' had grown up and were handling the family business, my grandfather suggested that perhaps even before he was able to visit New York, either his son, Mohamed, or his nephew, Ahmed, would visit America in the course of their business. If they did, he would see to it that they visited Mr Adam in New York. As for Simon Lieberman, he was still trying to 'hook' some good business in pearls. Despite it being out of season and the prices dear, my grandfather wished him success, adding that 'we all wait for better times'.

Kanoo Travel Agency established officially

During the 1940s, Mubarak and Abdulaziz Kanoo (two of Jassim Kanoo's younger sons, and my father's brothers) completed their studies at the American University of Beirut. So did their cousin Abdulla (Ali Kanoo's second son, younger brother of Ahmed Kanoo). Hamed Kanoo (Ahmed and Abdulla's youngest brother, as yet a teenager), continued his education.

Back in Manama, Abdulla Kanoo learnt the procedures of cargo handling and customs clearance, tutored by Ahmed. In 1945, Mubarak joined the family company and paved the way to establish the Kanoo Travel Agency officially. Meanwhile his brother, Abdulaziz, learnt about other aspects of the business. In particular, he remembers some of our other employees: Saeed Hussain who looked after the money; Abdul Muhsin who assisted Abdulaziz Al Khadhar with cargo handling and ship chandlery; Abdulaziz Al-Aali (a loyal employee); Sayeed Mahmood (who, years later, was appointed as Bahrain's first Minister of Finance).

As time passed, the Kanoo 'school of hard knocks' became much sought-after. Many a Bahraini father considered that it was a highly-prized opportunity for his son to work in the House of Kanoo, renowned for its hard office discipline and international outlook. In fact, many fathers sent their sons to work with us to gain valuable experience and later go forward to become prominent businessmen or senior government officials.

But for now, my focus is the Kanoo Travel Agency. Although Haji Yusuf had, for many years, been involved with aspects of the travel business, during his lifetime he never formed an official travel agency. From about 1910 he was the Bahrain agent for various shipping companies which transported pilgrims to and from Jeddah. From the mid-1920s (apart from his APOC refuelling agency business), Haji Yusuf assisted Imperial Airways in Bahrain only on a casual basis. From the late 1930s, Y.B.A.Kanoo also assisted British Airways Limited (later merged with Imperial Airways in 1940 to form BOAC).

In response to post-Second World War demand, Mubarak Kanoo was convinced that the time was right for Y.B.A.Kanoo to form an official travel agency. Not only would this be the first of its kind in Bahrain, but also the only one to exist at that time, anywhere in the region. Established in 1946, the Kanoo Travel Agency soon became the 'talk of the town'. Mubarak recalls that soon after its opening, the Kanoo family was honoured to receive a visit from the Ruler of Bahrain, His Highness Shaikh Salman bin Hamad Al Khalifa. Coincidentally, the Ruler of Kuwait, His Highness Shaikh Ahmed Al Jabir, was visiting the island at that time. Together with my uncle and the agency staff, their Highnesses drank coffee in our small travel office on the ground-floor of our family house in Manama.

At first, Kanoo Travel Agency consisted of just my father Mohamed, Mubarak, a member of staff, an office with a telephone, and a station-wagon. Two staff increased to four, and so on. By trial and error, the two brothers learnt about the travel business together, generated mostly by oil companies whose expatriate employees and dependents began to fly in and out of the region.

Nevertheless, life was tough. Hiring local transport to taxi passengers to and from the airport was difficult. International communication still depended on cables. Direct-dial telephones, telexes and on-line computers were, for Bahrain or elsewhere, in the distant future. Mubarak Kanoo's premise was to offer a service which enabled him to become close friends with many people. He recalls that very few Bahrainis spoke English. Having been educated abroad and having had some experience of air travel, he had a head-start over some of his contemporaries. Gradually, he established a good relationship with large companies established in Bahrain by providing a comprehensive travel service. In particular, Mubarak, or our senior

Travel Manager, Mohamed Ali, often drove the Kanoo station-wagon to Awali (BAPCO's township in the centre of Bahrain island) where a large proportion of our travel agency's early business was generated. From there, passengers were taken to the airport, helped with ticket arrangements, passport formalities (such as they were at that time), baggage-handling and any other reasonable assistance they required. When passengers returned, the process was reversed.

Mubarak Kanoo's approach in those pioneering days was quite simple. If he knew someone who planned to travel, he would go to him and say: 'Look, I am your friend. I would like to help you. Can I take care of your travel business?' Although it was difficult work, confidence grew because of relationships he developed with Bahrainis and their families, expatriates and their families, and company executives who wished to travel overseas, as well as visiting businessmen. In Mubarak's opinion, the Kanoo Travel Agency was established on the principles of courtesy, good manners and dependability, while making the most of post-war opportunities.

When BOAC completed its return to a peacetime basis during 1946, the airline began to adapt and expand. Early in January that year, Ensign-class aircraft were withdrawn from the Cairo – Karachi schedule and their place taken by 'C' class flying-boats. In the same month, BOAC formed a European division called the British European Airways Corporation (BEA), although this company was not formally established until 1 August 1946.

Also that year, the special services which the British Royal Air Force (RAF) had begun during the war, were abolished and some of BOAC's previous services discontinued. The trunk-route service from the United Kingdom to the Far East was extended to include Singapore, operated by Sunderland flying-boats. Then, towards the end of 1946, we received notice that these too were to be withdrawn and replaced by new Tudor land-aircraft. However, when the Tudors proved to be too heavy for Muharraq's modest runway, Bahrain ceased to be a stop-over on both the Durban–Calcutta and the Cairo–Karachi schedules. Thus, the air-link between Bahrain and the Trucial Coast (now the United Arab Emirates), was broken. This left just the United Kingdom–Singapore service as the one commercial air route serving Bahrain.

This was a great disappointment to us as it became practically impossible to obtain passages on these through-services. However, BOAC did agree to operate a weekly Plymouth flying-boat service between the UK and Bahrain, and augment it with a Bahrain–Karachi shuttle service. Soon after negotiations were completed in May 1946 the shuttle was introduced. But it was never profitable. So when BOAC discontinued this short-lived experiment towards the end of 1947, Bahrain island was served by only one dedicated route: the airline's Bahrain–UK service.

However, by now, this had developed into something rather special. On 2 May 1947, the *London Evening Standard* ran a story with the headline: 'Oilfields Air Express Starts'. On that very day, a new Plymouth-class flying-boat had taken off from Poole harbour (on the south coast of England) to launch BOAC's new weekly service to Bahrain. The reporter commented: 'Making night stops at Augusta, Sicily, and Cairo, the Plymouth with 22 passengers, will take just over two-and-half days for the 3,700 miles (5,953 km). The service has been started in response to the large demand by passengers from Britain to the rich oil-wells around the Persian Gulf'.

In other respects, too, BOAC and its agents enjoyed a commercial upturn. After the USA withdrew its wartime post office facilities in Bahrain and started to transport US Government personnel on commercial airlines, BOAC reverted to carrying airmail for British and American employees serving in Bahrain. The result was that, in 1947, the airline embarked 5,299 kilograms of post office mail, 21,173 kilograms of freight and 1,435 passengers. The disembarkation figures were even higher: mail, 8,539 kilograms; freight 88,783 kilograms; and 1,621 passengers.

Perhaps the most significant figure in terms of our business potential was that some 11,009 airline passengers transited through Muharraq aerodrome in 1947, despite the facilities being no more than a small, spartan single-storey building and a makeshift Second World War runway. In his memoirs, *This Strange Eventful History,* the late Edward Henderson (former oil company representative and British Ambassador to Qatar) described taking off from Muharraq in an RAF Valetta aircraft during 1948–9. On this sector of its weekly 'milk-run' to Sharjah, the RAF allowed civilians to buy tickets for these flights, if there were seats to spare. The Valettas, usually heavily laden with RAF stores and equipment and just a few passengers, 'lumbered into the air after a bumpy ride down the strip' over the perforated steel plates laid out on the rolled salt-flats. If the aircraft's wheels happened to hit unrepaired plates which had curled in the sun, take-off was a dangerous experience. Of course, landing in similar conditions, was just as much a hazard.

Widening our scope – IATA membership

In terms of what later became a Kanoo hallmark, the 'meet and assist' concept, clearly there was a ready market and much business to be done, not only in Bahrain but also in Saudi Arabia. In 1946, the Kingdom's first international airport was opened in Dhahran where, some twenty-three years earlier, a landing strip had been graded in preparation for the first flight ever to land there in 1923.

Meanwhile, in 1945, the Government of Saudi Arabia had taken delivery of its first aeroplane, a Dakota (DC-3), a personal gift from President Roosevelt to King Abdul-Aziz Al Saud. This became the first aircraft to be used by the Saudi Arabian Airline Corporation (SDI), the national airline set up by the King in 1947 to operate between Riyadh and Jeddah. Management and technical service were provided by TWA, the only international airline serving Dhahran airport at that time. (Later SDI became known as Saudi Arabian Airline, and more recently, Saudia.) By 1950, Convair 340s, DC-4s and Bristol freighters had joined the fleet. On 16 April that year, KLM began its service to Dhahran, as did Middle East Airlines (MEA) and Pan Am, also in 1950.

BOAC transited at Dubai *en route* to the Far East. Since Kuwait, Qatar, Abu Dhabi and Oman were not, as yet, served by international airlines, passengers from those countries wishing to fly beyond the Arabian Gulf region, had first to travel to Dhahran, Bahrain or Dubai from where they could connect with an appropriate international flight.

At that time, few people in the Middle East had heard of IATA, even fewer knew what it did. In 1945 the International Air Transport Association had been established in Geneva as the trade association of the world's scheduled international airline industry which itself had been founded in 1919. Our application to join IATA was an obvious step towards widening the scope of Kanoo Travel Agency. On 18 March 1948, Monsieur V. de Boursac, Secretary of IATA's Paris branch office, notified us that the Travel, Shipping and Forwarding Office of Yusuf bin Ahmed Kanoo, Manama, Bahrain Island, had been registered on the official IATA Agency List. The effective date of this approval was the day on which we had submitted our application: 12 November 1947. Not only was our family company the first travel agent in the Arabian Gulf region to join IATA, but also we were now eligible to be appointed by any IATA member airline wishing to enter into an agency agreement with us, thereby enabling us to sell international air passenger and air cargo transport.

Since its formation, Kanoo Travel has worked on a percentage basis. In the late 1940s, the standard IATA travel agency commission was 6 per cent of the total cost of the ticket-value sold. (In April 1979, this increased to 9 per cent.) IATA also claims an annual fee from its agents, not a slice of the travel agencies' commission. As the General Sales Agent (GSA) of such-and-such airline, Kanoo Travel Agency received 3 per cent commission to reimburse it for expenses incurred while carrying out GSA husbandry: preparing accounts and looking after the airline's needs, its representatives and dedicated travel outlets. The value of a ticket sold, less IATA and GSA commission, then had to be submitted to the relevant airline every fifteen days. (In the past, travel agencies were allowed to be a member of IATA and a GSA. Now, a travel agency must choose between the two, unless it decides to set up two separate companies. An IATA agency may service *all* airlines and sell any of their tickets. A General Sales Agency may serve only the airline for which it has contracted to be the GSA. Hence, today, no one outlet can offer both IATA and GSA services.)

It was on 20 September 1949 that Kanoo Travel became the General Sales Agent for the Dutch national airline, KLM. Although no surviving records provide us with a date we had also been GSA for Imperial Airways, followed by BOAC, because of our refuelling contracts to the airlines.

Until the mid-1950s very few Gulf nationals travelled far from home. Things had always been rather different for our family. As a young man, Haji Yusuf had travelled overseas on a regular basis. Several of my uncles had flown to and from Beirut to attend school, including Ahmed Kanoo who by now regularly visited India. For them flying was no longer so exciting. But for others, air travel was a great adventure. People would greet Ahmed and ask about the wonders he had seen: 'What is it like to fly? How do foreigners live? What do they eat? How do they dress? I hear that it was foggy in London. What is fog?

When someone left Bahrain by air, the whole family went to the airport and gathered by the fence on the tarmac. It was a commotion, something which happened only once in a while. When I left for school abroad, my entire family was at the airport to see me off. My mother cried, my aunts waved and my father prayed that all would go well. In those days, it was very special for people to fly away from Arabia in a contraption called an aeroplane.

In the late 1940s, the notion that Bahrainis might wish to spend their vacations overseas was certainly a novel idea, too. Taking the initiative in July 1946, the Foreign Manager of the official Dutch Tourist Office (ANVV) based in The Hague, informed us of their intention to attract the interest of foreigners to the possibilities of tourism in the Netherlands. To this end, Mr. Calkoen sought our co-operation to allow Y.B.A.Kanoo's name to be placed on ANVV's mailing list. In this way, we would receive promotional posters, folders etc. to display in our travel office.

Although he cannot remember the year, Mubarak Kanoo recalls flying in a Constellation aircraft (first used by BOAC in 1946) from London to New York, then an eleven-hour flight. Somewhere among his treasured memorabilia he has a certificate documenting his flight by Stratocruiser from San Francisco to Honolulu. BOAC confirms that it began to operate Stratocruisers in 1949, as well as Argonauts. In 1950, Hermes aircraft came into service. Before long, piston engines and propellers would be relics of a bygone age to be replaced by jet engines. The Comet-1, introduced in 1952, was one of the world's first jet-powered commercial aircraft.

Before the advent of on-line computers, one might wonder how international booking communication worked. Quite simply, cables were sent via the telephone network. However, it was not until 1949 that, finally, the region's first automatic public telephone system was installed in Bahrain. Even so, it still took a very long time to receive seat reservation confirmations from London, then BOAC's world-wide reservation centre.

In those days, the airline allocated Kanoo Travel two or three seats per aircraft (usually with a capacity of some seventy passengers in one class), permitting us to sell seats on various sectors such as from Dhahran to Cairo, Paris or Geneva; or from Bahrain to London, or Bombay. If we needed more seats, we asked. In the 1940s, the *ABC guide* (the travel agents' scheduled airline timetable), was a slim, 200-page volume. Today, its 2,000 pages are bound in two volumes, witness to the industry's remarkable expansion.

Chapter 7

Tankers, Tugs and Teacups

In 1946, when Abdulaziz Al Khadhar joined Y.B.A.Kanoo as a cargo superintendent, our company was still very small. From what both he and Ahmed Kanoo recall, there were only six senior managers working in the Kanoo office in Manama: Ali Kanoo (my maternal grandfather); his eldest son Ahmed (now the Group Chairman); Jassim Kanoo (my paternal grandfather); his eldest son Mohamed (my father); Mr. Diwan (an Indian secretary who had been employed by us for some time), and Abdulaziz Al Khadhar, plus a sprinkling of clerical and operational staff.

While the upturn in commerce during the immediate post-war years was welcomed by everyone, of more than passing interest to our family business was the need to pay urgent attention to the island's port facilities which still lacked adequate cargo-handling facilities, lighting, marker buoys and safe, sheltered anchorages. Mina Manama, the main artery for almost all commercial and personal items arriving in Bahrain, and those being re-exported to Qatar and the eastern province of Saudi Arabia, was continually congested with dhows and small inshore craft. For decades, the shallow harbour obliged ocean-going vessels to anchor some eight kilometres out to sea from where they were served by lighters.

It was a quaint sight to see small crowds gather round the port, the post office and Gray Mackenzie office (BISN's handling agent in Bahrain) as they keenly awaited the arrival of a ship's appearance on the horizon and, later, the arrival of their mail and other expected items. The Eastern Bank and the Imperial Bank of Iran, respectively the first and second foreign banks to open in Bahrain, relied on that service to bring currency from Bombay. The exceptions were shipments bound for BAPCO in Bahrain and ARAMCO in Saudi Arabia which operated their own dedicated landing facilities; and military cargo which was handled by the RAF at Muharraq. However, crowds did not always gather alongside the quay to witness happy occasions. Accidents within port limits still occurred with embarrassing regularity and invited their fair share of curious, if not morbid, spectators.

Cargoes and crews – their care, our concern

On 9 February 1946, a foreign dhow bound for Qatar's port of Doha, laden with 400 *gallas* of dates (a *galla* being a 'gunny bag' containing about 23 kg of dates) and 12 tins of date syrup, sank north of Muharraq island. The craft was wrecked and all the cargo lost. On the same day, an Iranian vessel was wrecked near Fasht Al-Adham. Although the cargo and vessel were lost, the crew was rescued.

Eight months later, a dhow carrying 400 bags of cement discharged from the British India Steam Navigation Company's SS *Vasna,* capsized near Manama pier. While the vessel was a write-off, the cargo was recovered, although in what condition, remains unknown. Then on 2 November 1946, another dhow, laden with cement bags, sank near a local shoal. This time the cargo was lost, but the craft was salvaged and the crew saved.

All this was nothing new. For many years, masters of vessels who visited Bahrain had long considered Mina Manama unsafe. Apart from winds whipping up the waves and causing small craft to capsize, the inshore anchorage at Manama was considered too shallow for steamers which drew more than 22 feet (6.7m) of water.

However, this notion was contradicted when, in December 1946, SS *Saminver* arrived from Canada laden with 9,000 tons of wheat. Although she drew 27 feet (8.2m) of water, her master reported that for the length of his course into port, he never had less than 32 feet (9.8m) of water beneath the ship's hull. Gray Mackenzie suspected the accuracy of previous surveys. We shared their view that the Bahrain Government should willingly contribute towards the cost of a new survey which would benefit everyone who used the port.

Meanwhile, the Bahrain General Merchants' Association (forerunner of the Chamber of Commerce) voiced numerous complaints about the loading and unloading arrangements provided by the Landing Company (operated by Gray Mackenzie). Cargo was badly stowed and roughly handled. No discrimination was made between different kinds of goods. Manama pier did not possess any modern equipment to off-load cargo efficiently. The one and only crane was 'a slow and antique piece of mechanism'. New landing craft and equipment were badly needed. Even the beacons and buoys were inadequate, as proved by SS *Pitt River* on the night of 17 August 1946.

Laden with a full cargo of BAPCO's petroleum products destined for Italy, the ship ran aground on the Shah Allam shoal. In order to refloat the vessel, many heavy drums had to be discharged manually without the aid of any heavy lifting gear. No one, it seems, had learnt the lessons of a similar experience earlier that year when the U.S. Navy tanker, *Cacapon,* had run aground on the same unmarked shoal. Then there had been no need to discharge cargo, which perhaps explains why nothing had been done to mark the hazard.

Meanwhile, the saga at Mina Manama continued to fray nerves and generate friction. In 1947 the problem came to a head because, during that year, no less than 723 commercial vessels called into Bahrain, a 28 per cent increase on the previous year. The national flags under which the ships operated had increased to include American, British, Danish, Dutch, Finnish, Italian, Norwegian, Palestinian, Pan-American, Portuguese, Spanish and Swedish vessels. While this post-war growth in trade was greatly welcomed by Bahraini merchants, it also fuelled their frustrations and their fury. Their new complaint was that Gray Mackenzie monopolised both Sitra oil terminal and Bahrain's general port, Mina Manama, and were not as efficient as required. As a result, the exasperated merchants decided to form a new company to discharge commercial vessels, and thus presented the necessary application.

After three high-level but inconclusive meetings held during April and May 1947, a fourth meeting was convened on 1 June to persuade the merchants not to create a rival landing company. They agreed, but only if Gray Mackenzie accepted certain conditions regarding the delivery and care of cargo discharged at Manama, reduced the scale of their landing fees by 20 per cent, and agreed to the Bahrain Government reviewing landing charges every year.

Having made their point, the merchants did obtain a reduction in landing fees (albeit only 15 per cent), and a promise that monthly meetings would be convened so that grievances could be aired. After withdrawing their application to form a rival company, the merchants agreed to co-operate with, rather than compete against Gray Mackenzie. As before, this left Y.B.A.Kanoo as the oldest Bahraini shipping agency 'to fight it out' with its traditional 'adversary'.

Contemporary with these events, my story moves to Sitra, an island lying to the east of Bahrain island. By now, shipping agency work was the 'senior service' of our family business. Yet none of this accumulated experience made life any easier when it came to coping with oil industry restrictions imposed on commercial shipping agents like ourselves.

One of BAPCO's first post-war projects was the creation of its new Sitra marine terminal: a four-berth wharf for ocean-going vessels, connected to Sitra island by a new causeway just under five kilometres long. Any aspirations that we, as shipping agents, might benefit from this new terminal were merely wishful thinking. All cargo required by Bahrain's oil industry was the responsibility of BAPCO and the shipping agents involved (including ourselves). This was discharged at Sitra terminal. Commercial cargo, despite arriving in the same vessels, had to be off-loaded into lighters at Sitra, and then ferried to Mina Manama for discharge. Two reasons explain this.

First, the distance which ocean-going merchant ships would have to sail north from Sitra island to an appropriate anchorage offshore from Manama was three times greater than that required by inshore craft such as barges and dhows. Obviously, this would have added to the actual sailing times and shipping costs.

Secondly, at that time, almost every vessel originating from Japan, Europe and the USA carried cargo for BAPCO. Clearly, it was more convenient to off-load commercial cargo from the same anchorage, namely Sitra. Thus, shipping agents did not have to wait for BAPCO cargo to be discharged first: commercial and oil industry cargo were discharged simultaneously.

BAPCO did not, however, allow the use of its jetty for commercial use. All non-oil-industry cargo had to be discharged either ship-to-barge at the Sitra offshore anchorage, or into lighters moored beside cargo vessels tied up at Sitra jetty, but not into trucks parked on the jetty itself. From there, tugs towed the barges to the Mina Manama customs shed, or wooden dhows sailed there under their own power. These inshore craft were obliged to sail north then west through the sea channel between Bahrain and Muharraq islands, pass by the open swing bridge which, after 1942, linked them, and south into Mina Manama where the pier, local landing facilities and customs shed were located. Even in fair weather and favourable tides, the journey from Manama to Sitra, or *vice versa,* could take more than one day, particularly when boats were laden with cargo on the Sitra to Manama run. In time Y.B.A.Kanoo acted as both a shipping agent, and a tug/barge contractor.

For several years, my father and Abdulaziz Al Khadhar spent much of their time at Sitra, often working on the ships themselves. This was not without danger. Al Khadhar once told me how my father, while stepping from a tug-boat to a barge, fell into the water between the two vessels as the barge moved away from him. Luckily, my father was a good swimmer. Even more fortunate was his instinct to swim under the tug to surface on the clear side to safety. If he had swum under the barge moored alongside the ship, he would not have survived.

If Y.B.A.Kanoo happened to be the agent for the shipping line concerned, it was usually my father who travelled to BAPCO's shipping office in Awali to have the manifests signed and returned to the ship's captain. The original manifests were then sent by airmail to the shipping line. A ship's chandler boarded an incoming ship after it dropped anchor or berthed to determine the ships' needs, such as food, water, laundry, dry goods and medicines. For the ship-to-shore work, a 'boarding clerk' handled all the paperwork and ship-to-port activities. In turn, the Port Manager orchestrated all the shipping activity in port under his agency.

Al Khadhar also told me that during the immediate post-war years, we had no equipment, no permanent tally clerks to service the ships, no motor launch, no barges, no tugs, almost nothing. The lighters which we hired were mostly inshore wooden sailing boats capable of going alongside ocean-going vessels. In 1948 we started to buy wooden barges and launches to do the job.

Al Khadhar and his assistant, Abdulmuhsin Abdulghani (both permanent Kanoo staff), recruited the supervisors, plus the temporary Bahraini tally clerks and casual labourers on a daily basis. The tally clerk day-rate was eight rupees, while the casual labourers were paid five rupees per day. This pool was 'on call' to service any ship for which we were the agent, or when we had a specific need for their help. The process worked liked this.

The ship advised the agent how many hatches needed 'working'. The ship had a foreman (*sehang*). Each hatch was allocated one gang consisting of one supervisor (*tindel*), two winchmen who operated the hatch cranes, thirteen labourers and one tally clerk. All the gangs worked under the foreman who liaised with the ship's Chief Officer about the required work-load.

Tally clerks recorded every drum, package and bale which was off-loaded. Literally, everything that was moved was noted. Did it tally with the manifest? If something was missing an insurance claim was submitted. When the ship had been discharged we had no further need for tally clerks and labourers until the next vessel for which we were the agent came into port. However, when these men were employed by us, their working-hours were long. Shipping companies never want their vessels idle in port, or at anchor, longer than necessary.

In the case of offshore work, it was less easy to organise shift-changes so it was quite normal for labourers and tally clerks to arrive for duty at 7.00 a.m. and then work a straight shift of some seventeen hours (including meal-times, tea-breaks and rest periods) until the ship was discharged. (The 8-hour shift system was introduced in 1962.)

The Kanoo fleet

No account of our shipping agency network would be complete without recalling a few anecdotes about the early development of our barge and tug fleet. According to Abdulaziz Al Khadhar, after the Second World War when our company was 'standing on its feet' and had saved some money, my family bought eight 50-ton barges which the River Thames authority in London was selling for about £500 each. To tow them, we purchased an ex-RAF rescue boat.

The eight barges were a real innovation for us. The initiative for the purchase had come from a British company called Intrade Limited, building and civil engineering contractors based in Brentwood, Essex. On 22 July 1948, Intrade's General Manager, Mr G. L. O. Shiner, contacted my grandfathers Jassim and Ali Kanoo, explaining that Henry Finch of the Anglo-Iranian Oil Company had recently called into his office, mentioning that Kanoo needed some 150 to 250-ton barges for their ship-to-shore work. It so happened that Intrade had several Thames dumb-barges available for sale. If, upon inspection, these second-hand craft suited our work, they could be supplied almost immediately. If we required special craft to be built, Intrade could provide us with fairly prompt delivery. Either way, Shiner was happy to help us.

For many years, Gray Mackenzie remained our competitor and unhappy about our progress. According to Ahmed Kanoo, they always tried to belittle us and liked to give the impression that they did not really care about what we did. While he could do nothing about British control of Bahrain at the time, and their support of Gray Mackenzie as a British company, Ahmed continually fought to gain respect for Y.B.A.Kanoo's shipping services. He remembers one occasion when Gray Mackenzie's local manager walked into his office and asked: 'Do you really think that you can compete with us with those new "teacups" of yours?' In his matter-of-fact style, Ahmed Kanoo replied: 'Yes. You will see.'

Such incidents deterred neither my uncle, nor my father whose determination and refusal to accept 'no' for an answer became legendary. Before long, my father purchased four more second-hand barges (this time from Holland) and a small launch from BAPCO.

During the course of time, we commissioned several wooden launches to be built for us as work-boats. They had numbers not names, for example, a wooden dhow Launch 2. By the end of 1949, the Y.B.A.Kanoo shipping division owned four launches and twelve barges. (Launch 2, now fifty years old and refurbished for the third time, is preserved today as an example and reminder of our humble beginning in the shipping business. Occasionally, it is still used for inshore fishing trips.)

As business grew, Abdulaziz Al Khadhar asked my father to buy some tugs capable of towing our wooden and steel barges, especially in rough weather. These operated ship-to-shore, and *vice versa*. The first arrived from Holland during 1949, a 125-horsepower tug which we named *Kanoo*. In 1950, we acquired a similar tug, also from Holland. This we called *Bahrain*. Before long, *Yusuf, Awal* and *Damman* had joined the fleet, bought in 1951 and 1952. Al Khadhar also remembers four of our later acquisitions, the larger 250 horse-power tugs called *Manama, Riyadh, Al-Khobar* and *Buraydah*.

In the same period we established our Saudi-based barge fleet by re-deploying some of our existing craft from Bahrain for up to three months at a time, depending on how long they were needed. Later on, barges (flat, one-hatch and two-hatch types) as well as tugs were bought specifically for Saudi Arabia. In particular, Mohammed Jassim remembers KB (Kanoo barge) 51 and 52 being towed by our tugs Faisal and Ali. According to his recollection, only the Dammam Port Authority and Y.B.A.Kanoo operated barges as ship-to-shore lighters in Saudi Arabia during the early 1950s. None of the other agents operated barges or tugs. (We later acted as Gray Mackenzie's sub-agent when they ceased operating in Saudi Arabia.)

Eventually, Y.B.A.Kanoo's shipping division comprised a total of 57 barges (38 hatch and 19 flat-topped), 21 tugs, several small launches and 2 fast (25 knots) crew-boats. Many of these vessels were deployed off the Trucial Coast and Saudi Arabia where we worked them until the mid-1980s. By that time, regional deep-water container terminals and ports with adequate berthing facilities had rendered most ship-to-shore barge services obsolete.

Shipping lines served by Y.B.A.Kanoo

By the late 1940s, some familiar shipping names had disappeared, either through amalgamation with, or acquisition by, other shipping companies. For instance, the Mahadi Namazi Line, originally an Iranian company which later moved its head office to London and kept a branch in Tehran, ceased to trade. Arab Steamers, for which we had been shipping agents, became another name of the past. The Mogul Line, associated with Turner Morrissons and Mackinnon Mackenzie, was later taken over by P. & O. which, in 1960, sold its interest to the Indian Government.

In May 1950, we added the Maersk Line ('flag-ship' company of Denmark's A. P. Moller group), to our shipping agency portfolio. Kanoo's long-established relationship with the Silver Java Pacific Line continued. Its vessels arrived from the Indonesian island of Java to discharge cargo, mainly sugar, which we re-exported to Dubai, Qatar and Saudi Arabia. On their return voyages, Silver Java Pacific Line vessels carried cargo from Bahrain to Bombay and Karachi. (In 1966, Silver Java Pacific Line became part of Royal Interocean Lines which, in 1977, was automatically integrated into the newly-formed Koninkuke-Nedlloyd Group. Near the fourth-floor lift in our main Manama office, a framed certificate hangs on the wall celebrating our fifty years' association with Nedlloyd Lines.)

The Holland-Persian Gulf Line ceased when it became the Kerk Line, a colloquial name for the VNS Dutch shipping company whose vessels were named after Dutch churches, hence *Leider Kerk, Laadar Kerk* and *Lely Kerk,* for instance. Preference for the colloquial and readily identifiable name Kerk was understandable. Vereenigde Nederlandsche Scheepvaartmaatschappij is not easy to remember, let alone pronounce!

Mohammed Jassim Al Dhawadi, a veteran employee of our shipping department in Saudi Arabia, remembers the names of these vessels which were regular visitors to Dammam port. The story goes that, during the 1940s VNS ships were regularly delayed at anchorage for unacceptable periods of time. When the company found out that Gray Mackenzie first discharged all British-flagged ships, then the other flagged vessels, the VNS Chairman came to Bahrain looking for a solution. He asked Y.B.A.Kanoo if we would like to represent the Dutch shipping company. Ahmed Kanoo said 'yes', the only difficulty being, at that time, we had had no experience of dealing with big ocean liners. The VNS Chairman quickly overcame this limitation by agreeing to send Dutchmen to train us in the various ports where we operated. This remained the case for many years but, as time passed, the situation reversed. VNS began to send young Dutchmen to Y.B.A.Kanoo for us to train and provide overseas experience. I myself worked as a trainee tally clerk during some of my school summer holidays. Most of this experience was gained on ships anchored offshore, in Bahrain port and on the tankers berthed at Sitra terminal. Two ships I remember in particular were the *Laader Kerk* and the *Leider Kerk*. Ultimately, Kerk Line was absorbed by Nedlloyd Lines, the result of several Dutch shipping companies having amalgamated.

The Norwegian Concordia Line also gave striking names to its ships, such as *Concordia Viking, Concordia Taj* and *Concordia Sun* (the last ship to be built for Concordia Line in 1954.) The principal for this shipping line which, for the most part, carried timber and general commodities, was based in Khorramshahr. Y.B.A.Kanoo was also the agent for the Swedish shipping line, Kons Baker which, like the Concordia Line, no longer trades. Hogg Line, also Norwegian by origin, is now part of the Hogg Robinson Group.

Meanwhile, Inchcape had bought the Frank C. Strick Shipping Line (for which Y.B.A.Kanoo was Gray Mackenzie's sub-agent in Saudi Arabia). The British India Steam Navigation Company (whose agent elsewhere in the Arabian Gulf was Gray Mackenzie), later became part of the P. & O. organisation.

I gleaned more about our shipping activities from an unexpected source, an International Air Transport Association questionnaire stapled to our application to register the Kanoo Travel Office in Al-Khobar as an IATA member. On 18 November 1950, Ahmed Ali Kanoo had answered: the Bahrain office of Y.B.A.Kanoo was also agent for the Holland-America Line, American Export Line, American President Line, Kerr-Silver Line and the Alexandria Navigation Company.

It was also during this immediate post-Second World War period that Ahmed Kanoo negotiated, through BAPCO, to become the Bahrain agent for the Overseas Tankship Corporation (OTC). On 12 June 1946, OTC was incorporated in Panama to handle the tanker requirements of BAPCO's subsidiary based in New York, the California Texas Oil Company (CALTEX). Since CALTEX marketed BAPCO's export products (and still does), it purchased forty surplus T2 tankers from the US government to increase its transportation capacity. In turn, this generated a new aspect of business which Ahmed secured for Y.B.A.Kanoo. Office space for the four CALTEX marine personnel based in Bahrain was established with BAPCO in Awali, while we expanded our shipping office at Sitra jetty. (At one time, I worked as a tanker boarding representative. This involved climbing from the work-boat onto a rope-ladder and up the side of the tanker. If the vessel was empty, the climb could be as much as thirty metres – a very scary experience.)

OTC's first tanker 'run' was from New York to Bahrain where the empty tanker was loaded with crude oil, sailed to Shanghai, discharged its cargo and then returned to Sitra to repeat the process. The Bahrain–Shanghai 'run' ended on 26 May 1949 after China's largest city fell to the troops of Mao Tse-tung's People's Liberation Army. By 1950, when it became clear that OTC could no longer command dollar freights, four other tanker companies were established outside the US and the T2 tankers were sold to them: Nederlandsche Pacific Tankvaart Mij, Outremer Navigaçion de Pétrole, Tokyo Tanker Company and Overseas Tankship (UK) Limited. While these changes had a far-reaching impact on international business, surviving documents confirm that Y.B.A.Kanoo maintained its relationship as a shipping agent with at least two of these companies for quite some years: the Tokyo Tanker Company and Overseas Tankship (UK).

In 1951, we acquired the agency for the American States Marine Line which was assisting the Marshall Plan. This aid programme, launched by US Secretary of State George C. Marshall in June 1947, was designed, by the provision of money and materials, to help Europe and other countries to recover economically after the Second World War. As part of the scheme, States Marine Line vessels visited Bahrain on a charter basis to load asphalt from BAPCO for delivery to Madagascar and other African countries.

By the early 1950s, Y.B.A.Kanoo had been appointed shipping agent for three other lines which regularly served Bahrain and later Saudi Arabia: Netherland Line and Royal Rotterdam Line (both later merged with Nedlloyd), and the Everett Star Line, an Asian shipping company. In 1951, Ahmed Kanoo saw the first Everett Star Line vessel to anchor offshore from Bahrain. (The company now trades as the Everett Steamship Corporation, although it was sold to Japanese freight forwarder, Kelvin Warehouse Company, in 1983.)

Ahmed Kanoo was also closely involved with the development the tanker division in Ras Tannurah. With the help of Cyril Jones, appointed General Manager of Y.B.A.Kanoo in 1952, he negotiated the Kanoo agency agreements with Esso and the Standard Vacuum fleet. (Esso was a trade name used by the Standard Oil Company (New Jersey) until November 1972, after which the company became the Exxon Corporation. Standard Vacuum's 'pedigree' began in 1931 after the Vacuum Oil Company and Standard Oil Company of New York (SOCONY) amalgamated to form Socony-Vacuum. In 1955, the company became Socony-Mobil, and in 1966 changed again to the now more familiar Mobil Oil Corporation.)

Forward frontier – Saudi Arabia

In 1949, after Abdulla Kanoo had served his 'apprenticeship' in our Manama office, my father assigned him the pioneering task of developing a Y.B.A.Kanoo presence in Saudi Arabia. Years later, Abdulla told me what a shock his first visit to Saudi Arabia had been. The urban sophistication of Beirut where he had studied and the familiar comfort of Bahrain had not prepared him for the harsh and very difficult conditions in Saudi Arabia at that time. Although the west coast of the Kingdom had been developed for many years as the pilgrim route to Mecca and, more recently, strong trading links had been formed in Jeddah, Mecca and Medina, Saudi Arabia's east coast did not develop until the discovery of oil.

After a year of hardship, Abdulla's reaction was to return home, march into my father's office and announce that he didn't wish to go to Saudi Arabia any more. Characteristically, my father told him: 'Fine, don't go. Stay here. We will give you somewhere to live and your salary will be paid, but we don't want you to work with us. You can sit here comfortably doing nothing.' Abdulla thought about this for a while. Then, the next day, he went back to Saudi Arabia. He had no intention of sitting around doing nothing. My father's approach had worked. He had not told Abdulla to return. Instead, he hoped that his more subtle tactic would motivate Abdulla to 'pick up the gauntlet'. So it was that Abdulla assumed the challenge. (Abdulla's feelings are familiar to me because I went through the same 'shock' after graduating from university in the USA, followed by a year of work experience in Bahrain. I was then sent to Abu Dhabi in late 1969, our new pioneering 'outback'.)

When Abdulla Kanoo arrived in the Kingdom in 1949, the development of the Eastern Province of Saudi Arabia was just beginning to move forward, although it was some years before it really 'took off'. The only tangible evidence of change was the construction which ARAMCO had achieved for both its own needs and those of the community. There were very few cars, and even fewer roads, most of which had been 'graded' by the oil company. As for greenery, there were only isolated palm trees, except for the Al-Hasa and Al Qatif areas which are famous for their gardens and dates, especially Khalas. Even then, the Eastern Province still relied upon essential consumer goods re-exported from Mina Manama to meet both the Eastern Province's regional needs and ARAMCO's industrial requirements.

By the late 1940s, Bahrain's port facilities were well developed at

Sitra and in Manama and capable of receiving ocean-going vessels with deep draughts. In contrast, Dammam's jetties were still modest and the water shallow. As a result, ships preferred to discharge in Bahrain rather than offshore from Saudi Arabia. This meant that our deep-draught, barge-pulling tugs had to find a different route from that used by the shallow-draught dhows. Eventually, as people began to see our tugs constantly plying the new route, the buoy in the approach to Al Khobar port became known as 'Kanoo Buoy'.

Because of the long distances between towns and industrial facilities in Saudi Arabia, cars became an essential part of life. The preferred vehicles were Ford, Chevrolet and GMC pick-ups and trucks, much sought-after because they withstood the rigours of Saudi Arabia's climate. The first pick-ups to be delivered had the numbers '1' and '8' on them, (perhaps the model number or size of the engine). As people began to Arabise this feature, a pick-up became known as a 'wanait', a nickname still used today.

International telephones were only available at ARAMCO and the Saudi Arabian Rail-Road (SARR) offices. Local telephones were primitive, the type which had to be cranked by hand to make contact with the operator. If a caller was nice to him when requesting a connection, the operator might oblige quickly (if the line was not busy or out-of-use). Otherwise you could wait for hours before your call was put through. When automatic dialling became available, it made a phenomenal difference by speeding up communication and business.

Staple food was plentiful locally. But if you wished to eat good steaks, for instance, then you needed a friend in ARAMCO which received regular food shipments by air and sea direct from the USA. Such contacts were invaluable since ARAMCO was everything: employer, provider, contractor and medical centre. Although its management was renowned for tough productivity targets and high standards, they behaved with human hearts too. Many of today's 'big-name' companies owe their start in business in the Eastern Province to ARAMCO; for example, families such as Al Olayan, Abdulaziz Tamimi, Abdulhadi Qahtani, Abdulla Fuad, Abdulla Ba Husain, Algosaibi, Al-Zamil, Al-Binali, Al-Turki, Al-Jumaih and Al-Moujil.

ARAMCO set a standard which officials in the Eastern Province tried to emulate. Dammam, as a city, was in its infancy. The Governor of the Eastern Province, the Amir Saud bin Jiluwi, also lived in Dammam which, for generations, had been just a small community. (King Abdul-Aziz's toughest lieutenant was Abdullah bin Jiluwi who, so it is said, stood in front of the King when he attacked Riyadh in 1902 as a preliminary to founding the Kingdom.)

Bin Jiluwi had a reputation for being tough, ensuring that discipline was maintained and that the oilfield facilities were secured. We should remember that the government infrastructure in Saudi Arabia at that time was in its early stages of development. The Kingdom's modern development was still young and 'raiding' was still prevalent. ARAMCO meant oil and hence the wealth of the nation which, in turn, meant that it had to be secured and protected from marauding bands of bedouins.

Abdullah bin Jiluwi was very strict and did not hesitate to implement the law, no matter how harsh it may have been. Without this enforcement, the oil-men could not have worked safely in the desert away from the cities since, we should not forget, the nomadic bedouin were living there too, trying to survive in the harsh desert environment. They needed supplies. The oil-men's food and equipment would have been a bonanza to them.

At first, Abdulla Kanoo based himself in Al-Khobar where he established a Kanoo shipping and travel agency presence. (The travel office is still there.) This town was chosen mainly for the convenience of ARAMCO whose staff and families used to shop there. The house in Al-Khobar had no water or electricity which meant no showers, electric fans or air-conditioning. In contrast, ARAMCO's camp in Dhahran had many facilities such as telephones, sweet water, a commissary and so on. In 1950, Mubarak Kanoo moved to Al-Khobar to relieve Abdulla of our travel business which, since the office's opening in 1949, had been managed by an Englishman, Mr Taylor, assisted by four clerks.

In 1953 Abdulla transferred himself and our shipping work to premises in Dammam. These became our head office in Saudi Arabia. Abdulaziz Al Khadhar transferred from Bahrain and became Abdulla's right-hand man in Saudi Arabia. By 1954 Abdulaziz Kanoo had also joined his cousin, assisted by Abdul Raouf Al Jishi, Mohammed Jassim and other staff also from Bahrain.

Our new head office in Dammam was a modest ten-room house. Offices occupied the ground floor. The first floor of the building was living accommodation of which one side comprised a wing of rooms used, from time to time, by various Kanoo family members: such as Abdulla, Abdulaziz, Mubarak and Hamed. The other side accommodated our senior bachelor staff. One kitchen served everyone. This was built adjacent to the office beside a little garden.

Port and petroleum – Dammam and ARAMCO

In 1950 we achieved a major coup when we secured a one-year lighterage contract from ARAMCO, a need generated because there was no proper jetty in Ras Tannurah for discharging local bulk cargo. The contract had been possible because, at that time, there were no professional local support services upon which ARAMCO could depend. Instead, local enterprises were encouraged to provide required specialities. ARAMCO invited bids, first on competence and secondly on price. Then they awarded an appropriate contract to the company which offered the best package. Through ARAMCO's support in this way, many local companies grew stronger, including ourselves.

The background to this opportunity was explained to me by Abdulaziz Al Khadhar. During the years that he worked for BAPCO in Bahrain (before joining Y.B.A.Kanoo in 1946) the oil company looked after its own chandlery needs. This involved supplying ships with fresh water and food, medical services and whatever they needed. As we knew from our own experience, the captain and crew of each vessel always wanted their personal mail first. The same situation applied to CASOC in Saudi Arabia until 1944 (when the company name changed to ARAMCO). Then, during the late 1940s, both BAPCO and ARAMCO were told by their respective host governments that ship chandlery had to be provided by commercial companies 'down-town'. Gray Mackenzie secured part of this business. We competed with them. On the occasions when Y.B.A.Kanoo was the shipping agent involved, our representative (the boarding clerk) received his instructions from the vessel's captain and chief officer whom he visited daily.

In Saudi Arabia we transported cargo from ships anchored offshore to ARAMCO's pier. The oil company supplied its own trucks and labourers to move the goods to its camp and oil drilling sites. To ensure an efficient service and to accelerate the work of our tally clerks, the oil company asked for cargo to be sorted at its port of origin. Each ship's hatch was assigned a tally clerk and a supervisor, the latter acting as a liaison between the tally clerk and the ship's Chief Officer.

Since it could take up to two weeks, sometimes longer, to discharge an entire ship's cargo, the men worked two shifts of eight hours, from 7 a.m. to 11 p.m., except on Fridays which was free time. As most of the cargo arriving in Dammam at that time was destined for ARAMCO, it was all separated into different divisions identified with a prefix, such as AA, DA, EA, RA. For example, a hold's hatch might be simply marked DA (Dhahran); AB (Abqaiq) and RT (Ras Tannurah). Handling staff would know immediately the destinations of that hold's cargo.

Tally clerks, based in Bahrain, were only called over to Saudi Arabia when a ship came into Dammam. They stayed in one of our staff houses in Al-Khobar. If a long wait was expected before the arrival of the next vessel, the tally clerks returned to Bahrain by launch. After Gulf Aviation was formed in 1950 and started a shuttle service between Bahrain and Dhahran, our personnel flew between the two destinations instead. Some of the five rupees-a-day tally clerks we employed in those days, are now senior managers in our Saudi Arabian company: Jasim Khalaf (Shipping Manager, Eastern Province); Abdulla Mutlaq (General Manager, Administration); Omer Amodi (Travel Manager, Eastern Province) and Abdul Raouf Al Jishi (Port Manager, Dammam).

Labour shortages were a major factor. Even until the 1960s, most available Saudi labourers were employed by ARAMCO and the Government of Saudi Arabia. This meant that shipping agents like ourselves had to rely on recruiting labour from the Trucial States (now the UAE) and Oman, particularly as the Sultanate's economy remained depressed until the accession of Sultan Qaboos in 1970. Supervisory staff were just as hard to find. Few Saudis spoke English, so we deployed cargo superintendents from Bahrain. Ships' stevedores were recruited from a labour pool, many also from Bahrain where we maintained a list of labourers, tally clerks and supervisory personnel whom we could call upon when needed.

As time went by, entrepreneurs started to compile their own lists of experienced personnel who were available on stand-by. Hence, when a shipping agent required labour, these independent entrepreneurs were asked to provide the necessary 'gangs', usually Iranians, or Bahrainis of Iranian descent. These tough labourers dominated the labour market. One such entrepreneurial agency was Al-Sharif Stevedoring in Bahrain. Until Dammam's new port, Mina King Abdul-Aziz, opened officially in January 1951, Mahmood Shakib (father of Khalil Shakib of General Stores) worked for the agency, his responsibility being to hire labour gangs to work at Ras Tannurah (where our office opened in 1950) and Ras Mishaab. (After 1951, Hamad Algosaibi took over the provision of labour in Saudi Arabia.) Labour gangs required to service ships for which we were the shipping agent in Bahrain were also hired from Al-Sharif Stevedoring.

In 1952, we established the Bahrain Shipping and Labour Agency (BSLA) to supply labour and ships' provisions. Its first manager, Mr Abdulghani was a very capable man. He assembled a good team to work with him, found his own supply of Iranian and Omani labour for Bahrain, and sourced a good range of consumable and non-consumable supplies. Even now, more than forty years later, BSLA remains the stevedoring arm of Kanoo in Bahrain.

From the outset, Mina King Abdul-Aziz in Dammam was planned to accommodate deep-draught cargo ships. One notable feature, a trussel causeway, had been constructed out to Dammam pier, the port's new deep-water pier comprising two berths, east and west. A single-track railway had been laid on top of the causeway. Alongside the track, a path allowed access to pedestrians. However, since the deep-water pier was some eleven kilometres from the shore station, this would have been a considerable hike for those so inclined. Dammam pier also housed the port authority office and a small restaurant. Apart from the small south pier which was made for the use of inshore craft, this was the extent of Mina King Abdul-Aziz in 1951. (In 1962, four more deep-water berths were added.)

So that ocean-going ships could be loaded and unloaded with comparative ease, heavy-duty cranes were installed to unload cargo from the holds directly into the waiting railway wagons on the single-track causeway. Even this new facility did not provide enough berthing to meet the growing needs of the port authority, and so the practice of discharging from anchorage still operated. Dammam Rail-Road Authority, which ran the port in the early 1950s, owned some barges which could be hired by companies.

After the port authority health and customs officials had cleared the cargo, discharging into the barges could begin. When full, they were towed by tug to the inshore-craft pier, the south pier. From here, cargo was discharged into rail wagons and then taken on the final leg of its journey to the customs shed in Dammam. Cargo discharged offshore at the deep-water north pier was loaded onto freight trains which often comprised twenty-five wagons.

Once at the jetty, the cargo was stored temporarily in the warehouse, if there was not enough space available on the rail wagons, or it was taken directly by rail to the customs post on shore. At that point there was a steel bridge, the port entrance. In the 1950s, there was no centralised port directorate as we know it now. The entire port operation was run by the Rail-Road Director (Abdulaziz Al Quraishi), assisted by the Port Manager (Abdulatif Othman). Health, customs and security personnel, along with the coastguards, took their instructions (with reference to the port) from these two officials.

The rail-road itself comprised four stations: Dammam served the Rail-Road Headquarters and the town; Shore Lane served the customs sheds and port management; Small Jetty and Northern Jetty stations were used by personnel who boarded and disembarked on the jetty. The passenger train was a modest three-carriage affair, each carriage with a capacity of 200 people, and available to everyone who used the port: labourers, crews and so on. (Travellers who wished to connect with the inter-Gulf up-mail or down-mail steamers which called into Bahrain, sailed to the island by dhow. Although by now Gulf Aviation operated a service between Bahrain and Dhahran, not everyone used this shuttle service.)

The passenger train made three round-trips a day. The first started at 6.00 a.m from Dammam station. At Shore Lane and Small Jetty stations, the train stopped to allow passengers to embark or disembark. Forty-five minutes after leaving Dammam, the train arrived at the Northern Jetty station. After waiting for fifteen minutes, the train began its return trip to Dammam at 7.00 a.m., stopping at the two intermediate stations on its way. Forty-five minutes after leaving the Northern Jetty, the train completed its round-trip at 7.45 a.m.

The same routine started again at 2.00 p.m. and 10.00 p.m., each round-trip lasting one hour and forty-five minutes. If you were unlucky enough to miss the last train you had to sleep where you were until the first train the next day. Jassim Khalaf (then a tally clerk, today our Shipping Manager in Dammam), remembers how he and his colleagues used to sleep in the open wherever they could find somewhere 'comfortable' on the occasions that they had to complete discharging a ship after the last train left the Northern Jetty station at 11.00 p.m. They then had to wait until 7.00 a.m. the next day before returning to Dammam.

Until Mina King Abdul-Aziz opened in early 1951, discharging delays were quite usual because of congestion and bad weather. Previously, Dammam port had comprised one simple small jetty constructed in shallow coastal water, capable of accommodating vessels with a maximum draught of ten metres. Yet between twenty and thirty ships for which Y.B.A.Kanoo were the shipping agents arrived every month. As we were not the only shipping agent operating out of the little port, Algosaibi and Alireza being our main competitors, often we had to wait our turn. To accelerate the process, shipping companies sometimes chose to discharge their cargos at anchorage, at extra cost, since they did not want their vessels idle for a long time. Since the ship-to-shore lighters were flat-bottomed barges and tended to be unstable, it was dangerous to tow them in rough weather. The strain on the tow-rope often caused it to snap. When this happened, the tug had to chase and capture the barge in choppy water. In such conditions, the cargo was easily splashed. This, of course, tended to spoil the commodities in transit, particularly flour, rice, wheat and cement. So in rough weather trans-shipment stopped which, of course, increased the delays.

Even throughout the 1950s, it was not unusual to see fourteen ships, perhaps more, riding at anchor waiting to be discharged, sometimes for up to two months. Although shipping companies were unhappy with this situation, there was little they could do to improve their lot, other than ensure that their crews were well provided for. After all, they still needed provisions, medical care, their mail delivered and collected, and so on. When we happened to be the shipping agent involved, servicing such needs generated excellent business for us.

After Dammam port and the railway were built, supervisors and tally clerks were able to instruct labourers to off-load the contents of one hold into trucks, or rail wagons, destined for one location. Prior to this development (in the days when cargo was discharged into ship-to-shore lighters), shipments had to be sorted and re-handled to separate them according to their final destinations. The tally sheet comprised four pages: one for the ship's master indicating that the cargo had been discharged from the ship; one to the port authority which compared it with the manifest; one for the shipping agent and one for the consignee. Thus, if a merchant complained that his Bill of Lading stated 20 cartons but he was delivered only 15, then the tally sheet would be the reference document. If the tally sheet showed that only 15 cartons had been off-loaded, then the merchant would lodge a claim with the shipping company.

Basically, the claims system worked like this (and still does). First, a merchant placed an order with a supplier who, in turn, arranged for the goods to be shipped and a Bill of Lading (a legal document proving ownership and describing the consignment) would be sent to the merchant. After the cargo arrived at its destination and was discharged by the relevant local shipping agent, a tally was made. Thereafter, the cargo became the responsibility of the receiving port. The merchant collected his consignment after paying port and agents' fees and customs duty. If items were missing or damaged, he submitted a claim to the ship's agent who, in turn, checked at which stage the items disappeared or were damaged: with the shipper, on board ship, or in port. The merchant would be told of the findings. If the ship was deemed to be responsible, the agent notified the shipping company, which instructed the agent either to pay, or not to pay the claim.

In these circumstances, Abdulla Kanoo, and his younger brother Hamed (after he joined our Saudi company in 1956), frequently visited the dock. They were often seen driving a pick-up around the port as they dealt with their regular shipping agency tasks. (The late Ahmed Saleh Khajah was our Dammam Port Manager at that time. Later, he became a big merchant in Bahrain.) Abdulla visited ARAMCO too, not only to rest, but to maintain relationships and solicit new contracts. In the early 1950s, the ARAMCO camp comprised houses and pre-fabricated buildings. By the end of the decade, it had assumed the appearance of 'small-town USA', re-created in the desert of Saudi Arabia.

US Navy contract – big business in Ras Tannurah

In the same year that Mina King Abdul-Aziz opened, Ahmed Kanoo visited London to attend to Y.B.A.Kanoo business. At some point during his stay, Ahmed received a telephone call from my father. This set in motion a chain of events which took my uncle across the Atlantic Ocean for the first time and enabled him to win the Military Sea Transportation Services contract in October 1951.

As the Korean War was now in progress, most oil tankers loading at Bahrain and Saudi Arabia had been leased by their owners to the US Navy which, in turn, organised these charters through a division of the US Navy Transportation Department. This section was known as the Military Sea Transportation Services (MSTS). So it was that MSTS contracted oil tankers to transport gasoline and aviation fuel from the Arabian Gulf to the American forces serving in Korea. In practice, this meant that many oil tankers which belonged to various civilian companies were chartered by the US Navy to load with fuel at Ras Tannurah, sail to the Far East, discharge their cargo and then return to Saudi Arabia to repeat the procedure. At that time, Gray Mackenzie had the monopoly of all shipping agency contracts at the Ras Tannurah terminal, with one exception. Naturally enough, they had their eyes on the possibility of acquiring the MSTS contract.

Abdulla Kanoo already knew some of ARAMCO's personnel well. One day he came to know that the oil company no longer wished to act as a shipping agent for all the tanker companies using its Ras Tannurah terminal, a commitment which obliged the oil company to service between twenty and thirty tankers every month. Hence, ARAMCO intended to discontinue its immense MSTS contract: discharging tankers, customs clearance, victualling (provision of food and water), bunkering (refuelling), facilitating crew changes, arranging onshore shopping trips and medical visits for the crews, as well as handling their mail.

If Y.B.A.Kanoo was interested in bidding for this business, then Abdulla was told that a member of our family should visit Washington to discuss the proposal with the US Navy's Chief of Staff. The buzz was that if Y.B.A.Kanoo didn't act now, then Gray Mackenzie would take the business. When Abdulla received this information, he travelled to see my father in Bahrain. Apparently my father then told his good friend, a US Navy Admiral based in Bahrain, that Ahmed Kanoo was in London. He agreed to cable Washington immediately, brief the Chief of Staff and set up a meeting. True to his word, he did just that.

Ahmed Kanoo flew across the Atlantic Ocean on 5 October 1951. In New York he was met by his good friend, Hussain Yateem. The following morning Ahmed flew on to Washington where he met the Chief of Staff, 'a very kind person'. Instructions were duly issued to prepare introductory letters for my uncle to visit all the shipping companies concerned. Furthermore, arrangements were made for my uncle to tour America, seeing two or three companies in any one town on any one day.

Looking back on that experience, Ahmed Kanoo says that the satisfaction he felt at the time was not so much because he had won such a huge slice of shipping business for Y.B.A.Kanoo, or that he was seeing California, Baltimore, Philadelphia and New York for the first time, but because 'it was my first step towards beating Gray Mackenzie, who still thought I was "a small boy"'.

Upon Ahmed's return to Bahrain, he wrote official letters to all those companies involved, including ARAMCO. In the latter's case, Abdulla Kanoo delivered the letter personally on behalf of our company so that it could be endorsed officially. Thus, initiated by Abdulla and my father, the Military Sea Transportation Services contract marked the beginning of what became our big tanker business in Ras Tannurah. We learnt later that Gray Mackenzie had been close on our heels, but they were too late. At last they saw us as serious competition, although this was not the end of the rivalry. Well into the 1960s, the arrogance of Gray Mackenzie's British management intensely irritated Ahmed Kanoo, motivating

him and his team to work harder for the sake of beating their rival,
which they did.

Chapter 8

Pioneering Partners

Gulf Aviation Company owed its inception to Shaikh Salman bin Hamad Al Khalifa who, in about 1945, thought about forming a regional airline. However, it was not until 1949 that his idea became reality, made possible by the timely arrival in Bahrain of Fredrick Bosworth, an ex-RAF officer. For several years, he had tried unsuccessfully to form a charter airline company in Iraq where he had been based. In the end, Bosworth decided to seek better luck elsewhere and flew his seven-seater fabric-covered Anson MK1 aircraft to Bahrain.

According to Charles Belgrave's *Personal Column,* 'Bosworth was a man of energy and enterprise and not easily disheartened', even though he had only a small amount of capital. Having abandoned his earlier plans, he now aimed to form an aviation company in Bahrain to carry passengers and freight to and from places in the Gulf region not served by BOAC. He also intended to pilot regional charter flights when there was a demand for them. He overcame his first hurdle, lack of cash, by approaching Hussain Yateem for a loan of Rs 2,000 so that he could buy spare parts for the Anson. Hussain gladly obliged.

Before long, Bosworth returned to Hussain, this time to suggest that they form an aviation company. Once again, Hussain agreed. Khalifa Algosaibi was invited to join the enterprise. So, with Bosworth as the third partner, a company was registered in England with capital of £1,500. Mrs Bosworth became the Company Secretary and Charles Belgrave its Chairman. It was obvious, however, that more funds were needed to buy new aircraft. Hence, Abdulla Darwish and Saleh Al-Manea joined the Board, as did Khalil Kanoo. (Later on, Saleh sold his share to Y.B.A.Kanoo, through Ahmed Kanoo.) Thus, with the support of local businessmen, Bosworth began a service of pleasure flights around the islands of Bahrain in 1949. Hussain Yateem remembers when a nine-seater two-propeller Heron aircraft was bought. Bosworth removed the toilet to make space for a tenth passenger seat. Before long, it became apparent that a structured airline transport company was necessary to service the growing commercial links between the Gulf region and the rest of the world.

Gulf Aviation Company – a new era in air travel

On 24 March 1950 His Highness Shaikh Salman bin Hamed Al Khalifa approved the registration of Gulf Aviation Company as a private enterprise, chaired by Charles Belgrave, and backed by prominent regional businessmen: Hussain Yateem and Ahmed Kanoo (both Bahraini); Abdulla Darwish and Saleh Al-Manea (from Qatar); and Khalifa Algosaibi (Saudi Arabian). Fredrick Bosworth was both Managing Director and Chief Pilot, while his wife remained the Company Secretary.

Less than four months later, Gulf Aviation began its scheduled operations on 5 July 1950, with a Bahrain–Doha–Sharjah service operated by an Avro Anson aircraft: four flights a week to Doha with one flight continuing to Sharjah. Twenty days later, the company started a thrice-daily service between Bahrain and Dhahran using a de Havilland (DH 86A) aircraft. This was affectionately called *Um Ahmed* (Mother of Ahmed) by the Bahraini mechanics, welders and office clerks who commuted between their island homes and their employment with ARAMCO in Saudi Arabia.

But before this shuttle could begin, Saudi Arabian permission was needed to land in Dhahran. Khalifa Algosaibi undertook this task and went to Riyadh to seek out someone who could help. As commercial air transport in the Kingdom was in its infancy, and no legislation for civil aviation existed, it took Algosaibi some time to persuade the Saudi authorities to grant the required landing permission. Meanwhile, aeroplanes were stuck in Bahrain.

Abdulrahman Ali Al-Turki (then a young man, now a leading businessman in the Eastern Province) was sent from Riyadh to take charge of the passport and immigration formalities at Dhahran's new airport. He remembers Abdulla and Mubarak Kanoo visiting him to obtain the long-awaited permission. Al-Turki then took my uncles to Salim Naghshabandi (Dhahran's Airport Manager), who controlled all matters related to the airport. He gave them a letter on the spot to permit Gulf Aviation to land in Dhahran. Meanwhile Khalifa Algosaibi also obtained landing permission from Riyadh.

Gulf Aviation's new service was a great asset to Y.B.A.Kanoo. Until now, travel between Saudi Arabia and Bahrain meant being on the deck of a wooden dhow with no amenities for up to three hours. There was no fixed departure time. The dhow sailed when it was full.

By late 1950, Gulf Aviation's service to Dhahran was quicker, more reliable and comfortable. The cost of a one-way ticket bought in Bahrain was Rs 17 and SR 17 when purchased in Saudi Arabia.

Now, we could send and receive mail-pouches between Bahrain and Saudi Arabia twice a day instead of waiting for a launch to arrive by sea. Because of the importance of personal mail to ships' and tanker crews, we had a special car which collected mail-bags from the airport. In these we also received ships' manifests sent from Bahrain. These then had to be translated into Arabic, then typed onto special port forms and presented to Dammam's port authorities who would not accept documents in English. To achieve this, we employed special translators, sometimes working on 24-hour shifts to cope with the volume of cargo. (Until the 1960s, few airlines flew into Dhahran so it was much quicker for mail to come via Bahrain, providing that it was not forwarded to Riyadh for central sorting only to be returned to Dammam after a long delay. Instead, correspondents could collect mail from their post office boxes at the airport, for example: Y.B.A.Kanoo, Dhahran Airport, PO Box 37, Dammam, KSA.)

By 1951 Gulf Aviation faced two major predicaments: money was still short; and the company found it difficult to encourage suitable pilots and engineers to join the small, new airline in the Arabian Gulf region. To overcome the cash-flow difficulty, Gulf Aviation secured a loan of Rs 400,000 from the Bahrain Government to buy several more aircraft. Tragically, Captain Bosworth was killed on 10 June 1951 in a night-time flying accident in the UK. He had been testing a de Havilland Dove, one of the aircraft he planned to buy. During the next day, George Beeby Thompson (Petroleum Inspector for the Government of Bahrain) assumed the management of Gulf Aviation and, for many years, remained its Chairman. Meanwhile, despite Bosworth's tragic accident, Gulf Aviation bought another Dove. This came into service on 15 August 1951.

While this was a positive development, Bosworth's widow was left with the loan, repayable over five years at five per cent interest. On 1 October 1951, after lengthy negotiations led by Hussain Yateem and my father, BOAC agreed to purchase 51 per cent of Gulf Aviation Company's shares, including those held by Mrs. Bosworth. The Ruler of Bahrain and some members of his family also expressed a wish to invest money in the scheme. Following their example, a number of Bahraini merchants bought shares in Gulf Aviation. The new Board consisted of G. H. C. Lee (Chairman), Hussain Yateem, Mohamed Kanoo (my father), Adil Algosaibi (Khalifa's brother) and

Sami Gayed (a businessman who represented Qatar), together with J. Linstead, B. H. Bamfylde and R. D. H. Wilson.

Meanwhile, earlier that year on 31 January 1951, the Yusuf bin Ahmed Kanoo Travel Agency in Al-Khobar had been appointed as IATA's first 'Approved Agent' in Saudi Arabia, and registered on the official IATA Agency List. Incidentally, the questionnaire which we had been asked to complete as part of our application form, listed the twelve airlines which our Bahrain office represented at that time. While many of the names themselves are of historical interest, the extent to which international airline routes to Arabia had developed by 1951 is also quite surprising. The airlines were: British Overseas Airways Corporation (BOAC), Pan American World Airlines (PAN AM), Trans World Airlines (TWA), Air France, Swiss Air, Iraqi Airways, Cyprus Airways, KLM Royal Dutch Airlines, Middle East Airlines (MEA), British European Airways (BEA), Aden Airways and Air Djibouti.

By 1952, Mubarak Kanoo was busy developing our air-travel business in Al-Khobar even more aggressively. His new focus was the ARAMCO camp where he made regular visits, stationing himself in the commissary, the restaurant or some other convenient place where people could see him and readily make contact. After a while, he was less of a stranger. If he did good work for one family, the head of the household would tell his friends. Those friends told their friends, and so on. A wife might telephone our travel office and ask: 'Can your representative come and see us at five o'clock when my husband is here?' Then the family would discuss their proposed trip with my uncle who then worked it out for them. Once we were seen to be giving a service, people began to telephone our agency office to discuss their travel requirements, rather than ask a representative to visit their homes.

At other times, my uncle simply 'cold-called'. As he walked from house to house in the oil camp, he knocked on doors and announced that he was a travel agent. Could he do anything for the family? Were they travelling? He could do this, or offer that. He remembers well that, at first, people didn't respond to him, not believing that an Arab could create an itinerary or check details with the airlines. One sceptic in particular was Mr Scardino, ARAMCO's District Manager. He disapproved of Mubarak Kanoo's activities around the camp to the extent that, on one occasion, he asked my uncle to leave. Mubarak did so, only to return later. Undaunted, he slowly gained the confidence of American personnel and their families wanting a good, effective service and so managed to build a credible reputation within ARAMCO. Later, Mr Scardino and Mubarak Kanoo became good friends!

Meanwhile, the Indian staff who manned our Al-Khobar travel office provided superb back-up to my uncle's efforts, being both well trained and technically effective in caring for our customers' needs. So much so that 'Canoe Travel' became part of ARAMCO folklore (also among BAPCO's American personnel), some customers even believing that this was the place which specialised in river-rafting or canoeing holidays! In time, this myth became a joke, but the colloquial name stuck. In the 1950s, many people found Kanoo Travel in Al-Khobar, and Bahrain, to be the only places where they could make travel bookings for either business or holidays.

By the end of the decade, Gulf Aviation's fleet included two 28-passenger Dakotas (DC3s), four 9- or 10-passenger Herons and two 11-passenger Doves. When George Beeby Thompson retired, Captain Bulmer took over, succeeded by Captain Alan Bodger in 1959. As a Gulf Aviation Board member, my father, Mohamed, took a special interest in the airline's affairs and worked hard with Captain Bodger to make it a success. Between them they ensured the small airline prospered. At first, only British pilots were employed. However, during the course of time, my father pioneered the 'Arabisation' of the airline's staff. Not only did he encourage Bahrainis to handle the aircraft on the airport apron, but he also forced the airline to train Bahrainis as pilots. Shaikh Rashid bin Hassan Al Khalifa, whose training was not sponsored by Gulf Aviation, joined the airline as its first Bahraini pilot in 1968. In 1971, Captain Abdulrahman Al-Ghood was appointed as Gulf Aviation's first Bahraini aircraft commander. (He was Gulf Air's Executive Vice-President – Airline Operations, when he retired in 1996.)

Meanwhile, in 1958, Aircraft Services Gulf Limited (ASGUL) was formed, forerunner to Bahrain Airport Services (BAS). The background to this development began soon after Gulf Aviation started operations. Initially, the new airline's aircraft servicing was taken care of by BOAC. Gulf Aviation personnel looked after its own passengers and aircraft handling. But as the young airline started to grow, these tasks became a burden to its management. It was obvious that a dedicated new unit should be established. It was this impetus which persuaded my father and Captain Bodger to form ASGUL, their objective being that it should assume all Gulf Aviation's ramp and passenger handling, as well as that required by other civil airlines using Bahrain airport. ASGUL was jointly owned by Y.B.A.Kanoo (51 per cent) and Gulf Aviation (49 per cent). Captain Alan Bodger was appointed as its first Executive Director, while my father, a Board director, was recognised as the driving force which solved many of ASGUL's problems, particularly those which concerned Government liaison and operations management.

Nineteen years later, in 1977, ASGUL shares were sold to new partners and a new company, Bahrain Airport Services (BAS), was formed. Inevitably, this stimulated yet another new development phase. However, for now, my story reverts to 1950. In the same year that Gulf Aviation was formed, Y.B.A.Kanoo embarked on another voyage of exploration, this time to Norwich, the county town of Norfolk in England.

Norwich Union – our introduction to insurance

Given our involvement with the shipping and travel industries, it was a natural progression to establish an insurance service. The Kanoo family approached Charles Belgrave (Adviser to the Bahrain Government), to seek his thoughts as to how we might effect an introduction to a reputable insurance company, perhaps one based in the United Kingdom.

As luck would have it, Charles Belgrave's brother-in-law, Sir Richard Barrett-Lennard, was then a director of Norwich Union. The company already had representation in various parts of the world, but nowhere in the Middle East. Sir Richard was briefed about our company, and assured that Charles Belgrave would help to set things up in Bahrain. Arrangements were then made for Ahmed Kanoo to visit the insurance company's head office in Norwich, England.

Almost immediately, Norwich Union's directors and Ahmed Kanoo shook hands on a deal. Their first agreement was signed on 10 May 1950, whereby Norwich Union Fire Insurance Society Limited appointed Y.B.A.Kanoo as its agents in Bahrain. W. G. Wylie (Norwich Union's Fire Society Manager for the East, based in Calcutta) wrote: 'Messrs. Yusuf bin Ahmed Kanoo of Manama (Bahrain) are sole and principal agents of this Society for the Bahrain islands and are empowered by us to issue cover, collect premiums, issue receipts and do such other things as are normally associated with the conduct of a Principal Agency business.'

The next significant development occurred during the following summer. At midnight on Sunday, 21 August 1950, Jack Spelman (Norwich Union's Life Society's Manager for the East, based in Bombay), arrived in Bahrain for the first time. Upon leaving the

Argonaut aircraft he expected to find someone from Y.B.A.Kanoo waiting to meet him. But the letter to our office advising us of Spelman's arrival had gone astray. Instead, he made his 'lonely way in a decrepit BOAC bus to the then BOAC hostel'.

At 7.30 a.m. the next day, Spelman reported to our office where he was warmly received by my father, but told that Ahmed Kanoo was absent. Furthermore, the insurance file could not be traced, and the parcel of Norwich Union stationery (which had been sent ahead from Calcutta) had also been misplaced. This unlucky start to Spelman's visit did not, he feared, bode well for a successful outcome. He need not have worried. A cable requesting replacement stocks of stationery was despatched, and stocks delivered quickly. (Years later, Spelman remarked that this speedy service had spoken well of the then airmail service between Calcutta and Bahrain, 'very much better than that presently [in 1975] existing between North America and Europe'.)

Despite the inauspicious start to Jack Spelman's first visit to Bahrain, five days after his arrival he issued Norwich Union's first policy in Bahrain. A list of policy-holders, dated 1950, revealed a variety of names and insurance requirements. The first All Risks Policy, dated 27 August 1950, was taken out by Mr Ahmad M. A. Kazim. The premium required to insure his personal belongings was Rs 10 13a. In September 1950, Abdulaziz Kanoo and Jack Spelman took out travellers' insurance policies, the premiums costing Rs 14 11a, and Rs 21 respectively. Y.B.A.Kanoo insured three vehicles, type unknown. Motor car policies issued in October 1950 suggest that the premiums were quite high: Messrs Kanian, Yusuf Essa Buhijji, Rachid Alawar, Jassim Mohammed Albaker and Abdulrahman Khunjee were charged Rs 525, Rs 348, Rs 205, Rs 375 and Rs 414 respectively.

Items of marine insurance were also included in the list, premiums being levied weekly or monthly. Messrs Sadary & Sons, the Eastern Trading House and Khalil bin M. Dawani & Sons, were among the policy holders. Not surprisingly, the banks protected their interests too. For example, on 4 October 1950, the British Bank of Iran and the Middle East insured itself against fire and burglary for a premium of Rs 20. In the same month, Abdulla Kanoo insured himself against personal accident at a cost of Rs 225, while my father, Mohamed Kanoo, took out a traveller's policy for Rs 57 3a. Also during October, Y.B.A.Kanoo's premises were insured against fire and burglary.

If these examples are anything to go by, it would seem that the concept of insurance was beginning to be accepted, even if at that time it was not widely acknowledged as a prudent, or even a permissible, undertaking. The total premium value for life policies taken out during October 1950 (Rs 772 3a), suggests that even in those cautious days, not everyone took a fatalistic view of life. Sometimes, despite their caution, clients even displayed a remarkable sense of humour, as the next story demonstrates.

During a later visit to Bahrain, Jack Spelman documented how my father and Ahmed Kanoo persuaded one of their wealthy Kuwaiti friends to become a holder of one of the first traveller's policies to be issued by Norwich Union in Bahrain.

Just as the Kuwaiti was about to leave our travel office for the airport, my father and uncle 'required' this gentleman to make a purchase from their insurance department. In no time at all, Spelman had sold the obliging Kuwaiti a twenty-four hour travel policy. Sensing his distinct nervousness about the whole procedure, Ahmed Kanoo and my father invited Spelman to join them while they escorted their new client to the airport in a large, open Cadillac car. Jack Spelman continues the story.

'I was asked to sit in the rear seat with my new client who, throughout the road-trip, sat with his policy in his hands and his eyes firmly glued to my face. As we approached the airport, without taking his eyes from me, he directed a question to Ahmed. He translated to the effect that his friend understood that, in the event of the plane crashing on landing in Kuwait, resulting in his death, then his estate would receive the sum of 100,000 rupees. However, the Kuwaiti wished to know what he would receive if the plane crashed and he escaped completely unharmed. I replied that we would refund him his premium of four or five rupees plus a 100 per cent bonus. This reply was followed by a few seconds' silence and thereafter there was an explosion of laughter.'

During the following spring, Ester Bamji arrived in Bahrain to assist Y.B.A.Kanoo's life insurance business development. After leaving Karachi in what he called a noisy, 'hardy horse' (an Argonaut aircraft), he arrived in Bahrain on 4 April 1951. Of his journey, Bamji particularly remembers the cube-like little lounge in the tail of the aircraft where passengers could sit and read magazines or even try to talk with friends. However, the excessive volume of the aircraft's engines usually made conversation impossible. Three months later, on 31 July 1951, Y.B.A.Kanoo was appointed Norwich Union Life Society's agent for the entire Gulf region, and in particular, the Eastern Province of Saudi Arabia. At that time, all Norwich Union's Middle East operations reported to their relevant Manager for the

East. As mentioned earlier, the Fire Society's Manager for the East was W. G. Wylie, based in Calcutta. The Life Society's Manager for the East, Jack Spelman, was based in Bombay.

It would be easy to believe that with no competition, as yet, the Norwich Union/Y.B.A.Kanoo insurance partnership could not fail. But at that time, less than half a century ago, the situation was not quite so clear-cut. Many Moslems remained rigidly opposed to insurance policies in any form, in particular life insurance. Islamic teaching states that it is the will of Allah whether one lives or dies. Insurance companies take no such ethereal view, but simply 'bet' on the premise that their clients will not die during the 'currency' of life insurance policies. Gradually, resistance to the concept became less widespread to the extent that, today, many Islamic insurance companies have been established. Even as recently as the early 1970s, this was not so. Ester Bamji (Norwich Union Life Society's Regional Representative in Bahrain) observed how this thinking changed dramatically over time. He recalled two contrasting cases which illustrate the mood of that period.

One day, many years ago, a young Bahraini, who had held a Norwich Union life insurance policy for six or seven years, walked into the office and announced that the policy had to be cancelled. Naturally, Bamji was surprised and asked if there was anything he could do to assist the Bahraini to solve the problem. The Bahraini explained that he was preparing to attend the Haj for the first time. During the course of discussion with his *mullah,* the life insurance policy was mentioned. The *mullah* ruled that this was *haram* (forbidden according to the teaching of Islam). The Bahraini expressed his regret, explaining that he believed life insurance to be a good thing for his family, but now that he had been advised by his *mullah* to cancel it, he had no choice. The policy was cancelled.

For a long time, there was even opposition to fire insurance. Bamji's second story involved the Royal Air Force Officers' Club in Gudaibiyah, owned by an elderly Shaikh. It transpired that the Norwich Union Fire Society handled the RAF's insurance needs, including those relating to the contents of their Officers' Club. As part of the British Government's bureaucratic process, the RAF was required to send insurance documents back to London so that the Ministry of Defence could satisfy itself that everything was in order. Predictably, back came a request: please ascertain from the landlord if the building itself was insured.

The RAF people then arranged to visit the Shaikh so that during the conversation they could ask him directly if the building had been insured. The Shaikh, apparently a charming old gentleman, just looked very blank and said: 'What are you talking of? You mean that the walls which I have built can catch fire?' The RAF emissaries soon realised that the RAF Officers' Club building in Bahrain was not insured. Shortly afterwards, Norwich Union Fire Society had insured both the property and the contents against fire. As a postscript to this tale, Bamji added that fire insurance was perhaps the slowest of Norwich Union's 'products' to develop in Bahrain.

Before long, Gray Mackenzie became Norwich Union's major competitor in Bahrain, together with the Zayani family who established an insurance agency in Manama during the 1950s. During this decade, Norwich Union Fire Society's main business was accident insurance, although the company offered all types of policies. The only exceptions were life insurance and related products. These were handled by the Norwich Union Life Society.

In time, Y.B.A.Kanoo became the principal insurers of all Bahrain government departments. The Fire Society covered much of Gulf Aviation Company's needs. As for marine insurance, most insurance companies would not insure dhows, only offering cover in the event of loss or damage to cargo. Banks would not allow boxes of currency to be despatched on the high seas without some form of insurance protection.

In due course, Geoff W. H. Jones was appointed as Norwich Union's Representative in Bahrain. He remained on the island for a long time, before transferring to Norwich, England, where he became a senior manager. (As his daughters were born in Bahrain, Geoff often referred to them as his 'Bahraini daughters'.)

Years later, in 1975, as Y.B.A.Kanoo and Norwich Union prepared to celebrate the Silver Jubilee of their partnership, Jack Spelman wrote a nostalgic note to Geoff Jones (who, by then, was International Manager, General Business, Norwich Union International, UK). Spelman reflected: 'I can quite clearly recall signing that first policy, BPG/50, All Risks for $1,000. This covered the transfer of a rusty Ovaltine tin containing natural pearls from Bahrain to Aden'.

Staff structure develops – partnership principles defined

For many years, especially before the First World War, Haji Yusuf had relied heavily on Indian *karani* clerks, in particular his chief clerk Mr Thorb and V. C. Gallon and Narayan Kernaka. The reason was that in the early part of the twentieth century, few Bahrainis spoke or wrote English or were trained to undertake office work, even in Arabic. As a result, Haji Yusuf employed Arabs (including Omanis and Saudis) to take care of correspondence and accounts which had to be written in Arabic. Indians looked after all his office work involving the English language.

In time, two sections developed in our company: one for Arabic affairs; and another which dealt with foreign companies which had branch offices in Bahrain (including banks), and their head offices overseas. In this case, the language of communication was English, even though it was not necessarily the native language of those involved (for example, German and Japanese companies with whom Haji Yusuf had developed business).

The first inkling of organisational change for us took place in 1940 when Mr Andrews was appointed as Y.B.A.Kanoo's General Manager. (Not only was he the first Englishman to join our company but also, so I have been told by several people, he was the first Englishman to work for an Arab company anywhere in the Arabian Gulf region.) In 1950, he was followed by John Bradford.

By now, the international shipping industry had expanded greatly and was more sophisticated than before the Second World War. Clearly, Y.B.A.Kanoo needed a technically qualified manager to run its shipping department. It was noticeable, too, that several essential jobs (other than that of General Manager) were being performed by Europeans. This had evolved because, at that time, neither Ahmed Kanoo nor my father would allow Gray Mackenzie (an international company) to be the only company to employ European staff. As a result, our family sought to provide a very competitive service in commercial, shipping and travel activities.

This did not go down too well with Gray Mackenzie. It was not unheard of for their British staff to insult and obstruct our British shipping staff, and even blackball their applications for various club memberships, just because they were working for an Arab company. The result, however, was detrimental to Gray Mackenzie. Their British staff underestimated their fellow countrymen's sense of personal pride. While, no doubt, our British staff settled such injustices on a personal basis, how this was achieved is not the concern of my story. However, at a professional level, I do know that our British staff avenged this humiliating treatment and proved their prowess in the business area by working harder and longer hours. In turn, this added effort had a positive effect for us.

When our shipping operation as a whole could justifiably boast standards of excellence, and we had more agencies and ships at the

Gulf ports than our competitor could claim, this arrogant attitude mellowed. Gray Mackenzie started to watch us and follow our moves. We beat them at their own game. Relationships between Kanoo and Gray Mackenzie then began to improve and we regarded each other as professional equals. We started to co-operate and co-exist. We competed hard, but cleanly.

The significant changes took place in 1954. Y.B.A.Kanoo had already established the basis of a commercial department having entered into an arrangement with the Dutch company, Harmsey Vermey and Dunlop (HVD), traders in tinned vegetables and cigarettes. The manager of this operation was Henry Soek. Our shipping operations were then divided into two. The Kanoo Slipway in Muharraq, started in 1954 to maintain our fleet, was capable of taking vessels of up to 15 tons. The slipway was managed by the Dutch who also looked after the Dutch shipping lines for which we were the agent. Cyril Jones (who joined Y.B.A.Kanoo as our General Manager in 1952) was appointed the first manager of our newly-defined shipping department, responsible for all 'other' shipping, travel and insurance services.

In early 1954 he introduced the concept of management consultants to our family. Although Kanoo's business was expanding rapidly, the company's organisational structure and systems were not keeping up with development. A team of consultants from the British firm, Urwick Orr, was installed in our Manama office. The team's brief was not to reorganise Y.B.A.Kanoo, but to document our organisational structure and produce an operations manual.

Two years later our accounting system was reviewed. Hitherto, Yassin Mullah Ahmed, a Bahraini who had been a good friend and a loyal employee of the Kanoo family, had taken care of the Arabic accounts. As he tended to commit almost as much to memory as to paper, it was clear that sooner or later Yassin's 'personal computer' would run out of memory. So it was that Saba and Company was asked to implement a formal accounting system, capable of rapid expansion and accessible to more than one person.

In one special aspect, these transitions had prompted my maternal grandfather, Ali, to look further ahead. He engaged the help of some friends and together they wrote a paper in Arabic which they called the *Deed of Gift and Transfer*. This had been no impulsive whim, but the result of several years' thought which had evolved after Haji Yusuf's demise on 21 December 1945.

At that time, Haji Ali and Haji Jassim had inherited everything which Haji Yusuf had owned, including various properties and, of course, the business which he requested should retain his name, even after his death. In 1945, the family did not own a great deal of actual money, only about 10,000 rupees. With the memory of the 1930s recession still sharp in his mind, Haji Ali decided to make some formal, structured provision for the family business and future generations.

Thus, on 25 April 1954 (Sha'aban 22nd 1373) Jassim Mohamed Kanoo and Ali Mohamed Kanoo signed the *Deed of Gift and Transfer,* witnessed by representatives of the Court of Bahrain and the Government of Bahrain, Ahmed Hassan Ebrahim and Yassin Mulla Ahmed. Little was Haji Ali to know how timely his initiative had been, for just a few months later, in 1954, he too died.

It was a condition that the sons of Jassim and Ali Kanoo should form a company with the wealth granted to them by Haji Yusuf. In accordance with that ruling they agreed to appoint the eldest son, Ahmed Ali Kanoo, as Chairman of the Board with Mohamed Jassim Kanoo (my father) as Deputy Chairman. Abdulla Ali Kanoo and Mubarak Jassim Kanoo were nominated as members of the Board of Directors. The other sons would play an active role in the day-to-day affairs of the business. Together, they owned properties registered in their names, as well as two commercial firms: Yusuf bin Ahmed Kanoo, and Jassim and Ali Kanoo. They also represented local and foreign firms, maintained current and deposit accounts with banks in Bahrain and abroad, and owned shares in some other companies.

Although Jassim had five sons and Ali three sons, because of their love for each other they decided to share the combined inheritance equally between them all. (The alternative would have been for Jassim's five sons to have received a fifth each of their father's share, and Ali's three sons a third each of their father's share.) As Abdul Latif later abrogated his share, the inheritance was divided equally among the remaining shareholders. Thus, when Haji Ali died in 1954, just a few months after the *Deed of Gift and Transfer* had been signed and later, when Haji Jassim died in 1982, the document was our official family guide. It is for this reason that Ahmed Kanoo and his brothers and nephews attach great significance to its relevance and legal standing.

Y.B.A.Kanoo Commercial Division evolves

In essence, our fledgling commercial department began in 1951. BAPCO's new local purchase policy and its support of local industry was the catalyst for change. As a result, Y.B.A.Kanoo set up two construction and building maintenance companies, Arabian Construction and Mechanical Engineers (ACME) and Kanoo Construction Company (KCC), both of which secured lucrative contracts from BAPCO.

In 1951 Abdulla Al-Ghanim of Kuwait and Messrs D.&C.& William Press Limited formed ACME as a joint venture with Y.B.A.Kanoo as its partner in Bahrain. The idea was that ACME, an international company based in Bahrain, would provide specialist mechanical engineering services to maintain BAPCO's refinery.

KCC was a wholly-owned subsidiary of Y.B.A.Kanoo, a civil engineering company with Bill Docherty appointed as General Manager. KCC's main purpose was to maintain the Swedish pre-fabricated houses in Awali (built in the late 1940s), and BAPCO's older coral-stone '*gasht*' houses which had been constructed in the 1930s as the oil-camp's first dormitory houses.

In 1957, Bill Brien arrived in Bahrain as KCC's cost accountant the result of an 'accident'. While attending an accountancy conference in London during that year, an advertisement in the *Daily Telegraph* caught his eye. The company concerned, which to Brien looked like another George Wimpey type of construction company, needed the services of an accountant. Since qualifying, Brien had worked in nearly every industry except civil engineering, so he decided to 'kill two birds with one stone'. The advertised job gave him the chance to gain more accountancy experience and accumulate some ready cash. Like many people, he intended to be an expatriate for one tour only, in this case, two and a half years. He is still with us nearly forty years later, the only non-family member to be a Director of the Y.B.A.Kanoo Group.

When Brien found out that KCC was not 'another George Wimpey', he initially turned down the job but then changed his mind. Why, I do not know. He spent the next three years in Awali controlling KCC's financial management, with Bill Docherty still as the company's General Manager. According to Brien, there were two reasons why KCC did so well: BAPCO engaged local contractors, such as ourselves; we employed European supervision familiar with western construction procedures. So although in one sense KCC was perceived as a local contractor we were lucky enough to be awarded specialist jobs for which we could charge accordingly.

As time passed, ACME found it difficult to compete with other construction companies in Bahrain because of the burden of increased mechanical engineering overheads. Meanwhile, KCC continued to trade primarily because BAPCO had made no alternative provision for the houses in Awali to be maintained. Nevertheless, since KCC was a wholly-owned subsidiary of Y.B.A.Kanoo, the parent company controlled its destiny. In 1959, KCC was wound down. After ACME completed the construction of our new main office in Manama in 1960, Bill Docherty and Bill Brien were transferred to Y.B.A.Kanoo's mainstream operations, Docherty as Head of Administration and Property Maintenance, and Brien to install budgetary control in our Manama offices. Three years later, ACME was wound down and ceased trading in 1963.

Meanwhile, one of our most successful episodes of diversification had occurred in 1958 . Our family realised that when the proposed regional deep-water ports 'came on stream', lucrative lighterage business would decline, if not end. Since this activity generated about a third of Y.B.A.Kanoo's shipping department's sales income, the potential loss of this business was a serious threat to our profitability. So, as an adjunct to our existing activities, we formed the Mercantile Department (now the Commercial Division), to market industrial plant and machinery.

Although heavy-duty cranes, compressors and fork-lifts hardly have the same cachet as air travel, this diversification proved to be immensely prudent and profitable. Among the agencies we held were BASF chemical, Grove cranes, Hyster fork-lifts, Bedford dump-trucks, Lincoln welders, C.P.T. compressors and Perkins/Rolls Royce engines and generators.

The division was started by Ted Whitticks, a shrewd trader. He faced continual difficulties with the family as he was introducing a new business they did not understand, especially when it came to buying stock, from which there was always an unsold percentage. To my uncles, this meant 'losses'. They were used to the service industry where capital is not a major prerequisite. Left-over stock was not an issue. But Ted persevered and established the department. He collected first class agencies and tried marketing them in Bahrain. After the third year, he succeeded when BAPCO started to buy from him on a regular basis. The construction 'boom' had begun, too, during which Ted made sure that our name was known to all the local contractors.

As the commercial department in Bahrain grew in strength, it was emulated by our operation in Saudi Arabia. This concentrated on oil-field supplies, hence the formation of our company, Oilfield Supply and Services (OFSS) in 1958, managed by Max Rasquinha.

It was during this period, when I returned to Bahrain in the summer for my school holidays, that I was put to work in one department or another. Once I was sent to Whitticks. For two days, he kept me sitting on a chair doing nothing. On the third day, I objected and so he told me that he suspected that I was a service-man and not a mercantile-man. If that were not so, then I would have to prove myself to him. (I guess he really thought that I would prefer the comfort of an administrator's office to the hardship of an industrial site!)

Anyway, I decided to prove myself and Whitticks promptly sent me to the warehouse where we manufactured insulation blocks by steaming pellets of polyethylene into a steel mould. As it was summer, it was very hot in there. My job was to cut the insulation blocks into specific sizes, using a hand-saw. Much as I wished to, I did not complain. After I passed this test, Whitticks then sent me to the spare-parts warehouse to work with our 'crazy' Indian storekeeper Koko. He had memorised the location of every spare part we stocked, thousands of them spread out along rows of steel shelving which stretched the length and breadth of the warehouse, 100 feet (30.5 metres) long by 70 feet (21.5 metres) wide. But when Koko went on leave, everything stopped, or took a long time because no one else knew where to find things. As a result, we started to organise ourselves. My contribution was to help install cardex and 'bin' systems. After this, we knew in which bin, or part of a shelf, each spare part was stored.

Mohamed Kanoo and British American Tobacco

While all these changes were taking place, my father was carving out another niche for our company. Mubarak Kanoo often refers to him as General MacArthur because of his persistence, strength and stature. Ahmed Kanoo speaks of my father's kindness, generosity and sincerity, but above all, his determination. He didn't care for people telling him: 'I cannot do this' or 'I cannot do that'. Instead, he would do the task himself and shame his staff into following his example, or prove to others that the task could be done. Even His Highness, Shaikh Salman, called him *Al Midfa*, (the cannon), because if you needed something done and done properly, you gave it to Mohamed Kanoo and he would not rest until it was finished.

But, as I understand it, all this hard work was not directed at securing new agency contracts with foreign companies. My father's endeavours were simply enabling existing agency agreements to run properly within the resources he had available but in a way that was acceptable to the principals overseas. After all, why should a businessman sitting in his London or Rotterdam office either know or particularly care that, for instance, we had no regular electricity supply or mains water. A shipping company wanted its ships to be discharged and turned around quickly. How this was accomplished was left to Mohamed Kanoo, 'the cannon'.

To motivate the staff, to be efficient and to excel, was a tough 'act' to keep going and up to scratch, particularly as we were head-to-head with the then powerful Gray Mackenzie in most of our functions, especially shipping. To succeed against the competition, we knew we had to be that little bit better. In this respect, there are a lot of stories about my father.

For example, he would be the first to board an incoming vessel for which we were the agent. He was renowned, too, for standing out in front of the office at seven o'clock in the morning waiting for staff to arrive, greeting them with 'Good morning' or 'Good afternoon', depending on whether they were punctual or late. But for all this discipline, my father was always discreet, particularly if staff came to him with their personal problems. Without making a big deal or telling other people, he would try to solve their problems quietly, no matter what they were. He was also generous to all those around him. Giving was second nature to him, whether it was a present to a little child or to a VIP. He always kept a stock of little gifts.

Throughout this period, Ahmed Kanoo and my father worked as a team, as they had done since their youth. For instance, as the agents of the Rafidain Oil Company during the 1950s, Y.B.A.Kanoo was responsible for re-fuelling BOAC's flying boats which transitted through Bahrain. Ahmed Kanoo told me that twice a week when the planes arrived, either my father or he drove the fuel-barge out to the aircraft anchored in the Khor Qalai'yah area, (just beyond where the Guest Palace was built in Gudaibiyah, completed in 1955.) Using only hand-pumps, they refuelled the flying-boats themselves. This team-work had been their hallmark since they were young, each knowing the other's mind and moves. Hence Ahmed was the 'front man' who sought agencies, finance and contracts, while Mohamed operated them to make a profit.

During Ahmed's absences abroad on business trips, Mohamed led the family and the company. He worked them both hard but fairly. He was hot tempered and it was not unusual to hear his voice above others. But if he felt that he had hurt someone's feelings, he would always call that person back and apologise, no matter how minor a position he held.

My father was also known to be concerned for the community

around him. He was a leader and patron of the Al-Ahli Club, one of the old cultural and sports clubs in Bahrain which aims to improve young Bahrainis' opportunities and skills in sport and cultural activities. Abdulrahman, one of my father's brothers, now leads the Al-Ahli Club, looking after it as if it were his own, spending much time and money on it as one of his contributions to the community.

In his late years my father contracted Parkinson's Disease, an illness which attacks the nerves. During this period it gradually became physically difficult for him to move. But until his last days, he kept his house open to all the family and friends to visit him, drink and eat with him daily. He became a focal point: 'I will see you at Mohamed's house tonight' was heard by people of all walks of life, whether they happened to be a Minister or merchant, tally-clerk or typist. His house was open to all.

Several major agencies which became part of Y.B.A.Kanoo's portfolio during the 1950s and 1960s were because of my father's efforts (and to some extent, those of his own father, Haji Jassim). According to Brien: 'One very big pet of Mohamed's was British American Tobacco. He was the man who made it possible for us to take on that agency both in the local environment and with BAT itself. That was in 1958'.

While Bill Brien cannot recall how the initial approach was made, Ahmed Kanoo remembers the sequence of events. British American Tobacco had another agent in Bahrain but members of our family knew some of the BAT directors in London who, from time to time, visited Bahrain. Gradually, a friendly relationship developed. One day, BAT management hinted to my father rather indirectly that, since the death of Mr Aujan (a close friend of our family and the head of BAT's agency in Bahrain), BAT were not very happy with their agent's current performance. The inference was that Y.B.A.Kanoo was being offered 'first refusal'. Should we decline the agency, then BAT would offer it to another merchant family. BAT told us that Y.B.A.Kanoo seemed to be a well organised company and that if we took over the agency, BAT would support us in technical matters. In Ahmed Kanoo's words: 'Mohamed convinced me. I told him, "Let's go for it. If we don't take it, somebody else will".'

It was agreed and in April 1959, Y.B.A.Kanoo, Bahrain, was appointed distributor for the British American Tobacco Company. Brand names included Du Maurier, Embassy, Players Navy Cut, Lucky Strike and 555 State Express. In October 1963, Y.B.A.Kanoo, Abu Dhabi, was appointed BAT's distributor. For many years, this was one of our top three agencies in terms of sales generation in Bahrain, the other two being Maersk Line (one of the biggest shipping operators in the Gulf) and British Airways (with whom we have worked for over sixty years).

To this day our relationship with BAT has remained very cordial. To me the most poignant aspect of our long association with British American Tobacco is that, even during the many years of my father's long illness, not one of the BAT senior management ever failed to visit him during their visits to Bahrain.

Chapter 9

Portraits of Progress

Despite advances in the aviation industry during the 1950s, for many people travelling to and from Bahrain, sturdy if not stylish steamers remained the only available and reasonably-priced mode of international transport. R.B.Tandon, a former Kanoo senior accountant now retired in Canada, recalls his journey from India to take up his new appointment with our company in 1953.

Many passengers slept on the open deck which for most of the journey was covered. Only when the steamer called into port would the deck covering be removed so that cargo could be discharged and new consignments taken on board. This diversion to the routine of the week-long voyage to Bahrain, only occurred when the steamer called into Karachi, Muscat and Dubai ports.

The cabins were well appointed and comfortable, with two passengers assigned to each. The timings for breakfast, lunch and dinner were all fixed. In between times, facilities such as table tennis, darts and indoor games helped to break the monotony. As cabin passengers had the use of an upstairs deck, they could watch the ever-changing spectacle of wildlife enjoying the freedom of their natural habitat, the sea and sky. Flying fish, dolphins at play and birds flying in flowing formations provided a fascinating spectacle for hours on end. The hazards of such freedom became too apparent when the crew cast their lines or nets to catch the preferred main meal of the day, fresh fish, even though all food needed for the voyage was taken on board at both the port of origin, Bombay, and then Karachi.

The only aspect which tended to mar the experience, was the variation in weather patterns according to the season and geographical location. During the winter the Indian Ocean is very pleasant, but the Arabian Gulf at that time of the year can be stormy. Conversely, summer at sea in the Arabian Gulf tends to be calm, yet after steamers pass through the Straits of Hormuz into the exposed ocean, the sea is often choppy. Either way, any hardship caused by seasickness only lasted two or three days.

Once steamers anchored offshore from Bahrain, lighters sailed out to the deep water where passengers were transferred to large flat-bottomed boats which could be rowed, or which sometimes deployed an auxiliary sail. Many lighters, capable of carrying between twenty and twenty-five passengers, had seats arranged along each side of the boat with an open space in the centre for stowing baggage. In the lighters which had no fixed seating, the crew unrolled carpets across the wooden planking. They added both colour and comfort, and somewhere for passengers to sit. If there was little or no wind, sails were useless. Instead, the boats had to be rowed from the steamer to Manama pier (three or four crew members per boat), about a half-hour journey.

Manama – shoreline and souq

In the early 1950s, Manama's almost undeveloped shoreline was punctuated with very few landmarks. Hussain Yateem's filling station was a notable exception, opened in 1938 to sell BAPCO fuel near the dhow jetty on what was then Government Road (now Avenue), and remaining in service for more than half a century. According to folklore, no one in Bahrain during the 1930s knew what a filling station should look like, so the completed edifice bore a striking resemblence to a simple mosque. (Only Hussain Yateem really knows, but it makes a nice story, particularly since he decided in the early 1990s to have the filling station demolished to make way for a very fine 'real' mosque. For a brief moment in time, its striking architectural features held pride of place on that section of Government Road. Now, rather sadly, it is overshadowed by Batelco's adjacent new high-rise, glass-faced, commercial centre.)

Near Bab Al-Bahrain Square the shoreline was dominated by warehouses (on the site which the Regency Intercontinental Hotel now occupies) and the customs shed which served Mina Manama. The customs shed, later to be replaced by the new Manama Post Office, faced Bab Al-Bahrain Square.

Gray Mackenzie's former office on Al-Khalifa Road (scheduled for demolition and re-development) now faces the modern Yateem Centre from where the sea ventured a little further inland. I always remember seeing as a boy the flag-poles in front of Gray Mackenzie's office. Meanwhile, until Government Road was extended as far as Ras Al-Rumaan (Headland of Pomegranates), better known today as Paradise roundabout, this strip of land was just a beach. (It was not until the late 1960s that the sea in front of the Government Road was reclaimed to form the land on which Government House, the Sheraton Commercial Complex and the Diplomatic Area were built.)

Inevitably, my memories of Manama as a ten-year-old school-boy are not those of an adult. Nevertheless, I was aware of the big 'names' of other established local trading houses (apart from Y.B.A.Kanoo), such as A.A.Zayani, Hussain Yateem, Yusuf Almoayyed, Ashrafs and Jashanmal. The Fakhro and Algosaibi families were well established, as were Gajaria, Al-Sharif, Al-Tajir, Darwish, Mudaifa, Al-Mattar, Garabali, Mannai, Shatter, Al-Majid and Aujan, to mention a few.

Most of the larger stores, many of which were run by Indians, were located on Government Road. Dorabjee ran a prominent shop selling sun-hats, shoes, shirts and Ecko radios. He was also more or less the principal importer of tinned foods. Clothing specialists, Rochiram, were situated nearby. Opposite, Jashanmals' store was housed just about on the sea-front in what used to be the Hilal building.

Alongside the Bab Al-Bahrain Road (which still leads to the souq), several stores sold household goods and garments, in particular clothing traders C. Kumar and Trikamadas, side-by-side with general merchants Khedouri (a prominent Jewish family) and Behbehani. Not far away, Al-Ajaji (General Motors' agent), Khalil Kanoo (the Ford distributor) and Bhatia's auto spares business were all well established.

Beyond Bab Al-Bahrain Road, lay the maze of the souq. Some shops had some sort of a display, but they were nothing compared to what we see now. During opening hours most traders folded back the wooden shutters which secured their shop-fronts so that customers could pause to see their entire stock stacked up in piles, perhaps make a purchase, and then continue on their way.

During the winter, when tides were very high, it was not uncommon for the sea to flood right up the Bab Al-Bahrain Road. The old Manama Post Office on Al Khalifa Avenue (now Bab Al-Bahrain Police Station) was the first casualty. Until BAPCO produced some shelves on which mail bags could be stacked off the floor, letters, cheques, bills and so on, were often soaked and ruined.

In 1953, R. B. Tandon's first impression was that Bahrain was a very small place, certainly when compared with Bombay. Very few people owned cars. There were few refrigerators. Cold water was produced by melting ice bought from ice factories. The blocks were one foot square by two feet long (30 sq cm x 60 cm), large enough to preserve for two or three days in large thermos flasks, before the ice completely melted. Ice-carts pulled by large white donkeys distributed the blocks (usually covered with jute bags) throughout Manama.

J. A. Court, who returned to Bahrain during 1951 as Manager of the Eastern Bank, found quite a contrast when compared with his first 'tour' in 1939 as a junior sub-accountant. In those days, drinking water supplies still came from Bombay by the 'slow mail' British India Steam Navigation Company's boats. He remembers having to send individual water drums out in launches, in all weathers, to the steamers anchored a mile or so offshore. Now, utilities were a little more sophisticated, including the installation in the bank of the latest York air-conditioning equipment. After the engineers who had commissioned the system left Bahrain, things began to go wrong. For some mysterious reason, despite a tank of chilled water being maintained at 36°F. in the garden, the room temperature in the building remained the same as that outside. After what Court described as some 'astringent' correspondence between himself and the bank's Head Office in London (one of his letters being described as 'intemperate'), the London architect agreed to come out to Bahrain to investigate, but only at the end of the hot weather. No-one had thought to check-out the strainers which, by now, were 'gummed up' with building contractors' rubble and other rubbish. After the pipework was cleaned out, 'the system worked like a dream and we were almost frozen out!'

Yet, for most organisations and homes, electric fans were the only internal cooling facility, except for those few traditional houses which had a windtower incorporated within their structure. During the summer months, most people slept in the open. Even when Mr V.A.Subermanian (Mani), joined our company a decade later, Bahrain still had little to offer in the way of a regular electricity supply and air-conditioning. As a paying-guest of a friend and his wife, Mani recalls the tedious summer evening routine. After returning to the house from the office in the evening, one man stationed himself at the top of the staircase which led up to the roof, while another operated a ground-floor tap attached to a stand-pipe. Together, they worked a system whereby the men would meet on the staircase and exchange buckets, the up-buckets being full of cold water and the down-buckets empty ready to be re-filled. Sufficient water had to be poured onto the roof until the plaster covering the terrace had been cooled, sometimes requiring as many as fifty or sixty buckets of water. After the plaster dried a little it was possible to spread out mattresses, sheets and pillows, lie down and attempt to sleep. But in the peak of the summer when the temperature and humidity were high, more than two or three hours' sleep a night were a rare luxury. By four o'clock in the morning, the sun had risen. Fifteen minutes later, its full rays together with swarms of buzzing flies, would render further sleep impossible.

Tandon lived in a district called Mutanajab, now the Mutanabi Road in the heart of the souq. This area, just behind our large family house, was known for its specialist jewellery shops where people came to deal in pearls, particularly at the end of the diving season. Tandon told me that when he prepared to sleep on his roof terrace, he always felt that if his employer could cope with the frustrations of the summer in this way, then there was nothing wrong in his living like that too.

Our Manama office, built on the site where the Kanoo Tower now stands, was not such a big office in the early 1950s. There were few departments and limited staff, maybe fifty employees. Our main activities were trading, travel and shipping, with the burgeoning insurance business being a significant addition to our operations.

Working in the accounts department on the ground floor, alongside other administrative offices, Tandon occupied most of his days 'pen-pushing'. Most records were handwritten in English, although Yassin Mullah Ahmed still maintained the Arabic accounting books. (Later, Yassin helped Mubarak in the UAE and Abdulla in Saudi Arabia.) Those were the days of fountain pens and bottles of ink. Tandon remembers that as the heat and humidity rose, perspiration trickled down his hand. Wet ledgers and smudged ink were unavoidable occupational hazards.

There were no telex machines and few telephones. It was possible to make international calls but the facility was very limited. Urgent cables were sent from the old Cable and Wireless office, then opposite what is now the Yateem Centre.

Milestones and landmarks

By 1953 I was eleven years of age and considered old enough to begin some basic grooming for the time when I too would join the family business. During the school holidays, in particular, I would go into the office to learn about our company. There, I met Peter Chaplin who arrived in Bahrain as a Ship Board Representative of Y.B.A.Kanoo. (Little did I know then, that many years later he would be such a great help to me in Abu Dhabi when I was launched there by my father to work and told to 'get on with it'.)

Peter Chaplin's career background was in shipping, having worked with Portline Limited, a subsidiary of Cunard. During that time, a man called Jimmy O'Dwyer had regularly called into Chaplin's office to collect bills of lading. O'Dwyer's employer was P. B. Broomhall, the forwarding company which was our London agent. O'Dwyer and Chaplin became friendly. In time, Chaplin met Garth Filton, Broomhall's Manager. It turned out that Broomhalls looked after Abdulaziz, Hamed and Abdul Latif Kanoo when they were in England, (as they did Khalil Shakib and Mohamed Zobari.) When my cousin Yusuf and I were at school in England, we were taken care of by Lt. Colonel Arnold C. Galloway, a senior manager in CALTEX's London office (then at Knightsbridge Green, near Harrods department store) who acted as BAPCO's UK representative between 1950 and 1968.

This was not our family's first encounter with Lt. Col. Galloway. Prior to this post, he had been Political Agent in Bahrain in 1946. Upon Haji Yusuf Kanoo's death on 21 December 1945, Galloway wrote to the British Resident in the Gulf informing him of this event, adding: 'You will doubtless let me know if the jewels of the various orders of which he was a member are returnable'. Since such decorations were given on the condition that they are returned to the Crown when the decorated person dies, the outcome was no surprise. The Political Agent collected Haji Yusuf's decorations from my grandfather, Jassim Kanoo.

In time, Jimmy O'Dwyer joined Y.B.A.Kanoo to set up its first London office, a company called Arabian Gulf Services (formed on 20 February 1957). Until then, most of Y.B.A.Kanoo's UK expatriate recruitment had been handled by P. B. Broomhall, through whom Peter Chaplin was recruited to join us in Bahrain.

At the same time, Haji Jassim had begun to concentrate on his Gulf-wide cement importing and distribution business. For a few years previously, he and his brother, Haji Ali, had managed the Y.B.A.Kanoo company. But little by little, Haji Jassim left the running of the company to Haji Ali, Ahmed Kanoo and my father. From the 1950s onwards, Haji Jassim focused his efforts on chartering ships to transport bagged cement to various ports up and down the Arabian Gulf where his appointed agents sold the cement in Kuwait, Saudi Arabia, Qatar, Abu Dhabi and Dubai. At one time, Haji Jassim imported and distributed more cement than anyone else in the area, often having between three and seven chartered ships operating up and down the Gulf.

It was also during the 1950s that our Manama office building

top *Al-Ahmadiah,* the first vessel to enter the new port in Abu Dhabi (1972), under the auspices of Kanoo Agency.

above Shaikh Zayed bin Sultan Al Nahayan and Shaikh Rashid bin Saeed Al Maktoum with Khalid Kanoo, representing the ship's agents, led by Said Al Darmaki, inspecting the berthed vessel.

top Abdulaziz Kanoo and James Hamed Belgrave
presenting a gift to Hafiz Wahba sitting with
Shaikh Salman Bin Hamed Al Khalifa, Ruler of
Bahrain (1953).

above The Kanoo senior family members:
Norwich Union Insurance magazine (1952).

right Kanoo Travel Agency 'Woody' Ford station wagon, which shuttled passengers to and from the airport (1950).

below Inaugurating Kanoo Travel office in Bahrain; from right, Shaikh Mubarak, Shaikh Salman (Ruler of Bahrain), Shaikh Jabir and Shaikh Mohamed (1946).

bottom First BAC I-II to join Gulf Aviation being met by Captain Bodger, Hussain Yateem and Ahmed Kanoo.

opposite First dedicated travel office in the Gulf. Mohamed and Mubarak Kanoo with BOAC station and airport managers Mr Parker and Mr Batt (1946).

inset Gulf Aviation last Board of Directors' meeting in London before creation of Gulf Air. From left, Ahmed Kanoo, Ali Wazan, Sami Gayid, Tom Urbin, Hussain Yateem, Khalaf Al Utaiba, Adil Algosaibi and Mohamed Kanoo (1973).

top Yusuf bin Ahmed Kanoo, the first licensed IATA Agency in the Gulf (1947).

above Bahrain Marine Airport at Juffair (1930).

left Two unexploded Italian bombs dropped on Bahrain during the Second World War.

top The second Kanoo office in Dubai (1965).

above Kanoo main building in Bahrain, the first in the Gulf with an all-steel structure (British Steel), opened in 1960 by the Ruler, Shaikh Salman bin Hamed Al Khalifa.

opposite ARAMCO geological survey party exploring the Eastern Desert of Saudi Arabia (1952).

above Ahmed Kanoo with his guests, King Saud bin Abdul-Aziz and Shaikh Salman al Khalifa (1954).

left Shaikh Shakhbut Al Nahayan, Ruler of Abu Dhabi, arriving in Bahrain on an official visit, Shaikh Mubarak on his left (1960).

began to show signs of stress in more ways than one. The number of employees had increased to the extent that we were nearly bursting at the seams. and the condition of the premises was shaky, to say the least. According to family folklore, it was during Hamed's wedding party in July 1958 that guests' minds were focused on more than the celebrations. With hundreds of people assembled on the second storey of the building, such was the precarious condition of the floor that everyone became quite worried that the structure was about to collapse, taking all the guests with it.

It is unclear exactly when a decision was made to rebuild the entire block. However, after Hamed's cousins, Mubarak, Abdulrahman and Abdulaziz were married at a combined ceremony in 1956 and Bill Brien had arrived in Bahrain during 1957, plans were made to lease temporary office accommodation, vacate and demolish our unsafe office building and rebuild it. With these arrangements in place, soon after Hamed's wedding in 1958 we moved into the Al-Wazzan building (on the site of the present Salahuddin building). There we maintained our temporary offices until 31 January 1960, the official opening date of the new building, the first to be constructed in the Arabian Gulf region using a steel beam structure. I remember Mr Omair bin Yousif, an Abu Dhabian leading merchant and travel agent, asking me in 1978 whether our large office block had collapsed or not. I told him, 'It is still standing, thank you, and why the question?' He replied that he was planning to construct a building using steel, and was just checking.

To complete the story, although momentarily it takes us forward in time, our on-going office development created a whole new dimension to our presence in Manama. Phase One of our office expansion programme entailed extending the 1960 building in the direction of the souq, away from Al Khalifa Road. In 1976, the penthouse was demolished to make way for the present fourth floor executive offices, Phase One extension. In 1977, Phase Two was completed, a new building next to Phase One, now Norwich Union's headquarters in Bahrain. Phase Three, generally known as Kanoo Tower, was also built in 1977 on the site of our original old family house adjacent to Tijjar Avenue. This provided offices for solicitors and consultants. Later, the first two floors of Kanoo Tower were converted to become a shopping mall called Zainah Plaza (named after Haji Yusuf's mother). This was the first retail enterprise in the history of our company.

Reverting to 1960, while our new office building took shape, plans were made to construct a guest-house and complex of family houses in the Mahooz area, near to the old race-course in Adliya. Apart from three houses and a block of four flats which had been built by an Italian, Gardechi, in 1956, there was nothing else on that compound at that time. The Kanoo Guest House was built first, constructed by ACME and opened on the same day as the Manama office building: 31 January 1960.

Then seven identical family houses were completed for the equal owners of Y.B.A.Kanoo: Mohamed, Mubarak, Abdulrahman and Abdulaziz (sons of Jassim); and Ahmed, Abdulla and Hamed (sons of Ali). After this, a bungalow was added to the complex specifically to house British American Tobacco personnel during their visits to Bahrain. This building-phase was completed with the construction of two more houses (built by CCC, a Lebanese company): one house each for the families of the late Haji Ali and Haji Jassim. Later, more villas were constructed to house our senior staff, including one for the Manager of Middle East Airlines.

Y.B.A.Kanoo – Gray Mackenzie's sub-agent in Saudi Arabia

From Bahrain, my story returns to Saudi Arabia where changes were also taking place. In 1954, ARAMCO altered its corporate policy. From operating an agency service itself, the oil company began to contract local Saudi Arabian companies. Thus, four agents established themselves in Ras Tannurah: Gray Mackenzie and Y.B.A.Kanoo, the largest, and Algosaibi and Alireza. In 1957, Y.B.A.Kanoo took over the provision of stevedoring in Ras Tannurah, managed for us by Abdulmihsin Abdulghani.

This *modus operandi* continued to operate fairly smoothly until 1964 when, for reasons explained shortly, Gray Mackenzie's operating licence was withdrawn and it decided to leave Saudi Arabia. Thereafter, Y.B.A.Kanoo came to an arrangement with Gray Mackenzie whereby, for the next five years, we acted as its sub-agent in the Kingdom. The origins of this change can be found many years earlier when, during the 1920s, the Saudi Arabians considered the Buraimi oasis area, and the region to the west of it, to belong to Saudi Arabia. In July 1933 King Abdul-Aziz Ibn Saud granted a petroleum concession to the Standard Oil Company of California (SOCAL) for 'the eastern portion' of the Kingdom, within its frontiers, including the Buraimi Oasis area. Since these frontiers were not defined, the United States Government was thus obliged to enquire of the British Government, the precise extent of the concession. The latter decreed that the eastern frontier of the

Kingdom was the so called Blue Line, as agreed by the British and Turkish Governments in the 1913–14 Convention.

Not surprisingly, the Government of the Kingdom did not accept the Blue Line definition of its eastern frontier. A series of protracted negotiations led to no agreement. In the late 1940s, when new exploration methods fostered the notion that oil might be present in the strata beneath the disputed territory, the prospect of finding an amicable solution seemed more unlikely than ever.

In 1949, the 'trigger' for conflict was released when ARAMCO despatched several parties to survey the coastal strip of Abu Dhabi's territory as far east as Abu Dhabi island. This precipitated another round of protests and counter-representations, all of which came to nothing. In August 1952, the Shaikh of Hamasah (one of the three Omani villages bordering Buraimi oasis) assembled a contingent of followers. In October 1952, an armed confrontation between Omani and Saudi forces was averted by a 'standstill agreement' negotiated in Jeddah between the British and Saudi Arabian Governments. In the following month, the British Government expressed the view that the disputed area was so large that the case should be submitted to an international court of arbitration. A tribunal opened on 11 September 1955. But these hearings, like previous efforts to resolve the dispute, broke down and the tribunal was never reconvened.

A month later, on 26 October 1955, the forces of the Sultan of Muscat and Oman and those those of the Ruler of Abu Dhabi, supported by the Trucial Oman Levies, with the backing of the British Government, confronted a Saudi Arabian military detachment. (Edward Henderson wrote a detailed account of this incident in his book, *This Strange Eventful History*.) Sir Anthony Eden, then the British Prime Minister, explained away his actions by declaring that the Riyadh Line, as amended in 1937, was unilaterally declared the frontier between Abu Dhabi and Saudi Arabia. For a while, the issue was left alone, but only for as long as the British Government remained legally the 'spokesman' for the emirate of Abu Dhabi. During the late 1960s, when Saudi Arabia's support was lobbied during the negotiations to form a new federation (later the United Arab Emirates), the frontier became a major topic of discussion once again.

This *fait accompli* from 1955 provoked the Government of Saudi Arabia into some form of retaliatory action against the British who, they believed, were against them. Their response was to withdraw the privilege which British companies had enjoyed for many years, namely their ability to operate in the Kingdom on a par with Saudi Arabian companies. British companies had a choice: leave the country entirely; enter into a joint-venture with a Saudi Arabian company; or appoint an agent to carry on their business. In the end Gray Mackenzie chose to appoint Y.B.A.Kanoo as its agent in Saudi Arabia. This greatly enhanced our shipping agency network since Gray Mackenzie represented several tanker companies whose vessels regularly used Ras Tannurah oil terminal.

The Abu Dhabi–Saudi border dispute was resolved eventually when Mahdi Al-Tajer, amongst others, became very involved in bringing the Abu Dhabian and Saudi Arabian government views closer so that, eventually, they came to an amicable conclusion. Once the Saudi–Abu Dhabi dispute was over, Abu Dhabi negotiated with Oman over Buraimi. In time, Buraimi and Al-Ain merged to appear as if they form one large town. A line was drawn indicating the boundary between the two communities. On one occasion, in 1980, I was shown an iron bar stuck in the side of the road, the only visible mark to separate the two towns. Now it is difficult to tell the two apart as there are no check-points between them.

While all this was going on, an important economic change was being implemented throughout the Arabian Gulf region. At that time, the British still controlled the financial affairs of the area, and maintained the Indian rupee as the region's unit of currency.

In 1959, the Government of India decided to introduce the Gulf rupee to replace the Indian rupee throughout the Arabian Gulf region in an effort to reduce smuggling and so protect the Indian economy. Although the value of the Gulf rupee was equal to the Indian rupee the various denominations for each currency were now printed on different coloured notes. By retaining the same coins for both currencies, however, inevitably the move was only partially successful. It became quite usual for people to transport sacks of silver and copper coins on the British India mail-steamers, rather than smaller, lighter volumes of paper notes. As a result, any benefits which the Government of India might have derived from this policy were more than matched by the confusion, if not inconvenience caused to residents of the Arabian Gulf region. This lasted until 16 October 1965, when the Bahrain dinar (BD) was created as the nation's own unit of currency.

Tied to the US dollar (BD 1 = US$ 2.70), the Bahrain dinar offered us new investment and business opportunities. From 1954 to 1966, Abu Dhabi used rupees, followed by the Bahrain dinar until 1973. Dubai followed a different route, using rupees until 1963 and then adopting the Qatari riyal until 1973. When both Abu Dhabi and Dubai became part of the United Arab Emirates in 1971, a new national currency was planned. The UAE dirham was launched in May 1973.

Bahrain – BASREC is born

Part of our 1960s diversification policy was to form the Bahrain Ship-Repairing and Engineering Company (BASREC) in 1962, under the general management of Mr Green. This occurred when we realised that we needed more ship-repairing capacity and capability, in addition to what we had in Muharraq to service our access needs and those of other marine craft owners.

For our Muharraq slipway (started in 1952), supervised by Abdulaziz Al-Khadhar, we employed fifty or sixty staff (welders, painters, platers and mechanics) under a Dutch engineer. He was responsible for maintaining and servicing our fleet of tugs, launches and barges. Even our craft based in Abu Dhabi and Dubai, as well as in the Ras Tannurah and Khafji terminals in Saudi Arabia, came to our marine base in Bahrain for maintenance. During my school summer holidays, my father decided that I should do something useful instead of lying about enjoying myself. I remember being sent to the slipway for practical training, helping to repair engines (big hot things confined in an engine-room) and to weld barges. The summer temperature in Bahrain averages 100-120°F and this, combined with the heat generated by the welding process, meant that it was impossible to hold a steel plate without gloves. Not surprisingly, my endurance was put to the test.

In about 1960, Ahmed Kanoo concluded that our Bahrain slipway operation was too small to cater for our own maintenance, let alone allow us to take on outside contract work. With this in mind, he decided to view our age-old rivalry with Gray Mackenzie in a new light and consider building a bigger slipway together. In a conciliatory mood, he approached our commercial adversary and suggested that we should get together. But they refused. Two or three more times Ahmed Kanoo visited their manager, a man called Mr. Alcock whom my uncle considers to have been quite unpleasant. At the last of these three meetings, Alcock suggested that we should go to the Ruler and ask him to help us form a new company. Quite amazed, Ahmed Kanoo asked: 'Do you really mean it?' Back came the provocative reply: 'Yes, go to your Shaikh'.

Typical of Ahmed Kanoo's style, he did not say 'no' as Alcock had expected. Instead, he went to the Ruler, Shaikh Salman, and told him the story from the beginning to the end. 'This is what he said? He told you that?', asked the Ruler. 'Yes,' replied my uncle. When His Highness asked Ahmed Kanoo what he wished to do, he answered that he wanted to form a company with the Government of Bahrain's support. Unfortunately, Shaikh Salman died in November 1961, the year before BASREC was formed. However, this new company was officially launched by his son and heir, His Highness Shaikh Isa on 17 December 1963. We bought a 51 per cent shareholding and sold 49 per cent to the public.

BASREC was designed to handle bigger craft than those maintained on our Muharraq slipway. Alongside its jetty any 'on board' repairs, mechanical, electrical or structural work could be undertaken. We were fortunate to have a very good manager in Mr Green, followed by the equally competent Eric Cockerill. (BASREC has been, and remains, a very successful company, consistently able to pay an annual dividend of 30 per cent. As a result, the company's shares are amongst the most sought-after in the Bahrain market.)

Meanwhile, Gray Mackenzie was running a slipway facility between Muharraq and Manama, the Bahrain Slipway Company. When BASREC started to operate, led by Ahmed Kanoo, it did so aggressively, soon able to perform most of the commercial marine work efficiently and more cheaply than the Bahrain Slipway Company. In the aftermath of this affair, Gray Mackenzie approached Ahmed Kanoo several times, requesting him to buy the Bahrain Slipway Company. But he refused. It was episodes like this which encouraged him not to let himself be 'slapped in the face' by anyone, and to strive for 'something more for our company'. Eventually, in February 1988, the Bahrain Slipway Company closed down.

The Kanoo network expands – Khafji, Riyadh and Jeddah

Until the early 1960s Ras Al-Khafji, the little port near the Kuwaiti border, was used mainly as a tanker terminal. Sometimes freighters discharged cargo there, rather than discharge it at Dammam for it to be transported by trailer some 300 km. north to Khafji. After a Saudi Arabian royal decree announced that oil companies operating in the Kingdom should use local service companies as far as possible we, and other Saudis, established offices at Ras Al-Khafji. We opened our office there in May 1964 to supply, service and provide travel facilities to the Arabian Oil Company (established in Khafji since 1958).

In those pioneering days, going to Khafji was no 'picnic'. The so-called roads were treacherous sandy tracks and trails. The saloon cars were not air-conditioned. In the winter, it was possible to drive from Dammam to Khafji, via Nariah, in five to six hours. In the summer, the journey could take the best part of a day. The procedure was to set off early in the cool hours of morning, making the most of them before the heat of the day set in. To avoid the vehicle over-heating, it was necessary to stop at midday for three– four hours, open the car bonnet and let the engine cool down. Meanwhile, so that the driver did not over-heat as well, it was essential to create some sort of make-shift shaded area where both vehicle and driver could wait until it was cool enough to move on. Since there was no cover on the desert road, Hamed Kanoo remembered many occasions when he would sleep under the car to get away from the sun. Now, it takes just three hours to drive from Khafji to Dammam, in air-conditioned comfort.

The effort was more physical than mental, especially avoiding wandering camels on the roads at night, whatever the season of the year. It was a serious 'health hazard' if you were unfortunate enough to hit one of them. Because of its height and one-ton weight, once knocked over, the animal would more than likely fall onto the bonnet and roof of the moving car.

At Khafji we became the agents for various shipping companies, satisfying the captains' requirements, such as providing supplies, delivering mail and undertaking port paperwork, as well as discharging cargo, ship-to-lighter, lighter-to-shore. When tanker crews changed duty, we would take those going off-duty to Dhahran airport. Then, there were only two oil companies in the Neutral Zone: American-owned Getty Oil (formed in 1958 and later moved to Kuwait) and the Japanese-owned Arabian Oil Company (AOC).

At that time, the Kanoo shipping staff had monthly meetings with AOC, attended regularly by Hamed Kanoo and Abdulaziz Al-Khadar. Since, at that time, Al-Khafji was decreed a Neutral Zone between Saudi Arabia and Kuwait, Kuwaiti companies also established themselves there. Hence, Saudi and Kuwaiti companies had an equal right to work in Khafji, even after it became part of the Kingdom's territory. Nevertheless, it maintained its neutral status, especially in the commercial field.

In 1964, Al-Ghanim was the Kuwaiti shipping agent for the Japanese-owned Arabian Oil Company. At that time, Al-Ghanim were charging US$7 per freight-ton to offload the Japanese cargo onto the pier. The Japanese company also had an office in Dammam which organised its purchasing and handled its affairs, Khafji still being a small village with limited facilities.

When we heard that the Japanese had put their stevedoring contract out to tender, Abdulaziz Al Khadar told my father, who was in Dammam at the time, that he could provide the same service for our company at half a dollar less than Al-Ghanim: US$6.5 as opposed to US$7. Apparently my father did not believe him, arguing that Khafji was too far away: 'you know that it is 300 kilometres from Dammam to Khafji!' Al Khadar told him: 'Don't worry. We can do it'.

Abdulla Kanoo approached the Arabian Oil Company. The Japanese gave us tender documents and we prepared our bid. When the tenders were opened in Dammam, it transpired that Al-Ghanim had submitted its bid from Kuwait, while Y.B.A.Kanoo had submitted theirs from the Saudi-side, at half a dollar less, just as Al Khadar had suggested.

When, in 1964, we secured this lighterage contract with the Arabian Oil Company, we charged US$6.5 per freight-ton, undercut the competition and still made a good profit. (For readers unfamiliar with shipping industry terms, a freight-ton costs more than a weight-ton. For instance, a cargo of plastic pipes might weigh only 5 tons, yet the freight-ton volume would exceed 15 tons, hence the greater figure is applied for costing purposes.)

Abdulaziz Al Khadar continued to operate the Khafji office until 1973, attending ships when they were discharged in port. He recalls that when he first went to Khafji, he found nothing but wooden huts to live in. Before long a small mosque was built and a large generator installed. Fresh water came by truck from Kuwait, as did food and other supplies. It was not until the 1973 oil price increases were really felt, by 1975, that Khafji became more civilized. Eventually we opened a travel office there, and Khafji village slowly developed into the strategic town today.

Meanwhile, in October 1967, Hamed Kanoo left Saudi Arabia to develop our business in Dubai. Abdulaziz and Abdulla began to look further west in Saudi Arabia. As our business grew larger in the Eastern Province, mainly in servicing the shipping, travel and oil industries, it became clear in the early 1960s that we needed to open an office in the capital, Riyadh. Abdulaziz Kanoo was selected for the task. With a few letters of introduction and names of our family friends in Riyadh, he started his uphill task of establishing our family name there. At first he found it difficult to be accepted in the Riyadh elite communities. He persisted however. His wife Sarah joined him and became a great help to him as she took care of the social life and its complicated dinner party arrangements.

One must remember that in Saudi Arabia, the sexes are segregated, hence there are men-only and women-only lunches and dinners. Although the princes and princesses, shaikhs and shaikhas have nomadic bedouin origins, 'society' in Saudi Arabia is based in towns and cities. There, strict protocol has to be observed.

Lulwa, Hamed Kanoo's wife, was also a great hostess and dinner organiser in Dubai. Greatly loved by everyone, she went through the entertaining acclimatisation, just like Sarah in Saudi Arabia, and Salwa (my wife) in Abu Dhabi. However, UAE protocol is very casual and informal when compared with Saudi Arabia. (After Hamed Kanoo died in 1994, Lulwa, his wife, chose to remain in Dubai.)

Soon people began to discover that Abdulaziz Kanoo was really a very nice man who was more of an asset than a threat to them. He became a great friend of Shaikh Abdulaziz bin Ahmed Al-Sudairi in Riyadh. They went everywhere together. After a year of this familiarisation process, my uncle was known to the majority of the merchants, and to the Royal family. He also became a close friend of Prince Salman, to the extent that Abdulaziz Kanoo was one of the few people privileged to receive and welcome Prince Salman's astronaut son, Prince Sultan, when he returned to earth (at NASA in Florida) on the Challenger space shuttle on 17 June 1985.)

Once the Riyadh office opened in 1963, Abdulaziz Kanoo recruited a manager, Amin Al-Sajeeni, to enhance Y.B.A.Kanoo's presence in the capital. Our activities were travel, commercial trading and joint ventures. As a family, we regard Abdulaziz as our pioneer in Riyadh who started something from nothing, just as Abdulla had done in Dammam, and Mubarak in the UAE.

Five years later in 1968, Abdulla Kanoo headed west to Jeddah. There, he opened an office on the ground floor of a big house on the Mecca Road. Staff housing was provided on the first and second floors. But business on the western shore of Saudi Arabia was not so good for us. Competition was severe as we soon found ourselves competing with old established families who had been trading in the port for hundreds of years. Most tribes and families in Mecca and Medina can trace their ancestry back to the time of the Prophet, some fourteen-hundred years ago. Losses started to mount up so the office became officially dormant.

While this satisfied our auditors, it did not please our principals for whom we had been the agents in Jeddah, particularly those involved in the commercial and shipping sectors. In due course, Abdulla decided that we should re-establish our presence in Jeddah. As a result, he built our present office on Medina Road, and spent a great deal of time in the city until the business was operating profitably. We have not looked back since. Trade slowly improved, as we found our niche in Saudi Arabia's west coast market.

Australian potential explored

While the infrastructure of Saudi Arabia and our business network in the Kingdom were being developed, Y.B.A.Kanoo's Main Board decided to explore the other side of the world: Australia. In 1968 Cyril Jones, by now our company's General Manager, pointed out that all the family fortune was tied up in the Arabian Gulf region. All the Kanoo eggs were in one basket.

Anticipating the risks and resistance, he persuaded the Board to adopt a conservative alternative by investing in a 'safe' country to secure the income of future generations and to generate a new source of funds. The Board agreed to the strategy, but could not agree on a country in which they could invest safely. The task of identifying such a place fell to Ahmed Kanoo and Cyril Jones who then spent some months travelling around the world trying to identify a country which met the Board's criteria. Eventually, they prepared a report which recommended Australia because of its political stability and future growth potential. The Board's agreement led to Y.B.A.Kanoo forming an Australian company as a vehicle to buy real estate, both vacant land and properties. We were already the Bahrain agent for Qantas Airlines, and Ahmed Kanoo had close personal ties with the airline's Chairman who, in turn, was able to point our new Australian venture in the right direction away from pitfalls.

Cyril also developed an association for us with the Weddel family in Australia. For the first time, chilled meat was brought to the Gulf region via Qantas airline air freighters. Under the supervision of Weddel's son in Bahrain, the 'undressed' beef and lamb was cut to suit the local taste. However, as time went by, the Chamber of Commerce received complaints that the Kanoo family was now in the food business and competing with smaller local firms. Ahmed Kanoo notified the Chamber of Commerce that it was not our intention to compete with, or jeopardise smaller firms. Within six months, he sold our food business to Universal Stores.

When Cyril Jones retired from Y.B.A.Kanoo's London office in 1981, Bill Brien (our Group Director) assumed the day-to-day management of both our Australian venture, and general overseas investment portfolio, (distinct from local investment portfolios, whereby a senior Y.B.A.Kanoo director in each territory invests in property, shares and joint venture companies as he sees fit).

Chapter 10

Transition in the Trucial States and Oman

Throughout the 1950s and 1960s, the Y.B.A.Kanoo organisation continued to expand in Bahrain and evolve in Saudi Arabia. Coinciding with this period, the Board decided that the time was right to investigate the possibilities of extending our network to the Trucial States, now the United Arab Emirates (UAE). But first a word about the Trucial States themselves.

During the late eighteenth and early nineteenth centuries, fast Arab dhows used to raid not only each other but also, on occasions, the East India company's ships carrying spices and other expensive goods from India to the United Kingdom. When a man-of-war naval gun-boat chased them, the dhows would hide amongst the shallow waters of the creeks, the sea inlets which were the predominant features of the Gulf coast between Abu Dhabi to the west and the Musandam Peninsula to the east. Eventually, in 1819, the British became tired of these raids and decided to put an end to them. They sent an expeditionary fighting force to land in Ras Al-Khaimah with naval guns and well-armed soldiers. The Bedouin armed with just their old muskets and swords had no chance.

After their boats were burnt, an agreement was negotiated which was signed in January 1820 by nine tribal shaikhs who agreed not to raid British vessels. The treaty was followed by other truces and agreements culminating in 1853 with the *Perpetual Treaty of Peace*. This began to change the relationship among the rulers of the lower Arabian Gulf coastal regions: through making a truce with the British authorities the rulers had made a truce with one another, hence the Trucial States.

Today, as aircraft fly low over the city of Dubai or Abu Dhabi on their approach to the airport, passengers enjoy a panoramic vista of high-rise buildings and urban development, parks and lush green golf courses, industrial projects, all linked by a sophisticated network of roads, bridges, flyovers and underpasses. From an altitude of several thousand feet, traffic resembles ants on the move.

Possibilities discovered

In the early 1950s, the Trucial Coast was vastly different. The coastline was still in its natural state with beautiful uninterrupted sand-dunes, mud-flats, ridges and slopes, their various patterns created by the irregularity of shifting winds, sand and waves. The late Edward Henderson's memoirs once again provide an excellent contemporary description of this scene in his first impressions of Dubai in the late 1940s:

> The coast was edged with white lines of surf, looking motionless from above, that divided the blue of the sea from the brownish yellow of the foreshore. The coast-line was breached in several places by creeks which seemed to have punched their way through the shore-line to find their way inland, to be finally soaked up in the sandy waste.

Mangroves appeared as dark patches among some of these winding creeks, deep enough to allow the traditional dhows and sailing boats of the Arabian Gulf to seek shelter and safe mooring. Inevitably, the focal points of such activity were small ports, then the only centres of population along the coast which, from the air, looked 'as if man could only maintain a feeble hold on the edge of the desert.'

When Mubarak Kanoo arrived in the late-1950s, the scene was much the same. He recalls Dubai being a small trading village on the south bank of the creek. The only office buildings were those belonging to the Ruler, the British Bank of the Middle East and one or two other companies. A promontory near the sea, also on this side of the creek, had been developed as a residential district called Shindagha where several shaikhs had built their homes. When strong winds whipped up the sea at high tide, this community was often isolated like an island.

Sprawling along the north bank of the creek was Deira. Here, a small business community was already active and this was where we established our first office with five staff. Whereas on the north bank (Deira side as it is known locally), there were quite a number of cars, there was less traffic on the Dubai side until the mid-1950s.

Deira and Dubai then began to grow side-by-side. But at that time, apart from the merchants' houses along the water-front with their distinctive wind-towers, perhaps the most impressive and obvious feature was the busy creek itself. *Booms* (dhows built for long-distance trade), plying the Arabian Gulf, the seaboard of Oman, the west coast of India and the east African coast as far south as Zanzibar, would present a fine spectacle when, with a fair wind, their lateen sails enabled them to tack gracefully up or down the creek. Meanwhile, their smaller sailing 'sisters', *jalboots* (derived from the British Navy's 'jolly boat'), would dodge out of their way, their mobility often assisted by spluttering little motor-engines. Like an artist who after completing his main subject concentrates on the background detail, the 'painter' of this maritime scene appears to have filled in with hundreds of ferry-men operating their two-oared *abras* (water taxis) back and forth across the creek, each boatman vociferously competing for custom as passengers approached the ferry stations.

Away from the hubbub of the waterfront life was moving at a measured pace in the quiet sandy alleys of Dubai and Deira. Mubarak Kanoo remembers that the buildings stretched ten or twenty houses back from the creek. Most were single storey, and none more than three or four storeys, built of lime, cement, or faroush (coral slabs extracted from the sea-bed.) Concrete blocks were yet to become a feature of the future. Traditional roofs were constructed with a lattice of painted mangrove poles, covered with palm-leaf matting which was sealed with pitch. This protected the structure from occasional rain, but wind-blown sand and intense summer humidity mixed with salt-laden sea-spray, created a destructive cocktail of natural elements.

The covered souq was another focal point, comprising a lane, perhaps 200 metres long, along which small open-fronted shops or stalls faced the thoroughfare. As in Bahrain, traders often sat in front of their shops on little stools, or cross-legged on carpets spread out on the floor, observing passers-by as they paused to look at at their wares. If they thought a transaction was likely, hesitant customers were invited to partake of their hospitality, each according to the trader's national tradition or the customer's personal preference. If the trader was a Gulf Arab, he might offer cardamom flavoured coffee from a brass *dalla* (coffee pot), poured into a *finjal* (a small coffee cup without a handle). If the merchant was Iranian, he might serve sweet tea in a small glass.

Abu Dhabi, a day's sailing to the west of Dubai, was not much different. Long-time resident of the town, Mr Bhojraj, remembers my grandfather Jassim's visits during the 1950s. According to Bhojraj, our family in Bahrain had business links on the island of Abu Dhabi even before the 1950s. Based on records relating to Jassim Kanoo's cement business and other trading interests, I am sure that this recollection is true. Until 1950, access between the two could only be achieved by wading (or driving a vehicle such as a Land Rover) through shallow water at low-tide. Abu Dhabi fort stood in prominent isolation beside a small collection of *faroush* (coral-stone) houses and *barasti* (palm frond) huts. This isolation ended in 1950 when Petroleum Development Trucial Coast (PDTC), then the oil concession-holder for the Trucial States, built a narrow stone causeway between the mainland and Abu Dhabi island. But apart from this modest improvement in communications, the scene changed little for several more years, except for the addition of the British Political Agency built in 1957 (now the British Embassy), followed by the British Bank of the Middle East. Equally fascinating, is the way in which Abu Dhabi changed out of all recognition after October 1960, when oil was discovered in commercial quantities in the Murban field, an area within the emirate's 67,000 square kilometres of territory.

During 1961, an airstrip was marked out behind the fort of Abu Dhabi. In the same year, an airstrip was constructed in Dubai to accommodate Dakotas and Herons. In 1962 Viscounts of Kuwait Airways started a thrice-weekly service to the emirate. A year later, construction began to extend Dubai's modest airport building and improve the runway, the latter work necessary to prevent flooding in the low-lying area. Initially, the British Overseas Airways Corporation (BOAC) was sceptical of any increased demand for its seats and so was reluctant to establish a weekly VC10 flight into Dubai. However, it soon changed its mind. Even before the new runway was ready for service in June 1965, other airlines were clamouring for landing rights. Then, in 1966, oil was discovered in Dubai and exports began in 1969. As revenues began to produce a reasonable national income, the creek was dredged to create a deeper draught for the increasing number of coastal cargo steamers and local craft, up to a capacity of about 500 tons. Single-track roads soon gave way to dual-carriageways.

With Dubai's oil revenues now heavily committed to many development projects, the emirate neared the limit of what it could reasonably afford. So it was that His Highness Shaikh Rashid bin Saeed Al Maktoum approached his son-in-law, the Ruler of Qatar, to seek a loan to help pay for the new Al Maktoum bridge which had exceeded its original budget. When this toll-bridge opened as the first road crossing over the creek between Dubai and Deira, already the faces of the two communities were being transformed into one big concrete city, overwhelmed by contractors, consultants, new companies and booming commerce. Now, it is almost impossible to differentiate between Dubai and Deira, especially as they are linked above ground by multi-lane highways elevated on flyovers and bridges, and by a tunnel under the creek.

New Kanoo offices – Abu Dhabi, Dubai and Sharjah

Our first approach towards starting an office in the Trucial States began in 1957 when my father, Mohamed Kanoo, accompanied Shaikh Mohamed bin Salman Al Khalifa, to visit Shaikh Zayed, the Governor of Al-Ain, an oasis lying to the east of the Shaikhdom of Abu Dhabi. In 1958 my father visited Abu Dhabi again, this time with Yassin Mulla Ahmed (our trusted family 'Man Friday') and approached Shaikh Shakhbut, the Ruler of Abu Dhabi, to seek a licence to operate there.

Thereafter, on a regular basis, Mubarak Kanoo and Yassin Mulla Ahmed continued to visit Shaikh Shakhbut until he granted us a trading licence in 1962. It had taken a long time to persuade him to do so. According to Mohamed Al Fahim, this is an understatement! In his book, *From Rags to Riches: A Story of Abu Dhabi,* Mohamed summarises the scenario: 'Given the Ruler's reluctance to put his signature to almost anything, their task was challenging.' Mubarak and Yassin had to convince Shaikh Shakhbut, first, that it was normal business procedure to open an office; secondly, that their proposal to represent shipping companies and airlines in Abu Dhabi would benefit its nationals by linking them to the outside world; and third, that the Ruler should support Mubarak and Yassin in what they were doing.

What Mohamed Al Fahim remembers most about Mubarak and Yassin's two-month stay in his father's house (which had no electricity, running water or indoor plumbing facilities) 'was the constant typing and retyping as they amended and rearranged the agreement, time after time, in an effort to achieve a set of conditions the Ruler would approve. In the end, their persistence paid off'. With considerable encouragement from Mohamed's father, Sheikh Shakhbut finally signed an agreement. 'The Kanoos, however, had to accept all of his terms and conditions in order to get permission to set up their office in Abu Dhabi.'

Now, with Shaikh Shakhbut's approval, the way was prepared for Mubarak to open our first office in Abu Dhabi in 1963, with the help of Yassin and Nasir Al Ta'i (the office's first manager). The premises consisted of one room within the Abduljalil Al Fahim building, by the water-front where barges and dhows were offloaded onto the beach. (The house was just about where the clock roundabout stands on the Corniche today). A barge would be run aground on the beach, sand would be shovelled around its bow to stabilise the hull, then the cargo, including cars and caterpillar bulldozers, would be discharged. Later, a short stone jetty was built. Sometimes a wooden plank was laid on the sand onto which the coolies stacked the boxes and bags discharged from the barge.

When this system proved to be inadequate, a stone jetty was constructed in a more protected area at the eastern end of the island sheltered from the wind. Barge discharge moved to this facility known as the Ruler's Jetty. Shaikh Shakhbut's yacht *Shuja'a* (Brave), purchased from Prince Rainier of Monaco and re-furbished by BASREC in Bahrain, was moored nearby.

At first, there were no hotels in Abu Dhabi, so Mubarak Kanoo often stayed with Abduljalil Al Fahim who in turn used to stay in our house in Bahrain when he visited the island. Mubarak and Abduljalil enjoyed a very warm relationship for a long time, until it soured because of a commercial dispute. (I should add, however, that Abduljalil's son Mohamed and I have always maintained a close friendship. Undoubtedly, his business acumen and hard work were major factors in the development of his family's small business into an international one.) In 1965, we moved from our one-room office in the Al Fahim building into bigger premises located in the Shaikh Khalid bin Sultan building on the new Corniche Road. By now, our business activities included commercial trading in machinery and equipment, shipping agencies, as well as selling cigarettes and insurance.

Meanwhile, almost simultaneously, Mubarak had been busy making arrangements for us to establish an office in Dubai. After 1958, both he and Yassin Mulla Ahmed (who became the first manager of our Dubai office) regularly visited the emirate. Yassin's closeness to our family, his wide experience and diplomacy in business and local affairs made him indispensable. Dubai, like Abu Dhabi, shared similarities with Saudi Arabia in so far as it was arid, had few amenities and was inhabited by a society with tribal bedouin origins. Dubai also supported a modest maritime community. As yet, this boasted few modern amenities.

In 1961, Shaikh Rashid bin Saeed Al Maktoum granted us a trading licence to operate in Dubai, the territory under his authority. (Later, he gave us a piece of land beside the beach in the Jumairah neighbourhood on which we built a family house, which we still use.) Because we did not own any property in Dubai initially, both Mubarak and Yassin lived in the Carlton Tower, a hotel beside the creek on Deira-side.

By now, a few large villas had been built in Jumairah, and more were being constructed. (Among these was the Ruler's Guest House, and the home of Mahdi Al-Tajir, a Bahraini who came to Dubai as Customs Manager. As his natural skills in trading became obvious to Shaikh Rashid bin Saeed, Al-Tajir was employed by the Amiri Court as the Ruler's close adviser and executor of his plans.) Otherwise, most houses outside Dubai and Deira during the 1950s and 1960s were coral stone and mud constructions, traditional *barastis*, tents or shelters made of any available material, located by the sea. What a difference thirty years has made. Compare the housing then with the ultra-modern development of Dubai today. This evolution is now presented in an audio-visual-cum-model exhibition in Dubai's new museum.

Initially, Y.B.A.Kanoo's business activity in Dubai was mainly confined to shipping agency work, although we also sold items to the construction industry, such as commercial paints, chipboard and other supplies. Gray Mackenzie had the monopoly of lighterage work for Dubai and in fact for the whole of the Trucial States. We soon changed that! As a family company, we do not care for monopolies, so one of Mubarak's first objectives was to establish a new service and acquire a respectable lighterage fleet capable of competing with Gray Mackenzie. Whether it was a joke or 'sour grapes' we shall never know, but gossip in Dubai let us know Gray Mackenzie's opinion of our tugs and Westminster barges which was similar to the earlier sarcastic remark made to Ahmed Kanoo in Bahrain. Y.B.A.Kanoo's tugs and barges were considered inconsequential in terms of their size and durability. It was our competitor's view that in no time we would crash our entire fleet of 'teacups'!

Mr N. A. Khan, who joined Y.B.A.Kanoo in 1963 as a shipping supervisor in Dubai (later, promoted to Deputy Shipping Manager for the Northern Emirates), remembers that thirty years ago, only three shipping lines called into Dubai: Dutch-owned V. N. S. whose ships put into port perhaps twelve times per year; Royal Nedlloyd, a joint-service with the American Hoegh Line which had just nine annual scheduled arrivals; and the Maersk Line whose vessels arrived perhaps eighteen times per year from the Far East. A few Russian and Polish tramp ships also appeared from time to time. Between them all, a monthly average of five or six vessels put into Dubai, their total cargo rarely exceeding 7,000 dead-weight tonnes. Today, we cope with between sixty to sixty-five ships per month in Dubai and Jebel Ali ports, handling some 100,000 tonnes of cargo.

Following the successes of being allowed to open offices in Abu Dhabi and Dubai, in 1963 Mubarak Kanoo was granted a licence by the Ruler of Sharjah, Shaikh Saqir Al-Qasimi, to open a travel office in his emirate. Unlike now, Sharjah was then separated from Dubai by some dozen kilometres of desolate *sabkha* (salt flats). When our Sharjah office opened, Y.B.A.Kanoo business was confined to travel, mostly serving Sharjah airport (originally opened in 1932 as a stop-over point on the route to India). This office was also managed by Mubarak Kanoo and Yassin Mulla Ahmed, but it soon became obvious that they could not be in several places at the same time. So, in 1965 Mr Mohammed Yusuf Darwish became manager of the Sharjah office which, after Khalid Port opened in 1966, diversified into shipping agency activities, too.

At this time there was still no deep-water port in any of the Trucial States and so tall ships had to anchor offshore and wait their turn for cargo to be discharged into lighters and taken ashore. Just as earlier in Bahrain and Saudi Arabia, deep-water ports were finally constructed in various developing cities on the Trucial Coast, Y.B.A.Kanoo was the shipping agent in place with our barges and tugs available to handle discharging requirements. The whole system was very demanding and needed considerable commitment to keep on top of the work-load. Often, our staff were kept busy twenty-four hours a day (with meal breaks and rest periods). I have no doubt that this is one reason why Y.B.A.Kanoo earned its legendary name throughout Arabia's shipping agency network.

Also in 1963, the year we opened our Sharjah office, my father's efforts to enhance our business relationship with British-American Tobacco paid off. Y.B.A.Kanoo's Mercantile Department in Bahrain was appointed as BAT's sole importer of its cigarette brands sold in Abu Dhabi. Part of the agreement was that we would not sell competitors' brands without BAT's consent. (Gallaher, whom we also represented, was not part of BAT.)

Given the limited development of Abu Dhabi at that time, it is interesting that BAT asked us to 'provide adequate air-conditioned storage and maintain sufficient supplies at all times for the market's full requirements'. Our letter of appointment also requested us to appoint sub-distributors in Abu Dhabi town, and in key points throughout the 'Sheikhdom', namely Al-Ain, Jebal Dhana and Tarif. It was intended that these sub-distributors would service this new trade by following the system used by the Bahraini Tobacco Trading Company, adapted to conditions in Abu Dhabi. In the end, however, we did not adopt this procedure but set up our own distribution in Abu Dhabi town and in Al-Ain. Until 1963 BAT's Dubai agency was with Ali & Saleh Al-Osami, from whom local traders bought their stocks. In June 1964, Easa Saleh Al-Gurg (a leading Dubai merchant who was a friend of my late Uncle Hamed and is now the UAE Ambassador in London) became the BAT agent for Dubai and the Northern Trucial States.

The Trucial States – tentative development takes off

Until 1966, His Highness Shaikh Shakhbut bin Sultan Al Nahayan ruled Abu Dhabi with what some people describe as a 'very tight rein'. He was reluctant to spend much, if any, of the emirate's newly-acquired petro-dollars on modernisation. He wanted development to move at his pace, primarily because he was suspicious of foreigners who were buzzing like flies around a honey pot with a 'let us modernise you' approach. As Shaikh Shakhbut saw it, the intensity of this foreign interest was purely a means of trying to take the emirate's newly-acquired wealth away from him. As a result, he paid very close attention to what went on, as illustrated by a letter he sent to us on 12 July 1966. In this, Shaikh Shakhbut asked why Kanoo was contravening our agreement with him: namely, we were licenced as a shipping agent, not to sell oil. Our reply on 18 July explained that we were not in the oil business, but that as a shipping agent, we provided a bunkering service (fuel for the ship's engines) as required. We assured Shaikh Shakhbut that we would abide by the agreement and licence granted to us earlier.

Just one month after we received our reprimand, Shaikh Zayed bin Sultan Al Nahayan (then Governor of the eastern region around Al-Ain) succeeded his brother as Ruler of Abu Dhabi on 6 August 1966. Shaikh Zayed had lived in Al-Ain for a long time which, like the rest of Abu Dhabi emirate, still lacked many amenities. The electricity service, where available, was very erratic. Water was usually trucked to each house. There was a semblance of graded roads, but none were asphalted. A few unreliable telephones provided basic communication. The Government infrastructure was non-existent. The emirate was run by the Ruler's office and the Municipality Council. So it was that Shaikh Zayed set about spending most 'generously' to turn things around.

When I first visited Abu Dhabi in 1964, five years before I was assigned there as Assistant Branch Manager, my first impressions were those of economic and environmental inhospitality. There was no airport building, just a desert strip half way up the island on which Dakotas could land. Baggage was unloaded onto the sand because there was nowhere else to put it. Our company driver, Mr Matter, arrived with his Landrover, slung our bags into the back and off we went along the so-called road to Abu Dhabi town, mostly compacted sand-tracks running in parallel.

The modest little town of Abu Dhabi occupied a small part of a small island, the only prominent landmark being a fort surrounded by barasti dwellings and mud houses. (Now you cannot even see the fort because of the surrounding modern high-rise buildings.) The Beach Hotel was the only hotel; guests could only rent a 'space' in a room, not the room itself. Although the rate was high, if more people came to stay than could be accommodated on a single-occupancy basis, then you had to allow strangers to share your room. If you did not like this arrangement, then you could sleep on the beach. A second hotel, the Al-Ain Palace, was in the process of construction, managed by a legendary Greek, Demitri. We called him 'Shaikh Al-Haara' (the head of the area) as many prominent people used to have coffee with him in the evenings.

After the accession of Shaikh Zayed in 1966, the foundations of a modern state were laid. The first shipments of oil from the offshore facilities at Das Island greatly increased Abu Dhabi's revenues from 1962. Production also started onshore in 1964 and the revenues increased in leaps and bounds thereafter, fuelling an amazing development. With an enthusiastic leader, available finance and the importation of know-how, technology and skilled workers, progress took place very, very swiftly.

Abu Dhabi began to flourish and achieved a stage in its development which had taken some European countries centuries to reach. To achieve this, many needs had to be satisfied. As oilmen started to arrive to work the oil-fields onshore and offshore, they required supplies, services and expertise. Almost immediately, Abu Dhabians recognised the opportunities. Very soon many had gravitated from a comparatively relaxed bedouin way of life to that of energetic entrepreneur, not least of all in the booming building industry. For among the most important needs were houses and flats to accommodate the massive influx of foreign entrepreneurs and workers which the boom had attracted.

Shaikh Zayed's brother, Shaikh Khalid, quickly recognised the dearth of accommodation for expatriate employees and managers who, by now, were flowing into the country. He looked around for a piece of land on which he could build houses to let. He selected an area, later named Al-Khalidiah, where he constructed houses and apartments. As this was the only decent accommodation available at the time, he rented them out at a high price. Many foreign and Arab company managers used them. Later, I was one of them.

No building regulations existed at that time. I remember one case which exemplified many hallmarks of haphazard planning. One of Shaikh Zayed's first decisions was to commission the construction of more roads. The project of building a road between Abu Dhabi city and Al-Ain oasis, a distance of 160 kilometres, was begun in Shaikh Shakbut's time, but completed in 1969. The stretch, covering low-lying *sabkha* and high dunes was divided into sections. Four companies were contracted and allocated one sector each so that the entire road could be finished quickly. With no overall professional supervision, the result was four different road surfaces of differing quality, each contractor having achieved what they could with the available resources.

From 1968 onwards, Abu Dhabi was a big construction site as the town infrastructure rose from the desert, alongside private enterprise houses and buildings. With astonishing speed, it seemed as if the desert had begun to 'bloom', almost literally. To do this Shaikh Zayed sought the help of many other countries.

With imaginative insight, Shaikh Zayed envisioned Abu Dhabi emirate being the most modern in the Gulf region. His love of gardens, trees and greenery drove him hard too. He spent millions upon millions of dirhams to convert these two visions into reality – the result is Abu Dhabi as it is today. Intuition also told him that he had to move fast to catch up with the rest of the world. Using his natural initiative, he imported essential know-how, believing that the Abu Dhabians would learn quickly from the foreign recruits. He was proved right. Today, the emirate of Abu Dhabi is run by its own nationals.

But in 1966 this process had only just begun. For a start, there were no schools of any note in Abu Dhabi. Yet, because Shaikh Zayed always said that he wished to build a strong future for the emirate, one based on a well-educated younger generation, he gave priority to creating a strong educational system. Before this could begin, teachers were needed. Bahraini teachers were among the first to lend a hand. Teachers from many other Arab nations also greatly contributed to this educational process, particularly Egyptian, Iraqi, Lebanese, Palestinian and Syrian teachers.

I do not know who was the first Bahraini to work in Abu Dhabi, Dubai or Sharjah. I do know, however, that the then rulers of the Trucial States asked the Bahrain Government to send Bahrainis to help them set up their respective infrastructures. Unlike Kuwait, Bahrain did not have massive oil reserves to provide wealth and abundant employment opportunities for its nationals. Thus, the Bahrain government agreed to help with the modernisation of Abu Dhabi, in particular, by seconding hundreds of Bahrainis to fill many of the vacant skilled positions. Bahrainis were also chosen because they had qualifications and were willing to seek new opportunities. Because they spoke the same language and had the same cultural background as Abu Dhabians, they fitted easily into that society. Some Omanis also worked in Abu Dhabi. Citizens of other neighbouring countries were either not available to travel or too occupied working in their own countries.

While this transition began in Abu Dhabi soon after Shaikh Zayed's accession in 1966, the period between 1968 and 1971 also coincided with the transition of the Trucial States into an independent federation, the United Arab Emirates (of which more later). On 2 December 1971, the new State of the United Arab Emirates was proclaimed. After this ceremony, Shaikh Zayed bin Sultan Al-Nahayan was elected as the UAE's first President, Shaikh Rashid bin Saeed Al Maktoum as Vice-President, and his son Shaikh Maktoum bin Rashid was appointed Prime Minister. On 9 December 1971, the UAE became a member of the United Nations.

During this evolution, buildings were needed to house central and local government departments. Defence, internal security, treasury policy and foreign affairs were to be administered from Abu Dhabi, the federal capital, while each member-emirate required its own local government departments (such as education, health, agriculture and commerce). To create and implement this new infrastructure, professional expertise had to be imported. Bahrainis answered the call. Together with expertise from many other countries, they helped to establish a new nation and to train Abu Dhabians. To some extent, this still applies today.

Bahrainis, considering themselves as one family with other nationals of the Arabian Gulf region, had done the same thing in Kuwait, (including Dr Abdul Latif Kanoo who, between 1961 and 1964, worked in the Ministry of Works). And, as mentioned previously, in the early days of Saudi Arabia's development, Bahrainis were the backbone of ARAMCO's multi-disciplined workforce.

At first, most Bahraini teachers arrived in Abu Dhabi on secondment, then later as new recruits. Every year more of them moved to the fast developing towns on the Trucial Coast. Khalid Al-Hashmi, an Iraqi, established the Department of Education in 1967 in Abu Dhabi. Soon afterwards Abdulmalik Al-Hamer (later, Deputy Minister of Education of Abu Dhabi), literally put together many of the text books which the students studied so that they reflected our Arabian Gulf heritage. Previously, most text books had been imported from Egypt.

Hassan Shams arrived from Bahrain in Abu Dhabi to set up the Customs services and systems, succeeded by Hamed Al Sabah and Abdulwahab Matter (who is still working there). Mahdi Al-Tajir (whose house in Jumairah was mentioned earlier) was sent to Dubai from Bahrain Customs to set up a similar operation. He did so well that Shaikh Rashid appointed him to the Ruler's Office. Mahdi, a natural leader and a very talented entrepreneur, became involved in all aspects of Dubai's development, including the two ports Mina Rashid and Jebel Ali Port (which opened in 1972 and 1979 respectively), the evolution of Jebel Ali Free Zone (launched in 1985) and the growth of Dubai's aluminium smelter. He was also an important negotiator with some of the toughest oil men around.

Abdulgafar Mohamed arrived from Bahrain's immigration department to set up and run a similar system in Abu Dhabi, which was later adapted by the federation of the United Arab Emirates (UAE). While Hassan Al-Sabah worked in the finance department at the palace, Abdulrahim Al-Mahmood helped H. E. Ahmed Al-Suwaidi in the foreign affairs department and assisted the latter in his endeavour to weld together the seven emirates into one state. Isa Al-Jam'a (now Bahrain's Ambassador to the UAE), headed the first population census in Abu Dhabi, in 1968, as part of a census of all the emirates under the direction of Habib Kassim (later, Minister of Commerce and Agriculture in Bahrain) and Dr Kevin Fenelon, a statistician, who had previously worked in Bahrain. Ibrahim Al-Sabagh set up the department for labour affairs and Ahmed Obaidly served as adviser to Shaikh Shakhbut, and later Shaikh Zayed. There were other Bahrainis, too, who worked in banks (such as Ibrahim Al Shakar), with Abu Dhabian and Dubaian merchants, in the oil services, transport, ports and airports.

But Bahrainis were not the only nationality who flocked to Abu Dhabi to work for the UAE Government, companies or themselves. When I was assigned to Abu Dhabi in 1969, it seemed to me that every nation was represented: Arabs of all nationalities, Europeans,

North and South Americans, Asians, Orientals, Africans and Australians. All of them, despite their different languages and cultures, worked together to build the United Arab Emirates, each in his/her own speciality. Many became extremely rich, while others just made a living, depending on their skills and luck.

Of the other nationalities who contributed between 1967 to 1970, I remember some in particular: two Iraqis, Abdulla Ismael who in 1968, established the oil department, in 1972 set up Abu Dhabi National Oil Company (ADNOC) and later became Deputy Oil Minister; and Fadhel Khan, ADNOC's Technical Manager. Two Englishman, Mr John Butter and Dr Horniblow, created the finance and health departments. Dr Abdulrahman Makhloof, an Egyptian, organised the town planning department. The Municipality's formation was undertaken by Alsuni Banaga, a Sudanese, while his fellow countryman Al-Sayed Saleh Farah assumed responsibility for the Department of Justice. Information functions were established by a Palestinian, Mohamed Al-Gusain. After the foundation of the United Arab Emirates, most of these departments were duplicated by federal Ministries.

Shaikh Zayed's strategy of importing know-how and utilising foreign knowledge had worked very well. He was able, in the short time of three decades, to catch up with the modern world and the UAE can now be compared favourably with other nations. Abu Dhabians were being educated as they rubbed shoulders with those who had knowledge. Now, all senior government posts are held by UAE nationals, as are the leading entrepreneurs and businessmen. Shaikh Zayed succeeded in fulfilling his vision. Who, in 1970, would have believed that so much could have been accomplished by today?

As it was not until 1966 that oil was discovered in Dubai (six years later than in Abu Dhabi), the emirate did not have as much oil wealth as its neighbour during the same period. Nevertheless, in time, Shaikh Rashid and his sons were successful in making Dubai the most important point in the Arabian Gulf for free-zone trading, providing services to companies, developing tourism, hosting international sports events (such as golf, power-boat and tennis championships), quite apart from becoming the most important entrepôt for re-exports to the entire region.

Abu Dhabi – 'an eastern place'

It was against this background that, in 1967, Hamed Kanoo left Saudi Arabia to join his cousin Mubarak in Dubai, the idea being that

Hamed would become Y.B.A.Kanoo's regional General Manager, while Mubarak became non-resident Area Director, paying one or two visits a month to monitor our activities. Hamed Kanoo's contemporary memories of the emirate were that it boasted just two hotels: the Carlton Hotel and the Lebanese-owned International hotel near to the airport.

In 1968 Y.B.A.Kanoo's Financial Controller in Bahrain sent out word through the supervisors that he was looking for someone willing to take up a challenge and go to 'an eastern place'. It would not be an easy job or as pleasant a life as in Bahrain, but the 'lucky' person might earn a little more money. V. A. Subermanian (Mani), then a senior accounts clerk in our Manama office, became that 'lucky' person. The 'eastern place' turned out to be Abu Dhabi.

One morning in October 1968, flying direct from Bahrain to Abu Dhabi in one of Gulf Aviation's Dakotas (a DC3), Mani landed at about 11 a.m. at the small airport near the eastern end of the island. The terminal building, serving only Gulf Aviation aircraft, was about as big as the Kanoo boardroom in Dubai. There was one clerk who stamped passports, but there were no customs procedures. When everyone had left, Abu Dhabi airport closed, just as people lock up their shops and go home at the end of business hours.

Accommodation was scarce, so Mani lodged with one of the shipping supervisors. Drinking water was a problem. Some mornings, he had to open a soda-water bottle and use the contents to wash his face before going to the office. Every second or third day, he depended on the water-tanker which came from Al-Ain, and other areas. At a cost of 1,500 dirhams per thousand gallons (4546 litres) of water, payable at the end of each month, this was more than Mani's monthly salary. Naturally, he was grateful for one company perk: Kanoo paid for the water used by their staff in their apartments.

Until 1965 Y.B.A.Kanoo rented a one-room office within Abduljalil Al-Fahim's small building. Later we rented two ground-floor shuttered shops on the sea-front, which eventually developed into what is now the Corniche. These two rooms measured about four and a half by nine metres. The floor above our offices comprised quarters occupied by the senior staff of the Abu Dhabi Petroleum Company (ADPC) which held the concession for Abu Dhabi's onshore oilfields.

Abu Dhabi Telegraph and Telephone Company (ADTT), a privately-owned subsidiary of Cable and Wireless, operated the local telecommunications system. Telephone numbers were four digits. Direct dialling, even to Dubai, was not possible so our staff used telex machines to contact Bahrain. We also used Gulf Aviation's daily mail service which simply involved handing our mail-bags to the captain of the aircraft. Everyday copies of letters were produced on manual typewriters with carbon paper. For longer runs, the now obsolete stencil and ink Roneo duplicating machines were used.

In the late 1960s, our office in Abu Dhabi was small, employing fewer than two dozen staff and their days were occupied with very limited business activity. This amounted to some shipping agency work, as well as cigarette and paint sales. The manager and the accountant were Omani, and the only supervisory control was exerted by frequent visits by someone from Bahrain, or from Dubai. Therefore, when Mani arrived, he was faced with 'a mess of things'. Everything was untidy. Nobody knew what was going on. Twenty-two people, a mix of several nationalities, were doing as many different types of work. Only the manager and the accountant could speak, read and write English. Within a week the accountant resigned. By the end of the month, the manager had resigned too.

For the first three months, Mani set himself a rigid routine. Each weekday at 7.00 a.m., he unlocked the padlocks on the heavy roller shutters securing our doubled-fronted office. After raising the shutters, he was 'open' for business. At one o'clock, he went home for half an hour to eat lunch, and then returned to the office until 11.00 p.m. Fortunately, there were some fans and a couple of window-type air-conditioning units in each of the two shop sections, but during the extreme summer heat, even these were inadequate.

As Mani sorted through paperwork, he identified our clients, found out who owed us money and who needed paying, and introduced a simple recording system. Each day, every numbered delivery order was matched with a corresponding sum of collected cash. Both were handed to the cashier who counted the money, reconciled it with the records and issued a receipt. Employees now had to pay for lunches and cigarettes from their salaries, not the most popular of the new regime's innovations! Within eight months, the accounts were under control. Our new focus became the development of the business.

What could we do other than service ships and sell cigarettes? A commercial manager was appointed to take charge and given the responsibility of seeking out additional agencies. In January 1969, Peter Chaplin was deployed from Bahrain to Abu Dhabi for a short stint until a new permanent manager could be recruited to replace the Omani who had resigned. Three months later Barry Cole was appointed, transferred from the shipping department in Bahrain.

British defence cuts – catalyst of change in Arabia

While Mubarak and Hamed Kanoo continued to develop our family business in the Trucial States, the prospect of immense political change had become the talk of the region. 'The event which re-directed the course of history in the Trucial States and led to the creation of the UAE was a result of totally unrelated events taking place in British domestic politics' is the opening sentence of the chapter on the formation of the the federation in Dr Frauke Heard-Bey's book *From Trucial States to United Arab Emirates*. In summary, towards the end of the 1960s, the rank and file of Britain's ruling Labour Party had become very critical of the British Government's defence budget. Such was the pressure of this lobby, that the Prime Minister and Leader of the Labour Party, Harold Wilson, promised a defence expenditure review. On 16 February 1967, a White Paper was published, its central thesis being a policy to liquidate almost all British military bases east of Suez. Part of this plan was the withdrawal of all British troops from southern Arabia by 1968, including Aden. Even so, this proposed drastic change in Britain's role east of Suez still did not satisfy many Labour Members of Parliament who were intent on accelerating the withdrawal.

Within weeks, the British Government considered withdrawing its troops from the Arabian Gulf countries as well. Not surprisingly, this indication was strongly criticised by the late King Faisal of Saudi Arabia during a visit to London in May 1967. He believed that such a hasty, relatively unplanned move would leave the region vulnerable to instability and possible turbulence. Some eminent scholars, including Dr Ghazi A. Algosaibi (Saudi Arabia's Ambassador to the United Kingdom), now believe that such an expression of the King's fears was more than prophetic. Most likely, he knew what might happen. Less than a month later, on 5 June 1967, Israel launched an air attack on seventeen Egyptian airfields. Thus began the Six Day War, the effects of which heightened fears throughout the Arab world.

Barely had tension subsided, when, during the following autumn, the British Government announced the devaluation of the pound sterling. Massive defence cuts were seen as an inevitable knock-on effect as nervous Arabian Gulf Rulers anticipated yet another announcement. They did not have to wait long. In November 1967, British Foreign Office Minister, Goronwy Roberts, was despatched to the Middle East to reassure the Shah of Iran and the rulers of the countries which bordered the Arabian Gulf's southern coastline, that the British military presence would be maintained at all its traditional bases. Perhaps, they thought, New Year 1968 would be worthy of celebration, not commiseration.

On 16 January Harold Wilson shattered that hope and with it, much of the British Government's credibility. He declared that because of further immense defence cuts, all British forces were to be completely withdrawn from Arabia by the end of 1971. An embarrassed Mr Roberts was then sent back to the area to face astonished rulers and diplomats as he informed them of the British decision. Although each had his own professional agenda and personal point of view, the combined effect was one of mutual stunned dismay throughout the Arabian Gulf region.

A significant consequence of Harold Wilson's announcement was that the emirates of Bahrain, Qatar and the Trucial States, together with the Sultanate of Oman would be obliged to conduct their external relations and prepare for their defence requirements themselves. The result was that, on the whole, the Rulers of these nations then drew together more closely for mutual support and contemplated a future federation. (Kuwait and Saudi Arabia were already sovereign states: the Kingdom of Saudi Arabia was formally proclaimed on 23 September 1932, while on 19 June 1961 Kuwait was proclaimed an independent sovereign state. Saudi Arabia and Kuwait were invited to support the future federation but they did not negotiate to join it.)

On 18 February 1968, Shaikh Zayed of Abu Dhabi and Shaikh Rashid of Dubai met on the border between their two territories and made a momentous and statesman-like decision. Formally, they agreed to merge the two emirates into one union. They followed this with an immediate invitation to the rulers of their neighbouring territories to participate in an expanded federation. Thus, a week later on 25 February 1968, the rulers of the seven Trucial States (Abu Dhabi, Ajman, Dubai, Fujairah, Ras Al-Khaimah, Sharjah and Um Al-Qaiwain) and those of Bahrain and Qatar, convened in Dubai for their first constitutional conference.

The reality of discovering a workable formula for the proposed federation was not easy. On 21 October 1969 the nine rulers arrived in Abu Dhabi for the sixth meeting of what was then known as the Supreme Council. (Shaikh Zayed ordered a big conference hall to be constructed, as well as six houses to be built in the Al-Khaldiah district to accommodate the visiting Rulers attending the meeting. Having been honoured with the opportunity to mix with the Bahraini delegation, I remember Mr Ahmed Al-Suwaidi, Shaikh Zayed's right-hand-man, often talking to the rulers, and their advisers, until two or three in the morning. With his tireless team, he solved one problem after another, and painstakingly explained the advantages of unification.) Meanwhile, Bahrain and Qatar continued to establish institutions at home, preparing for the moment when the British would withdraw their forces in 1971. As time passed, it became increasingly likely that both countries would opt out of the proposed federation.

On 24 July 1970, Sultan Saeed bin Taimur of Oman was replaced by his son, Qaboos bin Saeed. Although the logistics of integrating Oman would have been difficult, the idea that the Sultanate might join the proposed union of emirates did appeal to some of the nine leaders. However, on 20 October 1970, Oman's new Prime Minister, Tariq bin Taimur, declared that Oman would not become a member of the proposed United Arab Emirates.

The culmination of the negotiations occurred on 2 December, 1971, when the rulers of Abu Dhabi, Dubai, Sharjah, Ajman, Um Al-Qaiwain and Fujairah (but not yet Ras Al-Khaimah), signatories of a provisional constitution agreed upon in July that year, proclaimed the creation of the new State, the United Arab Emirates. The proposal to form a federation – much discussed for four years by the emirates in the region, was now a legal reality.

As forecast, in June 1971, the would-be partners of the nine Emirates were informed that Bahrain had decided to 'go it alone'. On 14 August 1971, His Highness Shaikh Isa bin Salman Al Khalifa broadcast the proclamation of independence announcing the creation of the State of Bahrain. Qatar followed suit on 1 September 1971. Thus, when the six Trucial States proclaimed the formation of the United Arab Emirates on 2 December 1971, this still left the opportunity for Ras Al-Khaimah to join the federation, if it chose to do so.

Ras Al-Khaimah settled its differences with the other federation members, and formally joined the United Arab Emirates on 10 February 1972. Thus, from the early warnings in 1967 to the conclusion of negotiations nearly five years later, the political and economic destiny of the Arabian Gulf region had been redefined and redirected. *De facto,* so had that of the Y.B.A.Kanoo Group.

Oman opens up

A new dimension emerged on 24 July 1970 when Sultan Qaboos bin Saeed took over as Oman's new ruler. Six months after this swift and peaceful revolution, Hamed Kanoo decided that it was time to investigate the possibilities of starting a business in the Sultanate which, by now, was showing signs of a change in its domestic policy. Not least of these, was a wish to emerge from economic isolation.

According to Hamed, when he first went to Oman to see the situation for himself, there were no roads at all, except one small stretch from Muttrah to Muscat. Now, it is completely different. From Seeb village into the city of Muscat, a distance of some sixty kilometres, the road is a paved highway and floodlit all the way. If I drive from Dubai, even with a stop at the Hatta border post, I can be in Muscat in just a few hours, not days. In 1971 it would have taken Hamed Kanoo a whole day to cover the same distance, most of which would have been sand and mountain tracks, preferably traversed with a four-wheel drive vehicle.

Our first office in Oman, located in Muttrah near to the port, was opened on 19 February 1975. The remnants of the old building overlooking the harbour, with grand railings round the verandah, still stand today. From our elevated position above the Corniche, we could observe people enter and leave the souq, well-known for its silverware even today, and watch our ships come into the harbour.

It took some two years to establish ourselves in Muttrah. During this period, Hamed negotiated with Petroleum Development Oman (PDO) for Y.B.A.Kanoo to act as its purchasing agent in Dubai. We also decided that we should take on an Omani partner. My uncle invited an old family friend, Dr Omar Al-Zawawi, to assume that role, a position he readily accepted. At first, with Dr Omar, we operated a shipping agency, and a clearing and forwarding operation. Later, construction and equipment departments were developed with another Omani partner, Mr Kamzooz, who previously had worked with Y.B.A.Kanoo in Dubai.

Before long we had established our core services in Oman: shipping agencies, clearing and forwarding, as well as a small travel office. To do this, we rented a four-storey building. Two floors were used as our offices. The other two were used as accommodation. My cousin, Yusuf (who, between 1967 and 1970, had worked in Ras Tannurah) occupied one apartment, while Allan Cottingham, our Manager at that time, lived in the other. (Allan Cottingham used to be our Clearing and Forwarding Manager in Abu Dhabi. He worked closely with our Omani partner, Mr Kamzooz.)

Electricity was provided by a generator, and water was delivered in a tanker, achieved only after we had bought both pieces of equipment. When Oman's infrastructure began to develop, mains electricity and water became available. Gradually, the roads were asphalted. Our commercial department was based in Ruwi, then a small village. Today, it is the commercial and banking centre of Oman's capital area through which an elevated section of the six-lane Seeb-to-Muscat motorway runs, slicing the district in half. Medinat Qaboos, a thriving new city consisting of villas, hotels and the residences of the diplomatic community, was still an architect's dream on paper.

In the mid-1970s, few aeroplanes flew into Seeb airport which had replaced the confined and dangerous airstrip at Bait Al-Falaj. Gray Mackenzie was responsible for passenger facilities there. When an aircraft was due, often about mid-morning, a representative drove from Gray Mackenzie's Muscat office to Seeb airport. Perhaps one or two passengers might arrive early, in which case they would have to wait for the Gray Mackenzie representative to arrive. After opening the company's small office, just a kiosk in those days, and organising the book of flight manifest records, the representative simply checked off the passengers' names. By this time, a black dot in the sky over the mountain had become large enough to recognise the shape of an aircraft as it began its steep descent down to the runway. After some dozen passengers had disembarked, usually replaced by some six joining passengers, the aircraft departed about half an hour after landing with as little ceremony as when it had arrived. That being the end of the airport's activity for the day, the doors were closed, the Gray Mackenzie representative returned to Muscat and all remained silent unless a flight from Bahrain was due later that day.

When Yusuf, Ahmed Kanoo's eldest son, moved to Oman as Area Manager in 1975, everything was very new. He stayed for five years, heading our operation in Muscat, until Hamed Kanoo recalled him to Dubai.

During the course of time, it became evident that Oman would not provide us with the business which we had anticipated. It is now ten years, or more, since we gave up our major operations in the Sultanate. We used to have commercial equipment and trading operations there, but that is no longer so as, somehow, business did not grow in the way we had anticipated. That being said, Oman is a beautiful country which has much to offer. As the nation's economic development continues to evolve, the Sultanate now offers new opportunities for growth. As a result, no doubt we shall seek other opportunities in Oman to nurture new ventures in the future, different from those associated with our traditional business activities.

Chapter 11

Challenge
and Change

My grooming for participation in the family business began at an early age. Although my formal education was complex, I cannot claim that my life as a student was devoid of fun. My serious schooling began in the same way as it does for many Moslem children, learning to recite the Holy Quran by heart. I attended the Quranic School in Bahrain, after which my studies continued at the Eastern Boys School, then at the Western Boys School.

It was at this point that my education became somewhat unconventional. First, I was sent to Gerrard High School in Sidon, a branch of the American University in Beirut. There I studied the Lebanese high school curriculum, different from the Bahraini version. My schooling then continued in England where I obtained my O (Ordinary) and A (Advanced) level certification, followed by a year in college. Thus prepared, I began a Bachelor of Science degree course in the USA. A year later, in June 1967, I married my wife Salwa in Bahrain and then returned to my university studies in earnest. In 1968, my first son, Nabeel, was born. A year later, I graduated with honours.

Prior to all this, during the school summer holidays I, like the rest of my cousins, regularly returned to Bahrain and gained work experience. The first year, I was a tally clerk in the port. The second year I was assigned to the Kanoo Slipway where I learned to weld steel plates onto our barges and repair tug engines. During the third year, I worked in our commercial warehouse, stacking spare-part shelves and delivering machines to clients. In the fourth year, I worked in the commercial department as a salesmen, then finally, in the fifth year, I spent my summer vacation climbing up and down the sides of tankers as boarding representative taking care of tanker needs. Whenever we came home from school, the usual joke was that we were sent to England in the winter to freeze to death, and were brought home to Bahrain in the summer to fry to death! Despite our adolescent protests, this family system of indoctrination continued.

For a while, after my return from the USA, I was set to work in the Manama office for the statutory three-month orientation in our operating divisions. Then when Bill Docherty, Head of Administration and Property Maintenance, fell seriously sick and went to London, I replaced him. Being young and eager, with fresh ideas in my mind and my university textbooks to hand, I started making inroads straight away. Together with a very capable Indian secretary who knew a great deal, and with some common sense between us, we started a big clean-up. I don't think anyone realised what I was doing until it was too late, particularly for those who wanted things to remain as they were.

After clearing all outstanding matters which had been pending on Bill Docherty's desk for some months, one of our first tasks was to start standardising. There appeared to be no staff forms, not even job application forms. Filing and other office procedures seemed to be very crude, even non-existent in certain cases. My secretary and I had a field-day. I would look at my references and management books and see whether we could adapt this or that to fit our company and our culture. If my experienced secretary said, 'Yes, this is adaptable', we would do it.

The implementation of the first Bahrainisation procedure and structured training was one of the first innovations we introduced in 1969, followed by various other organisational and administrative achievements. These included offering one of our Bahraini employees serious training, (Tawfiq Taqi was the first of our Bahraini employees to be trained properly overseas. He is still with us). We also standardised employment grades and salaries; helped to train staff locally and introduced proper induction into the company for female personnel. After eight months of this, my uncles and father thought that I had created enough havoc. So, in late 1969, they despatched me to our office in Abu Dhabi as Assistant Branch Manager, then the outback of our organisation!

The UAE – a new-born nation

By the end of the 1960s, Shaikh Zayed's zealous efforts to develop Abu Dhabi were much in evidence. Its physical character had changed beyond all recognition when compared with just a few years earlier. To me, Abu Dhabi town must be the prettiest landscaped city in the world with all its most beautifully manicured trees, grass, flowers and shrubs, not to mention its wide streets and modern high-rise skyline. However, development on such a scale depleted the emirate's financial reserves. As a result, over-spending precipitated a mini-recession which lasted until the late 1970s when the economy of Abu Dhabi began to stabilise.

During the course of the previous chapter, I tried to describe the essence of an Arab nation being born, how people of many nationalities interacted to create the UAE's infrastructure, led by Shaikh Zayed Al Nahayan (in Abu Dhabi), Shaikh Rashid bin Saeed Al Maktoum (in Dubai) and the rulers of the other member-emirates: Sharjah, Ajman, Fujairah, Ras Al-Khaimah and Um Al-Qaiwain. I do not think that in the history of the world, any nation can claim to have established itself in as short time a time as the UAE, and to such a level. Please forgive me therefore, if now, based on my own experiences, I try to explain how the attitudes of those around me, and irreversible change in many forms, helped the strong growth of both the UAE and Y.B.A.Kanoo's business network throughout its domain.

In retrospect, I genuinely believe that I was really privileged to be in Abu Dhabi during that era. For, in such a short space of time (fourteen years), I witnessed the birth of a new nation, the United Arab Emirates, and shared in its growth as it matured into 'adulthood' and became a fully-fledged united state. It was an honour for me, and an unrepeatable, unique experience. The Abu Dhabians and Dubaians welcomed us as part of their family.

Our company was also privileged to contribute in its small way to this astronomical growth. Abdulaziz Al Khadar (who joined our shipping department in Bahrain in 1946 and later served in Saudi Arabia) was assigned to Abu Dhabi for a short period during this time. His recollection of the experience was practical and to the point. 'There was nothing. We had to stay in a tent. The company had asked me to help them with some project but told me: "We are sorry. We have no rooms, nothing. You will have to take your food and sleep in a tent." It didn't matter. It was only temporary.' Abdulaziz has always been a tough guy.

Those were pioneering years in every way. Water, for instance, still came from one source, a tanker. If the water tanker didn't arrive, then you didn't drink or wash. Meat arrived at Spinneys supermarket once a week. If your wife was not there first thing on a Tuesday morning to buy whatever fresh meat and vegetables she could, then you could not entertain the next day, unless (as in our case) we knew somebody who was scheduled to arrive from Bahrain. Then we would telex an SOS: 'Please bring some fresh this or that with you'. That type of situation was commonplace. Of course, there were always local sheep and goats, as well as other supermarkets which supplied food. Nevertheless, people tended to shop where they felt most comfortable.

The electricity supply was erratic. Power-cuts occurred at any time of day, and lasted for equally unpredictable periods of time. If you did not have a generator, then you just had to sweat it out for anything between a few hours and a day-and-a-half, depending on what damage had been caused to the electricity supply.

Despite these difficulties our family company participated in the growing development of the UAE. We introduced companies to Abu Dhabi, Dubai and Sharjah which represented various commercial sectors, including shipping, oil, transportation, building equipment and insurance.

Every day, it seemed as though some new construction was going up, or something less obvious but equally significant was being achieved. In particular, we participated in the transition from discharging cargo onto the beach in Abu Dhabi to the transformation of the Ruler's Jetty (which I described earlier) into a multi-berth deep-water port, Mina Zayed. In late 1970, work began, Arthur D. Little having been commissioned to design and supervise the new port's construction. When Mina Zayed opened in June 1972, only twenty-six of the thirty-six planned berths had been built. Later, the port was expanded to include thirty-four berths.

The challenge

When I took up my appointment as Assistant Branch Manager of our Abu Dhabi office in 1969, there were fewer than two dozen members of staff, including the new Branch Manager, Barry Cole, Mr Lee (my secretary) who had followed Peter Chaplin, and Mani, of course. There was Mr Matter, our driver-cum-public relations man, an accountant, four other shipping staff and sixteen ships' representatives, drivers and salesmen. We sold BAT cigarettes, Blundel paints, Norwich Union insurance and handled four or so ships a month, discharging them offshore. Qureshi, who I mention later, joined Y.B.A.Kanoo in 1972, as did Richard Barnes (shipping) who, in 1976, emigrated to New Zealand. He was the Napoleonic type, short and very energetic. R. D. Chopra (insurance) left in 1974. David Oliver (commercial) joined one of our principals, BASF, in 1976.

From time to time, Peter Chaplin visited Abu Dhabi from Bahrain as the Kanoo Group representative. He, I believe, was one of the few people who really understood what was happening in the emirate during that era. Whenever he visited our office there, we spent most of our time together. He taught me practical managerial skills that I, as a young man, had not yet appreciated. We fought like cats and dogs during office hours because of my stubbornness, but in the evening we were always friends again. If I wanted to do something one way, Peter would ask if I had considered a different way. Invariably, I had not. So, together, we thought and discussed these points until we came to a decision. This was how I learnt. Not only was Peter Chaplin my mentor, but he also stuck his neck out for me several times.

In many ways, I look back on that time as the 'Khalid Kanoo Roadshow', partly because Hamed Kanoo was busy building our operation in Dubai and largely left me alone in Abu Dhabi. He had done his share of pioneering in Saudi Arabia. By the late 1960s, he had made his home in Dubai. There, he felt most comfortable and preferred to stay.

For me, Abu Dhabi was a challenge. In 1970, everyone in the business fraternity was friendly, each person trying to help one another. As yet, there was no cut-throat competition in the emirate. People were just trying to survive the recession. Money was scarce. There was none of the commercial 'violence' so evident after the mid-1970s by which time business practice had become really rough as everyone tried to gain a bigger share of the same pie.

My first task as Assistant Branch Manager was to enhance our company's ability to introduce Kanoo services and capabilities to the local market. This was very important since, at that time, the standard answer to most requests was: 'You have to have a local partner.' Shaikh Zayed wanted the Abu Dhabians to work with non-nationals so that they would learn about business and commerce. Consequently UAE nationals were placed in positions of influence.

To begin with, I found life in Abu Dhabi very tough and frustrating. Everything was a struggle, made worse by the lack of amenities that we take for granted today, such as power and water. I drove a Land-Rover because to drive anything else was asking to be stuck in the sand. Because of the lack of residential accommodation, I had to search for five months to find a house for myself and my family to live in.

The people, however, both local and expatriates, made life bearable. Everyone was kind and hospitable and I made great friends. Shaikh Mubarak bin Mohamed Al Nahayan (then the Minister of Interior) stands out. His moral and active support was invaluable to me. I admire and respect him like a father and he treats me like a son. His own son, Nahayan, is becoming like his father, a real gentleman, loved by everybody. Shaikh Mubarak, who had time for everyone, opened our new office building in Abu Dhabi in 1974. Now, I always make a point of visiting him first whenever I travel to Abu Dhabi. Shaikh Hamdan bin Mohamed, Shaikh Suroor bin Mohamed and Shaikh Saif bin Mohamed were also good to me. Of course, Shaikh Zayed bin Sultan Al Nahayan was unequalled. He was always fair and just.

Initially I had no business contacts in Abu Dhabi. When I needed guidance in commercial matters, I visited Ahmed Al-Masood, the then head of the Chamber of Commerce and a leading merchant. He was generous to a fault with a heart of gold, a true gentleman. (He died in London in 1978, a great loss to Abu Dhabi and myself.) Ahmed Al-Masood had worked hard together with his brothers Rahma and Abdulla, to create a reputable and prominent company. But the Al-Masood family strength was not in their money but, like many distinguished Arab families, in their generosity to those in need, their hospitality and care for their fellow men and country. As my grandfather Jassim's agent in Abu Dhabi, the Al-Masood family sold cement and provided labour for our ships. Their business dealings with us were very honourable. By the time that I arrived in Abu Dhabi, we had little work with them, but Ahmed Al-Masood was always there to help me if I needed his assistance. Arabs in business were bound by their verbal commitment. Even today, there are many who take more notice of verbal promises than signed agreements, which reminds me of one such episode.

Salim Al-Saman, a leading member of the Abu Dhabian commercial community, once told me that when he was a young dhow *nawkhadha* plying the Gulf waters, on one occasion he was stuck in Bahrain, his dhow engine broken down beyond the possibility of repair. Not having the financial resources at that time to buy a replacement, the enterprising *nawkhadha* visited Haji Khalil Kanoo, the agent in Bahrain for Kelvinator marine engines.

Salim had no money to pay for a new engine but said that, if Khalil would give him one 'on account', he would work hard to repay the debt quickly. After Haji Khalil had checked Salim's credentials, such as the name of his father, where he came from and whom he knew, he provided a new engine to be paid for when conditions permitted. True to his promise, Salim worked long hours so that he could repay Haji Khalil as soon as he could. No papers exchanged hands, just a man's word.

From the outset of my assignment to Abu Dhabi, I knew that I was more or less on my own and would have to work out the local etiquette for myself. My first step was to become known at the Ruler's *majlis,* as well as those of other Shaikhs, particularly Khalifa, Mubarak, Hamdan, Suroor and Saif, and the offices of other prominent Abu Dhabian merchants.

To start with, I would become friendly with one person, then I would say, 'I don't know Shaikh so-and-so who "sits" on such-and-such a day. I would like to go along with you next time you go'. When this happened, my companion would introduce me. Somehow, somewhere, Shaikh so-and-so would have heard of my family. At the *majlis,* usually in a building outside the home of the person who was 'sitting', I would make sure I was noticed without being offensive or obtrusive. The important thing was to ensure that the Shaikh's retainers noticed me and remembered my face, because once I had managed to be seen several times and my face had become familiar to the Shaikhs officials, then I would have frequent access to the *majlis.*

Government officials were always careful too, and avoided saying: 'Hey, you are not a national. You cannot do this or that.' On the whole, they gave me the impression that they said among themselves: 'He is always around the Shaikhs. The Kanoo family is well known. We will make an exception for him to do this or that', or something along those lines.

I cannot remember how I tackled each situation, but whatever technique I adopted, it seemed to work. Yes, it is true that I enjoyed and learnt from the years I spent in Abu Dhabi. But that is only because very early on I realised that to survive the environmental and economic hostility, I could either withdraw into my shell, or I could tackle the difficulties we faced head-on, and with a sense of humour.

With the support of Hamed Kanoo, my wife Salwa, Peter Chaplin, Abdulla Al-Kindi, Mani and a few other people who had more business experience than myself at that time, I told myself that I was going to make a success of it. I soon learnt to get problems 'off my chest', so that I was ready for the next one which came up and hit me, sometimes in the next few days, but more often within minutes. As I was alone in a completely new environment where things were developing fast, I had to learn very quickly how to handle shaikhs, customers, staff and competitors.

As anyone who is familiar with the Arab world knows, the generation of business is very much the result of successful public relations. My wife, Salwa, spent a great deal of time helping me out in this way, whether it was arranging a men-only official dinner party with shaikhs and prominent people, or having mixed social events, and even laying on 'emergency' dinners. For example, when Bahrain's national football team, led by Shaikh Isa bin Rashid Al Khalifa, won their match in Abu Dhabi, I was asked to arrange a celebration dinner for the entire Bahraini entourage. In total, there were thirty-six people. Knowing exactly what response I would get from my wife, I telephoned her nonetheless. I told her that although I appreciated it was 5.30 p.m., in just three hours, we were all coming to dinner. Would she please arrange for the food to be ready by 8.30 p.m.! Not surprisingly, she had a few choice words to tell me about planning ahead and where was she going to find plates, knifes and forks, let alone prepare food ready for three-dozen people in three hours? But when dinner-time came there was food for thirty-six people.

Another significant way in which Salwa helped me was by becoming accepted within the Abu Dhabi ladies' circles, including that of Shaikha Fatima, the wife of His Highness, Shaikh Zayed. Without my wife's understated yet significant role in this context, I doubt that I would have succeeded in Abu Dhabi.

It was important, too, that I could return to the comfort of a home at the end of a difficult day. By this, I do not mean just the material comforts of a typical Arab household, such as carpets, cushions and *gahwa* (coffee). I mean the opportunity to share the day's trials and tribulations with a supportive wife. Without this safety valve, life would have been very much more difficult. It was quite usual for me to leave home at seven o'clock in the morning, return twelve hours later, change and go out for dinner, not for relaxation but to continue the process of public relations. Then, at one o'clock in the morning, I would ask myself: 'What have I achieved today?' Often, I would conclude, zero. I might have followed the same routine all week, but at the end of it all, I would still feel that I hadn't achieved anything measurable. Sometimes, the frustration of appearing not to have done much or of having stayed still in terms of progress, made me quite depressed.

By 1973 all the hard work I had put in for four years came to fruition. Public recognition and income were 'measurable'. Even so, it was essential for me to have someone on my side and at my side, who understood what I was going through, who did not give me any conflict and who was there as both my confidante and personal companion. Certainly, my introduction to Abu Dhabi during those pioneering days was made much easier by having my wife with me.

Improvisation

I remember one night when I was hosting a big party. At about 9.00 p.m. there was a power-cut and I did not have a generator. Da'abis Kadri, a friend of mine, lived next door. Not only did he have a big living room, but also he owned a generator. So I called him and said: 'Look, I have people here and no electricity. What are you and your wife doing tonight?'

He invited us to join them, but explained that he and his wife were not dressed for a party. So I simply suggested that he took his wife out for a while so that I could bring my guests into his house to carry on with the party. So he did just that! Now, where can you get away with something like that now? I could not even call my cousin next door and say: 'Please take your wife out. I am going to have a party in your house.' But that was the co-operative spirit then. We all faced the same difficulties and we made the best of it.

By day the frustrations were, if anything, greater. Sand blew all over the place, in your face, nose, eyes, ears and hair. In some places, you would sink into the sand just trying to cross the road. But in this pioneering spirit, if your car became stuck in the sand, anyone who saw that you were in trouble would come and help push your car, regardless of who you, or they, were. This can be seen from an incident which happened soon after Abu Dhabi became the seat of government for the newly-formed United Arab Emirates.

One day, a big sand storm caused part of the beach to be blown across the new two-lane Corniche Road. At that time, my wife Salwa was driving her Toyota Crown along the road. Suddenly someone tried to overtake her, forcing my wife's car into the freshly blown sand on the edge of the road. There she came to a sudden stop, bogged down in deep soft sand. As she stepped out of the car, the British Ambassador's wife happened to pass by and offered her a lift. Later, when Salwa telephoned to tell me the tale, I was amazed: 'How can you get stuck in the sand on the Corniche Road?' She replied: 'Yes, there is enough sand for me not to be able to move my car'. Still sceptical, I told her that I must see this for myself! Sure enough, I found her car stuck in the sand on the Corniche.

While my driver went off to find a tow-rope, I stood waiting by the side of road. Coincidentally, a cabinet meeting was just about to start. Every few minutes, Ministers and other important people drove by: Shaikh Hamdan (Deputy Prime Minister), Shaikh Mubarak (Minister of the Interior), as well as several other people. In turn they stopped, some to offer help, others to tease: 'Hey Khalid, how can you get stuck on the Corniche? Can we help?' Very embarrassing indeed.

This 'Let us help you because you are in trouble' attitude, especially in times of physical trouble, was pre-eminent in Abu Dhabi and its neighbouring emirates at that time. Now manners have changed. Like many other parts of the world, you can get into difficulties and most people will just whizz by without stopping, either because they are in a hurry or, sadly, because they do not care anymore.

In those days, it was a different way of life. You could see your contribution and you would know that it would be appreciated. I could say to myself, I was the first to import these Hyster fork-lift trucks for the port or, those are my tugs operating out there, all helping to build a new country. Nowadays, this is no longer true as one jumps from one contract to another. It is every man for himself which, to my mind, is a pity. But then, that is progress...

Although Abu Dhabi boasted some 400 per cent more housing in 1970 than I had seen during my first visit in 1964, there remained an extreme shortage. For the most part, the road system still comprised just desert tracks. Perhaps 10 per cent of the new roads had an asphalt surface. The rest were either graded or sprayed with oil. For instance, the route from Abu Dhabi to Dubai was still desert. It would take three and a half hours, if you knew where you were going. There were tracks all over the place which you had to know. I remember two checkpoints on this particular stretch of road where you had to have your passport stamped, one for Abu Dhabi and one for Dubai. It was not unusual to hear of someone having died because he had turned right instead of left, and so had driven inland into the heart of the desert instead of heading for the coast. It was a long, rough ride during which you had to keep your eyes open and your wits about you. Foolish was the fellow who carried on driving after sunset. Not only would you lose your way, but also if it was your bad luck to hit a camel which you could not see in the darkness, the weight and force of the falling animal would almost certainly crush the vehicle and often its occupants.

Needless to say, these occupational hazards did not put me off desert driving. My first vehicle was a Land-Rover, after which I had a Toyota car, neither of which had air-conditioning. Like most young men in their early twenties who have both a passion for motor cars and a penchant for trying to impress their peers, I persuaded Ahmed Kanoo that he could not expect me to promote Kanoo business from a Land-Rover or a Toyota! So after some persuasion, he agreed to give me a budget to buy the car I liked: a Mercedes 250. But to meet the budget, it was very basic. It had no air-conditioning, no automatic transmission, and the windows had to be wound up and down by hand. Nevertheless, the important thing was that it was a Mercedes like my peers' vehicles.

That was my car for nine or ten years. Once the *nouveau riche* became prominent in Abu Dhabi and the new men became richer, they could afford to import all types of expensive cars, just to show off. So in my own innovative way, I joined them at their own game. As my car would get sand-blasted, particularly when I drove from Abu Dhabi to Dubai, every two or three years I would paint it a different colour so that it looked like a new car! As far as my father and uncles were concerned, the Kanoo family had to live and work with the resources that were given to us and I was no exception.

Measured success

In 1972, our main agencies in Abu Dhabi were for shipping lines, construction equipment manufacturers and British American Tobacco (BAT). Those were the days before government health warnings about the hazards of smoking when much of the population smoked with carefree abandon. Indeed, for a period of time, BAT became one of our three most profitable agencies in terms of income generation, the other two being the Maersk Line and Grove cranes. On average, we held 30 per cent of the cigarette market share in the Abu Dhabi emirate.

The major cigarette manufacturers, then part of BAT, were the American company Brown and Williamson, famous for its Lucky Strike brand. (Marlboro was its main rival.) The British manufacturers in the BAT Group were Benson and Hedges which produced State Express, and John D. Player, famous for their Senior Service brand. (Rothmans was the British competitor.)

Over the years, our trading practices improved and changes occurred. Now our salesmen regularly inspect the cigarettes on the retailers' shelves. Whenever they see that the product is out of date or discoloured, for example, they remove stock voluntarily and replace the defective items with fresh stock at no cost to the retailer. Then the reclaimed stock is destroyed, burnt under the supervision of an authorised person. My managers liked the cigarette trade. It was good business because nobody has ever brought a cigarette-end back for repair or maintenance. What we sold went up in smoke.

Being very conscious about efficiency and motivation, I am

reminded of a story concerning Subhan Qureshi, a Pakistani who joined our company in 1972 as our Sales Manager for Tobacco. (In the same year, I became Branch Manager in Abu Dhabi). More than twenty years later, Qureshi still works for us. Once we were established in our respective new routines, I visited him regularly to check on his sales and stock-control.

Rumour had it that Qureshi was on the fiddle and selling to his benefit from our stock. I did not believe it but I decided to put these rumours to rest. One day, unannounced, I went to the BAT warehouse with Qureshi, with the book-keeper following us. After numerous spot-checks, I could not find anything amiss.

Relieved that all seemed to be well, on my way out I noticed one cigar box without any sealed wrapping. I opened the box and saw three cigars missing. So I targeted that and asked: 'Where are the other cigars? Please show me the book.' Qureshi did as I had asked.

Sure enough, correctly documented, there was the entry: one box open and three cigars missing. 'What is this?,' I asked. 'Who opened the box and who took the cigars?' Very politely and patiently, Qureshi replied: 'Sir, it was you. When you came in the last time.' It was true. The cigars were from a new brand which I had wished to try to find out if it was good or not!

By the time I was based in Abu Dhabi with my family, Gray Mackenzie, our competitors, had established a base at Jebel Dhana. If you look at a modern map of Arabia, and follow the road south-west from Abu Dhabi for about 200 kilometres, you will see a town called Ruwais. Just off the road on the coast, there is a small promontory. This is Jebel Dhana. At that time, it was a desolate area comprising just a small village and an oil terminal from which Abu Dhabi's onshore oil was exported. (Das Island tanker terminal serves the offshore oil-field.) There was nothing of substance at Jebel Dhana. The only exceptions were a few industrial installations, such as chemical plants, required by the authorities to be sited near the onshore Habshan oilfield, located between Abu Dhabi and the Jebel Dhana oil-loading terminal. In our case, when a tanker for which we were responsible arrived offshore, one of us had to make the four-hour drive from Abu Dhabi to Jebel Dhana along a single carriageway road which degenerated into a sandy track some way before our destination.

In the early 1970s, the late Governor of the area, Shaikh Sultan bin Soroor Al-Dhahiry had his house and *majlis* built on top of the hill at Jebel Dhana. From this elevated vantage point, he could see everything going on around him. If, from his overview, the Shaikh noticed your arrival, he might sometimes send for you and enquire why you were in Jebel Dhana. If he liked you, he would invite you for Arabic coffee, lunch or dinner. Eventually, the time came when Kanoo senior management decided that I should approach Shaikh Sultan with a view to him agreeing to give our company a piece of land on which to build some permanent premises. After the customary round of courtesy calls and conversation a deal was reached and a fence was built round the allocated plot of land which, it so happened, was on the beach next to Gray Mackenzie's premises. Because we were short of budgeted cash I persuaded a local company which imported portable houses to deliver a sample to Jebel Dhana for people to see and then suggested that we would take care of it. To my surprise, the company agreed and so we used their demonstration house as Kanoo's Jebel Dhana office and staff accommodation.

There was really nothing to do in Jebel Dhana except work. The only entertainment available to those living there was during the evening when they invited each other for dinner to talk about work or whatever the gossip might have been. This isolation had one major compensation: living right beside a beautiful unpolluted beach with soft clean sand and turquoise coloured sea in which we could swim or go fishing.

In due time and particularly during the height of the oil boom, Y.B.A.Kanoo developed a very profitable niche for itself in Jebel Dhana by providing key services to the shipping industry: bunkering, ship's chandlery and lighterage. One of our biggest contracts was with the Saudi Arabia Transport Organization Limited (SATOL), an American-run Saudi-based company in joint-venture with us. It was through SATOL that the oil companies moved thousands of tons of oil exploration equipment on their big trucks to the oil well-heads. When the time came to build an oil refinery at Ruwais, this is where we came in. After the contracts were awarded to build the infrastructure and industrial plants at Jebel Dhana and Ruwais, we secured the main contract for lighterage: ship-to-shore, shore-to-site. It was a huge undertaking.

By 1977, I decided it was time to recruit a manager for Abu Dhabi. I had already interviewed a candidate called Alf Johnson, then employed by Alireza in Saudi Arabia. He seemed a good choice and so I offered him the job on the spot. He accepted and joined us three weeks later. His 'baptism of fire', as he calls it, began by arriving at Abu Dhabi airport at about eight-thirty one evening in mid-June, to be met by a rather large bearded gentleman who somehow recognised him.

A sandstorm was blowing and it was a miserable night. After Johnson's baggage was loaded into the car, the two men set off. After a while, Johnson asked his companion: 'Are you sure there is nothing wrong with your car?' Back came an unsurprised reply: 'Oh, yes. Both the front tyres are flat, punctured. And I don't fancy walking in a sand-storm carrying your bags'. So, in this condition, they drove all the way back to our Abu Dhabi office.

The driver was the legendary Norman Morris, generally known to us by his nickname Mick Morris. Johnson later told me, 'He was the best advertisement that Kanoo has ever had in the UAE'. He weighed about 146 kg, was an ex-wrestler and a former Coldstream Guards Sergeant, (the well-known regiment of soldiers which wears large bearskin 'hats' and guards Buckingham Palace in London), a huge man with a big black beard and a heart of gold. He managed our Cargo Services and anything else we gave him.

Having survived the bumpy, dusty ride, a shaken-up Johnson was brought up to my office. There he was introduced to 'two or three other guys' who told Johnson that he was to wait to meet me because he was to be appointed Branch Manager, there and then! After we had greeted each other and had a preliminary chat about this and that, I told Johnson that I would take him for dinner since I had a few things which I needed to explain to him. We set off for the Hilton Hotel, the only decent hotel in town at that time, and had them open up the restaurant at midnight so that we could order something to eat. During the course of our meal, I told Alf Johnson that my mother was very ill, that I had to take her to the United States and that I was leaving Abu Dhabi the next morning. I simply said: 'There are the keys to the office. The cheque-book is in the safe. Get on with it. I will see you when I get back'.

It was ten weeks before I saw Johnson again. When I returned, I asked him: 'Are you still here? You mean you haven't taken the money and gone?' An amazed Johnson looked me straight in the eye and simply replied: 'No. I'm still here!' And he is still 'here', based in Dubai as Y.B.A.Kanoo's General Manager of Joint Ventures and Associated Companies, UAE and Oman.

One of Alf Johnson's first jobs was to visit Jebel Dhana and Ruwais once a week to monitor our SATOL joint-venture activities. His Land-Rover had no air-conditioning and the road was still a compacted track. Certainly a conventional car could not reach the site. Despite his experience in Saudi Arabia, the conditions were terrible for Alf although picturesque to a tourist and normal to a bedouin.

As for Mick Morris, I first met him as the representative of Chicago Bridge, a tank-farm construction company. He worked for Larry Cooper, the Area Manager for whom we cleared cargo. Morris gave me such a hard time that when the job was finished I asked him to join us. I needed men who were loyal and hard-working and he never let me down.

Investment incentives

As far as we were concerned, it seemed that Gray Mackenzie had always been in the UAE. As a British company, part of the Raj operation, it was authorised by the British government to be the official British shipping agent in the Arabian Gulf. Prior to the 1970s, nobody wished to upset the British government because their Political Agent would simply talk to the Ruler and refer to this or that treaty to get his way.

African and Eastern was another British company which used to operate from Basrah through us as their agent in Bahrain representing the Arabian Gulf region. After we established the market for their products, they decided to establish themselves in Bahrain and the UAE, something that the locals could do nothing about until after the mid-1970s, by which time the local government had become sufficiently confident and strong to cause the British influence to decline.

Before Shaikh Zayed became Ruler of Abu Dhabi there was very little commercial activity in the emirate. Although many leading families worked there, those who prospered were the ones who dealt with international companies and other Gulf States business houses, and those who obtained the agencies of leading brands and service companies. Among the prominent names which come to mind in Abu Dhabi are the Al Fahim, Al Yousuf, Al Masood, bin Hamooda, Al-Nowais, Al-Khouri and Al-Gaith families. (Incidentally, the first few shops to open in the Abu Dhabi souq between 1961 and 1962 were owned by the Al Fahim, Al-Askari, Masood, Futtaim and Al-Yousuf families.)

After Shaikh Zayed had moulded a basic government mechanism and the emirate started to have surplus revenues, all foreign companies were forced to take partners. We were facing a big legal problem with a prominent Abu Dhabian, Mr Abduljalil Al Fahim, who felt that as he had introduced us to Abu Dhabi, then he was our partner. To settle this, Shaikh Zayed set up an arbitration committee, chaired by Mohamed Al-Habroosh (Head of Abu Dhabi's Finance

Department, at that time). A settlement of 10,000 Bahraini dinars was awarded to Abduljalil as fees for helping us in Abu Dhabi. We gladly paid this and maintained our friendly relationship with him.

Although there was no great pressure on us to take on a partner because of our history in Abu Dhabi, I decided to do so and avoid any future negative perceptions. I chose Faraj Hamooda, a fine character and shrewd businessman who co-operated fully with us. In practice I did not call on him to help unless it was essential, but nevertheless the congenial relationship we built up between us, allowed me to run our Abu Dhabi office without conflict. As a partner he received 25 per cent of our profit (the legal requirement defined in our Municipal Licence dated 31 January 1971). To this end, I insisted that our account should be audited professionally (by Whinney Murray) although Faraj Hamooda did not invest any of his own money into our company.

A major advantage of these changed circumstances was that, with the exception of Abu Dhabi where sale of land was a difficult process, we were now allowed to buy land in the UAE. We were no longer required to rent the land on which we built office and housing accommodation, only for it to revert back to the land-owner after the lease expired. In Abu Dhabi plots of land cannot usually be bought but must be gifts of the Ruler. In 1968, we were fortunate to receive such a gift from Shaikh Zayed.

After I became Branch Manager in Abu Dhabi (following the previous incumbent's resignation), one of my first decisions in 1972 was to commission the first Kanoo purpose-built premises in the emirate. After a year of nagging Ahmed Kanoo, the Group Chairman, he allocated me a budget of BD 150,000 for the building's construction. (As mentioned earlier, it was not until May 1973 that the UAE's national currency, the dirham, was launched. During this transitional period, the Bahrain dinar was used instead.) It was soon clear that BD 150,000 was not enough to pay for my ambitious scheme, a building of some eight or nine floors. I could afford just four floors, on three-quarters of the plot. So, to stop someone else encroaching on our land, I had a pavement laid out at the front and a store constructed at the back.

When our new office-block was completed in 1973 it was the tallest building on the road. Today, it is the shortest, overshadowed by buildings sixteen or more storeys high. But never mind, we owned our own office at last and it was decent enough. In our perception, and, we hoped, that of our clients, we had started to progress. Within eleven years, the eight staff we had when I arrived in 1969 had increased to some 300. When I left Abu Dhabi in 1982, this office was generating almost as much income as our Dubai operation.

Chapter 12

The Boom Years

For some time within the Arab world there had been a shift in weight and influence from the traditional political power centres of Cairo and Damascus to the Arabian peninsula. In 1973 what had been perceptible during the 1960s now became fully apparent. In his study, *A History of the Middle East,* Peter Mansfield shows how both skilled and unskilled workers, as well as professionals in many disciplines whose homes were in Egypt and the Levant states, had looked to the eldorado of the Arab Gulf countries as a means of transforming their living standards.

While this change was taking place, power politics were being played out by the OPEC membership. Investment of the 'petro-dollars' earned by its members' huge and growing surpluses had begun to affect both international currency markets and the business climate in many advanced industrial countries. However, amid all this debate, there was another undercurrent: increasing discontent with Israel's occupation of Arab lands. Little did we know at the time that the events of 1973 would have such a huge impact on the growth of our family business, and on the economies of the western nations.

During the summer of 1973, the Syrians and Egyptians co-ordinated their plans and launched an attack on Israel at 2.00 p.m. local time on 6 October which, that year, was the Jewish feast of Yom Kippur. The resultant war, which was to have far-reaching effects on the Arab world, was brought to a close on 25 October, after energetic diplomacy.

Meanwhile, on 1 October 1973, just five days before the outbreak of the Yom Kippur War, the price of crude oil was raised from US$1.80 to US$3.011. Realised market prices had begun to exceed the official posted price for the most widely traded crude oils, the result of a growing tightness in crude oil supply as oil companies found it difficult to expand their producing capacities at a rate compatible with world demand. Not surprisingly, the oil industry's problems were exacerbated by the new round of Arab–Israeli warfare.

Oil embargo and price explosion

Within two weeks two events occurred on successive days at the Sheraton Hotel, Kuwait City, which forced the world to face an Arab oil embargo of unprecedented proportions. Based on the findings of an OPEC working group and responding to some of the Arabian Gulf states' demand that the posted prices of crude oil should be raised, on 16 October 1973 the OPEC meeting made a dramatic announcement. The posted price of Saudi Arabian light crude, used by OPEC as a pricing bench-mark for crude, was increased on a 'take it or leave it' basis by 70 per cent to US$5.119 per barrel.

The second dramatic announcement was made the next day, 17 October 1973, this time during a meeting of nine oil ministers among the OAPEC members. The chief Iraqi delegate called upon the Arab states to target their anger specifically at the USA, namely to nationalise all American business in the Arab world, to withdraw all Arab funds from American banks and to institute a total oil embargo against the USA and other countries friendly to Israel. In his epic history, *The Prize,* Daniel Yergin noted that 'The chairman of the meeting, the Algerian minister, dismissed such a proposal as impractical and unacceptable'. Instead, the nine oil ministers agreed to reduce production by 5 per cent from the September level, and then a further 5 per cent every following month until 'their objectives were met'. Thus, the oil embargo began.

Yergin's assessment is that these two meetings in Kuwait City, on 16 and 17 October, were not formally connected. OPEC's price increase was a logical outcome of what had been evolving for some time. The OAPEC-backed oil embargo was seen more as a response to the new Arab–Israeli conflict (the Yom Kippur War).

Nevertheless, the desired effect was immediate. The posted price of Arabian light crude was more than doubled once again. By 1 January 1974, the price had shot up to US$11.65 per barrel. The impact of the Arab oil embargo and oil-price explosion was evident throughout the world. A new age had arrived.

At that time, people in the West and its media had many negative feelings regarding the oil price increase. I remember that King Faisal was put under great pressure by western leaders to ease the 'oil embargo' by increasing production and reducing prices. The astute monarch, one of my favourite politicians, was a very shrewd and subtle operator. When the same leaders threatened to stop supplying western goods to the Kingdom, King Faisal's response was typically pragmatic: 'western civilisation' had not yet reached a stage in Saudi

Arabia whereby the Kingdom could not revert to dependence upon dates and camel milk. 'We will survive.' The question he put to the western leaders was more to the point: 'Can *you* survive without our oil, and without our importing from you?' Not surprisingly, the leaders withdrew their threats and compromised with the King.

In fact, the West benefited because of the rising oil prices. After the price increases a typical economic reaction took place. Oil attained its true market price and the Arabian Gulf nations found themselves with a larger fund to improve the infrastructure of their countries, invest in services and industry and look after their citizens without taxation. This increased the natural entrepreneurial spirit of Arab traders. But from where did they buy all their services? The West, of course. There was a huge increase in demand for western companies to provide everything from paper and paper-clips, to nails, wood, cars, textiles, electrical products, power, water distribution, hospitals, schools, aeroplanes, airports, sea terminals, ships, telecommunications systems, and so on.

Arabia experienced an unparalleled metamorphosis. This was achieved in record time with the help of the 'developed' nations of the world. Let us not forget that each foreign country and company which participated in this phenomenal development benefited enormously too, as many still do today.

The dramatic increase in oil prices during 1973 stimulated a tremendous explosion of economic growth. According to Bill Brien, until then, the Y.B.A.Kanoo operation in Saudi Arabia was sometimes considered, because of its size and generated income, as a 'poor relation' to its 'sister' operation in the UAE, and the 'parent' business in Bahrain. So much so, that sometimes the Bahrain office had to send money to our office in Saudi Arabia to help finance its projects. The oil boom changed all that.

Coinciding with the oil-price explosion in the latter months of 1973, Bill Brien took over as Group General Manager of Y.B.A. Kanoo during the same year. Although all Kanoo family members involved with the business at that time were well aware of shifting trends, Bill Brien soon found himself assuming the role of financial adviser to the Group Chairman. From the perspective of monitoring world trading activity and investment opportunities, Brien reflected on the Y.B.A.Kanoo organisation's remarkable growth after the onset of the oil boom. Suddenly, the financial picture changed and overseas investment became attractive, if not desirable.

Portfolio management is something in which the Kanoo family, like many privately-owned family businesses, does not go into specifics. However, Bill Brien's brief account of what happened during the 1970s is an interesting commentary on the economic forces which affected the future development of our company, and that of similar organisations, too.

Suddenly, our family business, together with many others, found that we were obliged to offer credit and had to build up our inventories. We had to employ more staff and build additional accommodation. As Bill Brien 'crunched' the financial numbers, he soon recognised that the Y.B.A.Kanoo group was approaching a liquidity crisis because of its insistence on self-financing and on minimum borrowing from banks.

Fortunately our company responded to these danger signals early enough and managed to survive this crisis without having to borrow money. Before long, the Y.B.A.Kanoo Group began to ride on the crest of a new wave of good fortune, this time a financial surplus created during the latter years of the oil boom.

Once again, this prompted Bill Brien to discuss the company's financial strategy with the Group Chairman, his prime concern being the increasing uncertainties facing the financial world. To Brien, it didn't make sense for the Group to be exposed to volatile market fluctuations when our financial risk could be spread beyond Arabia. The days of boom and bonanza could not last forever. We all knew that. With typical pragmatism, Brien advised the Group Chairman that some form of investment overseas was the most prudent move.

The Main Board was not convinced. In the late 1970s, land prices were increasing rapidly, particularly in Saudi Arabia. To many Kanoo directors, real estate was a secure and saleable asset. In fact, Abdulaziz Kanoo in Saudi Arabia, Abdulrahman in Bahrain and Hamed in the UAE went ahead and bought property in their areas. However, when the Shah of Iran was deposed in 1979, followed by the onset of the Iranian-Iraqi war in 1980, economic uncertainty and national security concerns engulfed the Arabian Gulf region. At last, the Board agreed that the Kanoo Group should invest overseas.

Thus, with nervous caution the Directors adopted a new corporate financial strategy. The Group Chairman swiftly engaged a firm of London lawyers, gathered a team of trusted bankers with whom he had developed good relationships and instructed Bill Brien to prepare an investment plan: 'I had to dream up something which was going to give the family an element of security and not put too much at risk.' So he gave portfolio managers baskets of currencies and guide-lines and developed a conservative investment strategy. In retrospect, this bold move was more than risk management. The scope for greater diversification had become apparent, such as entry into Asian and Japanese markets which we had not explored.

Today, our family business activities in the Kingdom of Saudi Arabia account for the major part of the Y.B.A.Kanoo Group in terms of the range of offices we maintain and the number of employees required to service that extensive network. As for income generation, Y.B.A.Kanoo operations in Saudi Arabia are the most prolific in terms of our Group trading and service activities.

New age of technology and travel

Two dramatic changes which affected the world during the 1970s and 1980s were the rapid growth of computers and of communications systems, including major advances in air travel.

Our first encounter with computer technology began in 1965 when the Y.B.A.Kanoo Board decided to install the company's first computer. Our plans coincided with the Bahrain Government's 1965 census, conducted between 13 February and 12 March that year. In order to prepare a computer program to analyse the statistics (182,203 computer punched cards – one for each person who participated in the census) BAPCO had taken delivery of an IBM 1401 computer in late 1964. This utilised transistor technology, the first of its kind to be installed in the Middle East.

In our case, Kanoo Group Computer Services became a reality in May 1965 when our first computer was installed, not an IBM but an NCR390. We had asked IBM to quote. However, at that time, the company operated out of Beirut, Lebanon. Their attitude was: 'This is our price, this is our machine, sign this service agreement. Take it or leave it'. So we left it. NCR's attitude was much more flexible, with the result that Y.B.A.Kanoo was the first family business company to use NCR computer technology in the region and we have used their main-frame and mini-computers ever since. A General Ledger application was introduced. All accounting transactions were input through paper tape and then posted on magnetic ledger cards.

On 27 February 1971, Akber Sa'ati (now our Group General Manager) joined Y.B.A.Kanoo as a young computer programer. That same day he flew to Cairo to attend a computer training course at the American University, in preparation for the installation of our second computer in May 1971: an NCR Century 100 mainframe. Seven new applications were introduced, all transactions being input through cards instead of paper tape, and the data stored on '655' disks, quite an innovation in those days.

In June 1974, our NCR Century 100 mainframe computer was superseded by a faster, more sophisticated version, the NCR Century 101 mainframe. This enabled us to introduce several new applications including stock inventory control and management, travel ticket stock and sales, payroll and personnel, container control, and a computerized telex system.

Input for all the regions (Bahrain, Saudi Arabia, the UAE and Oman) was undertaken in Bahrain until August 1976. Then, in that year, a similar NCR Century 101 configuration was installed in Dubai so that documents pertaining to the UAE and Oman could be processed faster locally. It was not until October 1977 that another identical configuration was installed in Dammam for processing all our company's Saudi Arabian documents.

In June 1982 the Bahrain Century 101 computer was replaced with an even faster and more complex mainframe, the NCR V-8555 Criterion. Similar configurations were installed in Dammam in January 1983 and in Dubai in July 1988. Since then, we have designed and implemented many new systems, such as those required for expense control, sale and income analysis, asset control and management. As new technology has become available, such as mini-computers, we have continued to adapt to our changing needs. In 1992, we purchased a NCR 3000 mini-computer. After more than a decade of computer development, it became obvious that procedures and practices which had worked perfectly well since the Second World War now required change. The speed and scope of business had become faster and more complex. Although the entire Kanoo organisation is not as fully computerised as our management would like, PCs are evident everywhere. So far, our Shipping Division has been fully computerised by our programers who are now in the process of doing the same thing in the Travel Division. Once this is complete, the Commercial and Machinery Divisions will follow suit. In the end, computer chips have become just as important to our business growth as the vision of 'blue' chips.

Not only were computers adapting to this change. So were airlines as they responded to the growing needs of their passengers, both business and holiday travellers. Speed and capacity were key considerations. When the Sultanate of Oman and the United Arab Emirates became independent sovereign states, those nations were anxious to form a regional airline of their own. The obvious candidate was Gulf Aviation. (During that era, only the Kingdom of

Saudi Arabia and the Emirate of Kuwait had, so far, launched their own national airlines: Saudi Arabian Airline Corporation (SDI) in 1947, and Kuwait National Airways in 1954.)

So it was that my father and Hussain Yateem both became directors of the re-constituted Gulf Aviation (originally founded on 24 March 1950) and remained on its Board until the end of 1973. When Gulf Air began officially on 1 January 1974 they agreed to stay on as directors (Board members) of Gulf Air for a transitional period. The agreement was that Gulf Aviation's shares, owned by the Kanoo, Yateem and Algosaibi families, and British Airways, were bought by the Governments of Bahrain, Qatar, the United Arab Emirates and Oman. Thereafter, what had been a regional operation became the official airline of these participating countries.

Once this transition was complete, my father then retired from Gulf Air's Board. Captain Alan Bodger also retired as General Manager. It is an interesting coincidence that this new identity coincided more or less exactly with the dramatic January 1974 oil price increases, discussed already.

Within two years, Gulf Air had invested in new aircraft, its fleet in 1979 comprising a mix of VC10s, BAC 1-11s (bought in 1974), L10-11 Tristars (1976) and Boeing 737s (1979). Staff numbers had increased threefold to 3,400. The company also began the intensive development of maintenance and personnel training facilities.

Captain Abdulrahman Al-Ghood told me the story of his experience when he joined Gulf Aviation. All he wanted to do was to become a pilot. Instead, he was assigned to the ground handling section. Unhappy with what he saw as a 'dead-end' career, he quietly but clearly expressed his feelings by not standing up as a sign of respect when my father came to inspect his area of work. Afterwards, my father called him to his office to enquire why. Abdulrahman apologized for his behaviour, but explained that since Gulf Aviation refused to train Bahrainis as pilots he was depressed. My father telephoned Captain Alan Bodger to ask why Bahrainis were not allowed to be trained as pilots. Since the answer was not very convincing, he instructed Captain Bodger to establish a procedure for training Bahrainis as pilots and that he was sending the first candidate to him. He turned to Abdulrahman and told him to go immediately to Captain Alan Bodger for pilot training and may God look after him. So began the era of the Gulf nationals pilot scheme. The first student to qualify as a pilot was Captain Al-Ghood. (Just for the record, we scored another first in the airline industry. My son Faisal, at the age of eight, was the first passenger to disembark at the new

Abu Dhabi International Airport from the first official flight to be received in Abu Dhabi, a Gulf Air BAC 1-11A.)

Meanwhile, in 1969, a British Government enquiry recommended that British European Airways (BEA) and the British Overseas Airways Corporation (BOAC) should merge. The result was the creation in 1972 of a new-style British Airways. The integrated operations formally began on 1 April 1974.

Some two years later Bahrain was the scene of another episode in aviation history. British Airways' supersonic aircraft Concorde made its first ever commercial flight when it landed in Bahrain to do its final 'hot weather' evaluation in the Arabian Gulf before going into service. Kanoo Travel was the first agency in the Middle East to sell a ticket for passenger travel on this innovative supersonic aircraft which still operates today, although it no longer flies to and from Bahrain. This is because Concorde is restricted from flying over land, one reason being that the sonic boom sounds like an explosion. When Concorde began to over-fly the UAE, the camels, goats and other animals became frightened to the extent that Shaikh Zayed refused permission for the aircraft to fly over the UAE's territory. Later, the same restriction was imposed by Oman, Qatar, Saudi Arabia and some European countries. Now, Concorde is only allowed to fly over sea, principally the trans-Atlantic route between London and New York.

In 1981, Gulf Air became a member of the International Air Transport Association. During the early 1980s the airline expanded its network and, in 1982 and 1983, won the 'Best Airline to the Middle East' award. By 1985, Gulf Air's enhanced service had created employment for 4,500 staff who comprised forty-two nationalities and, between them, spoke twenty-three languages.

A decade earlier, another significant development had taken place in Bahrain's aviation industry. In 1975, Aircraft Services Gulf Limited (ASGUL) appointed its first Bahraini General Manager, Mr Hameed Al-Alawi. At the time, His Excellency Yousuf Shirawi, Minister of Development, felt that ASGUL should expand its operation and introduce new equipment. To do this, capital investment was required so some of ASGUL's shares were sold to additional equity partners and a new company, Bahrain Airport Services (BAS) was formed in 1977. Its shareholding was as follows: Y.B.A.Kanoo and Gulf Air, 30 per cent each; of the remaining 40 per cent, these shares were divided equally between five travel agents who each held 8 per cent. They were World Travel Service (WTS) owned by Unitag, Algosaibi Travel, Bahrain International Travel (BIT), Jalal Travel and

Delmon Travel. The first Chairman of BAS was Shaikh Isa bin Abdulla Al Khalifa, Director of Civil Aviation.

Since then, BAS has developed rapidly, providing services on equal terms comparable with those in other international airports. Today, Bahrain airport is one of the most modern, providing all the related services normally associated with aircraft, cargo and passenger handling, with the exception of aircraft maintenance. Although it accelerates my story forward by nearly twenty years, it is worth noting that BAS was selected as the best Duty Free facility in the world for the year 1994.

Containerisation heralds change

While significant changes were taking place in the computer and aviation industries, no less a transformation occurred in the shipping industry. By the late 1970s, the container age had arrived. Even a decade earlier, the need for change had become all too apparent. In Kanoo's case, our commercial agency portfolio in construction equipment had become really big business. Beginning with Bedford dump-trucks, we later became agents for Grove cranes, Hyster fork-lift trucks, Lincoln welders, Massey Fergusson tractors, C.P.T. compressors and about twenty-two other construction-related machines.

When, later, Arabia's boom gained momentum, companies competed to service the construction industry. It seemed that every conceivable type of equipment was on sale, ranging from gigantic Caterpillar earth-movers to five-horsepower Honda generators. Obviously, we were not the only company in the region importing heavy and delicate equipment. Gone were the days when it was feasible to beach an inshore lighter and manually handle this type of cargo onto the sand. The sheer weight and size of the equipment, and modern packaging, made this practice almost impossible.

Hitherto, most consignments were packed in an assortment of receptacles such as gunny bags (usually jute sacking), wooden crates and cardboard cartons, all of various dimensions stacked in haphazard fashion because of the constraints of the different shapes. Since there was no provision to isolate each consignee's goods, every piece had to be handled individually, bag by bag, box by box, in order to distinguish one person's shipment from another.

This labour-intensive and not so efficient system could not cope with the increased volumes of cargo and the changing product mixes. Fragile and sensitive items such as light fittings, large panes of glass, computers, domestic appliances, televisions, electrical and electronic equipment could not be lifted and passed from handler to handler in the way that bags of rice, sugar and cement could be discharged. Large metal containers provided the answer and introduced a whole new concept to cargo shipping.

Containerisation solved other problems, too. Cargo could be protected more from accidental damage. Misplacement was minimised and security against theft improved. A container could be handled easily, quickly and efficiently, even delivered from the port to the consignee's front door. Since containers are a regular shape and can be stacked symmetrically, storage space on each vessel was increased considerably and so helped to cope with the increasing volume of cargo. But without deep-water ports and quayside heavy-duty cranes, the new system could not work.

Partly in anticipation of these needs, Bahrain's new deep-water sea terminal, Mina Salman, opened in 1967. It so happened that the first ship to enter the port was *Linderkirk,* under our Nedlloyd agency. Dubai's importance as an international destination increased after Mina Rashid was opened officially on 5 October 1972. Almost overnight, our competition 'mushroomed'. Then, it was simply the united team spirit of every member of our staff which enabled us to keep ahead of the 'game' and ensure our company's continuing success.

When it was announced early in 1972 that Abu Dhabi's new port, Mina Zayed, was due to open in June that year, I thought: Why shouldn't Kanoo benefit from that? After all, I argued, the first vessel to arrive should be an Arab-flagged vessel. How much more thrilling if we happened to be the agent of that vessel as well. Amazingly, I managed to get everyone to agree. First, I persuaded the United Arab Shipping Company, the then Kuwaiti shipping line which we represented, to divert one of their vessels to Abu Dhabi for the occasion. Then I convinced the port authority that it should delay its opening ceremony for one day until the *Al-Ahmadiah* arrived to dock in the port. So it was that Y.B.A.Kanoo was successful in being the shipping agent of the first vessel to dock in the new port. A full opening ceremony took place in the presence of Shaikh Zayed and Shaikh Rashid and attended by many dignitaries. After inspecting the port's facilities, they then boarded our vessel for light refreshment.

We scored another first in 1972, spectacular in execution, but rather embarrassing for us. On this occasion, we were the agent of the first vessel to ram the jetty, only the fourth to enter the new port. The ship, *Smolny,* owned by Polish Ocean Line, happened to be on its maiden voyage. It seems that it came into port too fast and embedded the first five metres of its new bow right into the jetty beside its intended berth. Fortunately, there were no casualties and we were able to patch up the damage so that the vessel could continue with its voyage.

We were also the agent of the first vessel to catch fire in port, a Nedlloyd ship called *Neder Elbe*. This accident happened in 1974 at berth 5. Again, quick reaction saved the ship and prevented any loss of life or injury. As for the first ship to keel over, we were also the agent of that ship, a 500-ton coaster called *Mammoth Scan*. As cargo continued to be discharged from the port side at berth number 6, nobody paid attention to the vessel's increasing list until the ship rolled over onto its side!

While these episodes are interesting anecdotes, they are good examples of an unprecedented requirement to improve port management systems. The authorities were obliged to introduce operational procedures for the correct and secure movement of all vessels within port limits. Berths and temporary storage had to be allocated. Speed limits, safety regulations and security measures had to be introduced and implemented. Again, gone were the days of the 'free-for-all' approach. Since containers are manufactured to standardised dimensions, each consignment could now be kept as a group and not dispersed around the port according to where space could be found for irregular shapes.

The advent of containerisation had another far-reaching impact on the trans-shipment of cargo, particularly in the Kingdom of Saudi Arabia. The 'dry port' of Riyadh, opened by Prince Salman bin Abdul-Aziz in 1981, was created so that most cargo destined for the Central Province could arrive by sea at Dammam, be transferred by train to Riyadh and then cleared through customs there. The main effect of the new dry port was that it accelerated the throughput of goods through Dammam and made the whole process more efficient for both the Government and the merchants. Y.B.A.Kanoo was asked to bid for the handling and management of the new dry port, a contract which we won.

The origin of the Saudi Rail-Road goes back to 1947. Under ARAMCO supervision, a rail link was built between Dammam Port (where cargo was discharged), and Dhahran (the oil company's camp). In time, King Abdul-Aziz asked ARAMCO to study the feasibility of a passenger and cargo rail-link to Riyadh. (This began operations in 1952.) In 1958, the Saudi Railways Organization was formed as a new government authority to assume the railway management from ARAMCO. Then, the rail journey between Dammam and Riyadh took seven hours. Now, a new fast track (built at a cost of SR 115 million) enables cargo trains to cover the distance in four hours, and passenger trains in three hours.

Insurance joins the mega-money league

Containerisation was a welcome asset to the insurance industry, too. By the mid-1970s, Arabia's construction boom had spawned a whole new dimension to insurance premiums and pay-outs. Containerisation helped to offset some of the less desirable features of this phenomenon. The volume of equipment needed to service the construction industry created port congestion, particularly in Abu Dhabi. This generated fires, especially among the cardboard boxes, sacking and paper packages exposed to the sun. In turn, ships waiting offshore to enter port had their share of problems. Intense heat and humidity in the holds caused goods to deteriorate in all manner of ways – distortion, shrinkage, rotting, cracking, and so on – all of which rendered cargo useless by the time it was discharged. In all these situations, new forms of packaging and containerisation helped to minimise the number of claims. But then, on top of all that, there was the phenomenon of contractors' insurance. Iain Reid, now General Manager of Norwich Union in Bahrain, calls this the age of mega-money. Insurance premiums and claim pay-outs were in a league of their own. He remembers these as being very unusual times.

Iain first went to Abu Dhabi in the 1970s as Norwich Union Representative and soon gained the impression that insurance had always been part of our family business. Even though this is not strictly true since it was not until 1950 that our formal relationship with Norwich Union began, it is fair to say that as a family, we have always believed in the concept of insurance. Since the beginning of the century we have insured our ship's cargoes, barges, property and so on against damage or loss.

During the daily meetings which I held in Abu Dhabi, Iain Reid sat with his other functional counterparts, the managers of shipping, commercial, clearing and forwarding, travel, all of whom were on the Y.B.A.Kanoo pay-roll. Iain Reid was not. Even so, he was our branch Insurance Manager. Reid found all this very unusual, particularly the fact that we took such a very keen interest in what went on in the insurance business, and that we wished to help him and pushed his initiative hard.

But if this was a surprise to him, I have to admit that the way in which insurance became boom business for us in the late 1970s was something I could not have anticipated, particularly the goings-on in the port of Abu Dhabi. Enormous things would go missing just because the port was 'chock-a-block' with discharged cargo. Before long, importers were seeking to cover their consignments against being lost *after* having been discharged from the ship and cleared through customs. The cargoes would not be necessarily pilfered. They would just disappear into the mass of confusion and chaos. As a result, insurance companies honoured importers' claims on their insurance policies because they could produce documentation proving that their consignments had been discharged, yet later lost in the port. Every three years or so, the port authorities held an auction to clear some space. Reid remembers seeing some of the most amazing things sold under the auctioneer's hammer, such as two helicopter engines and big pleasure craft, just because the relevant importers hadn't been able to find the cargo!

Apart from genuinely misplaced goods, smuggling and pilfering had been easy 'lines of business' for those so inclined. To stop people helping themselves to goods on the quay, or using the confusion as a cover for illicit importing, a study was conducted as to how other major ports handled these problems.

In the case of the UAE, ships were arriving loaded with supplies to satisfy a country which was starting more or less from scratch, trying to catch up with the twentieth century. The momentum was breath-taking. Everything was needed. The civilian population, government, industry, oil companies, the airport, security services (the police and armed forces), hospitals, telecommunications facilities, schools, property developers and so on were all building their own installations. Everything was happening at once. As all the necessary materials were imported, inevitably the seaport became the focus for the distribution of incoming supplies. Inevitably, new port regulations and procedures had to be implemented to impose a sense of order.

What had once been the quiet, little-used Ruler's Jetty became a 26-berth international port. Only a limited number of trailers were available to go alongside ships to receive discharged cargo, and so accelerate its distribution to the consignments' destinations. Clearing agents often had to fend for themselves, scrambling over and among discharged shipments piled up within the port perimeter, as they sought to identify shipments and remove them by whatever transport they could command. The only way to keep things moving was to use one's initiative and ingenuity. Otherwise, cargo was often left unclaimed simply because it lay buried or misplaced among the confusion and congestion. Once containers became regular features, these chaotic situations ceased to exist.

Contractors' insurance was another remarkable characteristic of the times in which we then lived. Should some major mishap happen during the construction of a project, such as a rain-flood washing something away, or a fire, contractors could insure against the contingency of having to start the project all over again. As a result, premiums had to reflect the valuation of the assets under construction, often very high.

When Iain Reid was assigned to Saudi Arabia for a short time to help process the backlog of policy applications, he remembers finding them all piled into different categories. Those which involved premiums exceeding £100,000 received priority. The next category were premiums between £50,000 and £100,000. The third category went down to £10,000. As Iain observed: 'This was very big money. It's big money now. In 1977, it was mega-money.'

It was at that time that we were beginning to enter into joint-ventures with contractors. But to do so, we had to be sure what risks we were taking on. On one occasion, Reid flew over the new Yanbu site to assess the situation. Apart from the house in which Lawrence of Arabia once lived, almost nothing of permanence could be seen from the air. The most that he saw were masses of trucks and equipment. The contractors involved in the construction of Yanbu lived on dormitory ships anchored in the Red Sea and operated helicopters to and from the site. Construction being a very volatile business, problems may arise unexpectedly. Thus, construction insurance premiums are very high. But then, so are the pay-outs, if claims are authorised.

In cosmopolitan Dubai the insurance sector has always been relatively stable and is unlikely to increase for two reasons. Already, there are many insurance 'players', all competing with each other. Because of this, the authorities have closed the list of insurance licences. They don't want too many people spoiling the crowded market. In Abu Dhabi, other insurance companies have set up offices to satisfy the needs of the UAE's insurance market. But this does not bother Norwich Union unduly. Together with Y.B.A.Kanoo, Norwich Union has done very well out of insurance in the Middle East. Although the various emphases may change, people will always wish to insure against some contingency or another.

Y.B.A.Kanoo – divisionalisation and diversification

During the late 1970s, the Y.B.A.Kanoo Group reassessed its various interests in the United Kingdom. In 1976, twenty years after Arabian Gulf Services Limited had been formed in London, we decided to close the office located in 26 North Audley Street (very near to Selfridges department store). At first, apart from operating as a travel agent, the company rendered general services to Kanoo family members and other Arabian Gulf nationals who visited the UK. But as time passed, family friends and Gulf clients began to use the agency as a meeting place and demanded assistance in areas that the travel office could not handle. Hence, fewer business transactions took place and the office ran at a loss.

In 1977 Kanoo Group Limited was registered with its main office in London. This new company began business in July 1978 as a non-trading, non-profit company by providing services, within the UK, for shareholders of the Y.B.A.Kanoo Group and as a contact and liaison post which did not charge for its services. Cyril Jones retired as Group General Manager in Bahrain, but not from the company. Following the formation during that year of our UK 'arm', Kanoo Group Limited, Cyril transferred to 1 Balfour Place, London W1. to run the new company until 1981.

Meanwhile, in 1974, the Y.B.A.Kanoo Group submitted itself to another firm of management consultants: Cressep McCormack and Paget, a subsidiary of Citibank. Their brief was to see how Y.B.A.Kanoo could diversify. Their team studied our market and our organisation and recommended many industries and businesses into which our family business could diversify. But their presentation and supporting arguments were not convincing enough. Our Board of Directors were not persuaded to change from the course they had already laid, namely to stay in our traditional businesses of shipping, travel, commercial trading and insurance.

Despite this uncertainty, in 1981, the Arthur D. Little company was commissioned by Group Management to consider corporate reorganisation. This decision had been based on a discussion between Ahmed Kanoo (the Group Chairman) and Bill Brien. During this, Ahmed had said that he was not happy with the organisational structure of Y.B.A.Kanoo which, at that time, was arranged on a geographical basis: Bahrain, Saudi Arabia, and the UAE together with Oman. The only alternative was to organise the company into functional divisions: travel, shipping, commercial, and so on.

Divisionalisation was an idea much discussed by Bill Brien and myself. We were enthusiastic about it because we thought then, and still do today, that some of our company divisions are the size of trading companies. For example, the travel division in Saudi Arabia employs almost 500 staff. Feasibly, it could be a company in its own right, as could our shipping and commercial divisions.

Central control was another stumbling-block. At that time, mail, telephone messages and telexes of any importance had to be sent to Bahrain where a Group General Manager made decisions. The frustrations of coping with this cumbersome system were immense. Clearly, this was restricting company growth. A structural change was necessary to cope with our growing size.

However, the Arthur D. Little scenario did not work out quite as Bill Brien and I had expected. After a while, it seemed as if what we had been telling the consultants was echoing back to us. They were expressing themselves very nicely and charging handsome fees, but nonetheless, the consultants were repeating what Bill and I had told them. To be fair, they must have come to the same conclusion also. When challenged as to why they were doing this, the team leader simply told me: 'We are consultants. We borrow your watch and then tell you the time!' He was joking, or was he?

Despite this inauspicious start, Arthur D. Little's proposals were adopted for a while. Then it became clear that the new arrangement was not working any better than the one it had replaced. For one thing, it took our executive directors a long time to accept that they were responsible for a division, not a region. They all associated themselves with Bahrain, Saudi Arabia or the UAE, and not, say, the travel or shipping division. They felt, perhaps, that their roles had been weakened.

Divisionalisation was also costing a lot of money to operate yet by 1983 the oil boom had ended. Whereas we, as a family company, thought we were too big and needed more departmental specialisation in travel, shipping and so on, the reality was rather different. With the onset of the recession our business had begun to shrink. In the end, a compromise between divisionalisation and regional management was agreed. We maintained regional decentralisation and divisional management, but each area acts autonomously, while the Group controls major issues only. Thus, we reverted to the concept whereby each territory is looked after by an autonomous regional local Board, with senior directors and functional general managers reporting to a managing director. Yusuf was appointed Managing Director of the UAE and Oman; Fawzi (his brother), Managing Director of Bahrain; Saud (his cousin),

Managing Director of Y.B.A.Kanoo Property Company; and myself, Managing Director for Saudi Arabia. This structure is complemented by a specialist team based in Bahrain. Led by Akbar Sa'ati, the Group General Manager, this provides central support to each autonomous region, in various disciplines such as finance, legal affairs, manpower control, computers, administration. Joint ventures and investment remain in the hands of my elder uncles, each in his own area.

In complete contrast, during 1986 Abdulaziz became the first Kanoo family member to visit China. In fact, he is among the very few Saudis who have visited China officially, since Saudi nationals are not allowed to visit communist countries without specific permission. With the blessing of the Government, a group of Saudi businessmen visited Beijing and Shanghai, and even had the chance to visit the area where Moslem Chinese were living. Altogether, they were well received. When Abdulaziz Kanoo returned, the Saudi government sought my uncle's impression of China. He replied that it had been a fascinating contrast to the Saudi businessmen's delegation to America some time earlier. On that occasion, all the Saudis were transported from one area to another in two buses, with a bus-conductor as their guide and chaperon. When the same party went to China, every two delegates were designated a nice Mercedes 500. As my uncle said, that was communism versus capitalism!

At that time, China was more or less closed to business overtures from capitalist businessmen. Now, this is not the case. Following in his uncle's exploratory footsteps, my cousin Fawzi Kanoo visited China in 1992 to assess the business potential. His first coup occurred during the following year when our company was appointed General Sales Agent for Air China and the agents for some Chinese trading companies in Bahrain and Saudi Arabia.

Joint venture development

For twenty-eight years, Cyril N. Jones was closely associated with the Middle East. For the first two, he worked for the Anglo-Iranian Oil Company, and then in 1952 crossed the Arabian Gulf to join Y. B. A. Kanoo in Bahrain. After spending the first nine years of his service with our company in Manama, he was posted to London from where, until his retirement as a Director of the Main Board of Yusuf bin Ahmed Kanoo, he made constant sorties to the Arabian Gulf region during which he gained a remarkable insight into business opportunities, the benefits of which we reaped in many ways.

When, some three years ago, I wrote to Cyril seeking his

assessment of specific periods of our company history, his knowledge of our joint venture development proved to be a fountain of valuable information. Jones' essay, Formulating Plans for Joint Venture Companies in Saudi Arabia, published in an American business journal, is an immensely detailed study of the requirements for success in this complex form of business activity. In his introduction he wrote:

> The era of cheap energy from oil has gone forever. ... It is a solemn thought that the progress of civilization could be retarded by the failure of man to harness his genius and determination to the solution of the energy predicament that confronts him. Indeed, in all history there may never have been a more urgent need and a greater opportunity for vision than is presented today by the energy quandary.

In Jones' view, Saudi Arabia is deeply mindful of its vital and inescapable role as a supplier of world energy needs. The manner in which it fulfils that role is governed by a great sense of responsibility to both the world as a whole, and to its own people, now and in the future. As a result, the Kingdom's government concluded that a strategy of economic diversification by means of industrialisation, through the medium of joint ventures with foreign companies, was the most effective way of accomplishing that end. But to achieve this, the Saudi Arabian authorities recognised that potential foreign investors would require a programme of incentives. Referring to a remark once made by His Majesty, the late King Khalid bin Abdul-Aziz, Jones ended his essay by quoting: 'One day revenues from our industries will be equal to the revenues from our oil.'

His Majesty's prediction has not come to pass yet, but the immense and ambitious industrialisation movement in Saudi Arabia is moving fast in that area with the growth of the petrochemical industry and basic industries. The private sector has assumed the industrial mantle, to the extent that nearly every major company has a manufacturing company, either alone or in joint venture. The Saudi Arabian government has also provided encouragement through the Saudi Industrial Development Fund (SIDF). This offers long-term 'soft' loans and other facilities such as a 'tax holiday', all to encourage investment in factory development.

At first, the directors of Y.B.A.Kanoo did not like the idea of joint ventures. Then Uncle Abdulaziz in Saudi Arabia, aided by the then Saudi Arabia General Manager, Mr McNiven-Young (Mac) did very well in establishing our first joint venture in the Kingdom during 1976. The first was Saudi Arabia Transport Organization Limited

(SATOL), a collaboration with the Californian-based company, Crowley Maritime. This success was followed in the same year with the formation of two more joint ventures: Otis Saudi Limited and Foster Wheeler Saudi Arabia Company, the first specialising in oil and the second in construction.

Between 1976 and 1990, we established forty-one joint ventures of extraordinary diversity, all with international companies. These included Greyhound (buses); Cable and Wireless (communication); Ocean Inchcape (maintenance); Baroid (mud-drilling); Decca Survey (geodetic survey); Norwich Union (insurance); Exxon (lube oil additives); Strongwork Diving (pollution control and diving services); Elbar Turbine (turbine repairs); International Paint (paints); Container Terminals Services (container operations with Nedlloyd); Watson Grey (oil inspectors) and King Wilkinson (design engineers). When the development of Saudi Arabia's infrastructure was completed, many of these joint ventures were liquidated. Of the forty-one we had, only twenty-seven operate today.

Although several other joint ventures either lay dormant, were liquidated or ceased trading for some reason or another, our Joint Ventures Division could claim that between 1976 and 1993, they had formed forty-five companies in Saudi Arabia alone. For several years, the division flourished under the leadership of General Manager, Bob Harvey. (His daughter married his deputy, David Allen. After Bob retired, David assumed management of the division, keeping it in the family so to speak.)

More recently, we have formed other joint ventures, such as Saudi Formaldehyde Chemical Company (chemicals), J. C. Penney (fashion collections) franchise holder, Maersk Line Shipping Agency (port services and containers), Manhal Water (sweet water), Saudi Development and Training (with British Aerospace) and BASF (chemicals).

It is also worth documenting an episode which involved our insurance business joint ventures, although we had little control over the sequence of events. I am referring to the Norwich–Winterthur connection which lasted just twelve years from 1979 to 1991. The origins of this began in 1950 when Y.B.A.Kanoo was appointed Norwich Union's representative in Bahrain. In 1976 a joint venture was formed called Norwich Winterthur Holdings Limited, the partners being Norwich Union 45 per cent, Winterthur of Switzerland 45 per cent and Chiyoda of Japan 10 per cent.

Norwich Winterthur Insurance (Gulf) Limited was created to cover Bahrain, the UAE and Oman. This holding company, formed in 1976, did not start operating with Kanoo partners until 1979 as Norwich Winterthur Insurance (Arabia) Limited. In 1985, Norwich Winterthur Insurance (Saudi Arabia) EC was formed. Subsequently, various changes took place within the joint venture. In 1986, the Y.B.A.Kanoo Group became a 51 per cent shareholder of Norwich Winterthur Insurance (Saudi Arabia) EC; in December 1989, Bahrain Norwich Winterthur was formed so that Bahrain could separate itself from Norwich Winterthur Insurance (Gulf), based in Dubai. As occurred in Saudi Arabia, Y.B.A.Kanoo became a 51 per cent shareholder of the new company. No sooner had these companies settled into their new arrangements when, out of the blue, an announcement was made in April 1991 that Norwich Union was to acquire all Winterthur's interests in the Middle East. Effectively, this meant that Norwich Union was on its own again, apart from the Y.B.A.Kanoo shareholdings. A new company, Bahrain Norwich Union Insurance Co. BSC (C) was the outcome.

Despite this metamorphosis, Norwich Union and Y.B.A.Kanoo still have much in common. They regard insurance as a long-term business venture. In the boom years, the insurance sector was way down the line in terms of profit. Its contribution wasn't that meaningful to the Kanoo Group when compared with other major business sectors we were involved in. Now, the boom days have gone. Other divisions cannot repeat what happened in that era, yet the insurance business has steadily improved, and changed. Today there are many mischief-makers afoot, particularly in the sphere of professional indemnity. Speaking for Norwich Union, Iain Reid has seen the number of related claims increase dramatically to the extent that premiums have had to rise accordingly. Now, he says, the name of the game is not so much assessing the risk but sharpening the edge of fraudulent claim detection. Twenty years ago, this was a rare occurrence. Then, at the peak of the oil boom, everyone seemed blessed with the 'Midas touch', the fabled ability to turn all things to gold. With the onset of the world recession in the late 1980s, both moods and manners changed. But at no time and in no place were these more acutely felt than in Arabia on the morning of 2 August 1990. The invasion of Kuwait by Iraq was a turning point in history for the Y.B.A.Kanoo Group, and for the world community.

Chapter 13

Shield and Storm

Strategically choosing 17 July, the twenty-second anniversary of the Ba'ath party's accession to power, Saddam Hussain accused Kuwait and the United Arab Emirates of threatening the Iraqi economy. The crux of his complaint was that by exceeding their oil quotas Kuwait and the UAE had pushed the oil price down to $14 a barrel.

To many international observers, this televised speech was due warning that Iraq would be likely to add its long-standing border dispute with Kuwait to that of the simmering issue of oil quotas. By 21 July, intelligence sources had reported the movement of 30,000 Iraqi troops to the Kuwaiti border. Even so, William Webster, America's Director of Central Intelligence, did not consider that invasion was imminent. In his opinion, and that of many people including the people and rulers of Arabia, this was just another sabre-rattling exercise designed to hike the oil price at the forthcoming OPEC meeting, and to achieve other Iraqi objectives. On Saturday 28 July, just two days after OPEC delegates had convened at the Sheraton Hotel in Geneva, the Egyptian intelligence service reported to President Mubarak that an invasion of Kuwait was likely within a week. In Washington, satellite photographs revealed more troops heading south. By 29 July, the CIA knew that Iraqi forces comprising 100,000 men and 300 tanks had massed on the Kuwaiti border. In an effort to defuse the crisis, a high-level meeting was held in Jeddah during the evening of 31 July. The omens were not favourable. The following day, an emergency meeting was held in the White House, the CIA having concluded that the Iraqis were 'ready to go' and, in their view, would 'go'.

Kuwait invaded by Iraq

In the small hours of Thursday, 2 August 1990 Kuwait was invaded by Iraq. Satellite surveillance apart, Saddam Hussain had managed to camouflage his true intentions quite well. Immediately prior to the invasion, western military attachés not normally allowed to drive more than twenty-five miles beyond Baghdad, had been invited to

239

see what was going on along the Kuwaiti border. Many western embassies, well used to Iraqi rhetoric, had no clear idea of what was going on. The general feeling held by Kanoo senior management was that the situation would be contained, everyone and everything would settle down, and that would be the end of the episode until the next time sensibilities were offended. In any case, July and August being traditional vacation months, many nationals and expatriates had already left the Arabian peninsula believing there was no reason to change their plans. The Kanoo family and their staff were no exceptions.

By now, the Group Chairman, Ahmed Kanoo, was in London and I was several thousand miles away in Houston. When CNN announced the news, the only certainty in my mind was that I should return to Saudi Arabia. As it turned out, all members of the family returned to the Arabian Gulf, together with all members of our expatriate and local staff who were on leave. Even our retired Shipping General Manager, Bob Woodley, flew from Australia to give us a hand, a real show of commitment and faith. Meanwhile, in Dammam, the company took stock of the situation. Captain Nicholas Lane, General Manager of our shipping division in Saudi Arabia, telephoned United Arab Shipping company's office in Kuwait and asked if there any truth to what he had heard on the radio. The reply was short and succinct: 'Yes. I am sitting in the office and the tanks are outside.'

The first forty-eight hours after the occupation of Kuwait were a critical period. Until President Bush announced that American troops would be deployed and the first contingent had arrived in Saudi Arabia, the situation remained tense. Everyone knew perfectly well that if Iraqi tanks moved unchallenged at thirty or forty miles an hour along the road from Khafji, it would have been but a few hours' easy drive south to the oilfields, refineries and Dammam.

Already many residents in the Eastern Province of Saudi Arabia had ensured that their cars were full of petrol ready to head south or west, if necessary. For those nationals who wished to distance themselves from the zone of potential conflict, namely the oilfields, Jeddah was seen as a relatively safe haven. For nationals and expatriates who sought to leave the Kingdom entirely, Oman offered accessible beaches and deep ocean water where, if necessary, a sea-lift could be organised with little trouble. Airports in the UAE provided alternative options for a safe escape. Bahrain and the eastern seaboard of Saudi Arabia were a different matter. In all respects, their shallow shores and vulnerable airports created hazardous evacuation logistics.

Meanwhile, the Y.B.A.Kanoo organisation went about its business as usual. On the day of the invasion, Abdulla Kanoo (who was in Dammam) met with his senior managers in Saudi Arabia to assess the situation. He firmly maintained that this was a Kuwaiti incident. The Iraqis were not going to invade the Kingdom and Y.B.A.Kanoo, Saudi Arabia, would continue to trade. He, the Chairman, and the rest of the Kanoo family were there, and everyone was to carry on as usual. When asked what his immediate plans were, Abdulla Kanoo's unequivocal response was predictably business-like: 'I am going to stay here at my desk and the Iraqis can walk through the door and shoot me before I move.' Those who knew the Chairman understood precisely what that remark meant. Our services at oil installations, sea and airports were needed and so we would carry on, regardless of hazard or hiatus.

Throughout the crisis our company strategy was to maintain a high profile so that we could keep staff motivated. In Saudi Arabia, together with senior Saudi and British staff, I made regular visits to each Kanoo office, depot and outpost in the 'war zone'. The fact that we were seen conducting our lives and business apparently without fear soon had a calming influence on employees.

Nevertheless, one could not blame our staff for being jittery at that time. They were at the 'front line' manning airport and sea terminals. They supported oil company services in isolated areas. They handled tankers, and discharged ships loaded with war supplies. They supported the allied forces in the likely invasion areas such as Khafji, Ras Tannurah, Rahima and Jubail, let alone the communications facilities around Dammam. In all these places, our staff were likely targets for the Iraqis.

As I saw it, my task was to support our staff, 'wave the flag', motivate and pacify. If that meant working late at night, that was the way it had to be. My motto, 'Follow me', was no hollow rallying call. I had grown up learning that one should lead by example, like my father.

Largely because of the stance which our family adopted right from the start of the crisis, few employees resigned. Of course, there was understandable anxiety, particularly among the Asian and Indian staff who wondered what they should do. It swiftly became company policy that each expatriate employee had to assess the overall situation for himself and make his own decision as to whether he wished to remain in the Arabian Gulf region or leave. If he chose the latter, it would not be held against him and no formalities would be created to prevent his departure. In the end, 12 of our 2,300 employees decided to leave Saudi Arabia. Naturally enough, most of those who chose to stay, sent their families home to safety which the company arranged and paid for.

As time went by, the biggest stress factor was external pressure exerted by employees' families. On one occasion during the crisis, Indian television screened a city being bombed, claiming that it was Al-Khobar. Soon afterwards, many of our employees received desperate telephone calls from their families demanding that they should return home immediately. They had seen the bombing on television. What they had actually seen was a news-clip from the Iran–Iraq war. Such is the power of the media.

Military procurement – Sears and Zaina venture

Ironically, it just so happened that we had chosen Wednesday 1 August 1990 as the day on which to open Y.B.A.Kanoo's first retail store in Saudi Arabia. The plan was that this store, a venture with American-based Sears Roebuck called Zaina International, should open on that morning for weekend shopping.

This trial run had been designed to test our systems so that the official opening on Saturday 4 August would run smoothly. Everyone involved had worked long hours unpacking containers and arranging merchandise. Based on the scant information available at the time, all that we could say was that the project should go ahead as planned. Until more was known about the invasion, there was little that anyone could do except carry on. Nevertheless, this created a very strange feeling. Everyone had become so blinkered by the intensity of preparing the Sears' project for its opening day that the invasion was almost secondary.

When it became apparent that Saddam Hussain was not going to withdraw from Kuwait, the emphasis of concern shifted. We began to envisage the likely scenario if our potential Zaina clients left Saudi Arabia *en masse*. In this event, the store might well have gone out of business before it had even begun trading. We need not have worried. Almost as soon as the first wave of American troops arrived in Saudi Arabia, Zaina International became the talk of the town. First came the 82nd and 101st Airborne Divisions who were rushed to the Front line. Immediately, they were followed by other divisions: the 24th Infantry (Mechanized), 3rd/24th Helicopter, 3rd/69th Tank, 3rd and 4th Infantry, 1st and 7th Cavalry, the 13th Engineering Brigade and the 5th Army. We served them all, even the National Guards of the States of Arizona and New Mexico.

Much of the Kanoo attraction was attributed to the large unipole notice-board which had been erected outside the store in preparation for the August opening. Measuring some ten metres wide and five metres high it simply declared: 'Sears products sold here'. For the American troops, the name was familiar. So much so that they 'invaded' us for many of the tools they needed since the Sears brand was familiar to them. For quite a long time, Army 'humvees' and trucks dominated the car park.

Proof that the Kanoo organisation does not always just look at the 'bottom line' was our sympathy with the circumstances in which the troops found themselves. The health and hygiene of the troops who visited us became a priority. Soft drinks and candy bars were distributed free to all those who came into the store while, outside at the back, our staff rigged up a shower-stand. Those troops who were at the front line, nicknamed the 'animals', had to live in the desert for many weeks ready to fight, with no amenities, hot meals, showers or air-conditioning. When the men did visit us, most had to drive for several hours before reaching our store. Even for those based nearer, after days of desert-life with no facilities other than the packs on their backs, the tantalising sight of a shower must have seemed like a mirage.

Before long, the simple portable structures we erected, with a tank of water above and some elementary pipe-work below, became sought-after equipment for military camps. When asked if Zaina International adopted an aggressive marketing policy as 'Desert Shield' took shape, our Retail Manager replied: 'Did we attack the business? We were attacked first, and then we got our act together'.

'Desert Shield' sent the new Sears venture off in a totally different direction from what had been planned for the store. Along with other Saudi businessmen who experienced the phenomenon, we were fascinated by the way the American military did business. The buyers, or 'bike men' as they were called, tended to operate in pairs: one man made the selections while the other carried the money and signed for the goods. First, the 'buyer' would start by asking where, for example, he could obtain washing-bowls, toilet rolls, camouflage pattern, air-conditioners, video cameras, generators and so on. The shopping lists seemed endless. Then the 'banker' negotiated the price, signed for the goods and paid cash on the spot.

The first unusual event occurred when the military requested a photocopying machine to be sent up to Nu'ayriyah, a little town eighty miles south of the Kuwaiti border, the allies' forward military camp. Having agreed to deliver the machine over the weekend, Peter

Webber (our Retail Manager) set off, driving into the desert until he could not take the car any further. There he waited until the pre-arranged Army 'humvee' jeep appeared, its characteristic wide wheel-base being ideal for traversing soft sand. After the photocopying machine had been loaded into the back of the jeep, Peter was driven over the dunes for an hour-and-a-half until they reached the military camp. Reflecting on the experience, he believes that this was the first time that 'we really started building up a close relationship' with the desert armies.

Over time, this rapport grew until Y.B.A.Kanoo found itself sourcing a range of merchandise that Sears didn't normally deal with. The new Zaina store became the unofficial purchasing agents for some of the American military units to the extent that it became necessary to set up a one-man office in Nu'ayriyah, complete with fax and telephone. Military groups would appear with shopping lists for a variety of merchandise, have their orders faxed to the main store in Dammam where they would be sourced, and within forty eight hours, the goods would be delivered to their forward destination.

While the Sears store was being stocked I had been known to 'accuse' staff of importing items that we would never sell, such as twenty-five 14-pound sledge-hammers. Some three days after Zaina International opened, several burly GIs came in looking for something suitable to knock their tent pegs into the compacted sand. Not only did they buy all twenty-five sledge-hammers, but they also promptly ordered more to be shipped by air-freight.

Before long, the GIs returned. The sledge-hammers were doing their job, but broke the short tent pegs. No one, it would seem, had thought about hard, compacted desert sand and rock. Trying to pitch their tents in areas of softer, shifting sand was no easier. The pegs were not long enough to secure the guy-ropes, even when the pegs were hammered, unbroken, into the ground. So with the help of a local contractor, we manufactured especially strong and long tent pegs, a half-metre, one-metre and one-and-a-half-metres long, using angle irons. Once these new-fangled devices were doing their job successfully, then another use was found for the special pegs. It would seem that no one had anticipated the strong *shamals,* the fierce wind from the north which suddenly blows out of the desert. The pegs proved to be ideal anchor-points for the guy-ropes needed to tether parked helicopters which otherwise were flipped over by these winds.

Sand-ladders became another Kanoo product, as even the 'humvees' sank into the fine sand of the shifting dunes. So a few experimental sand-ladders were manufactured and put up for sale. In the end, we sold over 300 of them.

More than two years later, Peter Webber told me that while listening to an American Forces' programme he had heard how ingenious the American troops had been in overcoming the various problems of adapting to desert life in Saudi Arabia. They even mentioned *our* sand-ladders, which the Americans claimed they had invented and made themselves!

Y.B.A.Kanoo found a market for another unlikely product: leaf-blowers. Each device, a small engine secured in a back-harness, is attached to a pressure blower. When operated, air is emitted from the machine at a high velocity, ideal for blowing sand away from enemy mines planted in the desert. Demand was such that, on one occasion, an entire delivery of leaf-blowers was sold for military mine-clearing operations.

In turn, this stimulated a bizarre form of re-cycling. Discarded twenty foot (six metre) containers soon became much sought-after items. Wherever the military chose to build a semi-permanent base, they dug a suitably large hole, dropped in a container, covered it with sand and instantly, they had created a blast shelter for themselves.

In Jubail, the British Army regularly visited our offices to order what they needed, such as refrigerators, not only for storing drinks, food and medical supplies, but also helicopter seals which had to be maintained at low temperatures prior to fitting. An order for 5,000 coolers, or cold-boxes, came as no surprise either, particularly to our salesmen, Fahad Shahab and Ahmed Tablani, who had become well versed in the art of procuring the most obscure military requests from local sources.

Throughout the crisis, Sears support from Chicago, led by Carlos Humara and Dick Ford, was marvellous. Their performance both exceeded our expectations and, more often than not, delighted our customers who were surprised to see that no matter what they asked for and we ordered, Sears supplied. After all, if the Iraqis had invaded Saudi Arabia, Sears would have lost, with us, all their investment. But they had confidence that we would protect both their own and our interests, and that the Kingdom would be defended against invasion. Apart from all this, Sears wished to support the US Armed Forces who were serving there.

To Gordin, our Zaina International warehouseman, handling all these orders had become normal routine. For eighteen hours a day he controlled incoming and outgoing goods. In his 'spare time', he re-stocked the store. The vital need was to maintain our support to the allied armies. Whatever they needed, we located for them whether locally, or from abroad. As far as we were concerned, nothing was out of the ordinary any more. It was our obligation to find what was needed, quickly and at a fair price. This story is just one example of what was happening throughout the Kanoo network and how our staff, bless them, reacted in time of crisis.

Saudi Arabia – a mini-boom begins

In the opinion of many, Saudi Arabia has always been considered a safe and secure place, even throughout the Iran–Iraq War. The invasion of Kuwait changed that view and, inevitably, affected the Kanoo family business. The negative impact was on regular business throughout the Arabian Gulf region. Projects were suspended or cancelled; cargo shipments for civilian and commercial use were disrupted because of increased freight costs and insurance premiums; airports and sea terminals became congested with military activities; customers became unreliable, either because Saudi Arabian nationals living in the Eastern Province decided to relocate elsewhere in the Kingdom, or because expatriates resident throughout the Gulf States were obliged by their employers or embassies to leave altogether.

The fear that national gas plants, chemical facilities and communications installations might be sabotaged added to the uncertainty. In our case, many Kanoo offices were located in or near to these sensitive areas, such as oil towns, air and sea ports, all of which were potential targets for chemical or biological warfare. This applied to Saudi Arabia and Bahrain where business suffered badly.

The UAE and Oman were affected less as these countries were beyond Iraqi missile range and further away from the threat of invasion. Kanoo operations in those territories held steady, partly because airports in southern Arabia remained open to commercial airlines and became focal points for expatriate evacuation. Likewise, container ports such as Dubai and Fujairah remained busy terminals for cargo vessels which could not obtain insurance cover to proceed to ports in the war zone. Jubail and Dammam in Saudi Arabia, together with Mina Salman in Bahrain, were most affected.

In Saudi Arabia the positive impact of the invasion was that it spawned a new genre of business opportunities to support the war effort. As a result, the Saudi Arabian economy enjoyed a mini-boom. Abdulaziz Kanoo expressed the situation more graphically: 'We had 500,000 troops and 200,000 rich refugees from Kuwait. They all wanted to eat, buy consumer goods and find accommodation.' The practical mechanics of serving those needs was an immense exercise in logistics.

Dhahran airport remained open to aircraft which were engaged in civilian evacuation, but on the whole the airport was dedicated to military activities until war became imminent. Jeddah, therefore, became increasingly busier. Trucks and trailers were required to move commodities from the Western Province of Saudi Arabia to the east. People wanted to listen to news so the demand for radios and televisions caused stores to sell out. When the armies arrived, they wanted to dig trenches, create defences and build camps. The Kanoo commercial division responded by importing cranes and fork-lifts, and much more besides.

Respite from the desert heat could be bought in the form of air-conditioning units. These needed generators. Generators need fuel. And so the economic cycle of demand and supply created artificial and unprecedented markets and business movement. This enhanced the income of the Saudi Arabian merchants. In turn, the Government began to subsidise all food. A further knock-on effect was that local merchants were encouraged to import more rice, wheat and vegetables so that there would be no food shortages. Suddenly, business was there and everybody was buying and selling.

Meanwhile, the Kanoo Shipping Division quickly got to grips with evacuation procedures. One of the first opportunities occurred when we received a telephone call from the Getty Oil/Texaco refinery and sea terminal at Mina Saud, a few miles north of Khafji in Kuwait. They asked the Kanoo organisation to assist their employees' evacuation, if required. Within twenty-four hours after the invasion, Kanoo shipping offices from the Kuwaiti border to the Straits of Hormuz were on standby to receive a fleet of small craft laden with refinery personnel, if such a flotilla were to be organised. As it turned out, most Getty and Texaco oil men escaped by bus. The final contingent left Mina Saud in tugboats and sailed south to Khafji. Their leader, who happened to know the Kanoo office in town, walked in and announced their arrival. The Kanoo task then was to assist with the evacuation of the oil refinery personnel out of Saudi Arabia by air.

Naturally, this odd situation created a strange mixture of feelings. For the most part, Kanoo management believe that the overriding sense within the company was uncertainty. As for the general public, a perceptible aura of panic developed once they saw Kuwaiti refugee families arriving in the Kingdom. There was also a widely-held view that some embassies were responsible for fuelling heightened anxiety.

Immediately concerned with protecting their citizens, they generated a mass exodus and caused chaos at the airports. As military aircraft began to arrive laden with troops, commercial Jumbos departed packed with non-essential personnel. The influx of outgoing personal effects and incoming military cargo all added to the mayhem which, in the opinion of many Kanoo employees, created a sense of premature and unnecessary panic. Although Kanoo Travel was not involved with the movement of military personnel, the office was directly below the Dhahran flight-path. The thunderous noise of Galaxy (C5) transport planes and Jumbo jets, one aircraft passing overhead every twenty minutes, twenty-four hours a day, could hardly be ignored.

Throughout 'Desert Shield' until the start of 'Desert Storm' – the Gulf War – on 17 January 1991, Kanoo Travel's work focused on expatriate evacuation by air. In the first instance, their task was to arrange for other companies' employees and their families to leave Saudi Arabia, particularly after some companies closed down altogether. Often this meant working twenty-four hours a day, particularly when ARAMCO requested a round-the-clock service. Before long, commercial airlines changed their schedules. While some stopped serving the region altogether others introduced extra flights. When the Getty Oil and Texaco personnel established a base in the Dhahran International Hotel, Kanoo Travel set up a 'cell' within the Getty management organisation to arrange the repatriation of its stranded employees to their home countries.

Meanwhile, Kanoo Travel was presented with the challenge of repatriating 15,000 Sri Lankan housemaids who had arrived in Riyadh from Kuwait. Our company arranged not only temporary accommodation and pocket money, but the housemaids' home-bound flights and exit visas. If this undertaking had seemed immense, the repatriation of 106,000 Indian workers (on Air India), was an even more formidable enterprise, even though they were evacuated from various Gulf airports. To cope with this mass exodus, Kanoo Travel set up an evacuation facility at their airline centre in Al-Khobar specifically to arrange for the Indian workers' repatriation. When, eventually, Dhahran airport closed to commercial traffic, the evacuees were transported by bus to Qatar and the UAE from where they continued their homeward journeys by air. Even though, in each case, the evacuees' respective embassies paid Kanoo Travel by cheque or a book transfer, the full practical burden of their stay in the Kingdom fell on Kanoo Travel.

For Abdullah Abu Khamseen (General Manager of Kanoo Travel,

Saudi Arabia), his organisational task was simplified since, some fifteen years earlier, the Government of Saudi Arabia had built a huge housing complex to accommodate thousands of lower-income Saudis. (The project comprised six-bed apartments in 1,700 units in Dammam and 3,450 in Al-Khobar. Similar housing was built in Riyadh and Jeddah.) The units had never been occupied so, during the late summer of 1990, the Saudi Government did a speedy job in equipping them with basic furniture. Some of the complexes were occupied by allied military personnel, while some were allocated to Kuwaiti families who were not accommodated in hotels.

This was not the end of the refugee saga. The Municipality of Dammam contracted Kanoo Travel to cope with part of the influx of Kuwaiti families and all that this involved. At one stage, all the hotels in Dammam and Al-Khobar were fully occupied by Kuwaiti refugees and their expatriate domestic servants, with Lincolns and Mercedes lined up outside. To Abdullah Abu Khamseen, this was no joke. 'You know, some Kuwaiti families of say four members, might have three drivers, a cook, and three housemaids. They came with them all. ... The Saudi Government said: "OK, we will look after you, but we don't look after your domestic helpers. They have to go back home. It is much safer for them. ... You, Kanoo, set up something for us to despatch them."' So we did just that.

Y.B.A.Kanoo assists the allied war effort

Each Kanoo senior manager has his own story to tell as to how, throughout the company's diverse operations, he became involved in supporting the war effort. Some three weeks after the invasion of Kuwait, the Americans announced that they were to despatch 100,000 troops to Saudi Arabia and so an immense sea-lift began. By a stroke of good fortune, the Kanoo organisation attracted an estimated 60 per cent of the American sea-lift business, as Nick Lane, General Manager of our shipping division in Saudi Arabia, explained. The way they work is that the Military Sea-Lift Command, a non-offensive division of the US Navy, charters civilian ships to transport military equipment and personnel. All the sea-lift of the US military equipment fell into two categories: that carried by naval vessels and that which was contracted out to private companies such as Sealand, an American company which became a major bidder. Once having pre-qualified and qualified for the task, Sealand was contracted by the US Government to transport supplies to the war zone, and their subsequent discharge at Saudi ports, especially Jubail and Dammam.

In Saudi Arabia, Y.B.A.Kanoo was operating as Sealand's handling agent, or contract manager. By now, maritime insurance rates had risen dramatically, to the extent that the General Manager of our Shipping Agencies Division fully expected commercial cargo business in Saudi Arabia to 'drop off'. When Sealand approached him to discuss how the two companies could gear up to the task of handling military supplies, our staff were available for transfer to the new entity. Based in the Kanoo Tower in Dammam and staffed by a combination of Sealand and Kanoo personnel, an independent Sealand Military Unit was formed. Other existing Kanoo units remained independent and continued to support the company's established shipping lines and tramp ships so that at no time did they feel that Kanoo had diverted all of its energy to the war effort.

Kanoo Shipping Division's next target was the British Government's freight agents, Hogg Robinson. They had been contracted by the British Ministry of Defence to co-ordinate its army's sea-lift as part of the code-name: 'Operation Granby'. Some thirty-six hours after making a telephone call from Saudi Arabia to one of Hogg Robinson's company directors in London, Captain Nicholas Lane sat facing him, pitching in London on behalf of Y.B.A.Kanoo to become Hogg Robinson's handling agent in Saudi Arabia. The director telephoned round a few shipping companies to check out Lane's quote and Kanoo's ability to perform. The director accepted the bid and the deal was made. Our company became Hogg Robinson's agent contracted to handle 100 per cent of the British sea-lift operations in Saudi Arabia.

At roughly the same time, the British Army despatched a reconnaissance unit to Saudi Arabia. Once again, Captain Lane identified another commercial opportunity when the British Army's advance force, commanded by Lt.-Col. Barry Aitken, decided that Jubail was the port into which the British Army would land their freight. Captain Lane instructed Kanoo Shipping Division staff in Jubail to provide the unit with an office and all assistance until further notice. This gave the British Army an opportunity to operate locally, establish a presence in Dammam and Jubail with all essential conveniences and communications immediately at its disposal. The only thing asked of the army's Commander was that Y.B.A.Kanoo should be given the opportunity to quote for any business that he put 'out into the market'. The result of this initiative was that our company was appointed agent for the British Army, apparently the first time that it has ever made such a move.

So the momentum of the British mobilisation accelerated. The army designated the equipment to be transported. Hogg Robinson organised the logistics both in the UK, and in Germany, where the company had a permanent base servicing the British Army of the Rhine. Vessels loaded in England sailed from Marchwood Military Port, Southampton, while those leaving Germany sailed from Emden. The lead-time between their departure and arrival in Saudi Arabia was about three weeks, depending on whether ships from Emden were required to call into Southampton first.

Most vessels involved in the British sea-lift sailed round the Arabian peninsula, up through the Arabian Gulf and into Saudi Arabia's east coast ports of Jubail and Dammam. Some sailed only as far as the Red Sea, terminating either at Jeddah or Yanbu ports. Almost daily, we received updated lists from Hogg Robinson of expected forward movements.

As for the French, to say that Y.B.A.Kanoo had 100 per cent of their military shipping business in the Eastern Province is true but misleading. When France announced its intention to participate in 'Desert Shield', Captain Lane received a telephone call from a French company, saying that it had been approached by the French military. In the event of it organising a sea-lift, would Kanoo be able to assist? Of course, came our reply. Wherever the French wished to operate, all they had to do was to arrive and we would deal with their requirements. First of all, an aircraft-carrier and escorts arrived in Jubail, established a presence and basically told us: 'Go away. We don't need you. This is France and we shall do things our way.' Y.B.A.Kanoo only provided local liaison for the commercial ships which serviced the French requirements.

In the end, the French forces chose ports on the west coast of Saudi Arabia as their discharging points. Because of the small size of their contingent, when compared with those of the Americans and British, the French were able to do everything for themselves.

In comparison with their armies and navies, the allied air forces were relatively self-sufficient, in particular, the RAF. However, our Aircraft Handling Division did participate in 'Desert Shield' since, for twenty-five years, it had had the Military Airlift Command (MAC) contract to handle all US military aircraft which flew into Dhahran airport. Instead of dealing with a maximum of seventy movements a month, the staff now had to handle between sixty and eighty per *day*. The task became too much. We did not have the manpower to handle the cargo and personnel being discharged onto the tarmac from an avalanche of military transport: Galaxies (C5s), chartered Jumbo jets (Boeing 747s), C130 and C140-type aircraft.

The tremendous strain on our Aircraft Handling Division worsened when it became more difficult for us to hire extra staff to work at the airport. Prospective employees did not like to work in an environment which was a natural target for missile attack and, for security reasons, the local authorities declined to issue us with the necessary additional passes. The impact was immediate and far-reaching. MAC, however, came to the rescue by providing us with one hundred GIs who, under the direction of our supervisors, helped us to sort out the chaos.

As for the cargo, Khalil Buzaboon, General Manager of Y.B.A.Kanoo's Cargo Services in Saudi Arabia recalls that his division was not too involved in the military side of the business, since the US Army was exempt from clearing cargo through customs, and arranged its own sea, land and air transport. Instead, the Kanoo organisation became very involved with associated aspects such as dealing with the military's emergency needs and handling shipments of food and other supplies from Bahrain, Dubai and Jeddah.

Not surprisingly, the despatch of personal effects through Bahrain also became big business. Many expatriates, who did not envisage returning to the region, arrived at Kanoo's cargo offices with all their belongings ready to be shipped to their home countries. As a result, Kanoo Cargo Services Division was inundated with personal paraphernalia, including an extraordinary variety of pets.

The impact of the Gulf War

As the storm clouds gathered during the later months of 1990, the main concern was the threat of biological or chemical warfare. As a result we decided to make provision for wartime conditions. Gas masks were supplied to every Kanoo employee in Saudi Arabia. In Bahrain, gas masks were not as freely available as they were in the Kingdom, so we did all that we could to protect our employees. Plastic sheeting and tape were distributed to employees in both Bahrain and Saudi Arabia so that the windows of their offices and homes could be sealed. In the UAE and Oman we did not provide such facilities as it was believed that these areas were beyond Iraqi missile range.

In Dammam, instead of working the normal split day, employees worked from 7.00 a.m. until 3.00 p.m, our rationale being that staff should not have to drive to the office from their homes twice a day because Scud missiles, most likely, would be fired at us during the afternoons and at night. Yet the fact that staff disregarded this danger and worked extensive overtime, was evidence of their commitment to the war effort.

Because of the fear of chemical and biological warfare, we prepared a gas-proof area in every company office, house and flat, which included food and water for three days. The basement car-park of the Kanoo Tower in Dammam was converted into a bomb/gas shelter. At first, many staff brought their families to stay there at night. Curtained cubicles were constructed for family privacy, while a television set was rigged up so that everyone could watch CNN broadcasts. After a 'full house' in the first week, more and more, staff began to stay at home. By the end of the third week of war only a handful of people stayed in the shelter overnight.

As far as the Kanoo family was concerned, the prospect of war was no reason to change the policy which our family had practised since the invasion of Kuwait. We Kanoo family members, together with company staff, genuinely felt that we were required to support the war effort, each in our specialist roles. Apart from prudent personal protection against missile gas attack, the only other concession which Y.B.A.Kanoo made to the crisis was that important accounting documents and company records were despatched overseas to safety. At no time did we discuss closing down the business or leaving our posts. It was never on the agenda, not even on 16 January, what transpired to be the eve of war.

Abdullah Abu Khamseen remembers 13 January 1991, very well because some five hours before an Air India flight was due to take off from Bombay for Dhahran, the Saudi Arabian authorities told relevant travel offices that, forthwith, the Eastern Province of the Kingdom was closed to commercial aircraft. This was fair warning that war was imminent. As pilots and military aircraft increased their level of alertness, some well-informed British friends were saying: 'Watch for Wednesday evening/Thursday morning. It is going to start.' While in the American community, equally well-connected observers remarked: 'Two o'clock. Watch CNN and you will see it.' 'D Day' was an open secret.

And that, more or less, is what happened. Already security had been tightened at Jubail port, the general 'buzz' being: 'Come Thursday, it's for real.' There was a general evacuation of the Khafji area by all non-military personnel. As a result, we closed our shipping office in Khafji and told employees to travel south to Jubail. The same thing happened in the Khafji travel office, except that we had much trouble in persuading one employee to move as he was doing such good business issuing airline tickets to Kuwaitis. Eventually, on the promise that he could return to Khafji the following Saturday, if everything remained peaceful, this employee left his desk on the Wednesday evening. Hours later, the war began.

Forty-eight hours later, I received a telephone call in Dammam from our Saudi public relations officer in Khafji. He assured me that our office there was in good order and had not been damaged! Somehow, he had managed to talk his way back to check the office and collect some documents. I really had to lose my temper to persuade him to re-evacuate. Such conscientious staff spirit and bravado gave me nightmares.

The immediate impact of the Gulf War on Kanoo Travel was that commercial air traffic in and out of Dhahran and Bahrain ceased, both airports now being dedicated to military use. Yet, even on the first day of the war, Kanoo Travel was faced with a massive requirement to evacuate families and children from the Eastern Province. Our only choice was to organise a bus service to Dubai.

At first, we offered this to our own employees' families in the travel department. Then suddenly, Abdullah Abu Khamseen and his staff found people 'storming' Kanoo Travel offices demanding the same safe facility. The situation was distressing as families and children crowded our airline centre, by now a make-shift bus station, to bid farewell to loved ones whom they thought they might not see again.

For almost a month, the travel division ran as many as fifteen buses a day to Abu Dhabi and Dubai airports which remained open almost entirely throughout the crisis. The eighteen-hour road journey was hardly comfortable, particularly considering the customs and immigration checks at the Saudi-Qatari and UAE borders. Nevertheless, the bus service worked flat out until mid-February when both Bahrain and Riyadh airports reopened to commercial airlines. In mid-March 1991, two weeks after the end of the war, Dhahran airport re-opened to commercial traffic. By the second half of 1991, normal air travel had begun to re-establish itself.

Throughout the war, commercial cargo continued to enter Saudi Arabia, creating many problems for our shipping division. Under the normal terms of carriage in a war situation, a carrying vessel is not obliged to enter a war zone. In the case of 'Desert Storm', war risk insurance rose by about 7 per cent. Furthermore, it only provided seven days' cover from passing latitude 24° North. This gave a vessel just enough time to berth in Dubai, discharge, sail to Dammam, discharge and then leave the war zone. If the vessel stayed for one minute longer, another 7 per cent surcharge was levied. That, based on the average value of a container ship, amounted to between

top New Kanoo Abu Dhabi office building
opened in 1974 by Shaikh Mubarak Al Nahayan.

above National Bank of Bahrain. Chairman of
the Board, Ahmed Kanoo (fourth from left) with
Yousuf Almoayyed on his right and Isa Borshaid
on his left. Sitting, Haji Khalil Kanoo (left),
Hussain Yateem (right). Nooruddin, the Bank
General Manager (wearing a suit) with Abdulla
Alireza on his left.

top British Airways celebrates 60 years in the Gulf, 16 October 1992. From left: Abdulla Kanoo, Robert Ayling, Sir Colin Marshall, Khalid Kanoo.

above First official Saudi delegation to China, 1986. Abdulaziz Kanoo with Khalid Turki, Ahmed Abdullah, Abdulaziz Quraishi, Ebrahim Salman, Abdulaziz Sulaiman, Wahib bin Zager, and others.

above Abu Dhabi office (1974).

right Damman office (1992).

top The Amir of Bahrain Shaikh Isa bin Salman
Al Khalifa on his visit to the Kanoo office with
Ahmed Kanoo (1994).

above Sultan Qaboos of Oman being introduced
to Mubarak Kanoo by Nabil Qamber.

opposite Yusuf Kanoo Grand Mosque, Madinat
Hamed.

Ahmed Kanoo greeting King Fahd (1985).

top Former US President George Bush with Dr Abdul Latif Kanoo on an official visit to Bait Al-Quran (March 1996).

above Gen. Barry McCaffrey, 24th Inf (Mech) Division with Khalid Kanoo at Fort Stewart, Savannah, Ga., at the Divisional Mascot (camel) Induction Ceremony (1991).

right H H Sh. Rashid bin Saeed Al Maktoum with Hamed Ali Kanoo (Dubai 1974).

top From left: Haji Ali, Haji Yusuf and Haji
Jassim Kanoo. A painting by Abdulla Muharraqi.

above Kanoo Group Board chaired by Ahmed
Kanoo (1990).

US$450,000 and US$500,000 additional freight costs. In turn, these were charged-on to the consignee who, naturally enough, was unwilling to accept the extra charge, or passed it on to the consumer. Nevertheless, the reality was that any carrier had the right to say: 'I'll go as close as I safely can, discharge the cargo there and then it's up to the consignee to come and get it.'

The Saudi Arabian authorities were unhappy with this arrangement, as were many merchants. As a result, Nick Lane spent many evenings and nights, explaining the niceties of the insurance market to port officials and consignees. Led by Hassan Al-Ghamdi, our Shipping Operations Manager, they were required to write a detailed explanatory paper for the Director-General of Dammam Port. Initially, this was to be presented to Riyadh for submission to King Fahd, the Custodian of the Two Holy Mosques. The crux of the issue was that merchants had to ship military support-cargo on commercial terms. An added irritant was that since many consignments terminated in Dubai, the merchants were obliged to pay for the additional transport charges to Saudi Arabia.

After the storm

It was not until we started to repatriate military and civilian equipment used during the crisis, that the volume which had been imported became very apparent. Refrigerators, photocopiers, televisions, videos, Range Rovers, Land Cruisers and all the other luxury vehicles which military personnel had purchased, were just some of the 'consumer durables' which we packed up and shipped to the USA and Europe.

On its inward journey, military cargo had been off-loaded into marshalling areas on the same day that it had arrived in port. By the next morning, most of the cargo was gone, packed into convoys bound for the desert. When the same equipment came back to the marshalling areas, the procedures were more pedantic. Necessarily, the equipment was all carefully washed, cleaned and packed before being taken into the port for back-loading. Vast areas around Dammam and Jubail might be covered with tanks or trucks one day. Then, a week later, they would have left the country, only to be replaced by armoured personnel carriers, or mobile artillery waiting to be shipped. The main repatriation was completed in the second half of 1991, while the final repatriation was concluded in mid-1992.

It had been our expectation that when the war ended, there would be a marked drop in the volume of imported cargo. This did not happen. Throughout 1991 and 1992, incoming shipments were maintained as merchants began to restock in anticipation of evacuees returning. Even though civilian cargo handlings declined in 1993, the US military continued to import many containers into Dammam each month and our aircraft handling division continued to service military flights.

Another feature was that a noticeable amount of American non-offensive equipment, such as trucks, bulldozers and graders, was of Second World War vintage. Instead of shipping it all 'back home' the US Government took this opportunity to sell most of it at auctions. Despite the volume of equipment which was sold or shipped, an enormous amount was left behind to support the military peacetime presence in the Kingdom.

The switch from peace to war affected the confidence of international manufacturers with whom the Kanoo organisation primarily trades. However, because of its long relationship with principals and customers, much of Y.B.A.Kanoo's traditional business in Saudi Arabia, the UAE and Oman was not affected by the Gulf crisis. Y.B.A.Kanoo in Oman apparently made its biggest profit ever when it sold a mass of tents to the British army for a huge field hospital to be constructed in the Sultanate. In the end, when the tents were not used, the British tried unsuccessfully to sell them back to us.

Unfortunately, the economy of Bahrain suffered heavily, as did Y.B.A.Kanoo's business there. Our company had hoped that when the RAF and the US Air Force arrived on the island there would be new business opportunities. In practice, all branches of the military were very self-sufficient. Other than people wishing to leave Bahrain with personal effects and pets, the crisis generated little new business for our company. Instead, a tremendous down-turn in commercial activity occurred with the result that business continued to be depressed even in 1993.

On the other hand, Saudi Arabia enjoyed one its best trading years during the Gulf Crisis. As an Arab saying goes: 'Work and you will receive.' In Abdulaziz Kanoo's mind, this is no signal to be complacent. When asked what stood out in his mind as being the most far-reaching impact of the Gulf Crisis, not surprisingly my uncle focused on the region's priority to improve its defence. Unfortunately, yet inevitably, this will cost a great deal of money. Before the crisis, the governments of the Gulf Co-operation Council (GCC) countries were able to concentrate on economic development. Now, much of their income has to be invested in protection. Strengthening armies has never been a productive economic alternative. But even to this dark cloud there may be a silver commercial lining. If, through the establishment of national security, the confidence of investors, traders, customers and visitors can be ensured, then companies such as Y.B.A.Kanoo, together with the residents of the region, can position themselves for an optimistic future.

Chapter 14

Foundations of Future Growth

If someone should give Ahmed Kanoo, the Group Chairman, a box of mangoes as a gift, he would not keep all the fruit for himself but would have it distributed among the family. Selfishness is something which he does not care to see. His goal is to ensure that all family members work together for the benefit of the family company and not themselves. In essence, 'the young will respect their elders and the elders will be kind to the young'. This, in conjunction with self-discipline, living decently without extravagance and serving both community and country, is our family's basic credo as laid down by Haji Yusuf Kanoo at the beginning of the twentieth century, and still followed today.

Ahmed Kanoo, as Group Chairman and Head of the Family, instils in us all the importance of family values and ensures that everyone, from elders to children, practises what he preaches and understands our family traditions. Without labouring my point but to give examples, Ahmed Kanoo is well known for his attention to detail such as his checks to make sure that we are not overspending beyond what is 'reasonable' and his meticulous monitoring of our business operations. In this way, he tries to ensure that the Kanoo family and employees progress in a reasonable, responsible direction and maintain their course. He motivates, yet is a restraining influence. He is hard but he also has a heart of gold. He is there for any of us if we need him. Whatever the need, personal or professional, he is always there to help us.

As to the immediate future of our company, his role as instigator and moderator will remain important. Almost daily we are reminded to be careful and not to overdo things since excesses of any kind do not sit well with him. Caution and conservatism remain part of our family credo, even though it is hard to convince some of the younger generation that the trappings of life have to be paid for with money which has to be earned.

Balancing tradition with the 'tune' of today

All the Kanoo family members who work in our company have specialisations and personal characteristics which complement each other to achieve the family's goal, that of running a successful business. I have mentioned Ahmed in his role as father and moderator. I now turn to other family members.

Although Abdulla Kanoo is the Group Chief Executive Officer and Chairman of Y.B.A.Kanoo in Saudi Arabia he still does not mind rising at four or five o'clock in the morning to catch an aeroplane to attend a business meeting in some distant place. There are those who ask: 'Why does Abdulla Kanoo go himself? Why does he not send someone else in his place?' But that is his style. He is very much a 'hands on' person. He expects all to do their jobs well and does not mind telling them how to do it. He is extremely focused on company affairs.

Conversely, Mubarak Kanoo is aware of the younger generations wanting to 'do their own thing'. Already one or two of them wish to move away from what they perceive as the 'chains of tradition'. As Mubarak is the only member of the eldest generation to father only daughters, perhaps more than any other senior Kanoo family member, he has reflected on the younger generations' changing attitudes. He reads a lot, especially business management books and papers, and is very helpful when one needs his assistance. He also always accompanies the Amir of Bahrain when he travels overseas.

Abdulrahman spends much of his time promoting the family in a different fashion. He operates within the local community. He knows what is happening in the market. He heads the Al-Ahli Club, one of the leading sports and cultural clubs in Bahrain. He is a philanthropist who cares for the youth of Bahrain. He is also a property developer.

Abdulaziz is a superb public relations man liked by everyone for his willingness to help others. He is also a shrewd investor, as a result of which many people seek his advice or ask him to join them in their projects. He is very supportive of the younger generation and is, perhaps, the best 'listener' in the family.

Although Dr Abdul Latif Kanoo chose to work outside the family business (now as Under-Secretary in Bahrain's Ministry of Housing), he is still involved with family matters. Outside the Ministry, his interests vary from the foundation in 1986 of Bait Al-Quran (House of the Quran) and its continuing development, to collecting Islamic artefacts and manuscripts, writing newspaper articles and lecturing on Islamic affairs.

So, in this way, a balance is maintained. All of us work very hard to complement each other. In this respect, I can see their different points of view. On the one hand, as I am the oldest of the younger generations, I appreciate why my uncles are nervous about allowing the 'inexperienced' members of the family too much authority in the company. Often, we are still considered by the elders as 'inexperienced', even though, in my case, I am over fifty years old with twenty-eight years' work experience in the company. In some ways, this attitude has changed drastically over the last few years. Nevertheless, no matter how we excel, like any family-run business anywhere, we are still their 'children'.

On the other hand, I have been exposed to higher education and life in the USA, as have most of my cousins and my own children. Inevitably, none of us returned to Bahrain with the same outlook as before. Sometimes, we came back with attitudes and expectations quite different from the traditions of Arabia, and the expected norm of Y.B.A.Kanoo.

As the family looks to secure the future of its company, the threats as well as the opportunities must be assessed. To this end, my uncles continue to persuade the younger members of the family to accept advice, even though they all wish to have freedom to develop their own characters and careers, as they choose. To a great extent that flexibility is allowed with one basic proviso: The continued success of the family company must not be jeopardised by personal ambition. If there is a conflict of interests, then the company must come first.

Ahmed Kanoo believes that there is nothing which dictates that all must frame themselves within the tradition of the family company. In his view, this would be wrong. The new generation should be given opportunities and a chance. But being the old sage that he is, Ahmed Kanoo knows that through being given opportunities, we will make mistakes! But in the end, we will mould ourselves to follow in our fathers' footsteps, albeit in step with both family tradition and the 'tune' of today. Having said this, Ahmed accepts that the senior generation must adapt too. It must try to respect the opinion of the young generation, yet maintain some of the old conventions. It is this balance between tradition and a modern life-style that is crucial. As history has shown in the case of other family businesses, if one extreme overwhelms the other, disaster strikes and a family business will falter because of opposing points of view among the partners.

Fortunately, under my uncles' guidance, we have achieved an acceptable balance. The proof is that the family is still together after 100 years of trading. However, like family companies all over the world, we have our problems between the different generations. The elders wish to keep control of the business and the younger members feel that they are competent and should be given more authority and responsibility without constantly having to refer to the elder directors.

As a whole, we all respect family traditions and uphold them. For instance, why, as a family, do we 'sit' each Friday morning at the office in Manama for two hours? We do so to meet friends, business associates and retired employees who visit us. We drink coffee, discuss the latest rumours and market news and so on. We do so because Haji Yusuf did the same thing a century ago, as did his nephews Jassim and Ali, followed by their eldest sons, Mohamed (my father) and Ahmed. This tradition, still maintained by many old families, is continued by my uncles. In their case, they go to the office on Fridays at about 10.00 a.m. Visitors usually find Ahmed, Mubarak, Abdulrahman and Abdul Latif Kanoo 'sitting'. Sometimes, Abdulla and Abdulaziz join the morning *majlis* when they are in Bahrain. Later in the morning, they go to the mosque and pray.

Ahmed Kanoo senses that this era is in its twilight. It is only the elder generation which 'sits' in this way with friends and maintains the tradition. Members of the younger generations are infrequent participants. In Ahmed Kanoo's words: 'It is easy to say, why bother to sit and receive the few people of the old generation who may have nothing to do with the business any more. Why should I bother and leave my family to do this? But we feel we have to. There is something wrong with you if you don't do it. Unfortunately, our children are not doing this so regularly. I suppose after us, that will be it. Our Friday *majlis* will close.'

What Ahmed Kanoo has said is very true. I believe that our Friday *majlis* will cease after the older generation is no longer with us. The reason is not that the younger generations do not wish to continue with the tradition as their peer values have changed. On Fridays, they now prefer to spend more time with their families, go fishing, do some gardening, or simply sleep until prayer time. The reality is that the younger family members do not like to 'sit' on Fridays and talk. The culture has changed.

Focus on succession

Ironically, Ahmed Kanoo's poignant, if prophetic, remarks about the future of the family Friday *majlis* were made before my father, Mohamed, died in October 1991; before Ahmed himself suffered a serious, but mercifully brief, illness in early 1992; and before the untimely death of his youngest brother, Hamed, in February 1994.

After we had recovered from these severe shocks, we started to look at ourselves as a company more closely. According to my research, no matter which country one looks at, all family companies face four or five hurdles as they develop and mature. However, many companies face at least one, if not a combination of problems after the founder's death. The most important hurdle to overcome is the issue of succession. Other common problems include the separation of family affairs from business affairs; nepotism; father-and-son conflict; the in-laws gaining influence; and friction between the older and younger generations. If these 'normal' problems are not recognised and addressed to the satisfaction of the majority of the family members, disintegration will start. Issues that are unresolved in one generation will not go away. The next generation will be faced with the same issue. Only this time, it will become a bigger problem and harder to solve.

The bigger the size of the family company ownership, the more the collapse of that business becomes unavoidable. There are very few exceptions to this fact of life. The trick is to recognise the signs of dissension within the family and do something about it before the collapse. The usual solution is to go 'public', either wholly or in part, and so maintain family unity and company continuity. Irrespective of which country they operate in, many family companies collapse because they have not planned for a successor. To quote a phrase I once heard: 'Companies do not plan to fail, they fail to plan.' This is one significant weakness in Arab family business. In our case, it was only recently that the Kanoo Board established a succession plan.

Statistically, the odds against family-owned and controlled businesses continuing to thrive through successive generations is astronomical. Fewer than 30 per cent of all family businesses reach the second generation for two main reasons: either the children are not interested in their father's business or the business is mismanaged. Only 13 per cent of that remaining 30 per cent reach the third generation stage. When it comes to the fourth generation, the prognosis is dismal: just 4 per cent of that 13 per cent make it to the fourth generation. Less than 1 per cent of the remaining 4 per cent reach the fifth generation. When it comes to the sixth generation, only a very small percentage of that 1 per cent make it any further.

As our family-tree shows, Y.B.A.Kanoo is now in its sixth generation. While the company was growing throughout this time, the number of family members was increasing. Today, the Kanoo elders are aware of the pitfalls associated with family business and accept that planned succession is essential. As a result, the Y.B.A. Kanoo structure is slowly allowing more authority to the younger family members but the transition is not yet complete.

In many respects, the family *Deed of Gift and Transfer*, signed on 25 April 1954, laid the ground-rules for 'succession'. Forward-thinking for its time, this document, Ahmed Kanoo believes, is as relevant today as it was forty years ago. As discussed much earlier, this document defined Ahmed as Chairman; my father, Mohamed, as Deputy Chairman; and two Board Members, Abdulla and Mubarak Kanoo.

The first thing which happened which sent us all into shock, was my father's rapid decline in 1991. Even though he had been ill with Parkinson's Disease for many years, we had come to terms with his disabling condition. None of us anticipated such a final decline. Perhaps the experience should have cautioned us more. Nevertheless, before we had adapted to this change, Ahmed Kanoo underwent emergency surgery, an episode which produced an unprecedented moment of crisis. We faced the real risk that, suddenly, we could find ourselves with no captain and no navigation chart.

Now, four years have passed since this scare and the Group Chairman remains at the helm. However, in planning for the future, the shareholders have elected the next Deputy Group Chairman. He is Abdulla Kanoo, Chairman of Y.B.A.Kanoo, Saudi Arabia, and Group Chief Executive Officer, as he is the next most senior member of the family. If Abdulla should become the Group Chairman, then most likely his cousin, Abdulaziz Kanoo, will assume the Chairmanship of Y.B.A.Kanoo, Saudi Arabia. There will be a family meeting, all will be given the opportunity to air their views and a decision will be reached by consensus. We do not vote in our Board meetings. The Chairman asks for everyone's view and then sums up the sense of the meeting.

However, this has not yet explained how my father's seat on the Group Board was filled. Just like my cousins Yusuf, Fawzi, Ali, Saud and Bader, I was already attending the Group Board meetings but with limited privileges. We could make our voices heard and, indeed, listened to. If what any of us said made sense, then it was accepted. However, a full Group Board member is usually an owner of the company (one of the seven equal partners) and his voice will carry more weight than the non-shareholding Board members. The partners become involved in the important decisions related to the company or family. The Group Chairman is the ultimate arbitrator and, as such, it is not unusual for him to overrule a partner in favour of a younger non-shareholding Kanoo point of view.

When I was elected by the Group Board to fill my father's vacant seat, I became a full Group Board Director on 24 December 1992. Although I represented one share equal to those of the other owners, it was not automatic that I should become a full Group Board Director. It took fourteen months for the other Group Directors to be satisfied before they elected me. A similar procedure happened after Hamed Kanoo's death in 1994. His wife Lulwa and his children Maha, Bassim and Mishal inherited his share of the company. They selected Mishal as their representative on the Group Board and so the company continued to function as smoothly as it did before.

While Ahmed Kanoo is seen as the family arbitrator, I see my role as the mediator, even though I am variously regarded by my family as a rebel, an extrovert, even an eccentric! But in many ways, this is not surprising. The unfortunate position that I have always suffered from is that, although by birth I am a member of the younger generations, I am not always regarded as being such because I am the eldest of the younger ones. Let me explain.

My position has always been precarious because it is difficult to be the authoritative, accepted party in certain circumstances. If, for example, I walk into a room and Fawzi, my cousin, is there, he will stand up, open the door for me or let me go first, because I am the eldest of our generation. It is a sign of respect to the elders and our normal family tradition to act in this way. But if I were to sit in a room with my uncles and, for example, coffee was needed, one of my uncles might ask: 'Khalid, please go and get some coffee'. This is acceptable also because, in this case, I would be the youngest family member present. I have to be sensitive to each situation.

It is this oscillation between two different 'character roles' which has enabled me to develop a relationship with employees as their mediator. For example, if some of the boys come to me and complain that they need an extra bonus, they will find it easier to talk to me about it rather than approach my uncles out of respect for their age. I will try to persuade my senior uncle to authorise the bonus. I also act on behalf of my cousins if they need something from the family, or if a sensitive company subject arises which is related to them.

In another way, together with my managing director cousins, I try to bridge the gap between the way in which my uncles run the Group, and a more modern style of management that business demands today. My uncles worked very hard in the post-Second World War era to build the business into what it is today. However, during the last two decades or so, advanced technology, a volatile economic environment, innovative business practices and new theories often render old-style management 'out of step' with the times in which we operate. Today, our working procedures have to be handled in a different style, although the content may be very similar, if not the same. My uncles are 'men of action' brought up in the no-nonsense tradition that to get the job done, they must work with their bare hands, so to speak.

This is not limited to my family only. Other major families have grown in the same way: the Suliman Olayan and Ahmed Juffali groups in Saudi Arabia; Mohamed Jalal and Yusuf Almaoyyed in Bahrain; Al Darwish and Mannai in Qatar; Al-Ghanim in Kuwait and Al-Futtaim and Masood in the UAE, to mention but a few.

Conversely, many international companies which we work with today do not believe that the job-in-hand is being managed properly unless they commission studies, write reports and generate statistics. Thus, it has become the job of the younger generation to mediate between how the older generation perceives and achieves its business goals, and how these are interpreted to foreign major companies which tend to be run in a more structured way.

Complementary change

Whenever family members attend college or university overseas, it has always been the family expectation that they will return to take part in the family business. Nevertheless, we foresee a time towards the end of this century when many young family members may not wish to do that. Fortunately, this has not happened yet, except in the case of Dr Abdul Latif Kanoo. They may work outside the company after graduation to gain a few years' experience, after which they are expected to join the family business.

It is sometimes said that Y.B.A.Kanoo has always been a bastion of male preserve and that no Kanoo 'girls' are allowed to work for the company. The facts are quite different. For instance, before my sister Layla focused her energies on being a mother, she used to work in the Kanoo Travel Agency Division. Farida Kanoo works with Norwich Union; Maha (Hamed's daughter) is based in Dubai as Administration Manager of the Kanoo Group, UAE & Oman; Mubarak's youngest daughter, Dina (even after her marriage) is the Personnel Manager in Bahrain. My daughter, Nada, trained as a dealer in Gulf International Bank (GIB) with a view to her joining the family company at a later date. Abdulla's daughters, Hana and

Lamya, are being groomed to join the family business soon after they complete their higher education.

At the moment no female members of the Kanoo family have been promoted to Group Board level. But this is not because of any corporate or family policy which forbids such a move. Simply, we boys and girls must demonstrate both an aptitude and a degree of competence before we may be considered candidates for directorships, or even hold senior positions in the company. Without labouring the point, while no Kanoo women have yet achieved sufficient company experience to be promoted to senior positions, this does not mean that the 'winds of change' are not being felt now. A time will come when there is a move towards greater equality, more freedom of choice, and the possibility that one day, a talented and ambitious Kanoo woman may seek appointment to the Board, just as the Group Chairman foresees. Whether that happens next year or next century is not really the point. The certainty is that as part of our corporate evolution, that time will surely come.

The immediate priority of Y.B.A.Kanoo's senior management is to ensure that 'our house is in order' for the next generation of family graduates. In 1996, counting my two sons and their cousins who are are about to finish their education, the company must consider 'placements' for seven young Kanoo family members. Their diverse interests and characteristics mean that they will wish to bring fresh ideas and innovation to the company. Predictably, the 'old school' will resist rapid and risky change.

For example, in 1987, when I first suggested that our family should branch out into the retailing business, it was at a time when the company wished to launch a new Kanoo non-traditional business. I had already persuaded Sears Roebuck to venture overseas. At first, our Chairman did not like the idea, but after much study and consideration, he accepted my proposal and supported it. Eventually the Board approved the project and Zaina International (Saudi Arabia), opened to the public in 1990 to market Sears products. The same feasibility research was applied to the Zaina Sports Store which opened in Bahrain in 1991. Retailing has now become an accepted addition to the Y.B.A.Kanoo portfolio.

However, our Retailing Division faced a very difficult 'birth'. We made mistakes in our learning curve. Because of Y.B.A.Kanoo's inexperience in this business sector and my choosing a member of our staff with no retail background to be appointed as General Manager, we did not realise that 'Retail is detail'. Instead, in those early days, our company culture drove us to treat retailing as another

Kanoo industrial or service division. Now, we understand the problems of retailing, its weaknesses and strengths.

This experience led us to look at our Retail Division in a different light. We decided what type of companies we wished to represent and how we wished them to be managed. Our next experience was better. I was approached by Abdulla Nasser, an old friend from Abu Dhabi, who asked if I was interested in a joint venture to open a J.C.Penney Fashions department store in Bahrain, another outlet of the giant American fashion house. We registered Kanoo-Liwa Trading WLL, a company to 'hold' the joint-venture. Nine months later, the Bahrain J.C.Penney store opened on 30 November 1994. On 10 October 1996 J.C.Penney's Al-Khobar, Saudi Arabia, opened its door. Now we are negotiating with other international retail houses in the hope that they will come to the Arabian Gulf region and work with us.

While this new experience had its risks and rewards, as a family we must recognise the need to match an individual's personality, training and experience with what we have 'on offer' within the company. Our first priority is to avoid family fragmentation and precedents whereby individuals (whatever their age or experience) begin to set up satellite enterprises which may compete with Y.B.A.Kanoo's core businesses. So how do we resolve the problem?

Some directors feel that should one Kanoo family member prove not very interested in Y.B.A.Kanoo's traditional business but in something completely different, our attitude should be, if he or she is capable and proficient in something that we *could* do, then we should encourage that person to develop his or her talent in the chosen speciality. Then, if all circumstances are favourable, that enterprise can be attached to the family company as, say, a joint-venture. For instance, if someone is seriously interested in the film business, then let him or her work with a film company. If the person proves capable, then let us buy a film-related business and place that person in charge of it. If that company is successful, then we can attach it the Y.B.A.Kanoo Group. What is wrong with that? We have done stranger things before. Not all family members have the same abilities or like to do the same things.

It is fortunate that we, the working members of the Kanoo family, do not have jealousies or envy each other. Just because one drives a Mercedes, does not mean that the others must have a Mercedes too. If one person takes two extra weeks' holiday, or buys new furniture, it does not follow that other members will demand the same treatment. We know that many family companies have collapsed because each partner, or his son, became envious of the other and tried to 'out-take' each other from the company's fund. In this respect, I am not trying to suggest that we are smarter than anyone else, but at least we endeavour to learn from the lessons of such misfortunes and try to apply the principle of complementing each other, not competing with one another.

Sharing according to Sharia Law

Reverting to the beginning of my story for a moment, we know that when Ahmed Mohamed Kanoo (Haji Yusuf Ahmed Kanoo's father), passed his sole ownership business to his son, it was a very small and struggling business. As Haji Yusuf developed the Bait Kanoo (House of Kanoo) family business, it was his wish to pass that business, still a sole ownership company, to his heirs. As he had no children, he passed it on to his brother Mohamed's sons, Jassim and Ali. Hence the business had now become a partnership on a fifty-fifty basis between them.

In 1954 Jassim and Ali Kanoo signed the *Deed of Gift and Transfer* whereby they handed over the business known as 'Yusuf bin Ahmed Kanoo' to their male children. Although Jassim had five sons and Ali had three sons, Ali's sons decided to share the equity on an equal basis with Jassim's sons.

Then, on 13 July 1963, a Schedule was signed by the seven 'brothers'. This refers to the *Declaration of Gift* (the original document being called the *Deed of Gift and Transfer*). As a process of corporate evolution, an *Agreement for Sale of Business* was signed on 25 March 1965 by the same seven family members. In order of seniority, the signatories were Ahmed, Mohamed, Abdulla, Mubarak, Abdulrahman, Abdulaziz and Hamed. This legalised a new ownership arrangement, that of an equal partnership. Meanwhile, on 28 September 1964, our company known as Yusuf bin Ahmed Kanoo was incorporated by a special Charter, the first in Bahrain to be granted by His Highness Shaikh Isa bin Salman Al Khalifa, the Ruler of Bahrain. Thus, Y.B.A.Kanoo had become a limited liability company. Although company law became effective in Bahrain during 1975, it was not until 14 May 1981, that Y.B.A.Kanoo was registered as a company with limited liability (WLL).

As quite separate developments, when Abdulla and Abdulaziz went to Saudi Arabia, they created a partnership between them. Hamed, in the UAE, created a sole ownership company to operate there. Both companies are fully autonomous and independent legal entities. The Y.B.A.Kanoo Group Board helps and supports those companies whenever requested.

Nevertheless, complications regarding both the commercial and Sharia laws of each country where we trade, throughout the Arabian Gulf region and overseas, have to be addressed. We, as Muslims, are bound not only by the dictates of commercial law, but also by the Sharia Law which has clear rules, especially regarding heirs and inheritance. Since Y.B.A.Kanoo is a Muslim family business, we have to operate within the limits of the Sharia Law, no matter how ingenious lawyers may become. We cannot, nor do we wish to, ignore its established doctrine.

According to Sharia Law, one may gift someone anything one wishes during one's life-time. If one dies and has not gifted any assets, then Sharia Law comes into effect. Wills are only wishes. According to Sharia Law, they cannot be enforced, except for 30 per cent of the inheritance. Sharia Law also says 'no inheritance can be received before all the deceased's debts are paid.' What is left must be divided among the heirs according to a strictly layered arithmetical formula.

There is little doubt that my father's death brought the 1954 *Deed of Gift and Transfer* to the forefront because he was the first of the seven partners to die. This raised the question of how the partnership should reflect this change. To make the running of the company's affairs easier, my sister gave me a power-of-attorney to act on her behalf. I have now replaced my father as the owner (with my sister) of his share in the company. I received two-thirds of my father's inheritance, and my sister one third.

The reason for this is that in both our Arab and Muslim cultures it is expected that the man will be the breadwinner, and will be required to clothe, house and feed his family, as well as those relatives who require similar support. We still believe in family values, that the man should look after his mother, father, younger brothers and unmarried sisters, plus cousins, aunts and uncles who need help or shelter. So it is expected that a man will have more expense than a woman who may have a husband or a brother already looking after her. We look after our parents until they die. We do not believe in 'old people's homes' prevalent in the west.

Y.B.A.Kanoo – an evolving entity

Even though it is the practice for many companies to have a mission statement, often posted on corporate notice-boards to catch the attention of all who pass by, this is something we do not have in our company. There are those who believe that we should, but it has to be remembered that our family company is an evolving entity. Although we do not have a plan to say that we want to be in such-and-such a situation in five years' time, we do not drift with the market and happily arrive where the wind blows us. It was a family decision to be flexible in our forward planning. We have annual business plans and long-range goals, but these are amended as current conditions dictate. We live in volatile times and so must respond to change in order to stay ahead.

As a Group we are in constant touch with our customers. Management receives feedback, as do family members who often are in direct touch with our customers and principals, sometimes during the course of entertaining, at other times when courtesy calling or just as the result of receiving a letter or a telephone call. In this way, we try to keep improving our service. The travel agency division is just one area, where we are always trying to improve the quality of our services.

At the same time, we constantly watch and study both our own and other market statistics. We keep our ears to the ground and listen to what the market says. We employ consultants and analyse statistics. We watch our competitors and their progress. We visit our customers, principals, ministries and market-makers. Family members, starting with Ahmed Kanoo, approach companies with whom we believe we might develop business links. When Ahmed and other directors travel overseas, for instance, they always meet existing principals to keep in touch with them. We also visit potential companies that we may wish to work with. Whenever Kanoo members of senior management travel to a country, they allow time for these visits.

We also watch changing circumstances in world affairs. Take the case of the former Eastern bloc countries and the advent of new diplomatic missions all over the GCC. We do not take unnecessary risks, yet the Kanoo Group looks at regional or political change and considers whether it might be good business for us to develop contacts in countries which, hitherto, have been closed to western-style business. Today, we have shipping, airline or commercial agencies from Poland, Czechoslovakia, China, Russia and Uzbekistan. Hamed and Fawzi Kanoo have visited various eastern European countries several times, including Russia. As mentioned in a previous chapter, Abdulaziz visited China in 1986 as part of an official Saudi Arabian trade mission.

I have been asked how the outgoing activity of being a market leader fits with our traditional conservative family philosophy. In this context, we interpret conservative in the sense that we carefully evaluate new business opportunities before we launch ourselves into the unknown. We are no more immune from calamity than other companies to the extent that there is a calculated risk in everything we do. Yes, we are part of the 'risk business', but only up to a certain point. Like bankers (and after all Haji Yusuf operated an informal bank for a substantial part of his life), we are investors not gamblers. Unless we are convinced that a new business relationship is a good venture, we do not enter into it. Sometimes we are caught out and may miss an opportunity, but that is part of the game. As history has proved to us, we cannot expect to remain in the same markets for ever because change will take place. If we don't change to meet the future, the future will change us.

In the late 1940s, it was Ahmed Kanoo who made the promise to himself that the future business of Y.B.A.Kanoo should diversify into different business disciplines locally and invest in countries far beyond the shores of the Arabian Gulf region. By spreading the risk in this way, our family future would be much more secure and not dependent upon one industry or one country.

This policy remains as valid now as it was nearly fifty years ago. The main difference now is that we must look at different scenarios and take a realistic view. If, for example, our organisation wished to expand by 30 per cent in the travel sector, we would have to wipe out say, 30 per cent of the existing smaller travel companies' market share. That would be unacceptable as we do not believe that we should use our muscle to overwhelm smaller companies. The Kanoo philosophy prevents us from harming others intentionally. Yes, we compete aggressively. But we will stop if the community is adversely affected, as we did when – as explained before – we received complaints about our chilled meat business adversely affecting smaller retailers. As Group Chairman, Ahmed Kanoo felt an ethical and moral obligation not to compete against smaller, weaker companies. So we sold our chilled meat operation, although it was making a handsome profit.

Because we have grown as a family and as a company, we must be bold enough and brave enough to direct our destiny and not be followers of fashion. We must decide whether to launch internationally into manufacturing, industrial services, property, banking and finance, or consumer products, while keeping a firm grip on the services which remain the core of our traditional business in Arabia.

The new generation and its leaders must decide what, how, and when that diversification takes place. We cannot stand still but must move on to maintain our growth. We should not fear change. We have the tradition, the resources and the capability. Why should we not join the ranks of the world's leading companies? While avarice is considered a sin, as far as I know, there is nothing wrong with being ambitious.

Vision of the future

In the Kanoo family we have a strong commitment to the community. We feel that as we earn from and therefore live from a community, having reaped some of the harvest we should sow some of the harvested seed-corn to help the welfare of that community which helped us in the first place. Following the teaching of Islam, as observant Muslims we do not go around advertising our good deeds. Instead, we give quietly to those who require help, whether it is for a building for the community's specific needs, an individual facing a bad time, a charity looking after the handicapped or improving the lives of our youth.

In 1990, as a part of our centenary celebration, our family began to explore the idea of creating a foundation to provide scholarships or award prizes in various fields of endeavour such as history, art, music, engineering, sport, in fact in any discipline which we believe will encourage both the young and the old to develop their education or specialisations beyond conventional boundaries. Already, a sum of six million dollars has been set aside as a gift from the family to establish the Yusuf Kanoo Foundation. His Excellency Shaikh Abdulla bin Khalid Al Khalifa (Minister of Justice) and His Excellency Tariq Almoayyed (then, Minister of Information) were invited to assist the Group Chairman, Ahmed Kanoo, to develop this idea. Other local committees in Saudi Arabia, the UAE and Oman were formed. But the invasion of Kuwait interrupted the project's progress.

This pause was a blessing in disguise, since it caused us to rethink some of our ideas, reconsider some of the proposed rules and regulations, and take a longer view of the concept. Ahmed Kanoo sees the Yusuf Kanoo Foundation as being very similar to the Nobel Prize, although on a smaller scale. Candidates are nominated based on individual merit, not class or financial status. But like all grand schemes, the planning period must necessarily be cautious, which leads me to discuss future prospects for our family business.

The Y.B.A.Kanoo Group is a private company, is not listed on any stock exchange and does not publish annual accounts. Of course, the degree to which it succeeds is both a concern and a curiosity, depending upon one's perspective. Naturally enough, shareholders and senior managers know that employees are interested in its well-being. Clients have a vested interest in being well-informed. Competitors wish they knew more about us. As working family members, we know how well, or not, we are doing and we do not feel obliged to publish such information. For those who really wish to find out, they can look at any document which lists company and bank rankings, and then guess the financial success and size of our company. We do not feel the need to brag about our financial strength or trading size. We know it and that is enough for us.

We feel that our company future is secure as a family entity since, already, there are several members of the younger generation who have the potential to develop our business further. If these young people are given the opportunity now to work together as friends, then the potential danger of divisive rivalry will not become a major issue, a calamity we have seen befall other family enterprises. If the young generation think along the lines that 'Fawzi's achievement is Saud's achievement' or 'Yusuf's achievement is Ali's achievement' then we shall continue to complement each other and not compete jealously. The right seeds are there. Perhaps they have not yet grown, but at least the Group Chairman, supported by the other Group Directors, has planted them ready to be nurtured.

We should remember, too, that Arabia is no longer a limited area of trade and industry. It is a region of rapid development. I believe we have reached the stage where the export of knowledge in certain fields is a business opportunity waiting to be tapped. In this respect, my remarks embrace the Gulf Co-operation Council (GCC) countries as a whole, not just the Y.B.A.Kanoo Group.

For the last few decades, much of the Arabian Gulf region's economic activity has depended upon imported skills and services to compensate for those which the area lacks. While it may sound a novel idea to consider GCC countries as exporters of products (other than crude oil), this is not such a ludicrous notion. The region's industries now manufacture and export many products, ranging from everyday consumer necessities to specialist items, for example: aluminium ingots and derivative products, petrochemicals, air-conditioners, glass, furniture, clothes, jewellery, dairy products, agricultural and horticultural produce (even wheat and roses from Saudi Arabia, and strawberries from the UAE).

Consider Switzerland and Japan, for instance. These contrasting countries, both in size and culture, do not have natural resources, yet Switzerland is internationally renowned as an exporter of quality watches, and Japan for its cars and electronics. There is no reason why GCC countries cannot emulate them. Saudi Arabia, for example, could become a centre for solar energy products. Already, it has initiated a major research program. Bahrain might become a specialist in computer software. It has an interested and trainable young generation. The UAE is developing rapidly as an authority on arid agriculture technology. It is a matter of focusing on an industry applicable to the area. GCC countries undoubtedly have the prerequisites: entrepreneurs, funds, universities, training schools and a young population with the ability to develop.

Chapter 15

Reflections

When Haji Yusuf formed his company more than a century ago, no doubt he did so with the same idea with which most people begin a business: the hope that it would thrive in good times and survive the bad times for many years. Modern management textbooks abound with theories about how companies may plan to succeed. Business schools devote endless time to the study of case-histories. Obviously, hard work, planning and control will help an enterprise to survive, as will an element of good luck too. Yet, as we know, not all enterprises are successful. Economic volatility can hit companies very hard, as my family saw during the collapse of the pearl industry during the 1930s. Political turbulence can be both a blessing and a burden, as our family company also discovered during the Second World War and the recent Gulf War. While collecting material for this book, I was keen to find the deeper reasons for Y.B.A.Kanoo's success, something useful I could pass onto the next generation. As a family, perhaps we were all so close to the business that we have failed to recognise obscure opportunities, or lurking threats.

Obviously, discipline and respect are important. Authority goes to those who have proved themselves capable. We keep each other informed, especially senior directors. We move fast when 'trouble-shooting' and when seeking new projects for the company. But, clearly, there is more to success than that. As a clue, the Group Chairman often reminds senior members of the family that the company's employees are valuable assets. They walk out of the door at the end of each working day and there is nothing to guarantee that they will come back the following morning. Why do many remain loyal to the company for so many years, sometimes for their entire working lives? We are not known for paying the highest salaries, so curiosity encouraged me to seek out some other answers.

Our mentor's manifesto

When pressed on the subject of formulae for success, Ahmed Kanoo harks back to Haji Yusuf's policy of fairness and truth: if we wish people to respect us, we must respect other people, whoever they may be or whatever rank they may hold. In his personal view, and in his view as the Group Chairman, it is modesty and hard work which buy respect, not money.

All of us among the younger generations appreciate the role of Ahmed as our mentor and the financial architect of the Y.B.A.Kanoo Group as we know it today. When fledgling family members join the business, he counsels: work hard without incurring great risk; remain united; persevere and don't give up; avoid enmity; listen to advice; but most of all, respect your elders and be kind to the young.

Whether the Y.B.A.Kanoo Group should be self-financing or bank-reliant is constantly reviewed, as are the decisions whether, or how much, to invest locally or overseas; or whether to allocate funds to one project rather than another, and so on. In Bill Brien's view, Ahmed Kanoo has created a superb financial portfolio. However, not all projects can be successful. There is an element of risk in anything new and so financial provision has to be made to write off those projects which fail. For example, during the last ten years in Saudi Arabia alone, the Group Chairman readily admits to the fact that Y.B.A.Kanoo has lost nearly twenty million dollars in projects which were good in theory, but which just did not work out. Those losses were written off too. But then our company is not alone in making mistakes.

Ahmed Kanoo's financial philosophy, a view which his 'brothers' share, firmly stresses that it is one thing to put your own money at risk. It is quite another situation when the money belongs to someone else. If the lender happens to be a bank, the failure of a project could cause bankruptcy. To understand this point of view, several of my uncles still hark back to the financial losses which our family experienced when the pearl markets collapsed in the 1930s. With this memory still vivid in their minds, even though they were young boys at the time, those debts are not forgotten. Even today, many elderly people speak of that time when our family insisted that it should go round the souq paying off its debts, even though to do so meant that we had to sell a lot of our properties and assets.

This painful episode explains why, for decades, it has remained Kanoo Main Board policy to avoid bank loans and overdrafts, although until the 1960s this was not always possible. When it comes to financial risk, even today, we still prefer to avoid bank loans, even as part of an integrated investment plan. To illustrate the point, Bill Brien recalls a discussion he had with the Group Chairman several years ago, at a time when the company's financial position had strengthened. He suggested to Ahmed Kanoo that we could utilise our cash to better effect by running the company on borrowed money. Brien remembers that my uncle was totally outraged at the idea. It has been very difficult to satisfy the family that it is quite safe to borrow money.

To underscore his opinion, Ahmed Kanoo added another salient and sombre perspective. It is a fact that, whether we like to accept it or not, life on this earth is precarious. For one reason or another, any of us could die today. Relatively speaking, therefore, the accumulation of wealth is not that important. Instead, it is more relevant and responsible to consider the implications of debt. As a family company we do not rush into drawing conclusions on anything. Ahmed Kanoo prefers to walk before he runs which, he claims, works. 'Sometimes we are sorry for it because we miss an opportunity, but we can't be right in everything.'

We live in a volatile world and what better examples of this have we seen during the last few years than the Gulf crisis, the collapse of the Soviet Union, the disintegration of Yugoslavia and a series of civil wars with associated sanctions, all of which have had a far-reaching impact on world trade. When it comes to quantifying political risk, it is a Kanoo family decision. We pride ourselves on being non-political as much as we can. We will look at a proposed project's viability. If there is a perceived political risk, then the family adjudicates on whether or not a project should be developed.

I once asked my cousin, Fawzi, if he thought that perseverance was the same thing as aggressive marketing. Adamantly, he stressed that he did not see this as part of the Kanoo family credo. Nor, for that matter, is it normally associated with the Arab business psyche. In Fawzi's mind, his father Ahmed's philosophy of perseverance is synonymous with persistence. Mix this with politeness and patience, and one can achieve more than being aggressive and frustrated, common traits he sees in many western businessmen. After all, what is the point of giving yourself a heart attack unnecessarily, or losing friends, long-standing customers and loyal employees because of inappropriate attitudes and behaviour?

The Kanoo Group head office in the heart of Manama, Bahrain, the first steel-framed commercial structure to be built in the Arabian Gulf region, is a focal point at the edge of the souq's labyrinth. It is just a few strides from the site of our original family house where Haji Yusuf began our family business more than a century ago. Our present office block may lack the glamour of more recent counterparts elsewhere in town, but at over thirty years old, the building has a dignified and historic presence. It does not claim to be pretentious, nor does it need to be. Polished wooden panelling sits more comfortably with the Kanoo corporate image than manicured marble. Visitors comment on a perceptible sense of long-established dependability. As Fawzi once told me: 'Our buildings may look old by today's standards, but they are always very clean because our Group Chairman, God bless him, always comes round once in a while to check if there is dust!'

This observation may be light-hearted, but it suggests that attention to detail is one reason why our business has succeeded. Looking out of his office window, Fawzi Kanoo paused for thought. Amplified calls to prayer combined with a cacophony of car horns had curtailed our conversation, but not Fawzi's train of thought. Somehow, the interruption illustrated his next point well.

He, like all the Kanoo family's company executives, may not like coping with unscheduled visitors, particularly when busy. But, as part of his upbringing, Fawzi was instructed that, in the name of courtesy, he should learn to like this sometimes chaotic situation. Such an 'open-door' policy has always been a hallmark of the Kanoo management policy. Although, this phenomenon can be found throughout the Arabian Gulf countries, obviously some people support this tradition more than others. Hamed Kanoo, for example, was frequently heard to say: 'My door is always open'.

Legacy of loyalty

Dr Abdul Latif Kanoo, one of my late father's brothers, explained his perspective. Although he pursued a career in the Bahrain Government, Dr Kanoo remains within the Kanoo family system. 'We are brothers, irrespective of whether I work with the company or not. We are a family. This is an important aspect'. He maintains that if respect and understanding exist in family relationships, no matter what differences or feelings one may have, family ties will remain intact. Remove these factors, and there will be neither a cohesive family nor, in our case, a business.

As a family, we have a strong tradition of being supportive of one another. This is very pronounced when one of us is sick. The whole family is supportive. As many people as possible visit that person (depending, of course, where in the world that sick family member may be at the time.) Members of the family stay with the invalid. Flowers are sent, telephone calls and visits made until the sick person is on his, or her, feet again. The same is true for happy events such as engagements, weddings and special occasions. All the family will offer their congratulations. In our Arab culture, more distant relatives, friends and employees will also participate in sad occasions or joyful celebrations.

Uncle Abdulaziz, Deputy Chairman of our company in Saudi Arabia, extended this idea to the relationship between the Kanoo family and company employees: 'We have a loyalty which I always call a Catholic marriage between us and our employees. Once our employees join us and stay with our company for more than five years, you will find them here for thirty, forty, even forty-five years. They stay, not because they receive the best salary in the world, but because we build up relationships almost like those within an extended family. We have a certain time when we sit and talk with everyone, even the driver can come and play cards with us and so forth. There is nothing to tell him "No", he cannot do that. That is because of our Islamic teaching. It is very important.'

To many people brought up in the western culture, this is an alien concept. For instance, when Hamed Kanoo visited England, often he invited his British driver to join him for dinner or lunch, to sit and chat with him. But his driver did not feel comfortable with this arrangement. He preferred to sit at another table, alone. In Bahrain, the cultural convention is different. A junior employee will feel quite at ease to accept his employer's invitation to sit with him. He will not even think about it. They will talk, express opinions and so on. They may not agree, but they make their points. The older generation encourages all of us to treat our employees as though they are family members for this, they believe, is how you achieve employee loyalty. You do not buy it. You earn it. You have to work at building relationships, just as happens in every family.

Mr V.A. Subermanian (Mani), one of our longest-serving employees in the UAE, now retired, believes that the job security he enjoyed for twenty-four years counted for a lot. Experience taught him that unless an employee does something really unproductive, is terribly foolish or creates a financial loss to the company, he will not be fired. Disciplinary action may be taken but he will not lose his job.

Other long-serving employees firmly believe that a proper administrative and personnel system, together with a regular assessment of each person, means that employees can look forward to a better employment package if they perform well. This does not mean salary increases alone since Y.B.A.Kanoo is a performance-oriented company. Promotion to senior positions is open to all staff, regardless of their nationality, provided they 'measure up'.

I decided, in 1990, our centenary year, to give Y.B.A.Kanoo's long-serving staff in Saudi Arabia a special bonus, something extra to the centenary bonus we gave already. When I asked Administration for the names of all staff who had served the company for more than fifteen years, the result said a great deal about the special relationship we have with our employees.

There were 780 names from the 2,300 full-time staff we employed in the Kingdom at that time. 'Too many', I said. 'Give me a list of those people who have given 20 years service.' 320 names were provided. Even this surprised me. So, based on five-year increments, we worked out the number of employees who had served the company for so many years: 25 years, 180 names; 30 years, 80 names, 35 years, 22 names and over 35 years, 14 names. The oldest serving member of staff has been with us for 42 years. He must have joined the company when he was 15 years old.

The human touch

When, after the end of the Second World War, my father and uncles assumed greater responsibility for the development of the company, they managed to create an individual blend of self-discipline and dedication, a management combination which many employees adopted in their own working lives. Perhaps this was a formative example of what my cousins and I have always been taught: lead by example. The fact remains that our company has many employees who have worked with us for several decades. Inevitably, there comes a time when they should retire.

In many companies, this emotional process is executed with a familiar formula: check that the pension is in order, organise a party, cut a cake, present a long-service award, and then simply say 'Thank you, good luck and goodbye'. In the space of an hour or so, a working lifetime has been despatched to corporate oblivion. The employee may have done a good job, but as far as company productivity is concerned, his or her services are now obsolete. My uncles, however, neither care for this attitude nor allow it in our company. Instead, their way is in keeping with the Arab tradition of maintaining the concept of an extended family.

Mubarak Kanoo advocates this policy. He hopes that when a young employee joins our company, he will be committed and loyal and, if all goes well, the employee will devote his working life to our company. But as he ages, his productivity may decline. What does my uncle do then? He may suggest that the employee should retire, but if he replies: 'No. I have been happy working with you for so long. I am proud to carry on', then what happens?

Usually, a compromise is reached and the employee is allowed to continue working. Perhaps he is transferred to another job which is less performance-oriented. If the situation is not resolved this way, then another diplomatic solution will be found such as a 'golden handshake' to keep the employee going until he can find other gainful employment; or finding a job for him to his liking in other companies or in one of our joint-ventures; or, at least keeping him on a 'retainer' and using his services when needed. All the while, the employee's dignity must not be affected.

Abdulaziz Kanoo believes that this sort of arrangement creates self-respect. 'Every company wants to be more efficient, make more money with less expense. That goes without saying. But in Y.B.A.Kanoo, we do it differently. If an employee is sick or in trouble, he knows that his employer will visit him and stand by him. For example, if somebody tells me that his house has burnt down, I agree to help the unfortunate employee financially. Admittedly, I will not provide enough money to rebuild his house, but whatever the sum may be, it is a bonus which the employee will appreciate. If his wife is very sick or he needs a major operation, then our family will ensure that he is covered financially. Money by itself does not buy respect. People will show you respect, if you respect them.'

Recognition is another example. For many years, Yaseen Mulla Ahmed was a Kanoo employee in Bahrain. Later, he was a pioneer in the opening of Y.B.A.Kanoo, Dubai. Then he helped to kick-start our company in Saudi Arabia. As a mark of respect for the years of service he gave us, his portrait still hangs in our Dammam and Dubai boardrooms, beside those of the company's namesake and founder, Yusuf bin Ahmed Kanoo, and my paternal and maternal grandfathers, Jassim and Ali Kanoo.

One hundred years is a long time in the history of any family business. In our case, success is not measured by monetary gain alone. Involvement in the community has always been part of our corporate 'credo'. No association or individual who needs a financial gift or help is turned down. We believe that we should give to the community in recognition of what we have gained from it. In the Arabian Gulf countries there is no corporate or personal taxation, so what is given comes from the company or from individual direct income. But also as Moslems, our teaching obliges us to give to those less fortunate than us in the form of *zakat*.

Take Abdulrahman Kanoo, for example. Since most recreational clubs in Bahrain are voluntary, non-professional institutes for the cultural and sporting development of young Bahrainis, he has spent much of his time, effort and personal money in developing the Al-Ahli Club to which he is devoted. Ahmed Kanoo is one of Bahrain's best-known philanthropists and no one is refused funds for a worthy personal or community cause.

As a family we donated funds for the building of the Yusuf Kanoo Nursing School during the 1950s, the first nursing school in the Arabian Gulf region. We have funded youth clubs and community halls; thirteen mosques, ranging in size from the small Fatima Kanoo 'daily' mosque in Isa Town to the the Yusuf Kanoo Grand 'Friday' Mosque in Hamed Town, the third largest in Bahrain.

The Kanoo family have always had a keen interest in the building and refurbishing of mosques. The first of these on record, as told by Mohamed Juma, was the repair and refurbishment of a mosque which belonged to Mulla Mohamed by Ahmed Kanoo (the father of Haji Yusuf Kanoo) in about 1895. Haji Yusuf, who always prayed with Mulla Mohamed, again refurbished and improved the same mosque in about 1925. In 1970, that mosque was almost completely torn down and rebuilt by Ahmed Kanoo, our current Group Chairman. I recently discovered that Mulla Mohamed was the great-grandfather of H.E. Mohammed Ebrahim Al-Mutawa, the Minister of Cabinet Affairs and Information of Bahrain.

Regular and annual donations, *Sadaqa Al Jariah,* are made to charities and individuals in need. Prizes are given to charity events. Contributions are made to community projects such as *Bait Al-Quran,* and the University Student Scholarship Fund. Recently, we committed BD 2 million to build two clinics for the people of Bahrain.

While money helps us to provide community care, it is not the driving force. Our family attitude is that it is not enough to send a cable to someone who has reason to celebrate or who has been bereaved. We must make the effort to visit personally, not just one of us, but at least two or more members of the family. It is easy enough to share happiness. Learning to listen to grievances and support those who are grieving requires more self-discipline.

In times past, many families practised this philosophy. It was the philosophy of all Gulf Arabs. Unfortunately, not many of the younger generation accept this teaching, even though such advice does have direct compassionate as well as community benefits. Abdulaziz Kanoo explained this philosophy by describing a highly-regarded tradition maintained by the Governors in all three provinces of Saudi

Arabia. For example, from Abdulaziz's experience in the Eastern Province, traditionally each Monday Prince Mohamed bin Fahad invites local businessmen and Government officials to attend dinner with him at 9.00 p.m. This provides an excellent opportunity for this guest or that official to discuss any particular problem in an informal environment. The atmosphere is such that everyone is free to talk, not only among themselves, but also with the Governor. Abdulaziz has often said that he finds these occasions a most useful time to air differences of opinion, exchange information and to make business contacts, a tradition which we are continuing. Of course, there is a political aspect to such a gathering if the Prince wishes to pass a message to the community 'off the record', but there is a practical side too. Imagine needing to visit twenty people. If, instead of visiting everyone individually, everyone gathers around a dinner table, there is the chance to make a lot of contact in a very short time, all in one 'shot', and maintain our cultural traditions.

Bringing this philosophy closer to home, visiting each other's houses is a weekly ritual which Ahmed Kanoo insists upon for us all and practises himself. He feels, and most of us agree with him, that visiting on a regular basis keeps the family in touch with each other and enforces its unity.

For the men of the family, work and work-related matters are our hobbies and our life. We talk work after office-hours because we enjoy what we do. We are hands-on managers who enjoy each other's company (with a few exceptions!) and that of our employees. For the older members of our family, as in many other families, work comes first, and family life takes second place. The younger family members try to balance the two. Our wives understand what we are doing, supporting their husbands and accepting their workaholic tendencies. The Kanoo women have their own lives, either running small businesses such as boutiques, or engrossing themselves in social and charitable work.

The human touch also extends to the long-established financial arrangements within the Kanoo family. Maybe they are unfamiliar to some western readers, but they are by no means unique among Arabian families. All working Kanoo family members receive the same salary and similar housing. That is to say, that usually the salaries of the married male members of the family are the same and several houses are built at one time to house those of a similar age. Often, each group has the same architectural style with each house occupying a similar area of land. Kanoo wives receive similar salaries and allowances (with variations according to need), based upon whether or not they have children, and how many. Without getting into a complicated discussion, I should qualify that statement. While I have related the following three examples to my own family, the principles apply throughout the Kanoo family as a whole.

For example, now that one of my three children has married, my wife's allowance is slightly less, but always enough to cover household and personal expenses and the needs of my two other children. My daughter-in-law's allowance will increase pro-rata, when she has children. Conversely, if my daughter marries, then her allowance will be dependent on her husband's ability to maintain her. We help if needed or requested. Education, housing, travel and holidays are all paid for by the family, through a family fund especially set up for this purpose.

Professionalism in profile

While family convention and courtesies are part of our informal way of doing business, there is nothing informal about our operating systems. In my opinion, we have superb accounting procedures and computer systems which enable us to maintain modern management methods based on productivity and bottom-line criteria. To those who might wish to challenge such a claim, ask them how many major companies complete their full monthly accounts on the tenth day of the following month. In the West, it is not unusual (in my experience) for this process to take as long as forty-five days.

Not a dinar, dirham, riyal, dollar or pound enters or leaves any of our offices throughout the territories, or is signed in or away by cheque or draft, without our knowledge. The ultimate authority to approve major corporate finance and expenditure is the Group Chairman (Ahmed Kanoo), while territorial responsibilities lie with local Directors.

Having said that, Ahmed often cautions us to respect other people's attitudes towards their own businesses: 'You cannot go and pinch the other man's business just because you think you are more powerful.' Instead, we try to collaborate with other people, rather than work against them. After all, there is little point in wrecking a hard-won reputation out of sheer greed. We work on the win–win philosophy.

According to Bill Brien, Group Director of Y.B.A.Kanoo, another feature of success should be considered. Reflecting on nearly forty years of service with the company, he has seen many changes, not least those concerned with organizational structuring and management profiles. He believes that for many years, the Kanoo family recognised that, in Bahrain, it was very much to its advantage to maintain a mix of family directors and expatriate managers. Today, senior management is multinational and based on a dual ethos: capability and professionalism. Much the same can be said of our companies in the Kingdom of Saudi Arabia, the UAE, Oman, and Kuwait (the latter having been downgraded to representation status). In all cases, there is a mix of nationalities from around the world, a feature which was not evident among Y.B.A.Kanoo's competitors in the post-Second World War development era.

Even today, perhaps Y.B.A.Kanoo in Bahrain is unique. Admittedly, there has been quite a European staff turnover over the years, but there has always been a nucleus of western expatriate managers such as Cyril Jones, Alan McColl, John Bryant, Ted Whitticks, Captain Pettit and Peter Chaplin, all of whom are now retired. This does not mean that Y.B.A.Kanoo did not, and does not employ non-European expatriate managers. We operate on a person's capabilities and not their nationality. If a person qualifies for a job, then he is appointed, regardless of ethnic background. While a significant core of our junior, middle and some senior management comprises expatriate managers trained in western Europe, we have many others filling all levels of management posts who are originally from India, Asia and the Far East, as well as GCC nationals.

Nevertheless, reverting to the 1950s, even the 1960s, Bill Brien believes that Y.B.A.Kanoo maintained its 'edge' because the British managers understood how foreign companies operated and what they wanted. Thus, they were able to secure agency agreements from Europe, the USA and the Far East. Meanwhile, in Arabia, the Kanoo family members were familiar with local laws and so had the know-how to put these agency agreements into practice. Because of this, we got off to a tremendous start over the competition as we were able to manage our business considerably better than our local rivals. When they became wiser, the situation balanced out.

In the case of Y.B.A.Kanoo, Bahrain, the company developed naturally. For a long time, we had almost a monopoly of the islands' shipping agency business. Our main competitors were foreign companies such Gray Mackenzie and Gulf Agency. In Saudi Arabia, foreign shipping companies have never had it all their own way either. As Kanoo companies in Bahrain, Saudi Arabia and the UAE became more localised, we became even stronger as the foreign-owned shipping agents began to disappear.

While most prominent local families pursued domestic business interests, we derived our income from abroad, for instance through product sourcing (construction equipment and non-consumer goods), shipping and travel agency work. This concept of internationalism is an important factor. Ahmed Kanoo's contemporaries did not travel around the world as much as he did in the early 1950s. They were not in that sort of business. We started to compete with foreign companies rather than with local merchants. It was not until the 1980s that we met real competition from other local companies. But by then, we were leaders in our particular specialisms, not least in sea and air transportation, oil services and trading.

Consider the airline industry, where we worked closely with UK-based Imperial Airways during the 1930s. When, in 1940, it merged with its rival British Airways to form BOAC, Abdulaziz Kanoo's first assignment, after leaving the American University of Beirut in the early 1950s, was to gain work experience in BOAC's offices in Victoria, London. Until at least the mid-1950s, Y.B.A.Kanoo was the sole travel agency in Bahrain and the Eastern Province of Saudi Arabia. In 1958, we officially became BOAC's general sales agent in Bahrain. At one point during those heady, pioneering days, Y.B.A.Kanoo had the general sales agency of every air carrier that transited through Bahrain, and the majority of those which flew into the Eastern Province of Saudi Arabia.

During my research, I asked the International Air Transport Association if it might still have some material which I could include in this book. The Director of Agency Accreditation Services was kind enough to send me microfilm copies of documents that 'bear witness to our long commercial association'. Monsieur Gesinus also commented that since 1947, when our Bahrain travel office joined, IATA had seen many new developments in the agency world which had been 'fast and furious', stimulating growth on a big scale: 'Who, back in the fifties, might have been bold enough to talk about world-wide IATA passenger volumes running at almost 200 million? Who would have forecast almost 150 IATA Agents in Saudi Arabia alone?'

When asked how I would summarise the success of our family company, more than anything else effective leadership came to mind. Perhaps the Gulf War impressed this on me, for I firmly believe that by being around, and being prepared to do the same work as that of our employees, not only did we family members try to lead by example, but we were able to motivate people at the same time. In my case, throughout the Kuwait invasion crisis, I regularly visited our units at the seaports, airports and oil installations in Dammam, Al-

Khobar, Dhahran, Ras Tannurah, Ras Al-Khafji and Jubail, always with the possibility of being attacked at any time. We did not know the Iraqis' intention. We weren't sitting in London at a safe distance saying to our staff: 'Do this or that'. We were all at work and on the spot.

Our family policy throughout the Arabian Gulf region was that all of us should remain in our respective posts, side-by-side with employees, encouraging them, suffering with them and, when the occasions were right, laughing with them too. Without wishing to sound self-righteous, I do believe that this sense of 'togetherness' was the main reason why so very few people left our companies during the war, whereas other companies lost as many as 50 per cent of their staff. Some had to stop work altogether. Why? Because their owners and managers 'escaped' to Jeddah, London or some other safe haven.

This being said we were all scared stiff at times, particularly in Riyadh, Dhahran and Bahrain where our offices were in range of Iraq's Scud missiles which we often heard explode. But we were of a single mind that if we remained a united family and continued to manage our companies from the 'hot seats', then we would retain the commitment of our staff. With a few exceptions, that is what happened. It should be said also that we felt that it was our patriotic duty to stay and lead our employees because our company's services at seaports, airports and oil terminals were vital to the war effort. We had to do what we had to do and leave the rest to providence.

The public flotation debate

Six years have since passed. Now, in 1997, the Kanoo family is considering how to organise its business for the challenges of a new era: the twenty-first century. Among our deliberations is the debate as to whether or not the Y.B.A.Kanoo organisation should 'go public'.

In Dr Abdul Latif's view, corporate success can be measured in terms of how far a company has 'spread'. By this he does not just mean in a geographical sense in terms of premises and the number of employed personnel. In the case of Y.B.A.Kanoo, he also includes the way in which the youngest generation has been given management responsibility in a global sense. Guiding us in our respective regions, are three members of the senior generation: Ahmed, Abdulla and Mubarak Kanoo, all of whom help to run the holding company and the companies in Saudi Arabia, the UAE and Oman, and Bahrain.

Normally, a spread company is the sign of a successful company, that is if such diversification is evenly sustained and has not been the result of highly-geared, impulsive growth. In the case of a private family business, such as the Y.B.A.Kanoo Group, it would be impossible to control and maintain such a spread without the phased integration of the younger family members.

There is another factor. Companies which have dictated regional market trends, particularly in Saudi Arabia, are large traditional family businesses. Even today, many of them are run by traditional management systems whereby the head of the family is the chief executive officer of the establishment and his decisions are final. This is also the case in our family business on a corporate level.

However, times are changing, and quickly. Many business houses are rethinking their present structure and operation. Some are floating a percentage of their shares in the market. Other families form companies with the intention of going public.

In 1982, Kuwait opened *Souq Al-Manakh,* its stock exchange. Seven years later, Bahrain's Stock Exchange was established in 1989, followed by similar institutions in the UAE and Oman. Although many Arabian merchants and businessmen are quite familiar with the concept of a stock market, the idea that long-established private family companies should spread their financial risk by going public in this way, is something comparatively new. The Fataihi family of Jeddah is one of the pioneers, although it has not, as yet, been licensed as a public company. Other families are seriously considering doing the same thing, principally for the sake of family unity and ensuring the continuity of the business. In this way, there are fewer risks that family in-fighting will cause their companies to be split up.

No doubt all of these institutions have been very properly managed, but what will happen should some misfortune befall the head of the family and a problem of succession occurs, or there is a conflict between shareholders, or their children? One solution is public flotation. A minority share of a company's operations held by non-family shareholders will help to stabilise the family business and protect it from such a problem. Such a scenario would mean that non-family shareholders will expect profit, not family politics.

In our case, we have been through that pain barrier. When Ahmed Kanoo was seriously ill in 1992, our company Boards and shareholders were propelled into considering the succession issue and making some policy decisions. As it turned out, these were not based on going public. Our company's affairs and its ownership were reorganised so that Y.B.A.Kanoo as a corporate entity will not be affected if a partner dies.

Personal postscript

Perhaps, then, we may be allowed at least a sense of pride and reinforced purpose in the fact that our business has managed to survive for more than a century. Those hundred years are now behind us. How we tackle the future is another matter. According to one Chinese proverb, 'The best prophet of the future is the past', and that, perhaps expressed in a different way, is just what the older generation of the Kanoo family has been preaching to us younger members since our childhood.

As we sculpture and shape our family business for another century of survival and, we hope, continued success, all of us are aware that this depends on more than studying macro-economics and political risk. One of Ahmed Kanoo's remarks mentioned earlier, is worth repeating: 'Any of us could die today. Relatively speaking, therefore, the accumulation of wealth is not that important'. Our bottom line, as this chapter of reflections has highlighted, is not profit but the human factor.

With this thought in mind, I would like to end with a reflection from one of my uncles, based on his poignant memories of the Gulf War: 'One may', he said, 'gain business by arriving with guns, but that is short-lived. You have to win people's hearts to sustain longevity'.

Chronology of Main Events

1820	A General Treaty of Peace signed between the British and nine tribal shaikhs, after which the Arabian rulers make a truce with each other and agree to stop raiding British merchant ships, hence the Trucial States.
1862	British India Steam Navigation Company founded.
1868	Haji Yusuf bin Ahmed Kanoo born.

1868   Haji Yusuf bin Ahmed Kanoo born.
(For historical context: 1861-65, the American Civil War; in 1870, John D. Rockefeller formed the Standard Oil Company which, in 1929, became the parent company of the Bahrain Petroleum Company.)

1890   Haji Yusuf takes over the small family business, aged 22.

1900   J. Calcott Gaskin (lately British Vice-Consul in Bushire) assigned to Bahrain as the islands' first resident Assistant Political Agent.

1903–4   An epidemic of plague and cholera strikes Bahrain.

1904   Haji Yusuf's 25-year-old brother, Mohamed, dies of cholera.

1908   Oil discovered in Persia.

1909   Anglo-Persian Oil Company formed.
Eastern Bank established in London.

1910   Eastern Bank's first branch opened in Bombay.

1912   Eastern Bank open a branch in Baghdad.
Haji Yusuf awarded the Kaiser-i-Hind Medal.

1913   Haji Yusuf appointed Anglo-Persian Oil Company's agent in Bahrain.

1914   First World War begins.

1916   Eastern Bank applies to open a branch in Manama, but permission refused.
Kichimatsu Mikimoto perfects technique of cultured pearls.

1917   *7 August:* the Government of India confers on Haji Yusuf the Badge, Ribbon and Sanad of the title of Khan Sahib.

1918   *9 November:* an Armistice signed effecting the end of First World War.

1919   Al Falah, the first school for boys in Bahrain, formed by Mohammed Ali Zainal Alireza, helped by Haji Yusuf.
3 June: Haji Yusuf granted the MBE.
6 November: Major H. R. P. Dickson appointed Political Agent in Bahrain.
9 February: Passengers fly between London and Paris for the first time, heralding the world's first scheduled international air service.
Aircraft Transport and Travel Limited (forerunner of British Airways) formed during the year.

1920	29 January: Haji Yusuf sails for mainland Arabia to attend the Court of Abdul-Aziz Ibn Saud in Riyadh, his first visit to the capital.

1920   *29 January:* Haji Yusuf sails for mainland Arabia to attend the Court of Abdul-Aziz Ibn Saud in Riyadh, his first visit to the capital.

January: Mesopotamia Persia Corporation formed after Gray Mackenzie and Gray Paul, and Lynch Brothers amalgamate.

1 July: Eastern Bank commences business in Manama.

6 August: representatives of the London-based Eastern and General Syndicate arrive in Bahrain for the first time to bore water wells.

During 1920, a second car, a Ford Model A, appears in Bahrain, the Kanoo family's first motor vehicle. (Henry Ford had built his first motor car in 1896).

1921   Major C. K. Daly succeeds Major H. R. P. Dickson as Political Agent in Bahrain.

1923   Haji Yusuf decorated with the CIE .

May: Eastern and General Syndicate granted a concession in the Al-Hasa province of mainland Arabia by Ibn Saud, Sultan of Nejd.

1924   *1 April:* Britain's four main new airlines merge to form Imperial Airways.

May: Eastern and General Syndicate granted an oil concession in the Kuwait-Nejd Neutral Zone.

8 June: RAF aeroplanes land in Bahrain for the first time on a public relations visit.

1925   Following a bad storm in the Arabian Gulf during which many pearl dhows sink, *Sinat Al-Taba'a,* the 'Year of the Sinking', declared; during the same year, the Government of Bahrain introduces driving licences.

2 December: Shaikh Hamad bin Isa Al Khalifa, Deputy Ruler of Bahrain, grants the Eastern and General Syndicate an exclusive two-year oil exploration licence in Bahrain.

1926   Haji Yusuf, APOC's agent in Bahrain, begins to supply the RAF with fuel.

18 January: Amir Abdul-Aziz Ibn Saud (Sultan of Nejd) proclaimed King of the Hijaz, Nejd and its dependencies.

Charles Belgrave takes up his appointment as Adviser to the Ruler of Bahrain.

1927   *30 November:* the Eastern and General Syndicate assigns the Bahrain concession to Eastern Gulf Oil (a subsidiary of Gulf Oil Corporation, USA).

1928   *June:* Ali bin Mohamed Kanoo signs an agreement with American car manufacturer, the Studebaker Corporation, and becomes its Bahrain agent.

Khalil Kanoo and Mohammed Yateem begin to bore several water wells.

Geologist, Ralph Rhoades, optimistic that oil is present in Bahrain.

Croydon Airport, London (forerunner to Heathrow), opens.

21 December: Eastern Gulf Oil transfers its option on Bahrain's oil exploration rights to the Standard Oil Company of California.

1929   *11 January:* Bahrain Petroleum Company incorporated.

24 October: financial 'crash' of the New York Stock Exchange.

1931   *16 October:* Bahrain's Oil-well Number One 'spudded in'.

1932   *1 June:* oil discovered in Bahrain.

23 September: The Kingdom of Saudi Arabia proclaimed.

6 October: subsequent to Imperial Airways' creating a civil air-route along the eastern shores of Arabia early in 1932, its first commercial aircraft to pass through Bahrain arrives: *Hanno,* a Hannibal-class aeroplane.

9 December: The Ruler of Bahrain, Shaikh Isa bin Ali Al Khalifa, dies.

1933   Haji Yusuf's debts increase because of world-wide recession, causing him to mortgage property to the Eastern Bank for 75,000 rupees.

8 November: California Arabian Standard Oil Company formed.

1934   February: Haji Yusuf travels to Kuwait to secure a loan.

7 June: BAPCO's first shipment of crude oil leaves Bahrain aboard the *El Segundo* tanker, destined for Yokohama, Japan.

1935   Haji Yusuf sells a prime city block to Haji Hilal to repay his debts.

Oil discovered in Saudi Arabia, but not in commercial quantities.

6 May: on the occasion of the Silver Jubilee of King George V and Queen Mary, Haji Yusuf travels on a Hannibal aircraft from Sharjah to Bahrain.

21 May: Persia officially becomes Iran, thus the Anglo-Persian Oil Company becomes the Anglo-Iranian Oil Company.

1936   Mesopotamia Persia Corporation ceases trading, to be replaced by Gray Mackenzie and Company Limited (registered that year). British Airways Limited formed after several small airlines merge to rival Imperial Airways.

1937   *26 March:* pioneering aviator Colonel C. A. Lindbergh, accompanied by his wife, arrives in Bahrain from Delhi flying his own aeroplane.

1938   *3 March:* for the first time since oil was discovered in Saudi Arabia in 1935, oil 'gushes' from Dammam's Well Number 7 in commercial quantities.

30 September: In London, after Neville Chamberlain's historic meeting in Munich with Hitler, Mussolini and Daladier ends with a signed promise, the British Prime Minister declares: 'I believe it is peace for our time'.

Hussain Yateem opens his filling station near Bab Al-Bahrain.

1939   *1 May:* witnessed by King Abdul-Aziz, Saudi Arabia's first crude oil to be exported by tanker loaded aboard *D.G. Scofield*.

3 September: the Second World War declared.

1940   *1 April:* British Airways Limited and Imperial Airways merged to form the British Overseas Airways Corporation.

19 October: Italian aircraft attempt to destroy the Bahrain oil refinery; but most bombs fall outside perimeter and fail to explode.

1942   Shaikh Hamad bin Isa Al Khalifa, Ruler of Bahrain, dies. He is succeeded by his son, Shaikh Salman bin Hamad Al Khalifa.

The swing bridge between Muharraq and Bahrain islands is completed.

1944   *31 January:* CASOC changes its name officially to the Arabian American Oil Company.

Imperial Bank of Iran opens a branch in Bahrain.

1945   *7 May:* victory in Europe declared, after which the Second World War ends in Europe.

21 December: Haji Yusuf dies.

1946   Kanoo Travel Agency established officially.

Dhahran Airport opened.

1 August: British European Airways Corporation formed.

1947   India declares independence.

Ahmed Kanoo flies to London for the first time by flying-boat.

Saudi Arabian Airline Corporation formed.

5 June: US Secretary of State, George C. Marshall, launches the European aid program: the Marshall Plan.

12 November: the Bahrain office of Y.B.A.Kanoo applies to join the International Air Transport Association (IATA).

1948   *18 March:* Y.B.A.Kanoo (Bahrain) registered on IATA's list.

Cable and Wireless commissions an automatic telephone system to serve Manama and Muharraq towns, Bahrain.

The Kanoo fleet founded: Ali Kanoo buys eight second-hand 50-ton barges from the River Thames authority in London, and an ex-RAF rescue boat to tow them.

1949   Bahrain's first automatic telephone system becomes operational.

Y.B.A.Kanoo's first office telephone installed, number 25.

Abdulla Kanoo assigned to Saudi Arabia to open Kanoo's first office in the Kingdom.

Imperial Bank of Iran changes its name to the British Bank of Iran and the Middle East.

26 May: Shanghai falls to Mao Tse-tung's People's Liberation Army, ending the Bahrain/Shanghai oil tanker 'run'.

1950	Y.B.A.Kanoo secures its first lighterage contract with ARAMCO.
	Tug *Bahrain,* bought in Holland, joins the Kanoo fleet (as did *Yusuf* and *Awal* in 1951 and 1952 respectively).
	Maersk Line ('flag-ship' company of Denmark's A. P. Moller Group) joins Y.B.A.Kanoo's shipping agency portfolio.
	Y.B.A.Kanoo opens offices in Ras Tannurah and Ras Mishaab, Saudi Arabia.
	KLM, Middle East Airlines and Pan Am begin services to Dhahran.
	24 March: Gulf Aviation Company formed.
	10 May: Norwich Union Fire Insurance Society appoints Y.B.A.Kanoo as its agents in Bahrain.
	5 July: Gulf Aviation begins scheduled services with a Bahrain-Doha-Sharjah service using an Avro Anson aircraft.
	25 July: Gulf Aviation starts a thrice-daily shuttle service between Bahrain and Dhahran using a de Havilland aircraft, known as *Um Ahmed.*
1951	Y.B.A.Kanoo acquires the agency for the American States Marine Line which assists the Marshall Plan.
	Everett Star Line's first ship to serve Bahrain anchored offshore.
	January: Dammam port, Mina King Abdul-Aziz, opened officially.
	31 January: Y.B.A.Kanoo Travel Agency in Al-Khobar appointed as IATA's first Approved Agent in Saudi Arabia.
	10 June: Fredrick Bosworth, co-founder of Gulf Aviation, killed in a flying accident in the UK.
	31 July: Norwich Union Life Society appoints Y.B.A.Kanoo as its agent for the Arabian Gulf region.
	1 October: BOAC purchases 51 per cent of Gulf Aviation's shares, including those owned by Bosworth's widow
	October: the U.S. Navy awards Y.B.A.Kanoo its Military Sea Transportation Services contract.
	Arabian Construction and Mechanical Engineers formed.
1952	Y.B.A.Kanoo establishes the Bahrain Shipping and Labour Agency.
	British Bank of Iran and the Middle East shortens its name to the British Bank of the Middle East.
	Saudi Rail-Road in Dammam Port, begins operations.
1954	Kanoo Slipway Company formed in Muharraq.
	25 April: Jassim and Ali Kanoo sign the *Deed of Gift and Transfer.* Haji Ali dies later in the year.
	Urwick Orr (British management consultants) commissioned to document Y.B.A.Kanoo's organisational structure and produce an operations manual.
1955	Construction of the Gudaibiyah Guest Palace completed.

1957	Y.B.A.Kanoo takes over the provision of stevedoring in Ras Tannurah.
	20 February: Arabian Gulf Services formed in London.
1958	Aircraft Services Gulf Limited (ASGUL) formed.
	Oilfield Supply and Services formed.
	Japanese-owned Arabian Oil Company established at Khafji.
	Saudi Railways Organization formed.
1959	*April:* Y.B.A.Kanoo, Bahrain, appointed as the British American Tobacco Company's distributor.
	Kanoo Construction Company wound down.
	Oil discovered in Abu Dhabi in commercial quantities.
1960	*31 January:* the official opening day of Y.B.A.Kanoo's new steel-structure office block in Manama and the Kanoo Guest House in Mahooz.
1961	Shaikh Salman bin Hamad Al Khalifa, Ruler of Bahrain, dies. He is succeeded by son, His Highness Shaikh Isa bin Salman Al Khalifa.
	Abu Dhabi's first airport opens.
	Shaikh Rashid bin Saeed Al Maktoum grants Y.B.A.Kanoo a trading licence to operate in Dubai.
1962	Shaikh Shakhbut grants Y.B.A.Kanoo a licence to operate in Abu Dhabi.
1963	Y.B.A.Kanoo opens its first office in Abu Dhabi.
	Shaikh Saqir Al-Qasimi grants Y.B.A.Kanoo a licence to open a travel office in Sharjah.
	Arabian Construction and Mechanical Engineers wound down.
	13 July: a *Schedule* is signed, in order of seniority, by Ahmed, Mohamed, Abdulla, Mubarak, Abdulrahman, Abdulaziz and Hamed Kanoo. This document legalises a new Y.B.A.Kanoo ownership arrangement, that of an equal partnership.
	17 December: Bahrain Ship-Repairing and Engineering Company officially opened by His Highness Shaikh Isa bin Salman Al Khalifa.
	Y.B.A.Kanoo's Riyadh office established.
1964	*May:* Y.B.A.Kanoo opens an office in Khafji.
	28 September: Yusuf bin Ahmed Kanoo incorporated by special Charter.
	Thus, Y.B.A.Kanoo becomes a Limited Liability Company.
1965	Y.B.A.Kanoo installs its first computer, an NCR 390.
	25 March: an *Agreement for Sale of Business* signed by the same seven family members who had signed the Schedule on 13 July 1963.
	16 October: the Bahrain dinar created as the nation's unit of currency.
1966	Oil discovered in Dubai.

Silver Java Pacific Line, for which Y.B.A.Kanoo has been agent for many years, becomes part of Royal Interocean Lines.

6 August: Shaikh Zayed bin Sultan Al Nahayan (Governor of Al-Ain) succeeds his brother Shaikh Shakhbut as Ruler of Abu Dhabi.

1967   Hamed Kanoo leaves Saudi Arabia to develop the family business in Dubai.

16 February: the British Government publishes a White Paper which declares a policy to liquidate most British military bases east of Suez.

5 June: Israel launches the Six Day War.

Bahrain's new deep-water port, Mina Salman opens.

1968   Shaikh Rashid bin Hassan Al-Khalifa joins Gulf Aviation as its first Bahraini pilot.

Y.B.A.Kanoo's Jeddah office established.

BASF and Y.B.A.Kanoo enter into an agency agreement.

1970   *17 January:* Citibank opens its Bahrain branch in Y.B.A.Kanoo premises.

24 July: Sultan Saeed bin Taimur of Oman replaced by his son, Qaboos.

1971   Captain Abdulrahman Al-Ghood appointed as Gulf Aviation's first Bahraini aircraft commander.

14 August: His Highness Shaikh Isa bin Salman Al Khalifa announces the creation of the State of Bahrain.

21 September: the State of Bahrain admitted to the United Nations.

2 December: the State of the United Arab Emirates proclaimed by the Rulers of Abu Dhabi, Dubai, Sharjah, Ajman, Um Al-Qaiwain and Fujairah.

9 December: the UAE becomes a member of the United Nations.

1972   *10 February:* the emirate of Ras Al-Khaimah joins the UAE.

June: Abu Dhabi port, Mina Zayed, opens officially.

5 October: Dubai port, Mina Rashid, opens officially.

Abu Dhabi National Oil Company formed.

British European Airways and the British Overseas Airways Corporation merge to become a new-style British Airways, (formal operations begin on 1 April 1974).

1973   *May:* the UAE dirham launched as the federation's unit of currency.

1 October: the price of crude oil rises from US$1.80 to US$3.011 per barrel.

6 October: the Yom Kippur War begins.

16 October: the price of Saudi Arabian light crude rises by 70 per cent to US$ 5.119 per barrel.

17 October: President Sadat of Egypt and Shaikh Yamani

announce the possibility of an oil embargo against the western world which, later, is put into practice.

Y.B.A.Kanoo and Exxon enter into an agency agreement.

1974   *1 January:* Gulf Air comes into being officially.

January: the price of crude oil more than doubles to US$ 11.65 per barrel.

Later in the year, the oil embargo ends.

Management consultants, Cressep McCormack and Paget (a subsidiary of Citibank) commissioned to determine how Y.B.A.Kanoo can diversify.

1975   *19 February:* Y.B.A.Kanoo's office in Oman begins operations.

Early in the year, Y.B.A.Kanoo's first purpose-built premises in Abu Dhabi are opened officially.

Company Law becomes effective in Bahrain.

Y.B.A.Kanoo's office in Houston, USA, opened.

5 June: the Suez Canal re-opens to commercial shipping, having been closed for eight years following the 1967 Arab-Israeli War.

October: an offshore banking sector launched in Bahrain.

1976   *21 January:* supersonic aircraft Concorde lands in Bahrain for the first time.

Phase One extension of Y.B.A.Kanoo's Manama office block completed.

Y.B.A.Kanoo's first office building in Dubai completed.

Y.B.A.Kanoo Joint Venture Division formed.

1977   Phase Two extension of Y.B.A.Kanoo's Manama office block (now Norwich Union's head office in Bahrain) completed.

Phase Three (Kanoo Tower) of Y.B.A.Kanoo's Manama office development completed.

Kanoo Group Limited registered.

Bahrain Airport Services formed.

Royal Interocean Lines merges with the newly-formed Koninkuke-Nedlloyd Group (for which Y.B.A.Kanoo has been agent for more than 50 years).

1978   Kanoo Group Limited begins business in London.

1979   Jebel Ali Port opens.

The Shah of Iran deposed.

1980   Onset of the Iranian–Iraqi War.

1981   Arthur D. Little commissioned to consider Y.B.A.Kanoo reorganisation.

14 May: Y.B.A.Kanoo registered as a company With Limited Liability (WLL).

1982   Haji Jassim Mohamed Kanoo dies.

Kuwait opens Souq Al-Manakh, its stock exchange.

1984   *11 July:* Kanoo Tower, Dammam, 'the glass building', opened.

1985   Jebel Ali Free Zone launched.

	17 June: astronaut, Prince Sultan bin Salman of Saudi Arabia, returns to earth aboard the Challenger space shuttle, to be welcomed by Abdulaziz Kanoo at NASA.
1986	Abdulaziz Kanoo, part of a Saudi delegation, is the first Kanoo family member to visit China.
	The oil price collapses.
1987	Y.B.A.Kanoo's chemical section begins operations.
1988	*February:* Bahrain Slipway Company (owned by Gray Mackenzie) closes down.
1989	Bahrain's Stock Exchange established.
1990	*2 August:* Iraq invades Kuwait, following which the GCC countries together with their western allies, launch their defence response: 'Desert Shield'.
	August: the Kanoo/Sears retail store opens in Dammam.
1991	*January–February:* the Gulf War, code-named 'Desert Storm', is fought.
	October: Mohamed Kanoo dies.
1994	*February:* Hamed Kanoo dies.
	30 November: J. C. Penney store opens in Bahrain.
1995	Outram Cullinan & Co (strategic consultants of Coopers & Lybrand, UK) commissioned to review the Y.B.A.Kanoo Group.
	Y.B.A.Kanoo Group begins reorganisation to position itself for the twenty-first century.

Abbreviations and Acronyms

a	anna(s) formerly 16 to the rupee, now replaced by decimal coinage
ACME	Arabian Construction and Mechanical Engineers
ADNOC	Abu Dhabi National Oil Company
ADPC	Abu Dhabi Petroleum Company
ADTT	Abu Dhabi Telegraph and Telephone Company
AIOC	Anglo-Iranian Oil Company
ANVV	(Dutch Tourist Office)
AOC	Arabian Oil Company
APOC	Anglo-Persian Oil Company
ARAMCO	Arabian American Oil Company
ASGUL	Aircraft Services Gulf Limited
BMWT	British Ministry of War Transport
BP	British Petroleum
BA	British Airways
BAPCO	Bahrain Petroleum Company
BAS	Bahrain Airport Services
BASREC	Bahrain Ship-Repairing and Engineering Company
BAT	British American Tobacco Company
BBME	British Bank of the Middle East
BD	Bahraini Dinar
BEA	British European Airways
BISN	British India Steam Navigation Company
BIT	Bahrain International Travel
BOAC	British Overseas Airways Corporation
BSLA	Bahrain Shipping and Labour Agency
CALTEX	California Texas Oil Company Limited
CASOC	California Arabian Standard Oil Company
CIE	Companion of the Order of the Indian Empire
CIF	cost, insurance, freight
CNN	Cable News Network
Co.	Company
d	penny, pence (unit of sterling before decimalisation)
DDT	dichloro-diphenyl-trichloro-ethane (insecticide)
g.	gram, (unit of mass or weight in metric system)
GCC	Gulf Co-operation Council (full name Co-operation Council for the Arab States of the Gulf)
GSA	General Sales Agent
HMS	Her (His) Majesty's Ship
HVD	Harmsey Vermey and Dunlop (a Dutch company)
IATA	International Air Transport Association
KB	Kanoo barge
KCC	Kanoo Construction Company

kg.	kilogram(s) (1,000 grams)
KLM	Royal Dutch Airlines (Koninklijke Luchtvaart Maatschapij NV)
km.	kilometre(s) (1,000 metres)
kW	kilowatt (1,000 watts)
lb.	pound(s) (measure of weight – 2.2lb = 1 kg)
LLC	Limited Liability Company
MAC	Military Airlift Command
MBE	Member of the Order of the British Empire
MEA	Middle East Airlines
MPC	Mesopotamia Persia Corporation
MSTS	Military Sea Transportation Services
NASA	National Aeronautics and Space Administration
OAPEC	Organization of Arab Petroleum Exporting Countries
OC & C	Outram Cullinan & Co (strategic consultants of Coopers & Lybrand, UK)
OFSS	Oilfield Supply and Services
OPEC	Organization of Petroleum Exporting Countries
OTC	Overseas Tankship Corporation
oz.	ounce(s): measure of weight (16 oz. = 1 lb.)
PA	Political Agent
Pan Am	Pan American Airways
P. & O.	Peninsular and Oriental Steamship Company
PDO	Petroleum Development Oman
PDTC	Petroleum Development Trucial Coast
RAF	(British) Royal Air Force
Rs	rupees
s	shilling (unit of sterling before decimalisation)
SARR	Saudi Arabian Rail Road
SATOL	Saudi Arabia Transport Organization Limited
SDI	Saudi Arabian Airline Corporation (later known as Saudi Arabian Airline)
SIDF	Saudi Industrial Development Fund
SOCAL	Standard Oil Company of California
SOCONY	Standard Oil Company of New York
SR	Saudi Riyal
SS	Steamship (e.g., SS *Budrie*)
TWA	Trans World Airlines
UAE	United Arab Emirates
UK	United Kingdom
USA	United States of America
VNS	Vereenigde Nederlandsche Scheepvaartmaatschappij (a Dutch shipping line)
WLL	With Limited Liability
WTS	World Travel Service

Glossary

A'ain Al-Ghar – spring of bitumen (inferring that the fresh water tasted of bitumen seepages)

a'ain – a fresh-water spring

abra – water taxi

abu – father, as in Abu Dhabi

agal (or *ighal*) – black circular braided head–band which holds in place the *guttrah*

Al Falah – success in something good

Al Midfa – 'The Cannon'

Ashoora – refers to the first ten days of the month of Muharram

Bab Al-Bahrain – Gate of Bahrain

Bait Al-Quran – The House of the Quran

Bait Kanoo – House of Kanoo

Baladiya – Municipality

barastis – palm leaf huts

bin – son of (see also: *ibn*)

bint – daughter of

booms – dhows built for long-distance trade

chaw – a measurement used by Bombay merchants

coolie – an eastern, now obsolete expression, meaning unskilled labourer

dalla – traditional Arabic coffee pot

dhabi – gazelle, as in Abu Dhabi (literally meaning: father gazelle)

Eid Al-Adha – the Moslem feast and second annual holiday

Fananah – performing artiste (female)

faroush – coral slabs extracted from the sea-bed

Fasht Al-Adham – The Bones Reef

finjal – a small coffee cup without a handle

gahwa – Arabic coffee

ghar – bitumen

guttrah – the large kerchief comprising part of the traditional male head-dress worn by many Gulf Arabs with the exception of Omanis whose preference is for small embroidered pill-box hats

haram – forbidden according to the teaching of Islam

ibn – son of, as in Ibn Saud

Imshi – 'go away', the name of APOC's own-brand insecticide

jalboots – local craft, name derived from the British Navy's 'jolly boat'

Jebel Ad-Dukhan – Mountain of Smoke (focal point on Bahrain island)

Khal – Uncle

khor – bay or route (e.g. Khor Qalai'yah off the north coast of Bahrain island, formerly used by flying-boats for take-off and landing)

Khor Kanoo – Kanoo's route (a sea channel between Bahrain and Saudi Arabia)

lakh – Rs 100,000

majlis – sitting room outside a house, usually for men only

Mina King Abdul-Aziz – Port Abdul-Aziz, in Dammam, Saudi Arabia

Mina Saud – Port Saud, Kuwait

Mina Manama – Port of Manama, Bahrain

Mina Rashid – Port Rashid, Dubai

Mina Salman – Port Salman, Bahrain

Mina Zayed – Port Zayed, Abu Dhabi

mudharaba – underwrite the loss, or partake in the profit of a long-term, speculative deal (see also: *murabaha*)

Muharram – first month in the Islamic calender

mullah – Moslem religious leader

murabaha – a short-term, bridging-loan with minimum risk (see also: *mudharaba*)

Mutanajab – aristocratic, noble heritage

nawkhadha – boat captain, usually refers to a dhow

Nidd Kanoo – Kanoo's Rise (a sandy hill in Ras Al-Khaimah, UAE)

nowaakhdha – boat captains

pankah (also spelt *punkah*) – a Hindi word meaning a fan, referring to a portable fan, usually of palm leaf, or a large swinging cloth fan on a frame manually worked by pulling a cord or powered by electricity

Qhanoon – accepted law

Ras – head, top (e.g. top of a tent), or headland

Ras Al-Khaimah – (Top of the Tent) (place-name – one of the United Arab Emirates)

Ras Al-Rumaan – Headland of Pomegranates (beside Paradise roundabout, Manama and now surrounded by reclaimed land)

sabkha – mud or salt flats

Sadaf – mother-of-pearl

Sadaqa Al Jariah – regular and annual donations to charity

sehang – foreman

Shamal – a strong northerly wind

Shuja'a – Brave (name of the Ruler of Abu Dhabi's yacht)

Sinat Al-Taba'a – the 'Year of the Sinking', 1925 was so-named among the Arabian Gulf's pearl-fishing fraternity after a bad storm caused many pearling dhows to sink

souq – market

Souq Al-Manakh – Kuwait 'rogue' Stock Exchange which suffered a spectacular collapse

tindel – an Indian word meaning supervisor

Um – mother

Um Ahmed – Ahmed's mother

Um Al-Qaiwain – Mother of Qaiwain (place-name – a member emirate of the UAE)

Wazir – Minister

zakat – a percentage of a Moslem's wealth donated to charity and the needy

Bibliography

Annual Reports, Journals, Periodicals and Special Editions

Annual Administration Reports of the Persian Gulf Political Residency 1873-1947, re-printed and bound in 10 volumes entitled *The Persian Gulf Administration Reports,* Archive Editions, Gerrards Cross, England, 1986 (from original works in the India Office Library & Records, London)

Annual Reports, Bahrain Monetary Agency

Annual Reports, Gulf Air

Bahrain – an International Finance Centre, 4th edition, Economic Research Directorate, Bahrain Monetary Agency, 1991

Bahrain Government Annual Reports 1924-1970, re-printed and bound by Archive Editions, Gerrards Cross, England

Jones, Cyril N., 'Formulating Plans for Joint Venture Companies in Saudi Arabia', Essay written for Business Decision Makers, Volume, 4, 1978, pp. 161–169

Kingdom of Saudi Arabia, (special edition), Stacey International, 1979

Land and Marine Transportation, Ministry of Communications, Kingdom of Saudi Arabia, 1982

London Evening Standard, 'Oilfields air express starts', 2 May 1947

Saldanha, J. A. *The Persian Gulf Précis,* first printed in 18 volumes at Calcutta and Simla, 1903-1908; reprinted and bound in 8 volumes Archive Editions, Gerrards Cross, England, 1986 (from original works in the India Office Library & Records, London). Selected volume: *IV - Précis of Bahrein Affairs 1854-1904*

Arabic-Language Books

Al-Bassam, Khalid. *Those Were the Days - Stories and Photographs from Bahrain's Beginning,* Panorama Printing, 1987

Al-Khashrami, Abdulla. *Self-Made Men,* Al-Kashrami Printing and Publication, 1991

Al-Khater, Mubarak. *Judge (President) Qasim Al-Mehza 1847-1941,* 1986

Al-Maghrabi, Ali. *Leading Men of Hijaz,* 4 volumes, Dar Al Elm Printing and Publications, 1985

Al-Qo'od, Saleh Mohsin Fahad. *Ras Tannurah - Past and Present,* 1995

Al-Subai, Abdul Rehman bin Subai. *I Was With Abdulaziz,* Dar Mobeen Publications and Distribution, 1994

Al-Subai'i, Dr. Abdulla Nasir. *Discovery of Oil and Its Impact on the Eastern Province (Saudi Arabia) 1933 to 1960,* Al Shareef Printing 1989

Al-Watheekah. *Historic Documents Centre 10th year,* No. 19, Arabian Printing and Publishing, 1991

Al-Zaid, Khalid Saud. *Gulf Biographies in the Kuwaiti Press,* Al-Rian Publishing and Distribution, 1983

Clarke, Angela. *The Islands of Bahrain,* (Arabic edition), Government Printing Press, Bahrain, 1989

Sarkees, Adel Ahmed. *Personalities From Bahrain,* Fakhrawi Bookshop, 1995

Shattara, Asaad Saleem. *Rail Roads - Experience and Vision,* Al-Mutawa Printing and Publishing

Tahboob, Dr. Fayeq Hamdi. *The Political History of Bahrain 1783-1870,* Thatalsalasel Publications, 1983

Taylor, Andrew. *Travelling the Sands: Sagas of Exploration in the Arabian Peninsula,* Motivate Publishing (Dubai), 1995

Zayani, Rashid. *Memories and History,* (private publication), 1995

English-language Books

Abdulla, Mahdi. *Taste of the Past,* Bahrain, 1994

Abu-Hakima, Ahmad Mustafa. *Eastern Arabia: Historic Photographs Vol. I - Bahrain,* Hurtwood Press, 1984

Ajmi, Nassir. *Legacy of a Lifetime: An Essay on the Transformation of Saudi Arabia,* North Star Publishing (imprint of Al-Hilal UK), 1995

Al-Baharna, Dr Hussain M. *The Arabian Gulf States: Their Legal and Political Status and Their International Problems,* University of Manchester (England), 1968 and Librairie du Liban (Beirut), 1975

Al Fahim, Mohammed. *From Rags to Riches: A Story of Abu Dhabi,* The London Centre of Arab Studies, 1995

Algosaibi, Ghazi A. *Arabian Essays,* Kegan Paul International, 1982

Algosaibi, Ghazi A. *The Gulf Crisis: An Attempt to Understand,* Kegan Paul International, 1992

Al Khalifa, Shaikh Abdullah bin Khalid, and Rice, Michael (editors). *Bahrain Through the Ages: the History,* Kegan Paul International, 1993

Almana, Mohamed. *Arabia Unified: A Portrait of Ibn Saud,* Hutchinson Benham, 1980

Al-Muraikhi, Khalil M. *Glimpses of Bahrain From Its Past,* Ministry of Information, 1991

Belgrave, Charles. *Personal Column,* Hutchinson (London) 1960 and Librairie du Liban (Beirut), 1972

Bidwell, Robin. *Travellers in Arabia,* Garnet Publishing Ltd., Reading (UK); Hamlyn Publishing Group, 1994

Bulloch, John. *The Gulf: A Portrait of Kuwait, Qatar, Bahrain and the UAE,* Century Publishing, 1984

Carter, J. R. L. *Leading Merchant Families of Saudi Arabia,* Scorpion Publications, 1979

Clarke, Angela. *Bahrain Oil and Development 1929-1989,* Immel, 1991

Clarke, Angela. *The Islands of Bahrain,* Bahrain Historical and Archaeological Society, (English edition), 1981

Cornes, M.D. and C.D. *The Wild Flowering Plants of Bahrain: An Illustrated Guide,* Immel Publishing, 1989

Elmadani, Abdulla. *Finjan Gahwa and a Bit of Everything,* Al-Wafa Printing Press, Dammam, 1993

Facey, William. *Riyadh: The Old City*, Immel Publishing, 1992

Facey, William. *The Story of the Eastern Province of Saudi Arabia,* Stacey International, 1994

Fenelon, K. G. *The United Arab Emirates: An Economic and Social Survey,* Longman, 1973

Frater, Alexander. *Beyond the Blue Horizon: On the Track of Imperial Airways,* Penguin Books, 1987

Heard-Bey, Frauke. *From Trucial States to United Arab Emirates,* Longman, 1982

Henderson, Edward. *This Strange Eventful History: Memoirs of Earlier Days in the UAE and the Sultanate of Oman,* Quartet Books,London, 1988; Motivate Publishing, Dubai, 1993

Hornby, Ove. *A. P. Møller, Ship Owner 1876-1975,* J. H. Schultz (Copenhagen), 1988

Howarth, David, and Howarth, Stephen. *The Story of P & O: The Peninsula & Oriental Steam Navigation Company,* Weidenfeld & Nicolson, 1986; revised edition 1994

Ibrahim, Ibrahim. *The Gulf Crisis: Background and Consequences,* Center for Contemporary Arab Studies, Georgetown University, 1992

Izzard, Molly. *The Gulf: Arabia's Western Approaches,* John Murray, 1979

Jones, Stephanie. *Two Centuries of Overseas Trading: Origins and Growth of the Inchcape Group*, Macmillan Press (in association with the Business History Unit, University of London), 1986

Lacey, Robert. *The Kingdom,* Hutchinson, 1981

Legrand, Jacques. *Chronicle of the 20th Century,* Longman 1988

Mann, Major Clarence. *Abu Dhabi - Birth of an Oil Sheikhdom,* Lebanon, Khayats, 1964

Mansfield, Peter. *A History of the Middle East,* Viking, 1991; Penguin Books, 1992

Mansouri, Hussein. *Land and Marine Transportation (Saudi Arabia),* Ministry of Information, 1982

McLoughlin, Leslie. *Ibn Saud: Founder of a Kingdom,* Macmillan Press, 1993

Monroe, Elizabeth. *Philby of Arabia,* Faber & Faber 1973; Quartet 1980

Nawwab, Ismail I. Speers, Peter C., and Hoye, Paul F. (editors), *Aramco and its World: Arabia and the Middle East,* Arabian American Oil Company, 1980

Phillips, Diana Charles. *Wild Flowers of Bahrain: A Field Guide to Herbs, Shrubs and Trees,* (author's publication), Bahrain, 1988

Rashid, Dr Nasser Ibrahim Rashid, and Shaheen, Dr. Esber Ibrahim. S*audi Arabia: All You Need to Know,* International Institute of Technology, 1995

Sandwick, John A. (ed.), *The Gulf Co-operation Council: Moderation and Stability in an Interdependent World,* American Arab Affairs Council, and Westview Press, 1987

Sharif, Walid I. *Oil and Development in the Arab Gulf States,* Croom Helm, 1985

Strøm, Bjarne Aagaard. (translated by Karen White Haugan), *Christian Haaland A/S 1915-1990: A Brief Outline of the Shipping Company's History*

Taburiaux, Jean. *Pearls: Their Origin, Treatment and Identification,* (translated from the French edition *La Perle - et ses secrets*), English language edition 1985, Chilton Book Company, 1985

Tammam, Hamdi. *Zayed bin Sultan Al-Nahayyan: The Leader and the March,* (no credited publisher), UAE, 1981

Taylor, Andrew. *Travelling the Sands,* Motivate Publishing, 1995

Thesiger, Wilfred. *Arabian Sands,* Longman, 1959; Motivate Publishing, 1994

Twinam, Joseph Wright. *The Gulf, Cooperation and the Council: An American Perspective,* Washington DC, Middle East Policy Council, 1992

Wahba, Sheikh Hafiz. *Arabian Days,* Arthur Baker, 1964

Wheatcroft, Andrew, *The Life and Times of Shaikh Salman bin Hamed Al-Khalifa Ruler of Bahrain 1942-1961,* Kegan Paul, 1988

Wilson, Sir Arnold T. *The Persian Gulf,* Allen & Unwin Limited, 1959

Yateem, Aisha. *Bahrain Memoirs,* Pontifex Publishers, 1992

Yergin, Daniel. *The Prize: The Epic Quest for Oil, Money, and Power,* Simon & Schuster, 1991

Other Sources

Personal papers, Khalid Mohamed Kanoo Archive

Official company documents from the archives of:
    Aramco (Dammam), British Airways (London), BAS (Bahrain), Gulf Air (Bahrain), IATA (Geneva), Norwich Union (Bahrain), Standard Chartered Bank (London), Y.B.A.Kanoo Group (Bahrain, Saudi Arabia and the UAE)

Recorded interviews with members of the Kanoo family, their older staff and friends

Y.B.A.Kanoo – Six Generations of Family Business

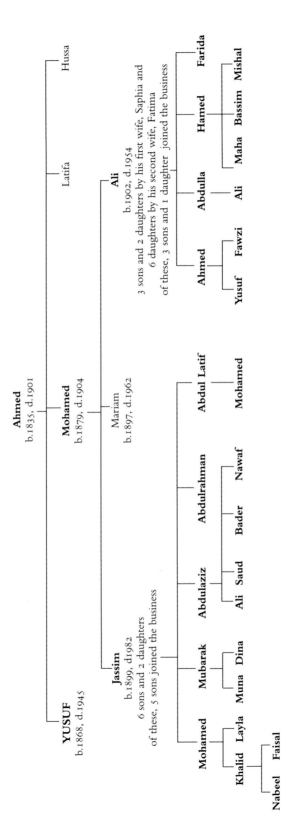

Figure 1   *Names in bold type are only those family members who have worked in the family business or continue to do so.*
This is a simplified abstract from the Kanoo family tree.

Index

311

Gaza 39
Geneva 239
Germany 16, 72, 75-6, 79, 88, 250-1
Getty Oil 173, 247-8
Gordin 245
Gray Mackenzie & Co. 4, 16-17, 54-5, 86-
    7, 101, 119-21, 124-7, 132, 137-9, 150-
    2, 157, 162, 168-72, 185, 198-9, 212-13,
    215, 287
Gray Paul & Co. 4, 8-9, 17
Greece 61
Green, Mr 171-2
Grenier, C.C. 36
Greyhound buses 237
Grove cranes 155
Gudaibiyah 14
Gulf
    Agency 287
    Air 225-26
    Aviation Company 133, 135, 141-6,
        150, 193-194, 224-5
    Co-operation Council (GCC) countries
        256-7, 271, 274-5
    International Bank (GIB) 267
    War 239-57, 279, 288-9
Gwadur 39

Haarmann & Reimer, Holzminden,
    Germany 75-6
Habshan oilfield 212
Hadden & Co. 73, 77
Hadrian 55-6
Haj 149
Hamasah, Shaikh of 169
Hamburg port 72
Hamburg-Amerika shipping line 16
Hamooda, Faraj 216
Hannibal 56
Hanno 39-40
Harmsey Vermey and Dunlop (HVD) 152
Harris 87
Harrison, Dr Paul W. 106
Harvey, Bob 237
Hassan, Syed Siddiq 13
Hatta border post 198
Hawar group of islands 2
Heard-Bey, Dr Frauke 195
Henderson, Edward 115, 169, 180
Hercules Export and Import Company
    90-3
Hijaz, Nejd and its dependencies 6, 12, 19
Himsworth, M.W. 26
Hitler, Adolf 79
H.M.S. *Juffair* 85
Hodeida 2

Hogg Line 127
Hogg Robinson Group 127, 250-1
Holland 107, 124-5
Holland-America Line 127
Holland-British Line 86
Holland-Nahas Import & Export
    Company 104-5
Holland-Persian Gulf Line 109, 126
Honda generators 227
Hong Kong 70
Horniblow, Dr 192
Humara, Carlos 245
Hungary 79
Hussain, Saddam 239, 242
Hussain, Saeed 112
Hyster fork-lifts 155, 210

IBM 223
Ibn Saud, Amir Abdul-Aziz 6, 15, 19, 30,
    37, 52, 53, 80, 116, 131, 168-9, 229 (*see
    also* Saud)
Imperial, Airways 32, 39-40, 54-7, 90, 95,
    113, 117, 288
    Aviation Spirit 32
    Bank of Iran 107-8, 119, *see also* British
        Bank of Iran and the Middle East
Inchcape 237
Inchcape, Lord 16, 127
India 3, 5-6, 15, 21-5, 28-30, 38, 40, 72,
    82-4, 88, 93, 117, 181 *see also* Bombay;
    Calcutta; Delhi
    Government 9, 13, 83, 169-70
        Administration Report (1889-90) 2
India Office 2-3
India Supply Mission 91-2
Indonesia, ports 88, *see also* Batavia and
    Semarang
International Air Transport Association
    (IATA) 116-18, 127, 144, 226, 288
International Paint 237
Intrade Limited, Brentwood 124
Iran 84, 108, *see also* Imperial Bank of Iran
    Shah of 195, 222
Iran-Iraq war (1980) 222
Iraq 14, 17, 32, 39, 239, 252, 289, *see also*
    Basrah
    Kuwait occupation 83, 238-42, 253, 273
    Petroleum Company 41
Iraqi Airways 144
Irwin, Commander 85
Ismael, Abdulla 192
Israel, Six Day War 195
Italian Somaliland 81
Italy 39, 71, 81, 107, 121